PEREGRINE BOOKS
Y 63

P9-AFQ-138

Individualism
and Nationalism
in American Ideology

YEHOSHUA ARIELI

Yehoshua Arieli was born in Czechoslovakia and emigrated to Palestine at the age of fifteen. His studies in history and philosophy at The Hebrew University were interrupted by service in the British Army during World War II and later in the Israeli Army. He received his Ph.D. in 1955. He was a graduate student in history at Harvard University between 1951 and 1953 and in 1960 was appointed Research Fellow at Harvard's Center for the Study of the History of Liberty in America. He is now Professor of Modern History at The Hebrew University, Jerusalem.

Individualism
and Nationalism
in American Ideology

YEHOSHUA ARIELI

PENGUIN BOOKS
Baltimore, Maryland

Penguin Books Inc
3300 Clipper Mill Road, Baltimore, Md. 21211

Copyright © 1964 by the President and Fellows
of Harvard College

This edition published 1966 by arrangement with
Harvard University Press

Printed in the United States of America

To the Memory of my Beloved Parents
Flora and Moritz Loebl
and my Teacher Richard Koebner

Foreword

Distinctive attitudes toward the relationship of the individual and the community played an important part in the history of American liberty. Altogether apart from any formal restraints upon the power of government to act, significant assumptions about the place of the individual personality in society generated beliefs basic to freedom in the United States.

The pattern of ideas embraced in individualism was more often examined analytically by Europeans than by Americans, who took it for granted. Visitors—Tocqueville notable among them—frequently focused their discussion of the differences between the Old World and the New on the traits associated with individualism. In fact, for some this became the central element of national character in the United States.

There was some validity to that judgment. Although the fully formed concept of individualism did not emerge until well into the nineteenth century—and, indeed, was first articulated by Europeans—its constituent elements originated in the eighteenth century and developed under the influence of the American quest for a national identity. The connection between nationalism and individualism, established in the early days of the Republic, long remained vitally important.

Although individualism was also expressed in many aspects of social and personal behavior, the primary concern of this volume is with ideology. Adequately to describe the conscious and deliberate articulation of the concept of individualism, it was necessary to recognize the strength of the intellectual ties that held together men on both sides of the Atlantic. No American idea was wholly indigenous, in the sense that it could not be traced back to a European antecedent or that it escaped the effects of alien influences. Yet, conversely, no European idea was simply transplanted, in the sense that it failed to be modified in the American context. Professor Arieli's subtle analysis has therefore had to distinguish the elements of connectedness and of separateness, of uniqueness and of generality, in the complex evolution of ideas that had a profound impact on the history of liberty in the United States.

OSCAR HANDLIN

Acknowledgments

The present work is the outcome of research which has occupied me for many years.

In its initial stages it owed much to the members of the History Department of Harvard University, in particular to Professors Arthur M. Schlesinger, Sr., the late Perry Miller, Samuel E. Morison and Oscar Handlin, with whom it was my privilege to study as a graduate student in 1951–1953.

Great is my indebtedness to the late Professor Richard Koebner, to whose inspired teaching at the Hebrew University I owe my approach to the historical discipline and who supervised my doctoral thesis in which the problem of the basic concepts of American thought was first raised.

No word can adequately express my gratitude to Professor Oscar Handlin and Mary F. Handlin whose untiring aid and inspiring work made this book possible. Professor Handlin's aid in revising and editing the manuscript was decisive for the shape of the work and it was through both Oscar and Mary Handlin's unremitting work that the book was made ready for the press.

I am deeply grateful to the President and Fellows of Harvard College for their invitation to become a Research Fellow in the Center for the Study of the History of Liberty in America in the year 1960–1961. Through their invitation and the grant-in-aid of the Hebrew University this research was made possible.

The exchange of views and opinions with the members of the Center was a fruitful and stimulating experience from which my work greatly profited. No less stimulating have been my talks with Robert E. Voitle of the English Department of the University of North Carolina. I wish also to express my gratitude to Miss Kathleen Ahern for preparing the manuscript, to Miss Betsy Top and Mrs. Nancy Jackson for coping with the proofs, and to members of the staff of the Widener Library for their assistance.

Yehoshua Arieli

The Hebrew University
Jerusalem

Contents

Contents

Contents

1

Introduction

"How does it happen that in the United States, where the inhabitants have only recently immigrated to the land which they now occupy . . . [bringing] neither customs nor traditions with them there; where they met one another for the first time with no previous acquaintance; where, in short, the instinctive love of country can scarcely exist . . . that everyone takes as zealous an interest in the affairs of his township, his county, and the whole state as if they were his own?" [1] This question, which Tocqueville set out to answer in his *Democracy in America,* indicates also the general direction of the present inquiry. This is an investigation into the nature of that collective identification through which a society, heterogeneous in structure and origin, recent in its history, and mobile and diverse in its character, came to consider itself a nation.

Nationalism is of fairly recent origin. It aims at the creation and maintenance of a community of life and destiny with a will and purpose expressed in the state and a unity embodied in the nation. Such unity is conscious and is maintained by a system of symbols, values, and notions which define and strengthen the awareness of a collective identity. Nationalism rises beyond the loyalties to ancient traditions or the attachment of men to their land, their homes, and the localities to which they belong. It is founded upon generalizations and a conceptual framework of orientation—in short, upon ideology.

This is particularly true of the structure of the American national consciousness. The American Revolution and the War for Independence, the establishment of the Confederation and of the Federal Union, form in the history of the Western world the first major expression of the principle of national self-determination.

Yet they represent at the same time the first conscious application of abstract principles to the political and social institutions of the commonwealth. Nationalism, constitutionalism, and republicanism were blended in the creative act through which a society established itself as a nation. The nature of the collective purpose through which so complex a result was achieved deserves careful examination. But it must be preceded by an inquiry into the relationship among national, political, and social orientations and into the functions which ideologies play in the formation of group orientations in the modern world. Only after we have clarified the relation between ideology and history in general, and between ideology and American history in particular, can we hope to gain a clearer concept of the structure of the American national consciousness.

The present study is mainly concerned with the rise and development of concepts which have played a major role in American public opinion and have served to crystallize a sense of collective identification. An analysis of their meaning and an evaluation of their historical significance will help to elucidate the nature of the American national consciousness.

1. HISTORY AND IDEOLOGY

Social and political concepts which have a hold on public opinion have their own inherent meanings. But they also fulfill definite needs in a historical situation and thus refer to a wider context of which they are indicative. They are constituent parts of the image the individual and society have of themselves and of the world around them. As such they are instruments of orientation and action, norms of behavior, and guides toward personal and social attitudes. Moreover, concepts expressed by the spoken or written word, are products of a concrete historical situation and serve social needs. They are the products of long-term trends and developments and embody significant collective attitudes. "The function which makes the spoken and written word an important element in the nexus of historical happenings is its instrumentality in shaping the consciousness of social bonds and cleavages, of loyalties and conflicts." [2] Concepts are significant, then, not only in terms of their inherent meanings, but also in terms of their capacity to become effective forces of social cohesion and action. Society can exist only insofar as the individuals of which it is composed carry with them the same ideas and images. We belong to a group because we see the same meanings in the world.[3]

The modes of maintaining and altering the structure and content of meanings have changed radically in modern times, with the growing mobility and instability of social relations and institutions. With the disappearance of organic frameworks of social organization, the traditional and partly unconscious conceptions of man's status in the universe have been supplanted more and more by conscious, abstract ideas. The awareness of social bonds and common purpose, the identification of the individual with the group, loyalty to national, religious, or social causes and the very sense of belonging have been formed and directed by conceptual frameworks or ideologies.[4]

The Reformation and the victorious progress of a scientific and rationalistic world view have furthered the breakdown of traditional attitudes. In the same degree that old loyalties and traditional patterns of status and occupation were destroyed, new social, religious, and political forces sought to legitimize their position by appealing to or by creating new norms and values to supplant or maintain traditional orientations.

By the second half of the eighteenth century, the Enlightenment had become aware of its power to reconstruct society, and ideological forces penetrated society on all levels. This process focused on the three great frameworks of social organization and action: on the state, on the nation, and on society. Though interrelated and interdependent, each became the object of trends which endeavored to reinterpret its meaning, purposes, and structure.

These political, national, and social ideologies tended to be complete systems of "cognitive assumptions and affective identification" which aimed, by interpreting reality in terms of their own basic views, to create norms of social life and direct its activities in accordance with their purposes and tendencies.[5] Each defined the proper field of action of the state, of the nation, and of society, and their interrelations in such a way that one of these categories represented the determining factor of a functional system, with the others variables. The functional relationship

among these three categories and their conceptual structure determined the individual physiognomy of each ideological system.

The development of each system followed a pattern of challenge
and response. Each was challenged by competing attitudes and
each responded by a strategy of incorporation or antithetical restatement, or of both. This dialectic process of conceptual attitude-
formations was related to concrete historical situations in which
it fulfilled the social function of creating, maintaining, or destroying consent.[6] Revolutionary or utopian ideologies sought to displace existing elements of social reality, while conservative
ideologies fortified them by setting them in a conceptual context
that legitimized and sanctified them.[7] Yet the distinction between
utopian and conservative ideologies deals with only one aspect of
the relationship between ideology and society.[8] The distinction
among political, national, and social ideologies is also necessary
to make clear the organizing principle inherent in each ideology.

2. TYPES OF IDEOLOGICAL ORIENTATION

The focus of all ideological endeavors has been the state, which
has been the ultimate framework of social obligation, social order,
and coercive power. Conceptions of the good life have turned
largely on the nature, purpose, and extent of political authority.
Every political ideology has therefore implied a total social philosophy. The problem of the nature of political authority, which first
gave rise to ideologies, has remained a central part of all ideological orientation.

Political ideology attempts to determine the extent and source
of legitimate authority. It defines the structure and functions of
the state, the nature and limit of its sovereign will, and its relationships to all other forms of social life. Political ideology aims to
establish, maintain, or destroy authority by relating it to a structure of norms, values, and data which are accepted as valid. The
divine-right theory, the philosophy of natural law, utilitarianism,
and organic theories of state and society are examples of such
meaning structures.

The rise of political ideology coincided with the emergence and
growth of the modern centralized state. Claiming unlimited power,
the rulers of the new monarchies relied on the support of political
theories to legitimize their claims against the traditional order.

The absolutism elaborated by Machiavelli, Bodin, Hobbes, and the jurists and theologians evoked in turn opposing theories which developed into rival political ideologies.[9]

Yet the conceptual framework of these new political ideologies contained elements which became in due course the formative centers of differently oriented attitudes, of social and national ideologies. Thus, the Puritan revolution, which first forged political ideologies for mass action and for the change of the political and social order, gave rudimentary expression to the ideas of constitutionalism, republicanism, democracy, socialism, liberalism, conservatism, and an incipient nationalism. Most of these tendencies were short-lived, but they had an important impact on later ideologies.[10] The Whig philosophy, heir to the Puritan revolution, reconciled the traditional and revolutionary tendencies of the seventeenth century into one ideological synthesis in terms of a rational conception of government, society, and man. Whiggism was at the same time a political, a national, and a social attitude. The common links among these three frames of reference were the concept of natural law and rights and the contract theory. The first limited sovereignty and circumscribed the spheres of government by well-defined functions. The second based the legitimacy of political authority on consent and established the principles of representation.[11]

Yet these political principles were also the basis on which a new concept of society and of the nation developed. The limitation of sovereignty and the establishment of a distinctive sphere of personal rights created a new intermediate plane between the individual and the state—society. In this field individuals cooperated for the mutual exchange of services and associated for common interests. Religion, morality, customs, culture, and economic activities tended to be regarded as liberated from the jurisdiction of the state. Instead, they were conceived as aspects of civil, nonpolitical society. The concepts of the economy elaborated by the physiocrats and Adam Smith, of culture, manners, and civilization described by Voltaire, Montesquieu, and David Hume, and of natural religion and morality as interpreted by the deists, all reflected a view of society independent of its political organization. This was the "natural order" as against the "positive order" of the physiocrats, the "civil society" of Adam Ferguson,

"Le système social ou principes naturals de la morale et de la politique" of the Marquis de Mirabeau.[12] The concept of society in the Whig philosophy proved the possibility of limited government and vindicated the claims for the increase of personal liberty. Regarded as the sphere of freedom, habit, and tradition, society was conceded to be autonomous but was not regarded as a determining factor in man's existence nor as the object of collective coercive action.

The emergence of fully developed social ideologies was bound up with the growing radicalism of the natural-rights theory and with the fusion of historical and sociological speculation into systematic bodies of thought. The radical interpretation of the natural-rights philosophy as expressed in the political slogans of the American and French revolutions changed the structure of both political power and society. The apostles of "liberty" and "equality" regarded political power as an instrument for changing the existing social order; for them, therefore, the political and the social spheres were interdependent. All the events of the revolutionary period focused attention on the fundamental importance of the social structure for the total human situation.

In addition, a new historical awareness tended more and more to define change in terms of alterations in the social order. The quick transformations caused by the industrial, technological, and democratic revolutions of the late eighteenth and early nineteenth centuries strengthened this inclination. Whether the new outlook led to conservative or to revolutionary interpretations of social reality, the center of gravity had shifted from political to social aims.

Such social ideologies were inspired by, and sought to translate into reality, an absolute value system. The natural-rights theories, the philosophies of religious and secular humanism basic to the ideologies of liberalism, democracy, and anarchism, aimed at the adoption of norms considered universally true. Their orientation was pluralistic rather than monistic; though they gave the social order primary importance, they recognized the autonomy of the political, national, and individual spheres.

The sociological ideologies, on the other hand, brought a new and revolutionary force into history. These referred to the totality of social existence and regarded all individual and social phenomena as expressions of one underlying principle of organization, or as fully determined factors of a closed system. Such views led necessarily to relativism, dogmatism, and totalitarianism. Sociological ideologies, whether revolutionary or reactionary, created ideological polarizations and tensions which endangered the very existence of society. Moreover, their influence had a radical impact on other ideological movements and increased the pattern of tension in every direction.

3. CITIZENSHIP AND NATIONALISM

This was particularly true in regard to the nationalistic ideologies of the nineteenth and twentieth centuries. Considering the state and society as expressions of the nation, nationalism was from its inception influenced by the prevailing political and social theories. To the degree that sociological views shaped any nationalistic ideology, that ideology, too, tended toward a monism that regarded all individual and social phenomena as the expression of one underlying principle, the nation, which absolutely determined the structure of the activities of its members. It too was relativistic toward others and dogmatic and totalitarian toward its constituents.[13] But in one respect nationalistic and sociological ideologies differed from each other. The latter tended to create new solidarities on the horizontal plane of supernational units, by destroying the state and the nation in order to unite humanity. Nationalistic ideologies, on the other hand, created vertical solidarity within the national state and destroyed the concept of human solidarity.

This antithetic relation arose from the very nature of nationalism, which aimed at the full absorption of state and society into a community of will and purpose—the nation. Nationalism considered the individual a citizen or member of the body politic because he was a part of the nation, a community bound by self-identification, which conceived of itself as absolute and self-determining. The state expressed the personality and group unity of the nation and was the embodiment of its will and being.[14]

The reinterpretation of the state and of society in the light of the idea of nationalism explained the claims which all systems of nationalism make upon the individual's absolute loyalty. The demand for total obedience which had been undermined by the natural-rights theory and by social ideologies thus received a new legitimacy. The state was not only the source of all power, the seat of all jurisdiction, and the ultimate framework of order and security but it was the expression of national unity, magnifying the nation through its power and sanctified in its power by the nation. To the degree that nationalism conceived the nation as a community of fate (*Schicksalsgemeinschaft*), it claimed also complete loyalty and authority.

The individual physiognomy of nationalistic ideologies depended upon the nature of the national identifications and upon the way in which the functional interrelations among state, society, and individual were defined and evaluated, and these in turn were determined by the historical situation in which they developed.[15]

The national movement arose in the age of absolutism as a reaction against the bureaucratic centralized state which had lost its legitimate authority and had come to be regarded as alien by a society aware of its own corporative existence. The centralized sovereign state had been a unifying and leveling force which had sought to forge everywhere homogeneous societies—"state-nations" —which became the bearers of the national movement. The state had welded its subjects into a nation, and the nation turned the state into an instrument of its own will and power. Furthermore, the centralized state compelled other societies to imitate its own political structure in order to survive. Dynastic, traditional monarchies turned into centralized states. Ethnic groups which had long lost political independence rediscovered the consciousness of national unity. And the modern nation-state became the general standard of political organization for all people who aimed at liberation from alien rule.

Yet though the nationalist movement changed the relation between society and government, it absorbed the outlook and the attitudes of its predecessor, the bureaucratic state. The sovereign state regarded itself as the embodiment of the natural order of human society, as the framework of social cooperation, and as the instrument for the social and moral perfection of humanity. From the perspective of the state, the nation consisted of all those united by their loyalty and the comprehensive social order established by the sovereign. This view maintained and applied to the territorial state the universalistic concepts of the Christian classical tradition, now to be realized in the idea of the *Rechtsstaat,* the Rule of Law, of the divinely established order of reason and of the supremacy of justice. Yet the sovereign state represented at the same time the principle of force in its relations with other states and with its own subjects, in which it was guided by the rules of war and power.[16] The permanent struggle for survival forced the state to aim at absolute independence and self-reliance. In its efforts to mobilize support, it had to emphasize more and more its national unity, and it increasingly demanded absolute loyalty and the separation of its society from all supernational bonds of community. Increasingly the state appealed to the loyalty of the people by emphasizing the identity of its interest with theirs and by glorifying its collective power.

The bureaucratic sovereign state transmitted to its heir, the national state, the dichotomy between rational norms and universal values on the one hand, and the cult of power, national egoism, and collective isolation on the other. The national state not only inherited the need to maintain its independence by permanent mobilization of power but it immensely strengthened the drive for power and prestige through its identification of the nation with the state.

Nationalism considered any weakening of state power a reflection on the nation's prestige and a sign of weakness. It projected individual competitive attitudes and concepts of courage, pride, honor, and strength in an increasing measure into international relations and it developed an in-group morality that did not have to be observed toward outsiders.

These tendencies appeared in all nation-states. They were the products of international rivalries and of pressures from within a closed system of power.[17] Tocqueville's description of the "irritable patriotism" of the American was valid for all national states. "As the American participates in all that is done in his country, he thinks himself obliged to defend whatever may be censured in it; for it is not only his country that is then attacked, it is himself." [18] Moreover, competitors for leadership inside the nation increased the drive for prestige and power in the attempts to gain support by appealing to the image of national greatness and expansion.[19]

Yet the role of the ideology of national power varied with the general pattern of identification. Nations welded together by a continued common rule, common historical experience, and common institutions developed differently from those in which national consciousness preceded political independence.

In the former, a common life under a common state imperceptibly and slowly created the feeling of community and the symbols of group identification. Community of language, of institutions, of political and religious symbols, of government and authority, created the nation before it became aware of itself. In these nation-states national consciousness and national ideologies developed through the political struggle for citizenship. The theories of natural rights, of the contractual character of state and government, and of popular sovereignty also became the basic concepts of national consciousness. The unity of society and state in the nation was achieved through the concept of citizenship. The nation was a real personality because its members were mutually united through common consent to a common rule and their collective will was expressed through the state.[20]

Political struggles in England and France in the seventeenth and eighteenth centuries were not directed toward political independence or national unity; both existed already and were taken for granted. They aimed at changes in the political structure and at the transfer of sovereign power. But they resulted also in the integration of society and state by turning both into a community of political power, rights, and responsibility. Until then, the "Multitude held together by Force, tho under one and the same Head," was "not properly united." Nor did "such a Body make *a People.*" Where there was no public or constitution, there was "no *Mother*-COUNTRY, OR NATION." [21] These struggles identified the nation with the body politic by defining as members those who shared duties and rights in the Commonwealth.

This new concept of the nation was most admirably expressed by the man who attempted to overthrow the contractual theory of the state and its revolutionary implications. Edmund Burke's *Reflections on the Revolution in France* invoked the image of society and of state as that of a partnership with a religious significance. The state "is not a partnership in things subservient only to the gross animal existence of a temporary and perishable nature. It is a partnership in all science; a partnership in all art; a partnership in every virtue, and in all perfection. As the ends of such a partnership cannot be obtained in many generations, it becomes a partnership not only between those who are living but between those who are living, those who are dead, and those who are to be born." [22]

The content of this national consciousness was formed by rationalistic and universalistic values and norms. The idea of citizenship, of the contractual and rational nature of the state, referred not to the nation as a unique collective being, but to the nature of man and to the structure of state and government in general. Man was part of a nation because the nation confirmed his humanity. The basic characteristic of the concept was that of consent of free individuals to be united together in a higher community which comprised their common ideals and interests. "A nation is a soul," Renan remarked, "a spiritual principle . . . it is summed up in the present by a tangible fact—consent, the clearly expressed will to continue a life in common. The existence of a nation is a *plébescite de touts les jours.*" [23]

The concept of citizenship had a decisive influence on the formation of the national consciousness in all countries in which the state created a homogeneous territorial society.[24] In England and France, and even in the German Reich, Spain, and Russia, the national movement developed at first through the quest for citizenship.[25] The extent to which nationalistic and universalistic elements predominated in each depended on the compatibility of the idea of citizenship with the prevailing structure of society and upon the strength of revolutionary forces in changing the political structure.

In England, tradition and the institutional pattern of society were integrated with rationalistic and universalistic views of civil and political liberties into a truly new conceptual pattern which thereafter dominated the English national consciousness.[26] The "rights of Englishmen" were oriented toward a liberal concept of society; yet they were truly national, since they derived their validity through tradition and bound the individual to the community of the Realm.[27]

In France, citizenship could be realized only through a total change in the structure of state and society. French nationalism therefore became identified with the universalistic and rationalistic outlook of the Revolution.[28] Yet the transformation of the constitutional movement for citizenship into the monistic concept of "la nation une et indivisible" based on Rousseau's "general will" created a cleavage between the living traditional elements and the revolutionary ones—which thereafter bedeviled French history.[29]

The same movement toward citizenship in the national awakening of Spain, Germany, and Russia in the first half of the nineteenth century was too weak to achieve its goal and collapsed. Yet the idea of the national state was too strong to be defeated and too dangerous to be left in the possession of revolutionary forces. The problem was how to separate the idea of the national state from that of citizenship and of the contractual theory of the sovereign people.

The Romantic theory of nationalism, which solved this problem, achieved the integration of state and society as nation by postulating the reality of the group personality, "the folk," and its priority over the individual. The nation was not a compact nor was it identical with political society; it was rather a fundamental fact of human existence which determined the total experience of man. The nation was united not by consent or by mutuality but by its objective uniqueness and individuality expressed in its institutions, habits and manners, culture and spirit. Herder's folk-poetry, Hegel's national state and folk-mind and Savigny's folk-right were steps in forging this ideology.[30]

This organic ideology of nationalism resembled the sociological ideologies in three ways.[31] It postulated the absolute subjection of the individual to the group. It denied the validity of absolute norms and values apprehensible by individual reason and thereby denied also the idea of humanity. Finally, it regarded history as the ultimate reality and as the totality of truth.

The romantic ideology of nationalism as foreshadowed and prepared by Burke, Herder, Fichte, and Hegel and developed by Adam Müller, Treitschke, and others proved both revolutionary and conservative, aggressive and quietistic.[32] It immensely strengthened the disruptive forces inside non-national empires and in societies governed by alien rule. It created a new principle of collective self-determination and state formation and awakened a consciousness of nationality and national community where it did not exist.

Yet it proved at the same time an immensely conservative force, especially in states in which society and ruler belonged to the same people, as in Germany and Russia, and later in France—all countries in which national unity was threatened by social and political conflicts and conflicting ideologies.

On the other hand, in societies in which nationalism became a movement for political independence or unity, the revolutionary idea of popular sovereignty and citizenship has been a major force in the emergence of a national independence movement, as in Italy, Belgium, Ireland, and Czechoslovakia.[33]

In most nations which attained political independence through the struggle for national emancipation, the idea of national unity and of national individuality weakened the rational norms and values of citizenship and responsible government. The emphasis on collective unity threatened the universalistic values of the concept of the rule of law and of the limited sphere of government. The conceptual unity of the nation tended to become a postulate of factual unity in thought, action, and political behavior.

The rise of ideology in modern history created mutually exclusive and antagonistic forces which contended with one another for the power to reform society. Democracy, nationalism, and socialism effectively destroyed existing patterns of political power and social organization, recast the map of the world, and fashioned new forms of communal life. History became a stage filled with visionaries who tried to make their dreams real by conquering the minds and hearts of men.

The ever-growing momentum of revolutionary change effaced all fixed points of orientation. Humanity turned into a free-moving mass, frenzied in mind and heated in emotion, which, burning up its past, sought new equilibrium.

The more mobile society has become, the greater has been its need for ideological guidance toward new patterns of stability. In some countries revolution turned into counterrevolution, liberalism into conservatism, democracy into dictatorship, and nationalism into fascism. But no country escaped the impact of ideology, for one ideology could only be resisted by another, as enemies equalize their position by adopting each other's weapon. In this context, Tocqueville's question had particular relevance and significance.

Part One

Ideology and American Nationalism

II

Ideology and the American Way of Life

1. THE IMPACT OF IDEOLOGY ON AMERICAN HISTORY

In the eyes of contemporaries the American Revolution heralded the triumph of reason, liberty, and human dignity. It was a decisive break with the past and the beginning of a new era in history. Here for the first time the Enlightenment realized its aims and confirmed its belief that history was the progress of humanity toward perfection. Taking courage from the American example, the intellectual *avant-garde* of Europe turned with greater confidence and resolution to shaping society "nearer to its heart's desire." [1]

The Declaration of Independence, the various bills of rights of the states, and the debates over the ratification of the Constitution revealed the ideological character of the movement. It was by its appeal to the rights of nature that the Continental Congress justified the independence of the colonies. It was upon the premises and corollaries of the natural-rights philosophy that the republican structure of representative government was built and political sovereignty established. [2]

The principles of the Revolution, legitimized by the very existence of the United States, could be neither abrogated nor curbed in their forward movement. Claiming absolute validity, they spread by the force of their own inner logic and created an ever-growing movement toward the democratization of American society. Yet the more the electorate became aware of its political power, the more vital it became to influence and control public opinion.

The fear of political democracy, at the heart of conservatism, reached back to the experiences of the Puritan revolution and became a constituent part of the Whig tradition. It seemed axiomatic that the political emancipation of the masses would create anarchy and class war, lead to social revolution, and end in despotism.[3] The apprehension of the radical demagogues made many a patriot into a Tory. It beset the minds of the Founding Fathers and constituted the hard core of federalism. The course of the French Revolution confirmed these fears and turned distrust into hatred of the tenets of radical enlightenment which had inspired the American Revolution. In the attempt to draw the line between the principles of American republicanism and those of French Jacobinism the Federalists sought to unmask the pretension of man to reconstruct society by reason and to challenge his faith in the efficacy of abstract schemes for social improvement. Washington's Farewell Address clearly reflected this fear when he exhorted the American people to "resist with care the spirit of innovation" and warned them against the inherent worthlessness of the ideological mentality, "that facility in changes upon the credit of mere hypothesis and opinion." [4]

Yet the conservatives failed. The very structure of political life, the victorious progress of democracy, and the growing power of public opinion compelled them to appeal to a common ground of consent by relating their own views to concepts which would bestow on them moral and national validity in the eyes of the public. Fisher Ames's view that "there is a kind of fatality in the affairs of republicks, that eludes the foresight of the wise, as much as it frustrates the toils and sacrifices of the patriot and the hero," though shared by many, became more and more out of harmony with public sentiment.[5]

Events proved the fears of the conservatives unfounded. Political democracy did not, as Fisher Ames expected, fall into "the control of the fiercest and most turbulent spirits in society." [6] Conservatives learned by experience that the only way to tame the spirit of democracy was to win its confidence by competition on the ideological level. The result was a permanent cross-fertilization and mutual adaptation of ideologies in America. Unlike the Old World, where the conflict between parties and ideologies became ever more sharply defined and ever more dangerous, the fundamental concepts of social life in America grew more similar, and the areas of dispute narrowed down to questions whch could be solved empirically within the existing institutional framework. The one great exception confirms this proposition: the crisis of the Civil War proved irrepressible because of incompatibility of ideologies and social attitudes rather than of practical interests. Apart from the southern heresy, American society proved surprisingly free of radical polarizations and revolutionary tensions. The unique stability of its institutions and their power of adaptation, the non-ideological character of its major parties, and the virtual absence of any revolutionary movement reflect the unifying and stabilizing force of its basic assumptions.

2. THE AMERICAN IDEOLOGY: THE PROBLEM STATED

The phenomenon of basic conformity in a free and democratic society, where no real attempt has ever been made to suppress thought or impose opinion by governmental coercion or indoctrination, poses a problem.

In England, Switzerland, and the Scandinavian countries, all of which achieved similar institutional stability and uniformity of outlook, the shock of political and ideological tensions has been absorbed by the vitality of inherited patterns of life and a strong consciousness of national community and unity. These democracies were not troubled, as was the United States, by the social mobility and uprootedness which provide the ideal breeding-ground for ideologies. Ethnic and cultural homogeneity, a common historical tradition, the primary conditions for the consciousness of national unity and community, were conspicuously lacking in American society. And yet an awarenes of common purpose and behavior emerged to astonish and puzzle foreign observers. None of them defined more lucidly the problem than Alexis de Tocqueville: "Picture to yourself . . . if you can," he wrote to a friend, "a society which comprises all the nations of the world . . . people differing from one another in language, in beliefs, in opinions; in a word a society possessing no roots, no memories, no prejudices, no routine, no common ideas, no national character, yet with a happiness a hundred times greater than our own. . . This, then, is our starting point! What is the connecting link between these so different elements How are they welded into one people?"[7] The same question recurred in *De la Démocratie en Amérique.* How did it happen that in the United States, to which the inhabitants had only recently immigrated, where the instinctive love of country scarcely existed, that everyone took as zealous an interest in the affairs of the state as if they were his own? [8]

The answer could come only through analysis of ideology. More than any of his contemporaries, Tocqueville was aware of the immense importance of ideologies in the creation of modern group cohesion and in the formation of political and social mass movements. He was probably the first to come to history with a "semantic approach"—that is, to study "the function which makes the spoken and written word an important element in the nexus of historical happenings." [9] The chapters in which he dealt with the emergence of general ideas in democratic societies were the first mature treatments of the "sociology of knowledge." [10] Since society could "exist only when a great number of men consider a great number of things under the same aspect, when they hold the same opinions upon many subjects, and when the same occurrences suggest the same thoughts and impressions to their minds," and since American society lacked a natural community of tradition, then its cohesion had to be the product of a community of values, beliefs, and ideas which replaced those created by tradition and homogeneity. [11]

Democracy, Tocqueville asserted, was the generating principle of American cohesion. It gave unity to the nation, animated and stabilized institutions, and controlled habits, feelings, and outlook. "What strikes me is that the immense majority of spirits join together in certain *common opinions*," he noted just a few months after his arrival in the United States. [12] In America all the laws originated, so to speak, in the same thought: all society rested on a single principle. [13]

It was, then, the correspondence between the values embodied in the social structure and those of its ideology that created a consciousness of national unity. [14] This thesis actually contained a statement which rarely has been made explicit. Democracy represented in America at one and the same time the principles of national, social, and political organization; national consciousness thus referred also to social and political ideals. The originality of this interpretation consisted in the functional relationship Tocqueville established between the political, social, and national spheres of action and orientation, a relationship determined by the social principle or by democracy as equality of condition.[15] His thesis was that social and political ideals and values determined American national consciousness.

Certain phenomena uniquely American confirmed this view. The expression, "the American way of life," assumed that a certain social-behavior pattern and value system was peculiarly American, though transferable to other nations and not limited by ethnic, racial, or historical group characteristics. Moreover, certain social ideologies were considered American while others were subversive and un-American. Individualism, humanitarian democracy, and "the free enterprise system" were among the former while all socialistic movements and ideologies were among the latter. The character of these social ideologies was different from those which claimed national significance in other countries. The claim of the American ideologies derived not from their compatibility with the nation's aspirations but from their absolute validity in the eyes of the American people. Democracy and liberty, "the American way of life," "the system of individualism," or "the free enterprise system" conveyed a message of universal truth, based upon a total world view. That truth was not subject to the narrow interest of the nation but rather modified the concept and structure of nationalism to its own standards.

The strength of American nationalism thus depended on its nonparochial and universal significance. The peculiar functional relationship between social ideology and national loyalty explained the absence of a strong socialist movement in the United States, the comparative ease with which radical or nonconformist thought became suspect, and the leadership assumed by the United States in the struggle with world communism. Like socialists and communists, Americans believed that their social system was universally applicable to all mankind.

This position was unique in the contemporary world. Socialism, communism, and humanitarian liberalism never identified themselves with the interest of any particular nation; their sphere of action transcended national boundaries and interests, although communism under certain conditions furthered nationalistic movements as a means toward an end. A clearcut division between social, political, and national ideas has sometimes permitted greater political realism and sometimes led to a dangerous collision of competing loyalties. But in countries other than the United States, such a division also encouraged the free ideological development of competing claims inside the political framework of the country without threatening the stability of society. A multi-ideological development in most countries of the Western world stimulated understanding of social and political systems differing from their own. The identification of an ideological attitude with America's national interests and aspirations has, on the other hand, made for a strangely unrealistic attitude toward the world at large and toward its own basic problems.

3. THE STRUCTURE OF THE AMERICAN IDEOLOGY: A PRELIMINARY ANSWER

Patterns of national identification have been achieved in several ways. One involved the imposition of a social philosophy on society by the state, as in the countries under totalitarian communist rule, and the creation of uniformity through the concept of a new social world order. National traditions and loyalties were destroyed and the loyalty and identification with the state achieved through the idea of a universally valid order of human life, sanctified by a scheme of ultimate salvation and redemption.

A similar integration was the product of totalitarian nationalism which imposed uniformity of belief through the idea of the fundamental organic unity and identity of the nation in which all social activities were coordinated and subordinated to the optimal functioning of the group. Totalitarian nationalism created a philosophy of social cooperation and tended toward the concept of the corporate state in which the position of the individual was defined by its function in the whole.[16]

Another type of national identification was achieved through the concept of citizenship. The feeling of national unity resulted from a long-established community of life, traditions, and institutions more than from a unitary ideology. The consciousness of national community did not lead toward conformity and ideological identification. It rather became an elastic framework for diversity of opinion and political orientation, kept in check through the consciousness of the common bonds of a national tradition. To the degree that ideals of citizenship and of political rights became

part of the institutional framework, the feeling of national identification increased in strength without threatening the autonomy
and variety of individual and group expression. Such has been the
development in states which gave birth to liberalism.[17]

The structure of the American national consciousness did not
correspond to any one of these types. Instead, the major characteristics of each of them were blended into a new variety. In the
United States, national consciousness was shaped by social and
political values which claimed universal validity and which were
nevertheless the American way of life. Unlike other Western
nations, America claimed to possess a "social system" fundamentally opposed to and a real alternative to socialism and communism, with which it competed by claiming to represent the way
to ultimate progress and true social happiness.

The claim to represent the real alternative to socialism was
expressed in the development of the concept of individualism in
the nineteenth and twentieth centuries. This concept, formed from
the beginning as the ideological antithesis to socialism, pervaded
almost all American politically significant thought in the late
nineteenth and early twentieth centuries. Nor did this attitude
materially change, though the term "individualism" fell into at
least temporary "disgrace" with the great depression and the New
Deal. In its stead other terms like "free enterprise system," the
philosophy of "a free society," took up the same burden and
claimed the same universal significance. The McCarthy years, like
the "Red panic" of the 1920's, the frequent denunciations of governmental participation in the national life as "creeping socialism,"
and the ideological nature of America's opposition to Russia and
China, all indicated the identification of the nation with a social
philosophy.

And yet, in contrast to socialism and communism, this social
ideology was, in addition, an ideology of nationalism. The "American way of life" was also a pattern of national behavior, beliefs,
and values; and its social ideology actually described and rationalized the general system of social relations existing in American
society.

From this point of view the American ideology resembled other
highly developed ideologies of nationalism. The American people
developed a strong sense of national mission and destiny, and

their aggressive nationalism expanded the territory of the United States from the Atlantic to the Pacific.[18] No other Western democracy so frequently applied loyalty tests or made ideological conformity the criterion of patriotism. The sense of national pride and the feeling of uniqueness were commented upon by almost all observers. "Not only are the Anglo-Americans united by these common opinions," observed Tocqueville, "but they are separated from all other nations by a feeling of pride. For the last fifty years no pains have been spared to convince the inhabitants of the United States that they are the only religious, enlightened, and free people . . . hence they conceive a high opinion of their superiority and are not very remote from believing themselves to be a distinct species of mankind." [19]

American nationalism rested on assumptions fundamentally different from those of other nations.[20] The American people were not a folk-nation or a federation of nations. They lacked ethnic, religious, or cultural unity, and all those traits which a common history impressed upon territorial societies.[21] This nation established its identity in patterns of political and social organization and in the benefits and powers deriving from its territory and its state. Citizenship was the only criterion which made the individual a member of the national community: and national loyalty meant loyalty to the Constitution. The formative force of American national unity has been, then, the idea of citizenship; through this concept the integration of state and society into a nation has been achieved.

The identification of the people with the state as citizens has meant participation in political power and the enjoyment of order and security, of civil rights and communal benefits. National identification has meant the will-to-power and prestige of the in-group in relation to the out-groups of other nations. The group feeling was created by the dividing wall of separate statehood, through the possession of sovereignty.

The strength of this nationalism rested upon the inevitable tension among closed systems of power, which forced the society inside each system to identify its welfare with the state. Its weakness stemmed from the struggle of the different sub-groups of the political society to use the state for the increase of their own power. Unless this nationalism is supported by a consciousness of intrinsic group unity, by a capacity to find areas of identification through which a community of purpose and belonging is created, nationalism may and has in American history become a disruptive rather than a unifying force. It is the character of this positive force of cohesion, of its national consciousness, and its concept of national unity which represents in America a unique configuration.

The singularity of this configuration lies in the fact that it refers exclusively to patterns of social and political values and to norms of thought and behavior and not to natural or historic factors of national unity and cohesion. Yet, the adoption of social and political values and norms as a framework for national identification is possible only if these values are based on some source of apparent ultimate truth or authority which confers on them the character of absolute validity—if they can claim universality. Universal citizenship implies always the incorporation of rationalistic and universal values into the national ideology.[22] But in no other nation have these values become the exclusive connotation of nationality or the exclusive framework of national identification.[23] On the contrary, having arisen in homogeneous societies whose national character has been welded by common historical experience, the nation was taken for granted, and the pattern of rational and universal values referred to the structure of the state and not to the identity of the nation.

In America, on the other hand, the same system of norms and values which justified the establishment of a new political structure, the republic, and brought about the victory of the concept of a citizen-state also brought about the establishment of national independence, the creation of a new nation. *This coincidence of the political and the national Revolution through the application of the same set of principles is the fundamental datum of American nationality and of the structure of its consciousness.*

The revolutionary separation from the mother country involved a radical break with its own past, the transformation of English subjects into American citizens and of the rights of Englishmen into the rights of nature. The very strongly developed consciousness of English national traditions and rights, of the continuity of history and belonging, had to be reinterpreted in new terms which replaced the traditional element by concepts taken from the natural-rights philosophy. The fact that the American nation was created by a revolutionary separation from the mother country brought about the adoption of rationalistic values and norms not only as the basis of an independent statehood, but as a definition of the nature of the new nation. Universal values and modes of thought which had served the British colonists in the struggle against England enabled them to interpret their own pattern of institutions and traditions in new terms. The interpretation of American nationality in terms of universally valid social and political ideals explains and maintains at one and the same time the character of the American nation as state-nation or citizen-nation. It is the paradoxical nature of its nationalism, its universalism, which has created the nation, welded the union, and given American nationalism its missionary and salvationist character. The same fact also explains the fixation of ideological patterns and the uniformity of its ideological developments.

If the unity of a nation is based on contrived grounds, on a conscious pattern of concepts and values, the state, society, and the individual will endeavor to maintain this unity under all conditions as the basis of social and political stability. In societies in which the principle of unity is a natural or a given datum, a variety of ideologies may compete with each other. But in a nation in which social and national cohesion is based on an ideological proposition, diversity can develop only within the framework of its ideological premises.

This interpretation of the American national consciousness has been challenged on the grounds that the American Revolution, unlike the French, hardly altered institutional and social patterns. Independence only changed the superstructure of society, or rather represented a final step in the process of a maturing nation. National character was thus a product of history, environment, and ethnic homogeneity, to which ideological premises or assumptions were irrelevant. This was the actual view of many of the conservative leaders of the Revolutionary generation and was to a certain degree shared by all of them. Washington's Farewell Address appealed to the sentiment of national unity by invoking tradition as well as principle: "The name of American, which belongs to you in your national capacity, must always exalt the just pride of patriotism more than any appellation derived from local discriminations. With slight shades of difference, you have the same religion, manners, habits and political principles. You have in a common cause fought and triumphed together. The independence and liberty you possess are the work of joint councils and joint efforts, of common dangers, sufferings, and successes." [24] Like their prototype and spiritual progenitors, the English Whigs, American Federalists and Whigs attempted to harmonize their own revolutionary inheritance with their tradition and to interpret the republican principles of American society and government as principles inherent in the national character and genius of its inhabitants and their religious heritage of liberty. This sentiment was particularly strong in New England and seemed to the young Tocqueville the ruling sentiment of this region.[25]

Franz Lieber, soon to become a shining light in political science and an authoritative interpreter of American nationalism, impressed upon the French visitor the uniqueness of the republican spirit of the American people which derived from the spirit of its mores and institutions—in short, from its national and racial inheritance.[26] The views of President Josiah Quincy of Harvard, of Jared Sparks, of John Quincy Adams, Daniel Webster, Alexander Everett, and Senator Francis C. Gray, were similar.[27] Josiah Quincy traced the American, and particularly the New England, spirit of liberty to the national genius of the American people: "Massachusetts was nearly as free before the revolution as to-day. We have put the name of the people where was the name of the king; otherwise nothing has been changed with us." [28]

Senator Gray emphasized the supreme importance of the common law for the spirit of American liberty and self-government. He also emphasized the tradition and inheritance of liberty: "We have been working for 200 years to form this spirit, and we had as a starting point the English spirit and an altogether republican religion." [29]

Jared Sparks traced the spirit of liberty and self-government in the American people to the ancient town meetings of their Saxon forefathers no less than to the conditions of an absolutely new beginning in a new world.[30] This viewpoint, colored in varying degrees with theories of racially inherited traits, dominated American historical thought from George Bancroft to Herbert Baxter Adams and was popularized by John Fiske, Josiah Strong, Theodore Roosevelt, and Lyman Abbott into a new organic concept of the nature of American nationality.[31]

This interpretation was basically conservative. It attempted to discredit the universal and rational premises of American democracy and the dynamic character of its concepts of nationality and to substitute an organic and traditional theory of American history and of American democracy. A more recent revival of this interpretation of American society and nationalism has re-emphasized the evolutionary and conservative character of the development of American society and the organic and tradition-rooted growth of American character traits.[32]

The authority of both Edmund Burke and Tocqueville also was invoked for this reinterpretation of American history. Burke's ambiguous support of the American cause, his hatred of the revolutionary dynamics of the French Revolution, and his reinterpretation of the English political status quo made him the paragon and teacher of American conservatism. Tocqueville, the prophet of a coming age of totalitarian despotism, has been cited to prove the basic difference between American democracy and European equalitarian tendencies, and his interpretation of the reconciliation of liberty with equality and public order has been accepted as the classical statement of this viewpoint.[33]

Yet the testimony of both witnesses is far from conclusive. Both were concerned to safeguard liberty and reconcile it with social order and stability. But Burke ignored all developments in America after 1776. Tocqueville, on the other hand, realized that the basic motive of American history and society was the social movement toward democracy. Though he noted that "this country is reaping the fruits of the democratic revolution which we are undergoing, without having had the revolution itself," and explained this organic growth of democratic institutions by the English heritage, the mores and principles of the early colonists, he realized that the transition from England to America was more than a transplantation. It involved a radical mutation of the social system by the selection of European patterns of social organization. "The emigrants who colonized the shores of America . . . somehow separated the democratic principle from all the principles that it had to contend with in the old communities of Europe and transplanted it alone."[34] Moreover, Tocqueville recognized the fundamental effect the American Revolution had on the pattern of social organization and ideas. "At this period [of the American Revolution] society was shaken to its center. The people, in whose name the struggle had taken place, conceived the desire of exercising the authority that it had acquired; its democratic tendencies were awakened; and having thrown off the yoke of the mother country, it aspired to independence of every kind." [35]

All Thirteen Colonies had developed institutional, social, and cultural patterns of life which created the basic conditions for independence and a national consciousness, and this pattern undoubtedly continued without radical change after the Revolution. Nor can it be doubted that a feeling of patriotism and of historical distinctiveness had arisen before the Revolution. For only when a society has become aware of its own corporate existence does it attempt to integrate the state with itself by the notion of nationality. Yet a political consciousness and a strongly homogeneous pattern of social life did not evolve within the American framework before 1765, but rather in the framework of each colony. The new national consciousness was the result of the contest between the colonies and the mother country and, finally, of the Revolution, and this consciousness was built upon the language and concepts of the natural-rights philosophy. Moreover, the establishment of the several states on the same grounds involved a radicalization of thought which brought about a change in all institutional patterns and in the structure of American society itself.

It has also been argued that the formative, historically elite group was ethnically homogeneous, of Anglo-American origin, and that the national pattern evolved in American society was its own pattern of life.[36] This pattern has been threatened, it is contended, by the deracination of American society, by the influx of other ethnic groups which have in the very act of accepting this way of life endangered its survival. Nativism from the beginning of the nineteenth century to our own times expresses the tension created by two competing types of national consciousness, the first universalistic in outlook, the second based on an awareness of belonging to a national organic community whose values are to a certain degree not transferable and whose aim is to determine the character of the nation and the activities of the state according to its own ideals. The interplay between these two tendencies has determined to a large degree the structure and course of American nationalism.

Yet, whatever the impact of universal concepts on the American historical experience, the conservative and nativistic interpreters of American history, no less than their opponents, concede that American nationality has to be defined, at least to some degree, by reference to certain political and social concepts; that it is a way of life and an attitude which somehow represents ultimate social values.[37]

III

National Unity: the American Interpretation

Wie an dem Tag, der dich der Welt verliehen,
  Die Sonne stand zum Grusse der Planeten,
  Bist alsobald und fort und fort gediehen
  Nach dem Gesetz, wonach du angetreten.
        So musst du sein, dir kannst du nicht entfliehen
  So sagten schon Sibyllen, so Propheten
  Und keine Zeit und keine Macht zerstückelt
  Geprägte Form, die lebend sich entwickelt.

Goethe, *Urworte. Orphisch*

The entire man is, so to speak, to be seen in the cradle of the child. The growth of nations presents something analogous to this; they all bear some marks of their origin. The circumstances that accompanied their birth and contributed to their development affected the whole term of their being.

Alexis de Tocqueville, *De la Démocratie en Amérique*

1. "A MORE PERFECT UNION"

National identification in America was achieved by the adoption of abstract, universal ideas which legitimized national independence and served as formative principles of the states and the Federal Union. The permanent influence of this system of ideas and values on the course of American history—the fixation of an ideological attitude—was due to the fact that the American people considered themselves a new kind of society. The very existence of the nation was bound up with the maintenance of those principles of social and political organization.

National identity was not a natural fact but an ideological structure. It was not the result of ethnic or historic unity, which accepts and realizes itself in a national state, nor could it be satisfied by citizenship and the desire for common power alone. Political unity had to be compatible with the meaning structure of national identification. The conceptual relation between society and state, between the American people and the Federal Union—in short, the meaning of the concept of the American nation—was revealed by the historic process which brought about the formation of the Federal Union.

From the beginning it was understood that some kind of national union was the necessary condition for independence, and the proposals for both were simultaneously considered by the Continental Congress. Common political action and the emergence of political unity developed largely through external pressures upon the colonies by Parliament and Crown.[1] The Stamp Act Congress, the Committees of Correspondence, the intercolonial boycott, and the Continental Congress were responses to a common challenge which created an awareness of a community of fate. The war with England developed the first institutional framework for united action. The Congress inherited the functions which had been exercised by the British Crown and substituted for the lost benefits of imperial union adequate forms of cooperation and unified force.

Emerging into a world of sovereign, centralized powers, of colonial empires, and mercantilist systems of economy, the new American states had to associate in order to survive and to enjoy the advantages of power. The decisive influence of foreign relations on the emergence of a unified national policy was expressed in the instructions of the Congress to its representatives abroad. The American ministers in France were to maintain "that these U S being by their constitution consolidated into one federal republic they be considered in all such treaties & in every case arising under them as one nation upon the principles of the federal Constitution."[2] Article III of the "Instructions to the Ministers Plenipotentiary Appointed to Negotiate Treaties of Commerce with the European Nations" stipulated "that these United States be considered in all such treaties, and in every case arising under them, as one nation."[3] In 1786 Jefferson explained that "to make us one nation as to foreign concern, and keep us distinct in domestic ones, gives the outlines of the proper division of powers between the general and particular governments." [4]

The concept of nationhood, then, was based not on the idea of intrinsic unity but on the awareness of the common needs of the people organized in political societies and compelled to deal with the outside world. The establishment of a national government thus rested on the purely rational and utilitarian grounds of the necessity for dealing effectively with other powers. Years later Jefferson summed up the motivations for the establishment of a federal government: "It could not but occur to every one, that these separate independencies, like the petty States of Greece, would be eternally at war with each other, and would become at length the mere partisans and satellites of the leading powers of Europe. All then must have looked forward to some further bond of union, which would insure eternal peace, and a political system of our own, independent of that of Europe." [5] In Europe the awareness of national unity created a desire for independence; in America independence antedated the will for national unity.

Though the Declaration of Independence was issued on behalf of the "United States of America" the Thirteen Colonies considered themselves free and independent states which took over, separately and together, the attributes of sovereignty. Justice Chase in Ware v. Hylton pointed out in 1796: "In *June* 1776, the Convention of *Virginia formally* declared, that *Virginia* was a free, sovereign, and independent state; and on the 4th of *July*, 1776, following the *United States*, in Congress assembled, declared the *Thirteen United Colonies* free and independent states." In the same case John Marshall, Counsel for Virginia, expressed even more clearly the absence of a political concept of nationality, by calling Virginia a nation. "It has been conceded," he remarked, "that independent nations have, in general, the right of confiscation; and that *Virginia,* at the time of passing her law [1777], was an independent nation." [6] Nor were the Articles of Confederation inspired by a clear concept of nationality; they rather created a league of independent states.[7] And the discussions of the Constitutional Convention of 1787 supported John Marshall's views.[8]

The very absence of any concept of national sovereignty made the breakdown of the Confederation inevitable, in the opinion of the prime initiators of constitutional change.[9] Gouverneur Morris distinguished between a federal and a national government. The former was merely a compact "resting on the good faith of the parties; the latter having a complete and *compulsive* operation." [10]

The very idea of the establishment of national government, advocated by the supporters of the Virginia plan, encountered passionate resistance. William Paterson argued that "the idea of a national Government, as contradistinguished from a federal one, never entered into the minds of any of them [the states and the people of America]. . . We have no power to go beyond the federal scheme. . . We must follow the people; the people will not follow us. . . If we are to be considered as a nation, all State distinctions must be abolished, the whole must be thrown into hotchpotch." [11]

Yet the term "national," used by James Madison, George Mason, Edmund Randolph, Gouverneur Morris, James Wilson, and others, did not refer to the awareness that the American people comprised a nation distinguished from others by its collective characteristics. Those inimical to the new Constitution were no less aware than their opponents of the common bonds and characteristics uniting the American people. Nor was the idea of "the national government" derived from an existing unity of the American people. It was conceived in contradistinction to state government and federation, and referred both to the method by which the government acted on the people and to the source of its authority. It referred, further, to the Americans' status of independence and common rights among the nations of the world. A national government operated directly on all the individuals of the United States. [12] It was supreme and subordinated to itself all other political authority. [13] Yet a centralized government could become a national government only if society identified itself with it and considered it as the embodiment of its own will. Such identification could be achieved through the idea of citizenship and responsible government or through that of natural and historic unity, or through both.

In America such concentration of political power as suggested by the nationalists in the convention could be legitimately exercised over the individual only if the government received its authority directly from the people. For this reason the nationalists in the convention insisted on the direct election of the national legislature. Republicanism alone did not account for the demand for direct representation. John Lansing, Luther Martin, and others were no less republican than the nationalists. It was rather the realization that a nation could be created only by citizenship. "Is it to be thought," asked George Mason, "that the people of America, so watchful over their interests; so jealous of their liberties, will give up their all, will surrender both the sword and the purse, to the same body, and that too not chosen immediately by themselves?" For the same reason James Wilson considered the election of the House of Representatives by the people "not only as the corner Stone, but as the foundation of the fabric: and that the difference between a mediate & immediate election was immense." [14]

The concept of nationalizing the state through citizenship and representative institutions explained also the insistence of some of the members on the direct election of the Senate and the Executive and their refusal to limit the rights of citizenship by property qualification.[15]

The main characteristics of the national-state were forged by the reciprocal impact of citizenship and representative government on the people of the United States understood as individuals and not as politically organized societies within their separate states. Yet the people became a nation by incorporating themselves as a political society through the compact of the Constitution.

The nationalists realized that the nation had to be thus established. During the debates the main argument for popular ratification was the fear that the states were unlikely to consent to the weakening of their own authority, and that any other procedure would renew the dependence on them of the national government, so that the Constitution would create a league, but in a different form.[16] Only popular ratification would make the Constitution the framework of a truly national union. Only the people "with whom all power remains" could accept and safeguard the Constitution. "It was of great moment," Mason observed, "that this doctrine should be cherished, as the basis of free government. . . In some of the States the Gov^{ts} were not derived from the clear & undisputed authority of the people. . . A National Constitution derived from such a source [ratification by the states] would be exposed to the severest criticisms." On the other hand, Madison pointed out, "a law violating a constitution established by the people themselves, would be considered by the Judges as null & void." [17] The Constitution was then to be the contract by which the people established a political society, which comprehended the states as integral parts of the nation.

Yet even this concept of the national state was not accepted by the Convention. The Constitution as adopted was, in the words of Madison, "neither a national nor a federal constitution; but a composition of both." [18] The terms "nation" and "sovereignty" were purposely omitted to conciliate the spokesmen of states' rights who proved adamant on this point.[19] The omission of these terms reflected the awareness of the incompatibility of the idea of national sovereignty with the concept of a compact on which the Constitution rested.

The idea of popular ratification and the provision of Article VI that "it was to be the supreme law of the land" endowed the Constitution with the character of a fundamental compact which created a national society. The dominance of the compact theory explained the hesitation to adopt the word "national." The concepts of social and political compact, of limited delegation of political power, expressed in the Preamble, dominated the idea of the nation no less than the independence movement and the establishment of the states. The same needs which led men to associate in civil societies led them also to federate in a wider framework for common protection and common welfare. The Constitution was the compact which defined the aims of this wider society, the powers delegated, the relations between the associated members, their institutions and the limits of political power.

The dominance of the natural-rights philosophy was reflected in the debates on the Constitution and those preceding its ratification. Thus the letter which transmitted the proposals of the Constitution to Congress stated: "It is obviously impracticable in the federal government of these states, to secure all rights of independent sovereignty to each, and yet provide for the interest and safety of all: Individuals entering into society must give up a share of liberty to preserve the rest." [20] Benjamin Franklin's suggestion that the Constitution might be imitated as a model for the unification of Europe revealed the purely rationalistic character of the concept of federal union.[21] The Union was built, according to Madison, on the analogy of a "fundamental compact by which individuals compose one Society, and which must in its theoretic origin at least, have been the unanimous act of the component members." [22]

The process of ratification emphasized the deliberate mode of creating a national union. The resolutions of the Massachusetts Constitutional Convention declared: "The Convention [of the people of Massachusetts] . . . acknowledging with grateful hearts, the goodness of the Supreme Ruler of the Universe in affording the people of the United States . . . an opportunity deliberately & peaceably without fraud or surprise of entering into an explicit & solemn Compact with each other by assenting to & ratifying a New Constitution in order to form a more perfect Union." [23] The ratifications of the states of Virginia, North Carolina, New York, and Rhode Island were all introduced by declarations which emphasized the purely contractual character of the Constitution and which limited further authority of the federal government. The Virginia declaration, like many others, endeavored to make the Preamble to the Declaration of Independence and of its own Bill of Rights an integral part of the Constitution, stating "that there are certain natural rights of which men, when they form a social compact, cannot deprive or divest their posterity." [24]

The theory of the contractual character of the Constitution contained an implicit conceptual distinction between the people of America and the federal union. The opponents of the Constitution maintained that the former were no more embodied in the Union than in the Confederation. "At the separation from the British Empire," declared Luther Martin, "the people of America preferred the establishment of themselves into thirteen separate sovereignties instead of incorporating themselves into one: to these they look up for the security of their lives, liberties & properties. . . The federal Gov^t they formed, to defend the whole agst foreign nations, in case of war, and to defend the lesser States agst the ambition of the larger." [25]

This distinction between the unity of the American people based upon common values and ideas, and political union was accepted by all sides. Even Alexander Hamilton, inimical to the equalitarian implications of the natural-rights philosophy, was compelled to use its arguments in *The Federalist* to defend the decisive national feature of the Constitution, Article VI. He argued that all laws which resulted from the contractual association of individuals must be supreme for this society. The laws of the federal government derived their authority from the contract by which the several political societies were fused into a larger one. "But it will not follow from this doctrine," Hamilton asserted, "that acts of the larger society which are *not pursuant* to its constitutional powers, but which are invasions of the residuary authorities of the smaller societies, will become the supreme law of the land. These will be merely acts of usurpation, and will deserve to be treated as such." [26]

Having accepted the purely contractual nature of the national government and its limited purpose, it remained to prove that the common interests of the people of America, their safety, well-being, and happiness could be secured only by federal union. The perils arising from the relations with the outside world and from the frictions among the states dominated the arguments of *The Federalist*. Though John Jay appealed to the unity and common nationhood of the American people, he did so in terms of common needs, common benefits, and dangers.[27] Emphasizing the necessity of national union for internal and external peace and for the security of all, he pointed out that "weakness and division at home would invite dangers from abroad," which nothing would avert more effectively than union, strength, and good government. Hamilton, too, warned that the alternative to union was internal weakness, rivalry, mutual war, and destruction.[28]

The right to interfere in the affairs of the states and to make general regulations was defended on the ground of common safety and tranquillity. "Laws in violation of private contracts, as they amount to aggression on the rights of those states, whose citizens are injured by them, may be considered as another probable source of hostility." [29] Without federal government the Republic would be destroyed by mutual tension, internal anarchy, and economic instability and would be replaced by military rule and monarchy. Madison examined and rejected for the same reasons the New Jersey plan proposed by Paterson as insufficient to prevent these dangers.[30]

From the necessity for survival the argument proceeded to the common benefits to be attained from the proposed Constitution—

stability, economic and political power, and good government. The Union was not favored on the grounds of common nationality but on the general principles of utility and necessity. It would combine all the benefits of the consolidated monarchical states of the Old World without the loss of liberty or civil rights and without the dangers of arbitrary rule. Federation, or the principle of the "enlarg[e]ment of the orbit," like checks and balances, was a "powerful means, by which the excellencies of republican government may be retained, and its imperfections lessened and avoided." [31] Characteristic was the reference to Montesquieu on the advantages of *confederate monarchy:* "This form of government is a convention, by which several smaller *states* agree to become members of a larger *one,* which they intend to form. It is a kind of assemblage of societies, that constitute a new one, capable of increasing by means of new associations, till they arrive to such degree of power as to be able to provide for the security of the united body." By their very extent and internal differentiation, they prevent the spread of tyranny or anarchy. "As this government is composed of small republics, it enjoys the internal happiness of each, and with respect to its external situation, it is possessed, by means of the association, of all the advantages of large monarchies." [32] The American nation had to be called into existence to secure for its people the advantages and benefits of federative association. It received its identity through its identification with the Union, with its strength, stability, security, and. power. "Let the Americans disdain to be the instruments of European greatness! Let the thirteen states, bound together in a strict and indissoluble union, concur in erecting one great American system, superior to the control of all transatlantic force or influence, and able to dictate the terms of the connection between the old and new world!" [33]

2. "WE THE PEOPLE OF THE UNITED STATES"

The appeal for a more perfect union was made to the "people of the United States," to "the people of America" and to "Americans." Though the term "the people of the United States" had a well-defined meaning, relating to the citizens of the several states, the expressions "the people" of the United States, "the people of

America" and "the Americans" possessed far more powerful emotional and evocative significance.

"The people of America" signified the aggregate of individuals living in the territory of the United States. It referred furthermore to the individuals, already members of the political societies of the several states, and thereby parts of a corporate entity. This double meaning of the world "people"—a sum of individuals, and an incorporated community—reflected the genetic and generic relation between the individual and society.

In the sense of the Enlightenment, the term "the people" meant "man"—sovereign over himself, the free associate of a political society, the bearer of individual inalienable rights. From the term "one people," used in the opening sentence of the Declaration of Independence, Jefferson immediately proceeded to the term "men" as the ultimate source of authority. The word "people" in the singular was used when speaking of the common government and in the plural when referring to the right to establish a "new Government, laying its foundation on such principles and organizing its powers in such form, as to them shall seem most likely to effect their Safety and Happiness." [34]

The people never lose their separate individualities even when entering society. They always retain their character though they exchange some of their natural rights for civil rights. George Mason, in the Resolutions drawn up for the Fairfax Independent Company, explained that ". . . men entered into compacts to give up some of their natural rights, that by union and mutual assistance they might secure them; but they gave up no more than the nature of things required." [35] They remain the ultimate judges and arbiters of their fate. This view underlies the practice and theory of government in all American states. It is made explicit in the bills of rights of the several states and inheres as a basic idea in the constitutions of the states and the federal union.

Jefferson expressed the same views in 1776. He distinguished between individual, self-enforceable rights and those which could be secured only through collective protection, the civil rights established by mutual compact. "They agree," he asserted, "to retain individually the first Class of Rights or those of personal Competency; and to detach from their personal possession the second Class . . . and to accept in lieu thereof a right to the whole power . . . These I conceive to be civil rights or rights of Compact and are distinguishable from Natural rights." [36] Identical views pervaded the thinking of the period. Samuel Adams stated that "the very end for which man alone can be supposed to submit to civil government, which is . . . that each individual, under the joint protection of the whole community, may be the Lord of his own possession." [37] The most succinct expression of this view is to be found in the Preamble to the Massachusetts Constitution of 1780: "The body politic is formed by a voluntary association of individuals." [38]

In all these statements the term "people" referred to free individuals creating societies and establishing a common rule for their own needs and according to the rights of nature and the light of reason. Whether the appeal was to the "people of the United States" or the "people of America," it was made to man as such. From this point of view, "the people" were timeless, beyond the contingencies of history, and they were identical with mankind. This timelessness and universality were transferred to the political structure, the states, the Union, and the nation. Growing out of the social compact, the nation had no other peculiarity than that which the land and men bestow on it. It was not a primary, concretely structured datum, but a fabricated and highly generalized community of men guided by nature and reason to secure the common benefits which social life could bestow on them.

This nation was highly articulate and purposive because citizenship and well-defined rules of common life were its only characteristics. The transparent simplicity of its structure created a feeling of community, unity, and identity, which was more intense than that of the historically formed nations of the time. And yet the simplicity of the national structure gained a definite character through the term "America." The word added to the political consciousness of unity through citizenship a natural and unique character. This collective awareness was expressed in the terms "the people of America," "the Americans." The people were more than a community of individuals guided by nature and reason. They were "Americans" united by history and geography, by a common country and a common future in the New World. The term "America" was juxtaposed to that of "Europe"; a "New World" was contrasted to the old, and a new system of government was set against the old régime.

3. THE NEW WORLD

The continent and the people were wedded to each other and blended into one idea and myth. Hardly any other land had such complex meaning—such symbolic significance. It was the Promised Land; the people were its Israel. They left their old homes in search of a better life, to gain the stature of men, to live according to their conscience, to build Utopia or the City of God—in short to realize their individual or collective dreams. America became endowed with all their emotions and saturated with their dreams until the continent personified the hope of a better world which transformed its people into a new race.[39]

Always, America had meant a new beginning, a new hope, and a new life—for the Puritans' Commonwealth, for Roger Williams' revolutionary civil government, for William Penn's "Holy Experiment," for the Moravians, Mennonites, and Dunkards, for the Scotch-Irish and the Huguenots, and for the thousands of the poor of England and the European continent who dared to cross the ocean, bound as indentured servants and redemptioners.[40] The land was not, as in the Old World, the land of the forefathers, the native country, *patria,* the place where home was. Nor was it the land of memories, of familiar landscape, or of the horizon of a rooted life. It was not even the setting of the wider community, of the nation, to which one belonged. The people did not give the land its name; rather the land made them a people—"Americans." [41] The land belonged to the future, not to the past. Its continental expanse, its virgin soil and primeval forests, stretched into space and time. America could not be compared to a country. It was as vast as mankind.

From the beginning it had held a unique place in the thought of Europeans. Amerigo Vespucci's vision of the *mundus novus* mingled the faint memories of a lost golden age, "the *ultima thule,*" and Paradise Lost. Sir Thomas More's "Utopia" was the first of the many dreams of a rejuvenation of mankind stimulated by the discovery of the New World.[42] Francis Bacon's New Atlantis joined memories of Plato's Lost Continent with visions of the newly found one.[43] John Smith's description of Virginia—"Heaven and earth never agreed better to frame for man's habitation"— chimed in harmony with Drayton's poem celebrating the first settling:

> VIRGINIA,
> Earth's only Paradise . . .
> To whome the golden Age
> Still Natures lawes doth give diue . . .

And Shakespeare's Gonzalo expressed the same composite image of new and old myths, Christian and pagan.

> All things in common nature should produce
> Without sweat or endeavor; treason, felony,
> Sword, pike, knife, gun, or need of any engine
> Would I not have; but nature should bring forth
> Of its own kind, all foison, all abundance
> To feed my innocent people.[44]

The religious vision of a redeemed and purified society in the seventeenth and eighteenth centuries added depth to the belief that a new earth was foreordained for the happiness of a renewed man. Puritans identified themselves as Israel; they were the chosen people and America their Promised Land. Their Messianism developed into a religious philosophy of history and progress. The future was the purpose of the movement of mankind through history; and America was to be the final scene in which the drama of history would come to a glorious conclusion, when all people would be "ruled by the Institutions, Laws, and Directions of the Word of God, not only in Church-Government and Administrations, but also in the government and administration of all affairs in the Commonwealth." [45] In Jonathan Edwards' *Thoughts on the Revival of Religion in New England,* history was still the scheme of redemption of the human race. The discovery of America, coinciding with the Reformation, opened up the possibility "for a glorious renovation of the World" of which the "great awakening" of New England was a conspicuous sign.[46]

In the eighteenth century, America becomes for Europe as well as for its own inhabitants the stage for the realization of mankind's hopes. "Nature," the magic masterwork of the Enlightenment, iridescent with the complex meanings which the revolutionary hopes for the transformation of society instilled, reigned in the

New World. Voltaire hailed the commonwealth of William Penn, where simplicity, tolerance, natural morality, and religion made life enviable and beautiful.[47] Abbé Raynal proved that American republican institutions and love of liberty reconciled Rousseau's critique of civilization with Voltaire's defense of its benefits. "Pennsylvania gives the lie to the imposture and flattery, that proclaim with impunity in temples and courts that man has need of gods and Kings. The righteous man, the free man, needs only his equals to be happy." [48] Guillard de Beaurien's *L'Elève de la nature* invoked Virginia as the ideal country which had neither towns nor luxuries nor crimes. "You are as Nature would have us all." [49] George Berkeley longed to establish an ideal community in America. The New English Humanism of the early eighteenth century, Christian piety, secular enlightenment, and the ideal of humanism fused in his vision of historical progress.

> In happy climes, the seat of innocence,
> Where nature guides and virtue rules,
> Where men shall not impose for truth and sense
> The pedantry of courts and schools:
> There shall be sung another golden age,
> The rise of empire and of arts,
> The good and great inspiring epic rage,
> The wisest heads and noblest hearts.
> Not such as Europe breeds in her decay:
> Such as she bred when fresh and young,
> When heavenly flame did animate her clay . . .
> Westward the course of empire take its way;
> The four first acts already past,
> A fifth shall close the drama with the day;
> Time's noblest offspring is the last.[50]

For the Age of Reason America had both a special and a moral meaning. The vast empty spaces, unobstructed by the past, invited man to live freely and not in crowds. Here the eternal beneficence of nature could be observed and reason became the guide of action. Unhampered by the accumulation of customs, prejudices, and the follies and crimes of ages, men could work out their own salvation by their own powers. Here humanity was created anew as one race out of the mixture of nations and religions. Here the process of civilization was repeated in the space of a few generations. Here, where the Indian proved that liberty and equality were the gifts of nature, the American could recapture these birthrights on a new and higher level of civilization. The circle closed. Man, created free and equal in the state of nature, having traversed countless ages, had on a higher level of enlightenment and civilization regained the stature of his first progenitor by building on the virgin continent a new society in which the rule of liberty harmoniously reconciled the individual's interest with that of his fellows.[51]

This structure of symbolic meanings was discovered by the Europeans before it had taken deep roots in America. Only with the approach of the Revolution was its meaning suddenly precipitated into national consciousness.[52]

As long as Americans considered themselves part of the British Empire, divided by colonial governments and united only by the Crown and by Parliament, the significance of being American could not fully reveal itself. Their national identification was that of free Englishmen, inheriting the liberties and rights of British subjects. The awakening of an American consciousness needed a point of observation and comparison from which the unity of life and the perspective of a continental future could be observed. It needed a revolutionary cause through which the colonists could identify themselves as members of one society.

4. BENJAMIN FRANKLIN, THE "FIRST AMERICAN"

Benjamin Franklin's intellectual development illustrated the transition from a provincial to a continental consciousness, from an identification with the British nation to the awareness of being an American. Because he was the most cosmopolitan of Americans, equally at home in London and Paris, he was the first to be aware of the basic community of fate and interests of the British colonies in America.

The Albany Plan, proposed by Franklin and calling for a voluntary union of the colonies, anticipated the Continental Congress and the Confederacy in its scheme of organization as well as in the scope of its proposed activity.[53] Franklin's thoughts moved in continental terms. He was aware of the unique possibilities which the continent offered to the colonies in well-being, in strength of population and economic power, and he realized the fundamental difference between the destiny of Europe and America.[54] Unlike

Europe, generally settled to its maximum capacity and unable to
increase its population except by the development of manufacturing, the basic fact of America was its superabundance of unoccupied land.[55] Given man's nature and the opportunities of the
environment, the American population would double every twenty
years. "But, notwithstanding this increase, so vast is the territory
of North America, that it will require many ages to settle fully,
and, till it is fully settled, labor will never be cheap here, where
no man continues long a laborer for others, but gets a plantation
of his own; no man continues long a journeyman to a trade, but
goes among those new settlers and sets up for himself. . ." [56]
Franklin surveyed the continent and envisioned a mighty empire
which would surpass England and Europe in population, wealth,
and happiness.[57] The Americans would "extend themselves almost
without bounds" and "increase infinitely from all causes; becoming
a numerous, hardy, independent people; possessed of a strong
country." [58]

And yet, up to the convocation of the First Continental Congress, Franklin could hardly be called an American nationalist
who strove for a complete emancipation from foreign dependence.
On the contrary, his awareness of the unity of the American people
was sustained by his feeling for their common British nationality.[59]
For many years he strenuously argued against the wisdom of
permitting the immigration of non-English settlers who "will never
adopt our language or customs any more than they can acquire
our complexion." [60] His insistence that the American people should
remain part of the British Empire emanated not only from utilitarian convictions but from a profound feeling for the natural,
historic, and spiritual unity between the American colonies and
the mother country. Only the most grievous tyranny and oppression could destroy such loyalty. Union with Great Britain through
an imperial Parliament would probably subsist as long as Britain
continued a nation.[61]

Franklin's concept of the Empire reconciled his growing awareness of the unique destiny of America with his identification with
the British nation. The empire was an association of free states
which should participate on equal terms in the government and
in the benefits accruing to all the members. It was bound together
by mutual protection, common force, and the advantages of an

imperial market economy, and by the common national heritage of descent, language, and the community of political rights, institutions, and ideals. The concepts of representation and responsible government, of the rule of law and individual liberty, inherent in the very rise of the British national consciousness, permitted this wider interpretation of English nationality.[62]

Yet Franklin could not be sure that the English themselves accepted this concept of the Empire. As early as 1766 Franklin doubted that Parliament would willingly forego its claims of supremacy over the American colonies. He realized more and more the purely mercantilistic character of British policy and the dangers, resulting from the rule of vested interests in Parliament and Cabinet, for the further development of the colonies. "It is time then to take care of ourselves by the best means in our power." [63] He realized, though with regret, that separation would inevitably follow from the British attitude.[64] His growing radicalism, and the emergence of a mature economic philosophy, made him increasingly critical of continental and English society and sharpened his awareness of the unique structure of American society.[65] "America, an immense territory, favored by nature with all the advantages of climate, soils, great navigable rivers, lakes, etc., must become a great country, populous and mighty; and will, in less time than is generally conceived, be able to shake off any shackles that may be imposed upon her, and perhaps place them on the imposers. . . In the meantime every act of oppression will, sour their tempers, lessen greatly, if not annihilate, the profits of your commerce with them, and hasten their final revolt; for the seeds of liberty are universally found there, and nothing can eradicate them." [66]

Reacting sharply against the English claims of sovereignty over the colonies, he spoke more and more of the "American people" in terms of a nation. When the First Continental Congress met, Franklin had come to think in terms of American nationality, in terms of a continental society and of a continental future. The relations with England and the Empire now were regarded solely in the light of political utility and of the risks involved in immediate independence. But these were the considerations of a man who had liberated himself completely from the sentiment of English nationality and looked at Great Britain as at a foreign nation.

"When I consider the extreme corruption prevalent among all orders of men in this old, rotten state, and the glorious public virtue so predominant in our own rising country, I cannot but apprehend more mischief than benefits from a closer union. I fear they will drag us after them in all the plundering wars which their desperate circumstances, injustice, and rapacity may prompt them to undertake." [67]

The development of Benjamin Franklin's political mind illustrated the growing impact of the continent and the New World on the rise of an American national consciousness and the abiding importance of these concepts in the structure of American identification. While the concepts of the national union and of the people retained the universalistic and rationalistic connotations which the natural-law theory and the philosophy of natural rights imparted to them, the concept of "America" endowed them with a concrete character basic to the formation of a national consciousness. Yet the tenets of the American revolutionary period which formed the pattern of national identification contained more than these elements; they also created a positive value system concerning man and society.

IV

The First National Creed: American Whiggism

The process of estrangement and of disassociation from the British nation and the emergence of a continental American consciousness, reflected in Franklin's thought, characterized also the ideological development of the leaders of the revolutionary movement in the period leading up to the Declaration of Independence. There were differences in the stages of development. The awareness of continental unity and of a unique destiny of the American people dominated Franklin's mind long before he recognized the necessity of separation. The majority of the patriot leaders, on the other hand, arrived at this conclusion through the clash of their own concepts of rights and of the nature of their status with those existing in Great Britain, and through the realization that the two sets of views were absolutely incompatible. That awareness was the product of a significant evolution.

By the mid-century the feeling of a community of values with Great Britain and of a common framework of authority had all but obliterated the older sense of separation and distinctiveness. The growing cultural sophistication in the seaboard colonies had strengthened this identification and created a provincial pride which fitted perfectly into the general pattern of British ideas about the nature of the Empire.[1]

British patriotism in America grew stronger with the participation of the colonial troops in the wars that brought the long-drawn-out struggle between Britain and France to a conclusion. The imperial consciousness, created by these conflicts with a common enemy and by the acquisition of the vast French territories, was English and not American.[2] Hopes for increased commerce and for the unlimited possibilities of extension of western settlement were important elements in this imperial patriotism. It seemed evident that the "foundations of the future grandeur and stability of the British Empire lie in America." [3] The Peace of Paris signified the triumph of "Protestantism, free government, and liberty." "The more independent and self-assertive the colonists became, the more anxious they seemed to sound like true-born Englishmen." [4] But the eighteenth-century Whig's interpretation of the British Constitution paradoxically created the ideological basis of American resistance to British imperial dominion and crystallized an American consciousness.

1. "THE FREEST PRINCIPLES OF THE ENGLISH CONSTITUTION"

Jefferson's statement that the principles of the American government were built on "the freest principles of the English constitution, with others derived from natural right and natural reason," was actually a description of the development of the American ideology.[5] That ideology proceeded from those "freest principles of the English Constitution," as understood by the eighteenth-century American, and disassociated them from their historic and factual background until they came to rest solely on the theory of natural rights and of natural reason. Liberty, constitutional limitation of power, and representative government were the main elements of the creed of the American Whig; and on this creed he based his loyalty to the British Crown, his pride as a British subject, and his identification with the mother country. "Eighteenth-century Virginia, indeed eighteenth-century America, was dedicated with astonishing unanimity to a 'party line'. . . . The principles of Whiggery, altered to American requirements, claimed the allegiance of all but a reactionary or radical handful of the colonists." [6] Through the eighteenth century these principles were increasingly saturated with the natural-rights philosophy and the outlook of an optimistic humanism, in which liberty and the ideal of active citizenship, wedded to a faith in the progress of men, became predominant.

Samuel Adams was sincere when he again and again protested his loyalty to King and Empire, in which the colonists envisioned the best guarantee for human happiness and colonial rights. "We beg that your Excellency would consider the people of this province as having the strongest affection for His Majesty, under whose happy government they have felt all the blessings of liberty: they have a warm sense of honor, freedom and independence of the subject of a patriot king. They have a just value of the inestimable rights which are derived to all men from nature, and are happily interwoven in the British Constitution." [7]

The equation of the rights and privileges of the subjects of Great Britain, with "the common rights of mankind" elevated the status of the colonists to that of citizens in an empire of equal rights and liberties and justified the independence of the colonial legislatures from the British Parliament.[8] It created a sense of nationality which was wholly determined by the idea of citizenship and to a large degree emancipated from the historic pattern of English loyalty. In this sense, Samuel Adams spoke of the "British nation" as a framework of identification and as a sanctuary of liberty and justice. In the era since the Glorious Revolution, "that grand era of British liberty," the blessings of English liberty had enabled the American colonies "to increase and multiply, till . . . a dreary wilderness is become a fruitful field, and a grand source of national wealth and glory." [9]

This interpretation of the rights of Englishmen under the Constitution rested on concepts the validity of which was never explicitly acknowledged by the ruling classes of Great Britain nor by those who sympathized with the American cause, the leaders of the different Whig circles and cliques.[10] The colonists turned a theoretical construction, or rather a theoretical fiction, into an instrument for defending their claim for equality against the Parliament while yet remaining loyal subjects of the Crown.[11] In this sense James Otis appealed against Parliament to the British Constitution as fundamental law which limited sovereignty and defined power in America. "No acts of Parliament can establish such a writ; though it should be made in the very words of the petition, it would be void. An act against the constitution is void." Such an interpretation was quite new and contravened the powers of the King in Parliament, though there were Englishmen who agreed with Otis. John Adams correctly stressed the fundamental importance of the theory propounded by Otis for the rise of independence.[12]

America's concept of the British Constitution was the first

expression of an independent mind and of a distinctive attitude toward government even though the colonists were not fully aware of the ideological significance.[13] The American patriots did not invent this concept but leaned heavily on those English and European writers and political philosophers who opposed the ruling powers of their time—James Harrington, Algernon Sidney, John Trenchard, Lord Bolingbroke and Montesquieu.[14] Yet, unlike the Europeans, the Americans acted upon this concept, and as in the case of the natural-rights theory, made the abstract idea a living institutional and legal force. For, despite its antecedents, the American concept of the constitution as fundamental law which preceded and defined legitimate authority was deeply rooted in its own historical experience and traditions.

The concept of the constitution as an agreement to form a civil compact developed both in England and America out of the sectarian and Calvinistic idea of the congregation under the impact of the political struggle against absolutism. It was the product of a debate which traversed all English history in the seventeenth century.[15] This debate was, of course, conducted in the context of medieval and Renaissance thought and subject to the influence of the classical revival.[16] Yet the Puritan-Calvinistic idea of the covenant transformed the ancient idea of a constitution. Having destroyed the fabric of traditional government, the Puritan revolutionaries had been compelled after 1642 to use the idea of covenants and political compacts to impart a new loyalty, order, and authority to their regimes. "The solemn League and Covenant" of the Parliament was followed by the constitutional proposals of the Levellers and the Army. "The agreement of the People," the "Heads of the Proposals" of the Army, the "Instrument of Government" and, finally, "the Humble Petition and Advice" were all constitutions in the American sense.[17] The turmoil of the Puritan Revolution transformed the Calvinistic and sectarian concept of the covenanted society into the civil compact of the natural-rights theory. The religious concept became saturated with elements of history, national, political and legal traditions, and ideas of natural law.[18]

The necessities of the Revolution in England were paralleled by those of planting new societies in the wilderness, and the same basic ideological developments were instrumental in laying the foundation for the construction of new societies in America.

The Puritan concept of the covenanted nature of the visible church of believers and of civil society was built into the very structure of the New England colonies.[19] The Mayflower Compact, the "Fundamental Orders of Connecticut," "The Fundamental Agreement or Original Constitution of the Colony of New Haven," were all true frames of government, or constitutions, agreed upon by those who associated with each other in their establishment. The "Fundamental Orders of Connecticut" stated: "we the Inhabitants . . . doe, for our selues and our Successors and such as shall be adioyned to vs . . . enter into Combination and Confederation togather, to mayntayne and presearue the liberty and purity of the gospell . . . As also in or Ciuell Affaires to be guided and gouerned according to such Lawes . . . as shall be made . . . as followeth." [20] "The Fundamental Agreement or Original Constitution of the Colony of New Haven" proclaimed itself "as a fundamental agreement concerning civil government." [21] In the same way the Compact of the Government of Rhode Island announced "that the Government which this Bodie Politick doth attend . . . is a DEMOCRACIE, or Popular Government." [22]

James Harrington, John Milton, Algernon Sidney, Henry Nevil, and John Locke, who formed the bridge between the revolutionary period and the eighteenth-century political theory of Whiggism in England, were to the same degree meaningful in America. Of this group of thinkers, Harrington and Milton distilled the whole force of the revolutionary theory of constitution into their political work, giving it a purely secular form. In both men the impact of the writers of antiquity and the Renaissance combined with that of their religious independence to create a theory of republican constitutionalism.

Milton's republicanism arose from his "being so conversant in Livy and the Roman authors, and the greatness he saw done by the Roman Commonwealth." In Hobbes's opinion, also, love of the Greek and Roman writers seduced such men as Milton to extol popular government "by the glorious name of Liberty." [23] While historical and sociological reflections often obscured the ideological nature of Harrington's theory, Milton clearly emphasized liberty as the supreme test of all government. In his *Ready and Easy Way to Establish a Free Commonwealth* and his *Present Means and Brief Delineation of a Free Commonwealth,* liberty was the constitutional principle which explained his theory of natural rights and social contract, his advocacy of the separation of state and church, and his hatred of monarchy.[24] Milton's concept of liberty was thus already dissociated from the "liberties" of the Englishmen. It had universal implications as the end and means of human felicity, the expression of human dignity, and the principle of all progress. "I behold," he observed, "the nations of the earth recovering that liberty which they so long had lost; and that the people of this island are . . . disseminating the blessings of civilization and freedom among the cities, kingdoms and nations." [25]

On the other hand, Harrington's *Oceana* and other projected frames and models of governments worked out the interrelation between forms of government and social conditions.[26] Like Jean Bodin in relation to the French Wars of Religion, Harrington distilled the experiences of the Puritan Revolution in his theory of the constitutions of government. He wished to determine the force which maintained or changed a given structure of government and which would reveal the principles that prevented the deterioration of republics or commonwealths. The constitutions, or principles of government, gave authority to power, which rested on the economic structure of society. The two were interrelated and determined each other.

A correct republican constitution changed the structure of society by preserving or creating a suitable pattern of economic power. *Oceana* was a model of a free commonwealth which possessed an intrinsic self-corrective mechanism for the preservation of the regime. "Government (to define it *de jure* . . .) is an art wherby a civil society of men is instituted and preserv'd upon the foundation of a common right or interest; or (to follow Aristotle and Livy) it is the empire of laws, and not of men." [27] The only natural government was a popular one, for it alone rested on the common rights and interests of all its members. In this sense, "a Commonwealth is but a civil society of men." [28]

The soul of the commonwealth was civil liberty, which was

obedience to the laws devised by reason and consented to by all.[29] As only men who lived under the dominion of reason were free, so "the liberty of a commonwealth" was "the empire of her laws, the absence thereof would betray her to the lust of tyrants." [30] A commonwealth was viable only if its government was constructed in the proper way, and if liberty and equality were determined by the fundamental law or constitution. "The center, or basis of every government, is no other than the fundamental laws of the same . . . Wherefore the fundamental laws of *Oceana*, or the center of this commonwealth, are the agrarian and the ballot." [31]

Harrington's constitutional projects and theories and his theory of the nature of free constitutions had a great influence on the proprietary projects of New Jersey, the Carolinas, and Pennsylvania. Among the founders of these colonies, Sir George Carteret, Anthony Ashley Cooper, third Earl of Shaftesbury, and William Penn all stood under the influence of the Cromwellian constitutional experiments as well as those of Harrington.[32] This is evident in "The Fundamental Constitution of Carolina" of 1669 which, whether constructed by John Locke or by Lord Shaftesbury, revealed, in spite of its medieval trappings, the thought and principles of the *Oceana*. "The Charter or Fundamental Laws of West New Jersey" expressly stated that "the common law or fundamental rights and privileges of West New Jersey . . . to be the foundation of the government, which is not to be altered by the legislative authority," [33] and Chapter XIV of that charter declared that "any who . . . subverts any of the fundamentals of the said laws in the Constitution of the government of this province" was to be considered traitor.[34]

William Penn's Frame of Government of Pennsylania (1682) followed Harrington not only in the use of the terms "frames" and "model" but also in the construction of its government. As in Harrington's commonwealth, the council proposed the laws which were decided upon by the elective assembly.[35] The same influence emerged in the preface to the Frame of Government which declared: *"any government is free to the people under it (whatever the frame) where the laws rule and the people are a party to these laws . . .* we have to the best of our skill, contrived and composed the *frame* and *laws* of this government, to the great end of all government viz: *to support power in reverence with the people,*

and to secure the people from the abuse of power . . . for liberty
without obedience is confusion, and obedience without liberty is
slavery. To carry out this evenness is partly owing to the Constitution, and partly to the magistracy." [36]

The concept of the constitution as the fundamental law of the
people's rights, though a good English doctrine of the seventeenth
century, was no longer recognized as valid in the eighteenth.[37]
The idea of the constitution as developed on both sides of the
Atlantic in the seventeenth century was revolutionary, unhistorical, and antitraditional. Its early association with the contractual
theory of government and that of man's natural rights made it part
of a rationalistic ideology which destroyed dynastic and national
loyalties. In the light of this theory, the constitution was a political
contract by which a society established itself as a state and its
people became a nation. In this sense the idea of the constitution
in seventeenth-century America was a force which set the American societies apart from England and destroyed their national
identification with the mother country.

Yet the Glorious Revolution of 1688 and the prolonged Whig
supremacy of the eighteenth century, together with the general
strengthening of imperial relations, created a new feeling of
national identity in America in which the idea of the British
Constitution played a decisive part. And yet, beyond the common
term used, there lay a gulf of misunderstanding and of differing
interpretations. The Americans continued to interpret the structure of British government and its principles in the light of seventeenth-century efforts to create a framework of civil liberty which
at least logically preceded the state and was set above its authority as its fundamental law. In this they were confirmed by writers
whom they took as representatives of the British mind—Sidney,
Locke, independent Whigs like John Trenchard and Thomas
Gordon; their successors, William Pitt, Lord Camden, and Lord
Shelburne; and the radicals of the second half of the century,
John Cartwright, Isaac Barré, John Wilkes, Richard Price, Joseph
Priestley, and others. From these writers the American settlers
derived a new concept of nationality and patriotism which eminently suited the colonial situation. British nationalism and patriotism, as developed in the eighteenth century, were built on the idea
of citizenship and liberty, on the feeling of a community of rights
and benefits which had sufficient nationalistic and universalistic

elements to encompass the colonists and their separate societies. This was probably the first modern theory—and the prototype—of European nationalism.[38]

No one expressed this feeling in a more felicitous way than the grandson of the founder of English Whiggism and the pupil of Locke, the third Earl of Shaftesbury: "OF all human Affections, the noblest and most becoming human Nature, is that of LOVE *to one's Country*. This, perhaps, will easily be allow'd by all Men, who have *really* a COUNTRY, and are of the number of those who may be call'd A PEOPLE, as enjoying the Happiness of a real Constitution and Polity, by which they are *Free* and *Independent*." [39] Yet this feeling was, though natural and even instinctive, a moral and rational attitude. The love of country was not that of the soil but of its free constitution. If a country were enslaved and its pepole emigrated, they would be still a nation.[40]

Shaftesbury directly pointed out the relevance of this concept of patriotism and of the nation to the colonists: "Surely, . . . wherever they might be then detain'd, to whatever Colonys sent, or whither-soever driven by any Accident . . . we shou'd be oblig'd still to consider our-selves as *Fellow-Citizens* . . . as honestly and heartily as the most inland Inhabitant or Native of the Soil." [41] Yet Shaftesbury's concept of the nation was firmly rooted in the universal tradition of the eighteenth century. The nation had meaning only insofar as it enlarged and confirmed the dignity of men. His reflections mirrored the birth of the concept of the nation out of the ideas of society, state, and citizenship. The seventeenth-century ideas of a civil society and of the contractual formation of the body politic were transformed into the eighteenth-century idea of the nation:

> The RELATION of *Country-man*, if it be allow'd any thing at all, must imply something *moral* and *social*. The Notion it-self pre-supposes a naturally *civil* and *political* State of MANKIND, and has reference to that particular part of Society to which we owe our chief Advantages as *Men*, and rational Creatures, such as are *naturally* and *necessarily* united for each other's Happiness and Support, and for the highest of all Happinesses and Enjoyments; "The Intercourse of *Minds*, the free Use of our *Reason*, and the Exercise of mutual Love and *Friendship*.[42]

Such public spirit could develop only in England and in other commonwealth states for such patriotism resulted from a "Social Feeling of Partnership with Human Kind." [43] Where absolute power ruled, no feelings of "community" could exist.[44] A multitude held together by force, though under one and the same head, was not a people. " 'Tis the social Ligue [League], Confederacy, and mutual Consent, founded in some common Good or Interest, which joins the Members of a Community, and make a People ONE. Absolute Power annuls *the Publick;* And where there is no *Publick,* or *Constitution,* there is in reality no *Mother*-COUNTRY, or NATION." [45]

The Glorious Revolution in England created the condition for a true nation, making the subjects fellows of one great partnership. A "happy Ballance of power" between the prince and the people saved their liberty and established stability of government. Only here a "*Free Government*" and a "*National Constitution*" were called into being.[46] "We have the Notion of a PUBLICK, and a CONSTITUTION; how a *Legislative,* and how *an Executive* is model'd. We understand Weight and Measure in this kind, and can reason justly on the *Ballance* of *Power* and *Property.* The Maxims we draw from hence, are as evident as those in *Mathematics.* Our increasing Knowledge shows us every day more and more, what COMMON SENSE is in Politicks." [47]

The terms "constitution," "balance of power" and "weight and measures" revealed the influence of the age of reason, its belief in progress and liberty through the gradual spread of knowledge.[48] Liberty and the rule of reason—this was the meaning of the British Constitution. No other people "ow'd so much to *a constitution,* and so little to *a soil* or *climate,*" as the British.[49]

The same concept of the constitution dominated *Cato's Letters* written by John Trenchard and Thomas Gordon, the independent Whigs whose essays "on Liberty, Civil and Religious" were immensely popular in eighteenth-century America.[50] Like all the liberal writers of the latter half of the seventeenth century and the eighteenth century, the authors of *Cato's Letters* were steeped in the spirit of classical republicanism and of religious independence which they fused into a humanistic concept of human liberty as the ultimate criterion of politics. *Cato's Letters* were dedicated to liberty. "Let us therefore," wrote Gordon in his dedication, "make general Liberty, the Interest and Choice . . . of all mankind; and brand those as Enemies to human Society, who are Enemies to equal and impartial Liberty." [51]

As for Algernon Sidney, whom the authors considered the best writer on government, liberty, both civil and religious, was the touchstone of all government and the purpose of the Constitution.[52] Though not commonwealth men, they were still rooted in the seventeenth-century tradition of revolutionary Whiggism and therefore suspicious and sharply critical of the coalition between the Crown and the ruling parliamentary and ministerial cliques. Yet a spirit of civil pride and British nationalism pervaded their attacks on government. The awareness of the fundamental difference between England's Constitution and the almost universal despotism in Europe and the remainder of the world made them unswerving critics of the post-revolutionary regimes in England. "Blessed be God, there are still some free Countries in *Europe* . . . Can we ever over-rate it [the blessings of liberty], or be too jealous of a Treasure which includes in it almost all human Felicities? . . . It is the Parent of Virtue, Pleasure, Plenty and Security; and 'tis innocent, as well as lovely."[53]

The central problem of all government was to master power, defend liberty, and avoid anarchy.[54] Power in a free state was a trust committed by all for their security and their common interest.[55] "There is something so wanton and monstrous in lawless Power, that there scarce ever was a human Spirit that could bear it; and the Mind of Man, which is weak and limited, ought never to be trusted with a Power that is boundless."[56] Power not kept subservient to the people and strictly defined turned into despotism. The principle of the constitution was to keep power within limits.[57]

Liberty, then, equal and impartial, was the meaning of the British Constitution. It was the security of owning one's soul, body, and property, the rule of law men have given to themselves, the absence of arbitrary power. For Trenchard and Gordon the Constitution stood above the actual legally invested powers of government and could be appealed to as against the latter's authority.[58] This liberty was "the essence of and reason for British pride and loyalty. But we have one thing more to boast of . . . and that is being freemen and not slaves in this unhappy age, when an universal deluge of tyranny has overpowered the face of the whole earth."

The same interpretation of the spirit of the constitution and of the nature of national loyalty appeared in Bolingbroke's *The Idea of a Patriot King*. The constitution was the sole means of defending civil liberty. It solved the dilemma of men who wished to maintain the liberty to which all were born and yet needed to live in society. "*The good of the people* is the ultimate and true *end* of government . . . now the greatest good of the people is their liberty . . . *Liberty* is to the collective body, what *health* is to every individual body . . . without *liberty* no happiness can be enjoyed by society. The obligation, therefore, to defend and maintain the freedom of such constitution will appear most sacred to a *patriot King*." [59]

Bolingbroke's *Dissertation upon Parties* was actually a systematic treatise on the British Constitution and contained many ideas and expressions which the American patriots borrowed verbatim. Montesquieu's famous treatment of the British Constitution probably owed much to Bolingbroke. "One nation there is also in the world that has for the direct end of its Constitution political liberty." [60]

That which made Bolingbroke's concept of the British Constitution so meaningful to the Americans was the distinction which he introduced between the government and the Constitution. "By constitution we mean . . . the assemblage of laws, institutions and customs, derived from certain fix'd principles of reason directed to certain fix'd objects of public good, that compose the general system, according to which the community hath agreed to be govern'd." [61]

Bolingbroke had introduced this distinction in order to attack the Whig supremacy which ruled the country through Parliament with the aid of the royal patronage. As against this legalized oppression, the Constitution was invoked to defend the liberty and welfare of the people. The situation and application suited that of America; moreover, Bolingbroke had already related the supreme authority of the Constitution to the natural-rights theory. Government was subordinated to the Constitution "that . . . [men] might preserve social, when they gave up natural liberty, and not be oppress'd by arbitrary will." [62]

It was in quest of liberty that constitutions were established to set limits to arbitrary power: "To govern a society of freemen by a constitution, founded on the eternal rules of right reason, and directed to promote the happiness of the whole, and of every individual, is the noblest prerogative, which can belong to humanity; and if man may be said, . . . to imitate God in any case, this is the case." It was the glory of the British nation that its history was that of liberty, of its permanent struggle against arbitrary power, and its final victory with the Glorious Revolution.[63] "If liberty be that delicious and wholesome fruit on which the British nation hath fed for so many ages, and to which we owe our riches, our strength, and all the advantages we boast of; the British constitution is the tree that bears this fruit, and will continue to bear it, as long as we are careful to fence it in, and trench it round, against the beasts of the field, and the insects of the earth." [64]

Liberty and constitutional government meant more than the principles of responsible government. Absolute democracy was no less tyranny than absolute monarchy. The form of a mixed government, established by the Constitution, alone secured liberty by stability and the rule of law.[65] This was the concept of the Constitution which enabled the colonists to fight as Englishmen against the prerogatives of Parliament. The identification of the British Constitution with the idea of free government had never been so clearly expressed before Bolingbroke.

Moreover, Bolingbroke had actually described the steps which led to revolutionary oppression and the loss of liberty in terms which eminently suited the American situation: the independence of Parliament from the people, its corruption through the utilization of patronage, the establishment of a Civil List which made government dependent on Parliament and made its members susceptible to bribery. "The increase and continuance of taxes acquire to the crown, by multiplying officers to the revenue, and by arming them with formidable powers against the rest of their fellow-subjects, a degree of power, the weight of which the inferior ranks of our people have long felt . . . how a full exercise of the powers . . . for the improvement of revenue, (that stale pretence for oppression) might oblige the greatest lord in the land to bow as low to a commissioner of customs, or to excise . . . as any nobleman . . . in France . . . to the intendant of his province." [66] Moreover, Bolingbroke gave the Americans the precise manner of their tactics, the appeal to the higher law of the Constitution. "The experience of many hundred years hath shewn, that by preserving this constitution inviolate, or by drawing it back to the principles on which it was originally founded . . . we may secure to ourselves, and to our latest posterity, the possession of that liberty, which we have long enjoy'd." [67] Bolingbroke's advice that "we cannot lose our liberty, unless we lose our constitution, nor lose our constitution, unless we are accomplices to the violations of it," [68] solved all dilemmas between self-government and national loyalty, between resistance to Parliament and remaining a radical Whig nationalist.

These ideas, then, shaped the Americans' image of England and *their* national identification. So powerful was the hold of this image on the revolutionary forces that the concepts of the Constitution and of the Patriot King, up to the outbreak of the fighting, became the greatest impediment to the breakthrough toward independence.

The immediate effect of this ideology of identification was, paradoxically, the full elaboration by the colonists of the concepts of citizenship, liberty, and equality of status. Disassociated as Americans were from the actual structure of England's political life and social forces, the application of these principles to the American scene could only mean the establishment of virtually sovereign states inside the British Empire. If the principles of nationalism aimed at the integration of society with the state, American nationalism was bound to arise as soon as the colonist realized that English rule could not be identified with the true interests of their own society, and that the ideals of full citizenship could not be achieved in the existing political framework. American national consciousness was therefore the dialectical development of the very strong British nationalism existing in the colonies. The transfer of loyalty and the change of identification evolved naturally from the premises of this prevalent ideology.

2. THE RISE OF AMERICAN PATRIOTISM

The emergence of an American consciousness followed a curious pattern, receding from the position of the eighteenth-century Whig ideology to that of the revolutionary creed of the seventeenth century. This American consciousness started out with the liberal concept of the nature of the British Constitution and ended with the pure natural-rights theory as the basis for a national identification. The elements inherent in the Whig philosophy were more and more identified in England with the existing pattern of society and government. The American had again to dissociate himself from them in order to defend his own claims for self-determination.

Samuel Adams had already perceived in his Master's thesis that the sole end of society was to safeguard men's natural rights and liberty. Like Shaftesbury, he recognized the functional relationship between liberty, citizenship, and national loyalty.[69] The concept of the nation was dissolved into that of society and citizenship based on the rights of men. On the same grounds, James Otis had severed the rights of the colonists from all historical prescriptive grounds. "There can be no prescription old enough to supersede the law of nature and the grant of God Almighty, who has given to all men a natural right to be free."[70] In this context the political philosophy of John Locke became a decisive influence. The purpose of civil government and the condition of its authority was the full enjoyment of political liberty.[71] "Whenever the legislators endeavor to take away and destroy the property of the people or to reduce them to slavery under arbitrary power, they put themselves in a state of war with the people, who are thereupon absolved from any further obedience, and are left to the common refuge, which God has provided for all men against all force and violence."[72]

The status of the British subject rested on a series of compacts which were embodied in the British Constitution. This is the meaning of the famous "Resolutions of the House of Representatives of Massachusetts" of October 29, 1765:

1. *Resolved,* That there are certain essential rights of the British Constitution of government, which are founded on the laws of God and nature, and are the common rights of mankind; therefore—
2. *Resolved,* That the inhabitants of this Province are unalienably entitled to those essential rights in common with all men; and that no law of society can, consistent with the law of God and nature, divest them of these rights.[73]

"The rights of the colonists," taking its grounds on the natural rights of men, had already fully disassociated the colonial theory of society and citizenship from its British background, and laid the foundation of political independence.[74]

Simultaneously with the rise of this ideology occurred a change in the evaluation of the historical relations between the American colonies and the mother country, which indicated a deepening awareness of the common experience of the settlers and of their separateness from England. In this perspective the plantations were seen as having developed independently from Great Britain through the exertion and bravery of those who left their old homes for the sake of civil and religious liberty and in search of a better life. Having conquered the wilderness by their own unaided exertions, they were masters of their destiny, the sole and lawful possessors of the land, and sovereign makers of their own societies. They were members of equal status with Great Britain in the Empire, bound by contractual loyalty to the King and the British Constitution.[75]

In this sense Franklin denied that the French and Indian Wars had been fought for the defense of the colonies.[76] He rejected at the same time the claim of Parliament to colonial jurisdiction by pointing out that the very motive for colonization was the desire of the settlers to live under their own laws.[77] America was "a country which had not been conquered by either King or Parliament, but was possessed by a free people."[78] The same argument gained increasing importance and emphasis in the colonial struggle. The Massachusetts House claimed that Parliamentary taxation canceled the conditions "upon which our ancestors settled this country; and enlarged his Majesty's dominions, with much toil and blood, and at their sole expense."[79] The newly awakened consciousness of historical independence fused, especially in New England, with the old spirit of separatism and its feeling of election for high purpose and produced an elated patriotism which gloried in dreams of American destiny.

It was for the sake of liberty that New England had been founded and because of English tyranny that the forefathers had left their mother country. In resisting the attempt to enslave it the present generation was only following in the steps of its forebears. In this sense Boston appealed to the Town of Plymouth, "that the Spirit of our venerable Forefathers, may revive and be defused. . . That Liberty Civil and Religeous, the grand Object of their View, may still be felt, enjoy'd & vindicated by the present Generation, and the fair Inheritance, transmitted to our latest Posterity."[80] With reverence and wonder, John Adams looked back on the settlement of America "as the opening of a grand scene and design in Providence for the illumination of the ignorant, and the emancipation of the slavish part of mankind all over the earth." [81]

This change of perspective created a consciousness of a common country and a common past and gave birth to a positive American identification. Richard Henry Lee spoke as early as 1764 of the dangers of British oppression of "North America" and defended the rights of the colonists not only by the laws of reason and nature but by virtue of the status their forefathers had acquired in settling the continent. "Can it be supposed that those brave, adventurous Britons, who originally conquered and settled these countries, through great dangers to themselves and benefit to the mother country, meant thereby to deprive themselves of the blessings of that free government of which they were members, and to which they had an unquestionable right?" [82] He saw the ultimate security for the rights of the "people of America" in their growing numerical and economic strength. [83] With the passage of the Stamp Act, Lee looked forward to the time "that America can find Arms as well as Arts, to remove the Demon Slavery far from its borders." [84]

The first important expression of this feeling of unity, John Dickinson's "Letters from a Farmer in Pennsylvania to the Inhabitants of the British Colonies," had an extraordinary effect which stemmed from their appeal to American patriotism. The address of the letters—to "My Dear Countrymen"—rang a new chord which reverberated through the colonies. This appeal was all the more effective because Dickinson clearly revealed his own deep attachment to the mother country in the awareness of the union of "religion, liberty, laws, affections, relation, language and commerce." [85] The "Letters" were motivated by the love of "humanity and liberty," the "sacred cause" of which had to be defended. Dickinson spoke as an American whose zeal was "for the happiness of British America," and in its name he refused to acknowledge the authority of Parliament in the internal affairs of America. [86]

The "Letters" kept a perfect balance—characteristic of the eighteenth century—between the concepts of mankind and of nation; between universal values and utilitarian considerations; between loyalty to the image of the British Empire and to his own country. They spoke in the name of liberty which was at once the right of man, the principle of the British Constitution, and the dimension of America's national unity. As in all contemporary political writings, the classical Roman concept of the citizen-people inspired Dickinson's patriotism. Believing that the cause of liberty had "too much dignity to be sullied by turbulence and tumult," he thought it "ought to be maintained in a manner suitable to her nature." Consequently he sought to express a spirit that would make it "impossible to determine whether an American's character is most distinguishable for his loyalty to his Sovereign, his duty to his mother country, his love of freedom, or his affection for his native soil." [87] Throughout, "Letters From a Farmer" dealt with the colonies as with one country, comparable to other exploited and subjected countries: the Sardinians under Carthage, Rome under Caesar, England under James II, and, above all, ruined Ireland under the British.[88] Consistently, Dickinson appealed to the colonies as one people: "Here then, my dear countrymen, ROUSE yourselves, and behold the ruin hanging over your heads. . . Let us all be united with one spirit, in one cause. . . A free people . . . can never be too quick . . . in opposing the beginnings of alteration." [89] The climax came in the magnificent conclusion of the last letter: "Let these truths be indelibly impressed on our minds—that we cannot be happy without being free . . . that therefore . . . unanimity of councils are essential to the welfare of the whole—and lastly, that . . . every man amongst us who in any manner would encourage either dissension, diffidence, or indifference between these colonies is an enemy to himself and to his country." [90]

Even more significant for the growth of American unity was Dickinson's "Patriotic Song," which was immediately adopted throughout the colonies.[91] The significance of this song lay in the appeal to defend liberty in the name of America and the Americans' birthright to liberty.

> Come, join hand in hand, brave Americans all,
> And rouse your bold hearts at fair liberty's call.
> No tyrannous acts shall suppress your just claim,
> Or stain with dishonour America's name.
>
> In freedom we're born, and in freedom we'll live!
> . . . our worthy forefathers . . .
> Through oceans to deserts for freedom they came,
> And, dying, bequeath'd us their freedom and fame.[92]

The song contained the elements of an American patriotism: a great and universal cause, the feelings of unity as expressed in the terms America and a common fatherland, the pride in its past and in a national inheritance, and the prospect of a future as a nation.

"The Rising Glory of America," written for the 1771 Commencement by two Princeton students, revealed a Franklinian vision of the future greatness of the continent which blended with that of Berkeley's "Westward the Course of Empire Take Its Way" and the belief of a mission to realize man's hope for liberty and happiness. At the same time these verses expressed a new feeling of home and of the brotherhood of people.[93]

> I see, I see
> Freedom's established reign; cities, and men,
> Numerous as sands upon the ocean shore,
> And empires rising where the sun descends!
>
> . . . We, too, shall boast
> Our Scipios, Solons, Catos, sages, chiefs
> That in the lap of time yet dormant lie,
> Waiting the joyous hour of life and light.[94]

This awareness and feeling of a common country and a common destiny, sporadic before the Townshend Acts, increasingly shaped the attitude of the patriots toward Great Britain and determined the course of their action. The boycott movement and the new non-importation agreements also showed awareness of America's economic strength and capacity to take care of itself.[95] The "Buy America" campaign was led by a moral crusade for the introduction of heroic and Spartan virtues becoming a free people which would make them economically independent of England. The advocacy of economic self-sufficiency was inspired by confidence in the immense resources of the country which strengthened the consciousness of unity and power.[96]

By 1770 Franklin's continental concept had fully taken possession of the mind of the American radical. America was bound to become the seat of a mighty empire and "no conduct on Great Britain's part can put a stop to this building. There is no contending with omnipotence, and the predispositions are so numerous, and so well adapted to the rise of America, that our success is indubitable."[97]

The vision of future power and imperial greatness mingled with the consciousness of spiritual and historical unity of the American people whose core was the defense of human rights and civil liberty. Writing to John Dickinson in 1768, Richard Henry Lee expressed this composite structure of the American: "As a friend to the just and proper rights of human nature, but particularly as an American, I acknowledge great obligation to you, for the wise and well-timed care, you have taken of our common liberty." [98] The meaning of the terms "rights of human nature" and "liberty" which rendered the "communication of sentiment" between the colonists so easy and which united, according to Richard Henry Lee, "the Americans, from one end of the continent to the other" was complex. [99] The rights of the Americans to self-rule were founded, as we have seen, on two complementary arguments. They rested on the rights of man and the laws of nature from which the "British Constitution" derived its legitimate authority; as such, they referred to the universal structure of civil life and claimed absolute validity. Yet these rights were in particular derived from the history of the American settlement, and inherited from the forefathers. But these historical rights in their turn were ultimately based on the law of nature and the rights of men. The fusion of the historical rights with those of nature became a decisive step toward independence. In James Wilson's "Considerations on the Authority of Parliament," the argument cut both ways. "Those who launched into the unknown deep, in quest of new countries and habitations, still considered themselves as subjects of the English monarchs . . . but it nowhere appears that they still . . . thought the authority of the English Parliament extended over them." And the same line was adopted in the Declaration and Resolves of the First Continental Congress, October 1774. [100]

Yet, in John Adams' *Novanglus,* the historical argument of emigration and colonization turned into a valid proof of the claim to full political self-determination inside the Empire with a purely contractual relationship with the Crown. The law that applied to the relation between England and America was the law of nations. Adams quoted James Harrington to the effect that the dependence of the colonies on the mother country continued only so long as they were not strong enough to maintain themselves unaided. [101]

Jefferson, with his uncommon gift of clear thought and happy expression, drew the final conclusion from the historical argument. Relating the rights of the Americans to the natural-rights theory of civil society and government, he cut loose from the constitutional debate. *The Summary View of the the Rights of British America* bluntly stated "that our ancestors . . . possessed a right which nature has given to all men, of departing from a country in which chance . . . has placed them, of going in quest of new habitations, and of there establishing new societies, under such laws and regulations as to them shall seem most likely to promote public happiness. . . America was conquered, and her settlement made, and firmly established, at the expense of individuals, and not of the British public. . . For themselves they fought, for themselves they conquered, and for themselves alone they have a right to hold." [102]

Jefferson drew from this position radical and far-reaching implications, which voided the claims of the Crown to the lands of the continent together with the claim of Parliament to regulate the trade of the colonies. "From the nature and purpose of civil institutions, all the lands within the limit, which any particular society has circumscribed around itself are assumed by that society, and subject to their allotment only . . . and if they are allotted in either of these ways, each individual of the society may appropriate to himself such lands as he finds vacant, and occupancy will give him title." [103] On the same ground, "The Declaration of Causes of Taking Up Arms" justified armed resistance. "In our own native land, in defence of the freedom that is our birthright . . . for the protection of our property . . . we have taken up arms." [104]

And yet, though Jefferson and his compatriots spoke in terms of one country and of one American people and claimed the right of self-determination, and though a few aimed at full independence, it was evident that the ties with their own English past and the idea of belonging to the British Empire had not been destroyed. As late as November 1774 Thomas Paine found "the disposition of the people such, that they might have been led by a thread and governed by a reed." [105] They still considered themselves the free subjects of the Crown and members of the Empire, being under a common tradition of rights and law provided by the Constitution.[106]

The past was more than a sentiment. It had shaped the living institutions. It provided the principles of legitimacy and authority for the total social order. It was the fountain of all rights, private

as well as public.[107] As John Adams put it: "All great Changes are
irksome to the human Mind, especially those which are attended
with great Dangers and uncertain Effects. No Man living can
foresee the Consequences of such a Measure [independence], and
therefore I think it ought not to have been undertaken untill the
Design of Providence by a Series of great Events had so plainly
marked out the Necessity of it that he who runs might read." [108]

Only the most compelling need to maintain effective military
resistance, preserve social order, and secure foreign aid, and the
final step of the British Crown's declaring the colonists rebels and
excluding them from its protection compelled them to declare for
independence.[109] Richard Henry Lee of Virginia put the situation
in a nutshell: "We cannot be Rebels excluded from the King's
protection and Magistrates acting under his authority at the same
time." [110]

The last step toward the final emancipation from the concept
of a common British nationality was the destruction of the image
of British freedom and of the idealization of its Constitution.
Franklin's letter to the Loyalist Joseph Galloway on the state of
general corruption in England was typical. John Adams believed
also that the causes of corruption had spread too widely in the
governing circles of England to hope for improvement, and that
only separation could save America from contagion.[111]

Friends of the American cause—Wilkes, Barré, radicals like Cartwright or Catharine Macaulay; Price, Priestley, and others—opened
the eyes of the Americans to the true state of British affairs. Events
in Britain proved at the same time that these circles lacked influence and that the government's policies toward America enjoyed
general support. The purchase of German "boors and vassals from
twenty hireling states" and the dispatch of an expeditionary force
of 30,000 Germans to America completed the process of emancipation.[112]

In this situation of practical independence and of the formation
of a *de facto* continental government, the urgent need was to
weave the main threads together into an image of a new America
and to furnish a final argument for the establishment of nationhood based not on necessity but on the promise of American life
and its inherent needs.

V

The American, the New Man: The Image of a New Nation

1. THE PROMISE OF AMERICAN LIFE

The great influence of *Common Sense* on the independence movement and on the rise of the American democracy cannot be explained solely by the skill with which Thomas Paine demolished the last remnants of the British image. This book, together with *The Crisis* and the *Rights of Man*, created a new image of America, of its destiny and of its promise.[1] In this image the universalistic values and norms of the rights of men, of faith in reason and natural justice, became the essence of a regenerated society; the continent was to be the setting of a mighty nation of free men, universal in scope.

The feelings engendered by the hopes for an absolutely new beginning destroyed the historic bonds with the English past. History taught Americans to avoid the errors of the past and to lay its foundation anew. This attitude earned Paine the undying hatred of the conservatives in his own times and in years to come.[2]

The language of *Common Sense* was that of a revolutionary genius, clear-cut, brisk, and imaginative. It conveyed a sense of urgency and of history pregnant with momentous decisions which recalled John Adams' words that as great a question as that of independence would never be decided among men. "'Tis not the affair of a city, a county, a province, or a kingdom," Paine wrote, "but of a continent—of at least one eighth part of the habitable globe. 'Tis not the concern of a day, a year, or an age; posterity are virtually involved in the contest, and will be more or less affected even to the end of time, by the proceedings now. Now is the seed-time of continental union, faith and honor."[3]

As a foreigner recently arrived, Paine, like James Wilson and Alexander Hamilton, was a "nationalist." Such men were more sensitive to the unity of the people, to their factual nationhood, than their American compatriots. For Paine, three factors determined the unity of America and of its people. The geopolitical possession of a continent of immense extent and possibilities made America a world in itself, which, as counterweight to Europe, was sovereign in its own fate and its economic development. America was strong enough to have the world for its market without becoming involved in its commotions. "In no instance hath nature made the satellite larger than its primary planet . . . England to Europe: America to itself."[4] Yet no less unifying was the common history of the nation. Not English descent—"Europe and not England is the parent country of America"—but the contrast between the Old and the New World, between tyranny and oppression, as against asylum for liberty and self-development, made it one. "Hither have they fled, not from the tender embraces of the mother, but from the cruelty of the monster."[5] This common experience created a new brotherhood of men which made them one people. But the expectation of a common future forged the strongest ties of all. The possibility of a dignified, free, and secure life, of a new society in which the happiness of each and the freedom of all would be the guiding forces, held them together.[6]

> Its first settlers were emigrants from different European nations . . . retiring from the governmental persecutions of the old world, and meeting in the new, not as enemies, but as brothers. The wants which necessarily accompany the cultivation of a wilderness produced among them a state of society . . . In such a situation man becomes what he ought. He sees his species . . . as kindred; and the example shews to the artificial world, that man must go back to Nature for information.[7]

This sense of creativity made the Americans one people.

> We have every opportunity and every encouragement before us, to form the noblest, purest constitution on the face of the earth. We have it in our power to begin the world over again. A situation, similar to the present, hath not happened since the days of Noah until now. The birthday of a new world is at hand, and a race of men, perhaps as numerous as all Europe contains, are to receive their portion of freedom from the events of a few months.[8]

The form of government would be as simple and as natural as the needs which led men to create political societies, that of a constitutional representative democracy.[9]

The image of a new world could be created only by a man who knew Europe well enough to hate its society and who longed desperately enough for salvation to envision in a flash of illumination the destiny of the New World as liberation from the Old. "O! ye that love mankind! Ye that dare oppose not only tyranny but the tyrant, stand forth! . . . Freedom hath been hunted round the globe. . . O! receive the fugitive, and prepare in time an asylum for mankind."[10]

Common Sense was written by a common man and spoke for the common people. Paine was one of the first great pamphleteers of the downtrodden, a man whose mind was kindled by the ideas of the Enlightenment. The projection of these dreams and hopes on the New World and on the American revolt against England revealed a profound awareness of the deeper undercurrents of history. *Common Sense* represented the meeting of Europe and America, the mutual impact of two different types of society. That meeting shaped the ideology of the new nation and helped create a sense of identity. Only with the experience of Europe in mind could the uniqueness of America and its awakening in the Revolution be perceived. "Here the value and quality of liberty, the nature of government, and the dignity of man, were known and understood, and the attachment of the Americans to these principles produced the revolution, as a natural and almost unavoidable consequence."[11] On these principles alone, Americans would be capable of uniting and forming a new nation, for "a union so extensive, continued and determined . . . must be something capable of reaching the whole soul of man and arming it with perpetual energy." It had to rest on a basis which "extends and promotes the principles of universal society; whose mind rises above the atmosphere of local thoughts, and considers mankind, of whatever nation or profession they may be, as the work of one Creator."[12]

The same perspective characterized Crèvecœur's *Letters from an American Farmer*. Undoubtedly the image of America projected by the *Letters* was colored by the nature-romanticism of the late eighteenth-century French culture, but they were more than rococo epistles, or, as Ludwig Lewisohn described them, "de-

lightful literature but fanciful sociology." [13] His commentaries on
the inhabitants of Nantucket and Martha's Vineyard and his
observations on the "Distresses of a Frontier Man" were written by
a keen observer aware of the ruthless power of nature and history,
and of the way of life of the pioneers.[14]

Crèvecœur lived in the American colonies for almost twenty
years before the War of Independence drove him to Europe, was
a naturalized subject of the Colony of New York and a well-to-do
farmer who considered himself an American by choice.[15] Though
the *Letters* were undoubtedly written with the object "of making
America loved," [16] they were a unique testimony of what the New
World meant to an American-by-choice. Crèvecœur was not concerned with politics. Nor was his aim to vindicate the fate of the
common man in the New World. And yet his perspective was
astonishingly similar to Paine's. For both men America represented a new attitude toward life. For both it was a radically new
type of society in which human nature, enlightened by reason,
created new rules of freedom and justice.

The concept of nature loomed even larger in Crèvecœur's
writings than in Paine's. It referred to the virginal lands of the continent hardly yet touched by man with their promise of "the
anticipated field of future cultivation and improvement . . . the
future extent of those generations which are to replenish and
embellish this boundless continent." [17] Nature became a formative
power which shaped the American, who expanded with the limit-
less extension of the lands and with the infinite possibilities of
work.[18]

> A European, when he first arrives, seems limited in his intentions as well
> as in his views, but he very suddenly alters his scale . . . He no sooner
> breathes our air than he forms schemes and embarks in designs he never
> would have thought of in his own country: There the plenitude of society
> confines many useful ideas, and often extinguishes the most laudable schemes
> which here ripen into maturity. Thus Europeans become Americans.[19]

In its primeval force nature destroyed all superfluities of civilization and compelled man to adjust himself to its laws in order to
survive. The Indian was the counterpart of this aspect of "nature."
Perfectly adapted to its laws, he was yet perfectly free. As his
reason had mastered the rules of the forest and its life, he was
master of his own life and represented man yet unfettered by the
artificial and corruptive influences of civilization. He was the

great temptation of the American, representative of a possible way of life which drew the pioneer and the outlaw to his own level of liberty.[20] The Indian was, at the same time, the archetype to be reached again on a higher level of civilization. The span of history reached from the Indian to the pioneer hunter, to the pioneer settler and the forest village, to the free community of farmer citizens. This chain connected natural liberty to that of a newly won social freedom and individual liberty.

Crèvecœur, like Thomas Paine, conceived of America as a melting pot in which the different nations of Europe were transformed into a new race of men.[21] "The American sees his species," wrote Thomas Paine, ". . . as kindred, and the example shews to the artificial world, that man must go back to Nature for information."[22] "In this great American asylum," wrote Crèvecœur,

the poor of Europe have by some means met together, and in consequence of various causes. . . Alas, two thirds of them had no country. Can a wretch, who wanders about, who works and starves, whose life is a continual scene of sore affliction or pinching penury, can that man call England or any other kingdom his country? . . . Everything has tended to regenerate them, new laws, a new mode of living, a new social system; here they are become men.[23]

Crèvecœur succeeded in describing and analyzing the process of "transplantation" and transformation which turned the European into a new man, the American. He described the process in terms of the totality of social and personal experience:

Here the rewards of his industry follow with equal steps the progress of his labour; his labour is founded on the basis of nature, self-interest; can it want a stronger allurement? The American is a new man, who acts upon new principles; he must therefore entertain new ideas, and form new opinions. From involuntary idleness, servile dependence, penury, and useless labour, he has passed to toils of a very different nature, rewarded by ample subsistence— this is an American.[24]

Crèvecœur was the first writer to realize that America represented "a new social system"; and he recognized in this conflux of social, environmental, and psychological forces the framework of a new national identification. New sociological concepts like those utilized by Voltaire, Montesquieu, the physiocrats, Ferguson, Hume, and Adam Smith pervaded his letters; yet his writing excelled that of his contemporaries in sensitivity of analysis and authenticity of insight.

The question, "What is an American?" was new, and disclosed

immediately the nature of the problem. "He is an American, who, leaving behind him all his ancient prejudices and manners, receives new ones—from a new mode of life he has embraced, the new government he obeys, and the new rank he holds. . . Here individuals of all nations are melted into a new race of men, whose labours and posterity will one day cause great changes in the world."[25]

Crèvecœur exemplifies the importance of *Fremdheitserlebniss,* or the experience of facing the alien and stranger, in the crystallization of a national consciousness in America.[26] The personality and its image, individual or collective, emerged only through the meeting and confrontation with "the stranger," who crystallized the consciousness of being a unified and definite personality.

The stranger coming to America and the American meeting Europe became sensitively aware of the collective personality of the respective societies. The whole development in the period between 1763 and 1776 was characterized by the experience of meeting the outside world. The formation of an American national consciousness was accelerated through confrontation with the harsh realities of England. For the same reason, English and European observers were more clairvoyant concerning the future of America than the Americans themselves. Benjamin Franklin, coming into close contact with Europe at a relatively early stage, was also among the first to realize the continental future of America and its distinctive pattern of social and political institutions and attitudes.[27] As early as 1772 he wrote from England to his American friends:

I thought often of the happiness of New England, where every man is a freeholder, has a vote in public affairs, lives in a tidy, warm house, has plenty of good food and fuel. . . But, if they should ever envy the trade of these countries, I can put them in a way to obtain a share of it. Let them, with three fourths of the people of Ireland, live the year round on potatoes and buttermilk, without shirts. . . Let them, with the generality of the common people of Scotland, go barefoot. . . Had I never been in the American colonies, but were to form my judgment of civil society by what I have lately seen, I should never advise a nation of savages to admit of civilization.[28]

It required the vision of Europeans, repeating the historical experiences of the first settlers to define the nature of the new nation by contradistinction to European political and social institutions. Such comparisons pervaded the *Letters* of Crèvecœur. "Europe has no such class of men. . . Europe contains hardly any other distinctions but lords and tenants; this fair country alone is settled by freeholders, the possessors of the soil they cultivate, members of the government they obey, and the framers of their own laws. . . A traveller in Europe becomes a stranger as soon as he quits his own kingdom. . . We know, properly speaking, no strangers; this is every person's country." [29]

Thomas Paine and Crèvecœur complemented each other. They advocated a political and national structure which would safeguard the patterns of liberty and self-government for the American people. Paine's political ideology was not advocated for the sake of political and national independence but as an adequate safeguard for "the rights of men," as a political framework for a free and equalitarian society. This correspondence of the political structure to a free society ruled by natural justice was the essence and destiny of the American nation. Crèvecœur, on the other hand, described and analyzed the character of American society as it had developed in his own time. He traced the process which transformed the European into an American, the natural and sociological factors through which "the individuals of all nations are melted into a new race of men" and made America "the most perfect society now existing in the world." Only in America could men become what nature and God have destined each individual to be and work toward their own happiness according to their own will and capacities. A "new social system" restored on a higher level the original equality and liberty of the natural man. The "free society" of Crèvecœur and the "free government" of Thomas Paine created in their interaction the framework of national identification and loyalty. In the last analysis, American nationality was based on an identification with a "social system" and its political superstructure, which were organically related to the opportunities of the open continent. Traditional elements of national loyalty, the ties to the native soil and the local structure of social life, pride in the historic achievements of the forefathers, were also woven into this texture of nationality.

The same view of their country intensified the nationalism of those Americans who traveled to Europe. The physical and moral oppression of the masses in Europe, compared to their happiness in America, overwhelmed Jefferson. The abyss which divided the upper from the lower classes, the corruption of the aristocracy, and the illiteracy and barbarity of the masses heightened his consciousness of the unity of the American people in their happy state of society, manners, morals, and way of life.[30] "Of twenty millions of people supposed to be in France, I am of opinion there are nineteen millions more wretched, more accursed in every circumstance of human existence than the most conspicuously wretched individual of the whole United States."[31]

The evidence of Europe turned Jefferson into a zealous democratic republican. The misery of Europe was created by the curse of bad government, by aristocratic and monarchial principles, by "kings, nobles, or priests" who formed an "abandoned confederacy against the happiness of the mass of the people."[32] The bottomless ignorance of the mass of the people seemed almost beyond hope. "A thousand years would not place them on that high ground on which our common people are now setting out. Ours could not have been . . . placed under the control of the common sense of the people, had they not been separated from the parent stock, and kept from contamination . . . from . . . the . . . people of the old world, by the intervention of so wide an ocean."[33] Europe taught Jefferson the danger of the concentration of political power and strong government which divided its nations into "wolves & sheep."[34] "It will make you adore your own country," Jefferson wrote to James Monroe, "it's soil, it's climate, it's equality, liberty, laws, people, & manners. My God! how little do my country men know what precious blessings they are in possession of, and which no other people on earth enjoy. I confess I had no idea of it myself."[35] He advised his American friends against sending their children to receive a European education, as the manners and spirit of the two continents were incompatible.[36]

The meaning of "American" and the "American people" had, then, a complex structure. It denoted a people possessing, or expecting to possess, a continent with immense possibilities of wealth, happiness, and power, which they conquered and turned into a settled habitation, a homeland, and a country. But it meant increasingly a society well defined in its pattern of life, its manners and outlook, and in its social and political institutions. This society was unique, absolutely different from all the historic societies.

Only here had the universal rights of men been translated into a living reality. This last stage in the evolution of the American consciousness took place with the Declaration of Independence, which made the rights of men the basic principle of the emancipated nation.

2. "THE FOUNDATIONS ARE LAID: THE NATION IS BORN"

The Declaration of Independence set forth "the causes which have impelled us to this mighty revolution, and the reasons which will justify it in the Sight of God and man." [37] Its famous Preamble stated the theory which entitled "one people to dissolve the political bands which have connected them with another, and to assume among the powers of the earth, the separate and equal station to which the laws of Nature and of Nature's God entitle them." This theory of the sovereignty of the people and the contractual nature of government, taken largely from Locke's apology for the Glorious Revolution, served its purpose as well as it had done in Locke's own time. [38]

Political power could legitimize itself in only one of three ways: through the authority of religion; through the appeal to history and tradition; or through reason. The Americans had fought for their rights on the basis of all three. Having failed to legitimize their rebellion on historical grounds and being compelled to choose independence, the only course left was to accept boldly the rationalistic concepts fitting the situation. And yet the Preamble overstated the argument. It would have been sufficient to state the grievances against the British Crown and to prove that the contract between the American people and the Crown had been dissolved through violation of its terms, as Jefferson's *Summary View,* Adams' *Novanglus,* and James Wilson's *Considerations* had done. [39] The Declaration itself cited Richard Henry Lee's resolution: "That these United Colonies are, and of right ought to be, free and independent States, that they are absolved from all allegiance to the British Crown." [40] John Adams, George Wythe, and others had defended the resolution for independence by the undoubted right of the colonies to separate, by the imposssibility of reconciliation, by the fact that independence had been established *de facto,* that "as to the King, we had been bound to him by allegiance, but that this bond was now dissolved by his assent . . .

by which he declares us out of his protection, and by his levying war on us . . . it being a certain position in law that allegiance & protection are reciprocal, the one ceasing when the other is withdrawn." [41]

The Preamble to the Declaration of Independence did more; it was the "credo" of the revolutionary party. John Lind, an English barrister, in "An Answer to the Declaration of the American Congress," pointed out that the theory of government proposed in the Preamble was "absurd and visionary" and that its political maxims were "subversive of every actual or imaginable kind of government." [42] The Declaration was nevertheless a model for all future state constitutions. In the words of Jefferson, "It was intended to be an expression of the American mind, and to give to that expression the proper tone and spirit." [43] The revolutionary principle of man's rights against government had been invoked by all radicals, especially those from New England, against Britain, even when its government had still been considered to possess legal authority. The philosophy of natural rights had been developed as a theory of free government long before the Declaration of Independence,[44] and "had been hackneyed in Congress for two years before." [45] Virginia had introduced the same principles in a Declaration of Rights "as the basis and foundation of government" almost a month before Lee introduced his Resolution to Congress. South Carolina had established her own government and so had New Jersey and Virginia. North Carolina had requested the same right since November 1775, when Congress had advised New Hampshire to call "a full and free representation of the people" in order to "establish such a form of government as, in their judgment, will best produce the happiness of the people and most effectually secure peace and good order." [46] The thoughts of all were turning to the question of the forms and principles which would shape the life of the American people. The Resolution of the Continental Congress on May 11, 1776, advising the colonies to establish their own governments, was considered by John Adams as an "epocha." [47]

Independence meant, then, first of all, the construction of government on new and revolutionary principles. This was the interpretation John Adams gave to the recommendation of Congress on May 11 and 15: "The decree is gone forth and it cannot be recalled, that a more equal liberty than has prevailed in other parts of the earth must be established in America"; and "every colony must be induced to institute a perfect government." [48]

Many of the "trimmers" and enemies of independence shared the opinion of Carter Braxton of Virginia that the radicals advocated independence to revolutionize society and government. "The best opportunity in the World being now offered them to throw off all subjection and embrace their darling Democracy they are determined to accept it." [49] Rutledge entreated John Jay to throw his vote against the resolution of independence in order to avoid the domination of eastern radicalism. "I dread," he wrote, "their low Cunning, and those levelling Principles which Men without Character and without Fortune in general possess, which are so captivating to the lower class of Mankind, and which will occasion such fluctuation of Property as to introduce the greatest disorder." [50] Thus, Thomas Paine was correct when he remarked that "the independence of America, considered merely as a separation from England, would have been a matter but of little importance, had it not been accompanied by a revolution in the principles and practice of governments." [51]

The Preamble in this context stated the principles on which the nation was to constitute its several states,[52] yet it signified both more and less than a philosophy of republicanism. Its basic aim was to establish the principles of a constitutionally limited republican government by a declaration of individual rights and by the voluntary social compact of individual men.[53]

The immense impact of the principles of the Revolution, as formulated in the Preamble, on the formation of the new states becomes evident by comparing the state constitutions created before and after the Declaration was signed. The First Constitution of New Hampshire, adopted on January 5, 1776, was framed in purely pragmatic terms: "For the preservation of peace and good order, and for the security of the lives and properties of the inhabitants of this colony, we conceive ourselves reduced to the necessity of establishing A FORM OF GOVERNMENT." [54] Framed for an emergency situation, it was concerned only with social stability and the establishment of a government adequate to the task.

The Constitution of New Jersey, framed in May and July 1776, was less ambiguous. It rested on the compact theory and used the phraseology of Locke. Government was established for the common interest of society and rested on a contract between the governed and the rulers, to be dissolved by the unilateral infringement of its terms by one of the parties—in this case, the Crown.[55] A Bill of Rights embodying the liberties conceived as the common inheritance of all Englishmen introduced the Constitution.[56] It established a republican form of government on the principles of the separation of powers and of checks and balances. It lacked, however, a basic philosophy of the nature, purpose, and limits of political power and statehood.

The introduction of these principles into the constitutions of Virginia, Pennsylvania, Vermont, New Hampshire, and Massachusetts during the first decade of independence meant more than a legitimation of independent republican forms of government. It signified the *creation of new societies,* the *abrogation of the British past,* the *revolutionary erasure of historic continuity,* and the *construction of society, government, and nationhood from their first foundations.* The deliberate creation of a political society by a social compact of free individuals was re-enacted, sometimes vicariously and sometimes factually, throughout the nineteenth century, with the recurrent act of establishing new societies and new states in the expanding West.

The Constitution of Alabama, ratified in 1819, was typical of this process of forming new societies and states on the principles of the natural-rights philosophy. It declared:

"We, the people of Alabama Territory . . . in order to establish justice, insure tranquility, provide for the common defence, promote the general welfare, and secure to ourselves and our posterity the rights of life, liberty and property, do ordain . . . the following constitution or form of government; and do mutually agree with each other to form ourselves into a free and independent State, by the name of. . ." [57]

After this Preamble, which defined the general object of political societies, a Declaration of Rights stated the terms of the social compact which limited the power of government and defined the relations between the members of society to each other and to the government: "That the general, great, and essential principle of liberty and free government may be recognized . . . we declare: . . . That all freemen,[58] when they form a social compact, are equal in rights." [59] The wording of the Constitution of Michigan emphasized even more emphatically the artificial, voluntary, and deliberate character of the formation of society and state: "We, the people of the Territory of Michigan . . . believing that the time has arrived when . . . the right of self-government be asserted . . . mutually agree to form ourselves into a free and independent state." [60] Vermont's Constitution of 1777 defined the just rules and original principles of "their future society." [61]

The impact of the natural-rights philosophy on the century of enlightenment has become an historical commonplace. Yet few have analyzed the actual impact of this theory on political action and the different functions it fulfilled in the concrete historical context of events. [62] In Europe the theory was accepted as interpretation, justification—or even as criterion and guide—for existing institutions and political actions; in America it served as blueprint for the construction of society, state, and government. [63] In America it dissolved existing loyalties and traditions and atomized society in order to build it anew on the most generalized, abstract, and universal principles of the Enlightenment. This process of dissolution and atomization, inherent in the very nature of the natural-rights philosophy, became a living force which shaped the basic concepts of social life, of the state, and the image of the nation, only in the United States.

Decisive in the development of the American ideology was the way in which the relation between constituent parts of the natural-rights theory was established. The European development tended to absorb the natural state in the civil state, individual rights in those of the community, the contracting members in the incorporated body politic. In these long-established, homogeneous, and thoroughly integrated societies, the natural rights of the citizen were assimilated in the concept of the sovereign state or nation. Rousseau and Burke, Bentham and Mazzini, Herder, Fichte and Hegel, in spite of their basic differences, operated in the same universe of discourse—that of the nation, the community, the society, and the state. Not so in America. The conceptual pairs of the theory—civil and natural states, individual and community, contracting members and incorporated society—were never fused but remained distinctive and opposite as permanent factors of one system the main characteristic of which was the idea of individual liberty. Society was a corporation with limited power and responsibility. Government was *"nothing more than a national association acting on the principles of society."* [64] The Preamble to the Declaration of Independence gave classic expression to this concept of society and, for this reason, in almost all state constitutions the declaration of rights was introduced with the phrase: "That the general, great, and essential principles of liberty and free Government may be recognized . . . we declare." [65] The Virginia Constitution set this pattern with its declaration "that all men are by nature equally free and independent, and have certain inherent rights, of which, when they enter into a state of society, they cannot, by any compact, deprive . . . their posterity." [66] Popular sovereignty was thus the logical result of the social compact; but its sphere extended only to the limits set by the terms of the compact, by the declarations of rights, and the constitution itself. The relations between society, state, and government and the individual members of society were strictly determined by the motives which brought the individuals into compact to secure their individual rights and liberties. This may be seen by a comparison between the final version of the Declaration of Independence and the several bills of rights.

The Declaration read: ". . . that all men are created equal, that they are endowed . . . with certain unalienable rights . . . that to secure these rights, governments are instituted among men." The first draft of the Declaration read: ". . . that all men are created equal & independent." [67] The word "independent" was obviously not suitable for the purpose of the Declaration; yet it was all-important for that of setting up constitutions, and most of the state constitutions included it after the pattern of the Virginia Declaration of Rights, which read, "equally free and independent."

The other significant difference concerned the sentence, "to secure these rights, governments are instituted." The Virginia Declaration and most of the state constitutions emphasized the priority of these rights to the setting-up of governments, and, unlike the Declaration of Independence, spoke of the creation of *social compacts,* not of governments: "that all men . . . when they enter into a state of society, they cannot, by any compact . . . divest their posterity." [68] The primary aim of society, then, was to ensure the freedom and independence of the individual and his rights, or rather to secure them by the exchange of equivalent civil rights. This concept of the relation between the individual and society was explicitly expressed in the Second Constitution of New Hampshire, ratified in 1784. Article III of the Bill of Rights declared: "When men enter into a state of society, they surrender up some of their natural rights to that society, in order to insure the protection of others; and, without such an equivalent, the surrender is void." Article IV declared: "Among the natural rights, some are in their very nature unalienable, because no equivalent can be given or received for them." [69] The individual, then, lost neither his freedom nor his independence as a member of society; they were, rather, established for each and all on a surer basis. Society, state, and nation were still voluntary associations of individuals.

The Americans followed the political philosophy of John Locke in a peculiar way. They aimed to approximate as far as possible the civil state to the state of nature. "The *state of nature*," wrote Locke, "has a law of nature to govern it, which obliges every one: and reason, which is that law, teaches all mankind, who will but consult it, that being all *equal and independent,* no one ought to harm another in his life, health, liberty or possessions." [70] The main task of society was to enable man to live in accord with nature and reason by eliminating dangers caused by the clash of independent and unrestrained action. Society's rule secured and established, rather than eliminated, the freedom and independence of man. "*Law,* in its true notion," remarked Locke, "*is* not so much the limitation as *the direction of a free and intelligent agent* to his proper interest, and prescribes no farther, than is for the general good of those under the law. . . So that, however it may be mistaken, *the end of law is* not to abolish or restrain, but *to preserve and enlarge freedom. . .*" [71] The foundation of all the rest was that liberty "to dispose and order as he lists, his person, actions, possessions, and his whole property, within the allowance of those laws under which he is, and therein not to be subject to the arbitrary will of another, but freely to follow his own." [72] This freedom was grounded "*on his* having *reason,* which is able to instruct him in that law he is to govern himself by, and make him know how far he is left to the freedom of his own will." [73]

The originality of the Revolutionary period consisted in the literal application of the natural-rights philosophy and the ideals of constitutionalism to the formation of fundamental institutions. This application changed the relationship between Locke's natural and civil states, which had been regarded as succeeding one another after the social compact. Instead, the relationship became an interpenetration of coexisting modes of life whose common rule was the approximation to the state of nature and reason. The boundaries between the state of nature and that of society, between natural and civil rights, were determined by their inherent structure. Those rights in the exercise of which the individual was self-sufficient remained his natural rights. Those which demanded collective protection were civil rights and were made objects of the social contract and of legislation. This was the distinction made by Jefferson: "As all their rights, in the first case are natural rights, and the exercise of those rights supported only by their own natural individual power, they would begin by distinguishing between these rights they could individually exercise fully and perfectly and those they could not." [74]

In William Blackstone's *Commentaries* there were passages which described exactly the intention of the American constitutions. The principal aim of those constitutions was "to protect individuals in the enjoyment of those absolute rights, which were vested in them by the immutable laws of nature; but which could not be preserved in peace without that mutual assistance and intercourse, which is gained by the institution of friendly and social communities." They agreed with Blackstone that "the first and primary end of human laws is to maintain and regulate these *absolute* rights of individuals" and that "Political . . . or civil liberty . . . is no other than natural liberty so far restrained by human laws (and no farther) as is necessary and expedient for the general advantage of the public." [75] Yet, after all, Blackstone's natural-law concepts were commentaries on the laws of England. The American constitutions attempted to institute these natural laws as the fundamental laws of the state, and the whole political structure of society was to be shaped accordingly. The positive law was to be dissolved into the natural law or, rather, the natural law was to become the rule of civil society in America.

In this process of creating a new society, all the traditions, concepts, and images of national identification were united and crystallized into permanent shape. The idea of the Constitution and of liberty, that of individual rights and of a voluntarily created contractual society, the images of the continent and of nature, the awareness of an American pattern of life, and the perspective of a common continental future were transformed into the idea of the American people, which permitted the reconciliation of unity and diversity. Unity lay in the identical structure of the societies and in the basic similarity of men. Having abstracted the concrete and individual men into the universal man, and the historically shaped traditions and institutions into universal concepts of society, states, and government, the relation between the separate states and the American people was the same as that between the nation and humanity. They were realizations of an identical pattern of social life and values in diverse forms.

In almost all the states the end of the institutions for the maintenance and administration of government was to "protect and to furnish the individuals, who compose it with the power of enjoying in safety and tranquillity their natural rights, and the blessings of life." In all the states the body politic was formed "by a voluntary association of individuals" and was a "social compact, by which the whole people covenants with each citizen, and each citizen with the whole people, that all shall be governed by certain laws for the common good." [76]

The "chords of affection" by which the people were knit together were created by kindred blood, common tradition, and a common country, but still more by their common fight for their natural rights and the common possession of principles of social life and common expectation for well-being and happiness.[77]

Because of this common possession of principles, the supporters of the new Federalist Constitution could invoke a feeling of identity. "Happily for America, happily, we trust, for the whole human race, they pursued a new and more noble course. They accomplished a revolution which has no parallel in the annals of human society. They reared the fabrics of government which have no model on the face of the globe." [78] This identity, then, had its own ideological structure. It is not that of ethnic or historically developed unity which accepted and realized itself in a unitary national state. The "manly spirit," which displayed its "fervor of private rights and public happiness," [79] obstructed by its very nature the emergence of a national sovereign state "one and indivisible." The idea of the contractual and voluntary character of society limited to the task of securing for its members—"by nature equally free and independent"—their rights created a paradoxical kind of nationality. The common bonds consisted, rather, of a common freedom; and political unity was sustained by the love for individual independence. Only if the state could completely satisfy the idea expressed in the concept of "self-government" would it be truly national. The violent opposition to the ratification of the proposed plan of the Constitution in almost all the states was explained by this paradox. Only through the Americanization of the proposed Constitution, through the addition of the Bill of Rights in the form of the first Ten Amendments, did it become acceptable.

The fateful years in which the Constitution was debated, attacked, and defended proved that the core of the national identification did not consist in the concept of unity through the state but in that of the relations between the individual, society, and government. The Constitution itself was permeated with the idea of the contractual nature of society and the limited sphere of political power. Its concept of "the people" was that of individual men, and the political superstructure it proposed was based on a somewhat less confident and more realistic perception of the "nature of man" according to his innate constitution and the experience of history. Its outlook was not less universal or rational than that of the states. Both forms of political organization contained a social philosophy which, being embedded in the very structure of the institutional framework of national life, secured its own continued survival and ideological dominance as the basis for all future national identification.

The character of American society as it had crystallized by the end of the eighteenth century could not be described in purely political terms. It could be described only by reference to the totality of human existence, to the attitudes, values, and norms of the individual as a member of society. America represented a new way of life and a new social and moral order.

All the attempts made by Americans to define the meaning of their independence and their Revolution showed an awareness that these signified more than a change in the form of government and nationality.[80] Madison spoke of the American government as one which has "no model on the face of the globe." [81] For Washington, the United States exhibited perhaps the first example of government erected on the simple principles of nature, and its establishment he considered as an era in human history.[82] Similarly, John Adams was convinced that a greater question than that of American Independence "will never be decided among men." [83] For Jefferson, America was the proof that under a form of government in accordance "with the rights of mankind," self-government would close the circle of human felicity and open a "widespread field for the blessings of freedom and equal laws." [84] Thomas Paine hailed the American Revolution as the beginning of the universal reformation of mankind and its society with the result "that man becomes what he ought." [85] For Emerson, America was "a nation of individuals . . . another word for opportunity . . . a last effort of the Divine Providence in behalf of the human race." [86] Edwin H. Chapin, Unitarian minister, defined the mission of America "to carry out the great ideas of a new dispensation, to elevate and improve the individual, to establish on the highest degree of the scale of human progress the standard of national greatness." [87] George Bancroft, the historian of the Republic, believed that America's mission in history was to realize fully the idea of liberty in its material and spiritual expressions. "First in the history of mankind," the American people "established mutual freedom by mutual acknowledgment of individual equality." [88]

VI

"Natural Society" – the Evolution of a Social Ideal

We believed . . . that man was a rational animal, endowed by nature with rights, and with an innate sense of justice; and that he could be restrained from wrong and protected in right, by moderate powers, confided to persons of his own choice, and held to their duties by dependence on his own will. . . We believed that men, enjoying in ease and security the full fruits of their own industry, enlisted by all their interests on the side of law and order, habituated to think for themselves, and to follow their reason as their guide, would be more easily and safely governed, than with minds nourished in error, and vitiated and debased, as in Europe, by ignorance, indigence and oppression.

—Jefferson to Judge William Johnson, June 12, 1823[1]

1. STATE AND SOCIETY

The dimension of freedom and of personal absolute rights was not identical with that of political society, nor was the state the only framework of liberty. Man's natural rights were not absorbed by political society; they interpenetrated one another without losing their identity. Nature and society existed side by side, or, rather, society was plastic enough to comprehend individual independence so that liberty could unfold its "blessings" on a higher level of rational life.

And yet, unless men were presumed to associate with each other because of inherent needs, interests, and affections in a "natural society," the discrepancy between liberty, or personal independence, and political society would lead either to confusion or to the gradual enlargement of political authority. Only on the assumption of a natural sociability could liberty and order be reconciled.

"Natural society" was voluntary, and its relation to political society was reciprocal. The sphere of its activities diminished or grew inversely with the increase or contraction of the authority and the scope of governmental action. But both were necessary and defined through their quantitative and qualitative relationship the nature of the society.[2]

This concept of society gained more and more prominence in the eighteenth century and became the dominant idea of the liberal movement in both Europe and America. In American ideology, the concept of the natural order of society became the system of coordinates which explained the relationship between freedom and authority, between the rights of the individual and the needs of society.

The idea of the natural society was plainly expressed in the first great exposition of American democracy, in Thomas Paine's *Common Sense* and *Rights of Man*. Paine, with the sure instinct of a great agitator, grasped the central importance of this idea of the natural society for the liberation of man from the oppressive and coercive authority of the state.

Some writers have so confounded society with government, as to leave little or no distinction between them; whereas they are not only different, but have different origins. Society is produced by our wants and government by our wickedness; the former promotes our happiness *positively* by uniting our affections, the latter *negatively* by restraining our vices. The one encourages intercourse, the other creates distinctions. The first is a patron, the last a punisher.

Society in every state is a blessing, but Government, even in its best state, is but a necessary evil; in its worst . . . an intolerable one. . . Government, like dress, is the badge of lost innocence; the palaces of kings are built upon the ruins of the bowers of paradise.[3]

The need to form society was, according to Paine, like a "gravitating" power, which drew strangers cast together into society, "the reciprocal blessings of which would supercede, and render the obligations of law and government unnecessary while they remained perfectly just to each other."[4]

Paine clearly intended to destroy the myth that the disruption of the existing structure of political power and legal authority would throw society into confusion, anarchy, and civil war. By postulating the autonomy of social life, its inherent rational structure of mutuality in exchange for service and aid, he aimed to rid the Americans of their fear and of their voluntary subjection to an

exploiting and parasitic class rule.[5] Individual freedom was reconciled with social order, not through the coercive powers of the
state but by the very nature of man's wants and affections. Not
freedom, but uncontrolled power and authority, endangered
society. The functions of government were limited and represented
only a small part of the activities of society, which were unlimited
and capable of infinite development. The development of arts and
sciences, of agriculture, commerce, and industry, the refinement of
manners and morals—all occurred in the social realm through the
impact of the ideas and common work of its members.

> The circle of civilization is yet incomplete. Mutual wants have formed
> the individuals of each country into a kind of national society, and here the
> progress of civilization has stopped. . . There is a greater fitness in mankind
> to extend and complete the civilization of nations with each other at this
> day. . . The present condition of the world . . . has given a new cast to the
> mind of man. . . The wants of the individual, which first produced the idea
> of society, are now augmented into the wants of the nation, and he is obliged
> to seek from another country what before he sought from the next person.[6]

The same idea was more succinctly stated in the *Rights of Man,*
considered by all Americans as the first systematic treatise and
defense of the American ideology.[7] The book helped to crystallize
both the conservative-federalist and the republican movements.[8]
Jefferson fully identified himself with Paine's views.[9] "I am extremely pleased to find it will be reprinted," he wrote of the
Rights of Man, "and that something is at length to be publickly
said against the political heresies which have sprung up among
us. I have no doubt our citizens will rally a *second* time round
the *standard* of Common Sense."[10]

Paine's theory of society proved that the order which reigned
among men was not the effect of government but resulted from
the natural sociability of men. This order existed prior to government and would exist if government were destroyed. The mutual
dependence and reciprocal interest which bound people together
and connected all parts of the civilized community "create that
great chain of connection which holds it together. . . Common
interest regulates their concerns, and forms their law, and the laws
which common usage ordains, have a greater influence than the
laws of government. In fine society performs for itself almost
everything which is ascribed to government."[11]

It followed that the authority and functions which government took upon itself were "mere imposition," a legitimation through which parasitic classes maintained their hold on society. "Government is no farther necessary than to supply the few cases to which society and civilisation are not conveniently competent; and instances are not wanting to show, that everything which government can usefully add thereto, has been performed by the common consent of society, without government. . . The instant formal government is abolished, society begins to act: a general association takes place, and common interest produces common security." [12] The principle of association and security was inherent in man's nature. As his natural wants were greater than his individual powers; and as experience, reason, science, and civilization increased those wants and increased their means of satisfaction, there arose a law of growth, progress, and perfection which constantly diminished coercive power and integrated government more and more with society. "The more perfect civilisation is, the less occasion has it for government, because the more does it regulate its own affairs, and govern itself." [13] Society, then, again approached nature on a higher level of being as reason; and the lawful relations inherent in the nature of things then ruled the affections and the social relations of man. "All the great laws of society are laws of nature. Those of trade and commerce . . . are laws of mutual and reciprocal interest. They are followed and obeyed, because it is the interest of the parties so to do, and not on account of any formal laws their governments may impose or interpose." [14]

Though in an ideal society government would be completely absorbed by its members, the lesson of America proved that the integration of government and society might be optimal. America demonstrated how different nations might be united by "the simple operation of constructing government on the principles of society and the rights of man" and *that government is nothing more than a national association acting on the principles of society."* [15] Its functions were strictly determined by the needs of society, which ruled itself by the device of representation. "The representative system takes society and civilisation for its basis; nature, reason, and experience, for its guide." [16] It recruited its leaders from all the members of society and as in the republic of letters, discovered worth by giving genius a universal and fair chance. Its laws, by being exposed to the public interest and collective experience, were the most likely to be wise.[17] This theory of society integrated the main elements of the American ideology into a social system. Liberty, the rights of man, the concept of a contractual political association, constitutionally limited in its sphere of action and achieving its ends by representative democracy, were the main aspects of the system.

There was an immense difference between this concept of a free and natural society and that of the democratic or republican theories developed in Europe in the wake of Rousseau's *Contrat social*. Paine believed that the state would be more and more absorbed by the activities of a spontaneously acting society. But society, in Rousseau's concept, was completely absorbed by the state. The individual did not remain sovereign of his own destiny but, as a citizen, abdicated his own for that of the general will of the community:

> On convient que tout ce que chacun aliène, par le pacte social, de sa puissance, de ses biens, de sa liberté, c'est seulement la partie de tout cela dont l'usage importe à la communauté, mais il faut convenir aussi que le Souverain seul est juge de cette importance.[18]

His freedom is that of being part of the sovereign state, and his rights are those which the sovereign grants him.

> Ces clauses bien entendues se réduisent toutes à une seule, savoir, l'aliénation totale de chaque associé avec tous ses droits à toute la communauté . . . Car l'Etat à l'égard de ses membres est maître de tous leurs biens par le contract social . . . Les possesseurs étant considérés comme dépositaires du bien public.[19]

Society and state were absolutely integrated with the citizen-nation, and the sovereignty of the people deprived the individual of his self-determination.[20]

According to the American concept, the individual became a member of the community through the incessant impact of mutual needs and through the exchange of services—the "unceasing circulation of interest, which, passing through its million channels, invigorates the whole mass of civilized man."[21] Rousseau's sovereign citizen-state, on the other hand, created by its very nature a uniform rule for all which regulated the individual through a web of laws.[22] "The body politic, therefore, is a moral being possessed of a will; and this general will, which tends always to the preservation and welfare of the whole and of every part, and which is the source of the laws, is with regard to all the members of the state the rule of what is just and unjust."[23] The sovereign nation, created by the social contract, thus dissolved autonomy and took over the functions of the natural society.[24] The republican movement which rose in the wake of Rousseau sought the unity and equality of the people in common citizenship in a national state.[25] Nationalism and democratic popular sovereignty coincided. Patriotism was the virtue of both.[26]

This difference between the American and European concept of democracy was foreshadowed in the "Déclaration des droits de l'homme et du citoyen" of the National Assembly, August 26, 1789. The American constitutions decisively influenced the form and content of the French declaration, but there were also significant differences.[27] The French declaration spoke about "le but de toute association politique," while the contractual concept of the American counterpart referred to society itself.[28] The French declaration was dominated by a concept of sovereignty foreign to American thought. Article Three of the French declaration read: "Le principe de toute souveraineté réside essentiellement dans la nation," while that of Virginia declared that "all power is vested in, and consequently derived from, the people," a term which meant something quite different from the term "nation."[29] "The people" referred to men freely associated; "nation" to an indivisible unity of society. The same difference reappeared in Article Sixteen of the French declaration: "Toute societé dans laquelle la garantie des droits n'est pas assurée . . . n'a point de constitution." That of New Hampshire stated: "When men enter into a state of society, they surrender up some of their natural rights to that society, in order to insure the protection of others; and without such an equivalent, the surrender is void."[30] While the French text indicated the total surrender of men's natural rights for certain political rights, the American text stressed the inalienability of certain individual rights. The real ground of divergence between the systems lay in the French concept of sovereignty and the American concept of the coexistence of natural and civil rights. The French frame of reference was that of the nation, the general will, and the idea of sovereignty. The suggested French Constitution, which represented the social contract that established the nation, did not secure the permanent rights of the individual against the state but rather incorporated them completely into the sovereign nation and in its *volonté général*. The oath of fidelity was rendered not to the Constitution,[31] but to the nation, an indivisible spiritual being possessed of will and personality which differed from that of its members.[32] The Constitution of 1793 declared: "La loi est l'expression libre et solennelle de la volonté générale. . . La souveraineté réside dans le peuple. Elle est une et indivisible. . . Le peuple souverain est l'universalité des citoyens français."[33] The concept of the nation had actually absorbed the concept of the individual.

The process of hypostasis through which the people became a nation, through which the will of its majority, the general will, and the delegated powers of its representatives became a sovereign power, changed also the meaning of the Constitution and the concept of man's natural rights. The state became the expression of the mystical unity of the nation which suffered no other loyalty but to itself. This deification of the state could be seen in the "Loi chapelier." It decreed:

> Il doit sans doute être permis à tous les citoyens de s'assembler, mais il ne doit être permis aux citoyens de certaines professions de s'assembler pour leur prétendus intérêts communs. Il n'y a plus de corporations dans l'Etat; il n'y a plus que l'intérêt particulier de chaque individu, et l'intérêt-général. Il n'est permis à personne d'inspirer aux citoyens un intérêt intermédiaire, de les séparer de la chose publique par un ésprit de corporation.[34]

The basic difference between the Jacobin and the liberal traditions lay in their attitudes toward politics. "The liberal approach assumes politics to be a matter of trial and error. . . It also recognizes a variety of levels of personal and collective endeavors, which are altogether outside the sphere of politics. The totalitarian democratic school, on the other hand . . . recognizes ultimately one plane of existence, the political. It widens the scope of politics to embrace the whole of human existence."[35]

The fixation on the idea of the sovereign nation and its general will was no less decisive for the development of the French national identification than the idea of a free society was for that in America. In America this idea replaced that of the British nationality and became therefore truly national; in France the revolutionary concept of the popular sovereign national state came into permanent conflict with the idea of the organic unity of the French nation as determined by history and its collective spirit. For both concepts the national state and its grandeur remained the supreme symbol of identification and the frame of reference for all moral and civil obligation. This situation "narrowed the field of political speculation to the main problem raised by the Revolution—that of the form of the State, and restricted the angle of vision to within the limits of narrow nationalism . . Neither in practice nor in theory did any criticism emerge of current conceptions of government as embodied in the *ancien régime;* the relation of the individual to the State, the nature of sovereignty, the nature of authority, the sphere and aims of law—all these were taken for granted." [36] The dominating concept of the sovereign nation did not impede the growth of French sociological thought. But, by contrast with American experience, such speculation developed in opposition to democracy and nationalism.

It is easier to demonstrate the influence of Thomas Paine's ideas than to discover their sources. Though the concept of the natural development of a social order had become the common property of the Enlightenment, it was Paine who integrated this concept with the ideal of self-government, the rights of man, and a republican system of government.[37] The concept was immensely significant in the development of the American attitude toward government and the state and toward the relation between the individual and society.

The image of a natural order of social life dominated the Jeffersonian tradition. The idea of a natural identity of interests, of a natural sociability, and the spontaneous growth of a social order explained the relation between individual rights and political authority, between the distrust of power and the concept of an equalitarian democracy. Society was the middle term which appeared both in the major and the minor premises, in the principle of individual rights and in the idea of the majority rule by a democratic government. This middle term transformed the ideal of American democracy into a social rather than a purely political philosophy.

Because most historians have interpreted the term "society" in purely political terms, they have been puzzled by the apparent contradictions in the American concept of democracy, its insistence on the rights of man and on the constitutionally limited powers of democracy. Thus, Charles M. Wiltse, in *The Jeffersonian Tradition in American Democracy,* defined its contradictions:

> The chief difficulty with Jefferson's political system is that of getting the individual into society, without the use of force. He argues that some form of social organization is necessary to protect and enforce individual rights; and at the same time he bases morality on innate social instincts. Logically these two arguments are incompatible; for a consistent individualism cannot admit instinctive social desires, any more than a natural social order can leave room for unrestricted personal rights.[38]

This criticism stemmed from a limited and historically distorted view of the basic concepts involved. The dichotomy was between the thesis that "the best government is that which governs least" and the idea of a democratic state which aimed at the realization of a common good existed only if state and society were considered identical,[39] as in the Rousseauan concept which subjected the individual to society. But the American ideology integrated man's natural and civil rights into a larger concept—that of a society which harmoniously coordinated spontaneous-voluntary and contractual-coercive social relations through the idea of social cooperation and self-government.[40]

2. "NATURAL SOCIETY"—THE EVOLUTION OF A CONCEPT; LORD SHAFTESBURY

The comparison between the French and the American concepts of government and society has revealed a fundamentally different outlook on the relation between the state and the individual. In the former the political society, the national citizen-state, completely absorbed the individual; in the latter, the polity was an association for limited purposes which performed only those functions which society could not perform for itself. In the United States men's needs were supplied by the natural and spontaneous order of association which stemmed from the innate sociability of humankind. The assumption of the existence of a natural order of society made feasible the contractual order of limited political obligation. The distinction between a natural social order and the political order rested on concepts which not only formed an integral part of the eighteenth-century Enlightenment but also became the very fundamental on which American democracy was reared. An analytic description of the evolution of these concepts must therefore precede any further study of the crystallization of American ideology.

The distinction between political and natural society could not be based on Locke, although certain elements were implicit in his description of the state of nature. He pointed out that man was social by nature, by necessity, convenience, and inclination; that the greater family actually formed a natural society; that a law of nature governed humanity in the state of nature; and that "reason, which is that law, teaches all mankind . . . that being all *equal and independent,* no one ought to harm another in his life, health, liberty, or possessions." [41]

Locke, furthermore, distinguished between the political compact and other contractual relations which still pertained to the state of nature: "For truth and keeping of faith belongs to men, as men, and not to members of society." [42] The distinction between the state of nature and the sociopolitical state explained the purpose and the just limits of political obligations and power. In this context Locke cited the habits of the American Indians, an example of a prepolitical society which lived according to the laws of nature in free association without government. [43]

Yet for Locke the natural state preceded political society and was superseded by it. In American thought, by contrast, both states existed simultaneously; new elements in the theory of natural society enlarged the conceptual framework.

The chief impetus for the enlargement of the idea of a natural society came from the pupil of Locke, and the grandson of the founder of the Whigs, Anthony Ashley Cooper, the third Earl of Shaftesbury. Shaftesbury's distinct contribution was his insistence on the primary and underived character of man's sociability and his rejection of the notion of a presocial state of nature. [44] Though many others preceded him in this, Shaftesbury was the first to connect man's sociability with a native moral sense, which even at the lowest level of human development directed his activities toward society and affirmed moral rules without reference to political authority. [45]

The moral sense was not solely the product of pure reason [46] but was rooted in the physical needs and in the affections, as well as in reason and reflection.[47] The moral sense was the compass with which nature endowed man to distinguish right from wrong and to prefer the right—that is, the good of humanity. Such sense, being based on reflection, was perfectible and grew in strength with the enlargement of reason and the refinement of culture. Like the sense of beauty, it sprang from awareness of the harmony of the cosmic order and was reflected in moral as well as aesthetic judgment. Virtue was therefore not blind and benevolent; it was inspired and directed by reflection and understanding. "And in this Case alone it is we call any Creature *Worthy* or *Virtuous*, when it . . . can attain the Speculation or Science of what is morally good or ill."[48] As the sense of beauty was the affection toward the fitness, compatibility, and harmony of interrelated parts, so the moral sense was an awarenes of the fitness, compatibility, and harmony of human action with that of the good of humanity.[49]

Shaftesbury's concept of morality rested on his concept of nature. Nature was the system of harmoniously adjusted, interrelated, and absolutely interdependent parts which encompassed the totality of being. That which disturbed the system was ill or bad and that which maintained it was good. There existed levels and chains of interrelatedness, systems within systems. Goodness referred at first to the immediate system to which a being belonged "who then only is suppos'd *Good*, when the Good or Ill of the System to which he has relation, is the immediate Object of some Passion or Affection moving him."[50] By this very definition, good and bad were equated with the natural and unnatural; "this too is certain; That the Admiration and Love of Order, Harmony and Proportion, in whatever kind, is naturally improving to the Temper, advantageous to social Affection, and highly assistant to *Virtue;* which is itself no other than the Love of Order and Beauty in Society."[51]

Through the notion of the moral sense, Shaftesbury liberated morality from religion and authority, and men from the need to live under a coercive power. Society, like morality, was autonomous and natural. Freedom and the moral sense were two aspects of man as well as elements of social life. The truly enlightened individual was capable of living in society without the rule of any other authority than that which nature had implanted in his heart.

The sense of "Right and Wrong therefore being as natural to us as *natural Affection* itself, and being a first Principle in our Constitution and Make; there is no speculative Opinion . . . which is capable *immediately* or *directly* to . . . destroy it. That which is of original and pure Nature, nothing beside contrary Habit or Custom (a second Nature) is able to displace."[52]

Through the moral sense, nature is introduced as an immanent principle of judgment and behavior into the realm of human and social relations. The voice of nature might be dimmed by institutions, false notions, habits, and artifice; yet its laws ruled society and could always be recovered. Underlying this argument was the notion that man's true state of nature was society and that sociability was the instinct which nature had implanted in men. That which distinguished Shaftesbury from Locke and the natural-law philosophers was not "whether the very philosophical propositions about right or wrong were innate; but whether the passion of affection toward society was such: that is to say, whether it was natural and came of itself or was taught by art."[53] Society was the natural system of human life just as the association of the particles in any body was the natural system of physical nature:

If *Eating* and *Drinking* be natural, *Herding* is so too. If any *Appetite* or *Sense* be natural, the *Sense of Fellowship* is the same. If there be any thing of Nature in that Affection which is between the Sexes, the Affection is certainly as natural towards the consequent Off-spring; and so again between Off-spring themselves. . . And thus a *Clan* or *Tribe* is gradually form'd: *a Publick* is recogniz'd: and besides the Pleasure found in social Entertainment, Language, and Discourse, there is so apparent a Necessity for continuing this good Correspondency and Union, that to have no *Sense* or Feeling of this kind, no Love of *Country, Community,* or any thing *in common,* would be the same as to be insensible even of the plainest Means of *Self-Preservation,* and most necessary Condition of *Self-Enjoyment.*[54]

Unlike Hobbes and Locke, Shaftesbury completely denied the proposition that self-interest and self-love were the dominant passions of man.[55] Though man pursued happiness, he did not pursue self-interest alone. The preservation of life did not imply preservation at any cost. "If he loses what is manly and worthy in these, he is as much lost to himself as when he loses his Memory and Understanding."[56] True happiness was a pattern of life created by the fulfillment of man's highest capacities and virtues. Therefore, selfishness destroyed happiness. Since sociability was coeval with man's existence, "herding" and fellowship were deep passions to which the individual was subject no less than to his desire to self-preservation. Yet this inborn sociability did not by necessity lead to the creation of that great and impersonal society, called the state or commonwealth. Shaftesbury introduced here the distinction that later became famous through the German sociologist Ferdinand Tönnies, between "community" and "society" (*Gemeinschaft* and *Gesellschaft*).[57]

Left to its own instinctive force, sociability created knots of fellowship. In society, in the state and the nation, this sociability was refined by reason and reflection, and thereby the moral sense became the guide of social life.

> The relation of *Country-Man,* if it be allow'd any thing at all, must imply something *moral* and *social.* The Notion it-self pre-supposes a natural *civil* and *political* State of Mankind, and has reference to that particular part of Society to which we owe our chief Advantages as *Men,* and rational Creatures, such as are *naturally* and *necessarily* united for each other's Happiness and Support.[58]

The postulate of man's social nature did not involve a derogation of the supreme value of individuality and liberty. All natural social relations were sustained by morality and reason no less than by affection and instinct. In Shaftesbury's view, fellowship and citizenship presupposed the existence of a free, self-determining personality.[59] For a rational creature, self-preservation and the public good were inseparable, as moral rectitude and virtue, reflecting the universal interrelatedness and harmony of nature, were the only guide to the true interest of the individual. "Vice," on the other hand, resulted in "the Injury and Disadvantage of every Creature." [60] Balance and harmony, being the secret core of nature, ruled man's attitudes toward himself and society. Social and self-centered affections were in themselves morally neutral. They could be morally evaluated only through their intentions toward a system of human relationship.[61]

Since self-preservation was the condition of existence, the failure to guard it was a dangerous negative moral attitude.

> And thus the Affections towards private Good become necessary and essential to Goodness. For tho no Creature can be call'd good, or virtuous, merely for possessing these Affections; yet since it is impossible that the

publick Good, or Good of the System, can be preserv'd without them; it follows that a Creature really wanting in them, is in reality wanting in some degree to Goodness.[62]

Morality was, then, a system of balanced passions and affections which reflected the "*œconomy of the passions*" through which nature preserved the species. In nature this balance was instinctive; in man it was the product of affections and reason and was therefore precarious. Religion, laws, and institutions created new habits, opinions, and passions which might be destructive, "so that 'tis hard to find in any Region a human Society which has *human* Laws. No wonder if in such Societys 'tis so hard to find a Man who lives NATURALLY, and as a MAN." [63]

The major concepts and attitudes of the Enlightenment found expression in Shaftesbury's moral philosophy. It fused reason and nature, transcendence and immanence, into a system of cognitive assumptions which supported the optimistic belief in man's progressive nature and in universal benevolence. Harmony and the law ruled in the moral and social world no less than in the physical one. The selfish impulses of man were socialized by their very objects of desire and by reflection and his moral sense. Though nature did not know the contrast between the ideal and the real, between history and the final design of mankind, man could and would, through reason and reflection, re-establish that harmony and sympathy between the individual and society.

The liberation of morality from the dictates of revealed religion, and of society from the guardianship of the state, explained the immense influence of Shaftesbury on eighteenth-century moral and social thought. Basing morality on the innate sociability of man, and society on the natural wants and affections of men, he opened a way for the psychological approach toward morality and for a sociological approach toward history and society. The Scottish school of moral philosophy—Francis Hutcheson, David Hume, Adam Smith, Adam Ferguson, Dugald Stewart, Thomas Reid, and Lord Kames—all stood under Shaftesbury's influence.[64] Montesquieu put him on the same level as Plato, Montaigne and Malebranche. Diderot translated his "Inquiry Concerning Virtue," and Rousseau's *Discours sur les arts et sciences* and *Discours sur l'origine et les fondements de l'inégalité* showed the effects of

Shaftesbury's thought. Even more profound was Shaftesbury's impact on the German Enlightenment, which revolted equally against Locke's sensualism and French materialism.[65]

3. LORD BOLINGBROKE

While Shaftesbury's concepts of society and morality developed in protest against the sensualism of Locke, Lord Bolingbroke arrived at essentially similar results by building on Locke's psychology. Like Shaftesbury, he aimed to prove the independence of morality from revealed religion and traditional political authority. A confirmed deist, he sought to discover the forces which created and maintained society and which instituted and fostered morality in man himself. Again, like all naturalists of his time, he had to refute Hobbes, the first to explain both in purely scientific terms of natural causation and vital needs.

Bolingbroke's political creed of constitutionalism and political liberty led him to emphasize the distinction between society and state and to uphold the relative autonomy and independence of society from political authority.[66] The Newtonian world view dominated the social philosophy of Bolingbroke. The concept of universal interdependence and of the harmony of natural forces, the belief in the perfect design of nature, were transferred to the moral and social realm and made to explain society.

Mankind was ruled by forces inherent in the individual and society, which assured the greatest well-being of the whole and of each member within it. Morality rested on the absolute need of man to live in society in order to survive and to develop all his capacities. On the other hand, morality was essentially the process of reasoning applied to the relations between the individual and society. It discovered its truth, like any other science, by observation, analysis, and generalization of natural data. It did not result from innate ideas but was created *a posteriori* by the observation of the necessary relations existing between men.[67] "Right reason consists in a conformity with truth, and truth in a conformity with nature. Nature, or the aggregate of things which are, is the great source from whence all the rivulets of real knowledge must be derived." [68] Moral truth, then, could be derived also from the scientific study of man as a social being.

Like most of his contemporaries, Bolingbroke distinguished

between nature and history, reason and the positive law. True morality returned forever to the law of nature, which was reason in the relation of things. History, on the other hand, was mostly the deviation of men moved by passions and affections and particular ends from the original scheme and balance of things. Return to nature, then, meant the breakthrough of reason and the re-establishment of natural harmony. Therefore it was necessary to distinguish between state and society, natural and civil society.

Moral obligation could never be derived from civil or religious law; its authority rested on the necessity to conform to those rules which inhered in the conditions of human happiness and survival. "Reason is in this case the obliger. A rational creature is the obliged; and he is so obliged as no law, made by mere will, can of itself oblige." [69] The authority of civil law was itself based on the needs of men to live in society.

Nature directed them to unite in societies and to submit to civil laws, for their common utility. Fraud betrayed them into the tyranny of mere will, and when various institutions and various customs had made them lose sight of the law of their nature, it was not hard to persuade them that the dictates of will, designed for particular not common utility, and even repugnant to this law, were deduced from it. . . When absolute power is once established, it may impose arbitrary will for law. It cannot make things just or unjust.[70]

Bolingbroke clearly recognized that no valid morality could be derived from the premises of Locke's natural-rights philosophy. The obvious discrepancy between the rights and interests of the individual and those of society were overcome by the concept of society as the basic framework of human existence.

I have said thus much, in order to show that political societies grow out of natural, and that civil governments were formed not by concurrence of individuals, but by the associations of families. It is the more necessary to repeat and to inculcate this distinction, because, for want of making it, and by representing mankind to themselves like a number of savage individuals out of all society in their natural state, . . . our best writers, even Mr. Hooker, and much more Mr. Locke, have reasoned both inconsistently, and on a false foundation.[71]

Society and man were, then, coeval. Yet, unlike Shaftesbury, Bolingbroke based the validity of moral obligation on utility in the first instance and only to a lesser degree on the evidence of nature, history, and social life.[72] Unable to rid himself of the atomistic attitude of his master, Locke, Bolingbroke reduced man's sociabilty to that which seemed the individual's fundamental drive—self-love and self-preservation. On that element Bolingbroke built his theory of society and sociability.

Sociability and the formation of society were derived from the primary motif of self-love, which experience and reason transformed into morality.[73] History became all-important. Experience and observation required time, and the reason that collected them and was improved by them ripened only through time. Reason itself worked too slowly and too imperfectly to regulate the conduct of human life if self-love, "the original spring of human actions," did not come to its aid through instinct.[74]

Self-love begat sociability; and reason . . . as well as instinct, improved it . . . extended it to relations more remote, and united several families into one community, as instinct had united several individuals into one family. . . . The natural obligation to exercise benevolence, to administer justice, and to keep compacts, is as evident to human reason, as the desire of happiness is agreeable to human instinct. We desire by instinct, we acquire by reason.[75]

Through the "genealogy of law" nature begot natural law, which begot sociability, which created human society and union by consent.[76]

Since Bolingbroke's theory did not explain the postulate of the primacy of society, he introduced the pleasure principle as auxiliary. Society was the source of all happiness. Benevolence, justice, and other moral virtues which alone maintained society then became desirable.[77] Thus necessity, utility, and pleasure above all, made man sociable and enforced upon him the "rules of the game," or social virtues. Their practice was "the law of our nature" because happiness could only be achieved by the dependence of private on public good.[78]

This was demonstrated also by the study of natural societies which existed without formal government or coercive power. There, order and cooperation, morality and personal freedom, were maintained by the manners and rules according to which they regulated their life. All barbarous tribes had customs equivalent to laws, with the recognized authority of the elders equivalent to magistrates, and they were better ruled and more virtuous than many civilized societies. It was the mistake of most writers that they had "nothing in their minds but political societies of human institution, and did not advert to those that are natural."[79] Individuality was a late product of civilization. Men formed in primitive and prepolitical communities such tightly knit societies that the attribute of individuality properly applied to the whole rather than to a single person.[80] The transition from natural to artificial society did not occur instinctively but rather by experience, necessity, force, and reason.[81] Bolingbroke restated here the distinction already made by Shaftesbury and fully developed by Ferguson. Natural societies were social organisms, communities—or, in the language of Tönnies, *Gemeinschaften*. Civil societies were nonorganic, maintained by interest, historical forces, and ideas. Their cohesion emanated from agreement and utility and was expressed by the state. Each individual was relatively isolated, and his relations with others were impersonal.[82]

Natural and civil societies were unlike—the one instinctive, the other deliberate; the one based on sociability, custom, and unconscious bonds; the other on reason, consent, and common interest.[83] The relation of the natural to the civil society was not an immediate one in the "genealogy of nature." This explained the tendency of all greater societies to deteriorate from their original purpose. "Societies were begun by instinct, and improved by experience. They were disturbed early, perhaps as soon as they were formed, both from within and from without, by the passions of men; and they have been maintained ever since, in opposition to them, very imperfectly, and under great vicissitudes, by human reason."[84] Reason was aided by government, which everyone concurred in maintaining because all agreed to control the passions and restrain the excesses of others.[85] The process of civilization tamed the passions, strengthened reason, and, by increasing social interdependence, increased the hold of morality. The paradox of history was that the farther society moved from nature as instinct, the more it approached nature as rule of reason and virtue.

These views opened up several different lines of inquiry. Alexander Pope immortalized them in his *Essay on Man*.[86] Bolingbroke's experimental and scientific attitude toward morality as a "natural" phenomenon opened the way for a sociological and historical study of the development of human societies.[87] His approach to morality, partly hedonistic and partly utilitarian, foreshadowed that of Hume, Adam Smith, and the social psychology of Condillac and Helvétius.[88]

4. FREEDOM AND DETERMINATION IN SOCIETY

Though most of the social philosophies of the eighteenth century abandoned the premises of Locke's political philosophy, his postulates of the natural liberty, equality, and personal independence of man remained the great inspiration of the age. The development of eighteenth-century social thought was decisively conditioned by the ideals of personal liberty and individuality. These remained the heuristic principles for the reformation of state and society.

The idea of the natural society proposed not to limit man's right to self-determination but rather to minimize the need for coercive power and to liberate him from the overbearing authority of the state, the positive law, and the church. The concept of innate sociability transferred the Newtonian image of the system of nature to society and created a social universe out of the motivations and drives of men. The harmony which ruled the great chain of being ruled also the sphere of social relations. Justice, morality, and utility coincided, and the interests of all were linked through the medium of society under the law of right reason.

The social and historical sciences emerged out of this synthesis as studies of the specific laws which ruled human society in time and space. Almost all eighteenth-century social thought assumed that society preceded the state in time and importance, and conceived the latter as a system of functions set up by the former. The structure of society, its mores, civilization, and the morality of its members determined the character of political power. The state became part of a system determined by social forces, with its functions strictly limited to the needs of society.

After the middle of the eighteenth century, the tendency to account for social and historical phenomena without reference to metaphysics became ever more pronounced.[89] Custom, habit, and environmental factors, together with biology and psychology, replaced earlier explanations. The rise of the concept of historical process and of the social system implied the conditioning power of impersonal and changing patterns of institutions, ideas, and social relations. This was already evident in the work of Voltaire and Montesquieu. It became prominent in Rousseau's *Discours sur l'inégalité*, in Hume's *Essays*, Helvétius' *De l'ésprit*, Holbach's *Systeme social ou principes naturals de la morale* . . . , Ferguson's *Essays on the History of Civil Society*, and Adam Smith's *Inquiry*.

And yet social sciences were still, at the end of the eighteenth century, considered a part of "moral philosophy." The Saint-Simonists and Auguste Comte, the founders of modern sociology, no less than the founders of modern historiography in Italy, England, France, and Germany, believed in the progress of humanity toward greater perfection and felicity. This belief and the confidence in the power of reason to liberate man—"aus Seiner selbstverschuldeten Unmündigkeit," [90]—did not decline but increased in strength toward an apogee in the American and French revolutions. This apparent contradiction between the development of the social sciences and the optimistic belief in progress, liberty, rationality, and benevolence was resolved by the eighteenth-century concept of man's nature. In spite of all evidence to the contrary, that concept was taken to be fundamentally the same at all times and places. The unity and uniformity of mankind were simply assumed.

"Practically every philosopher of Ferguson's period [based] his work upon what he thought of as ultimate fact, that is, the constitution of man. No scholar of the eighteenth century would have thought of questioning the scientific adequacy of such a foundation. Their science was thus, in Hume's phrase, very really 'the science of man.' " [91] This belief had been strengthened by the immense confidence in the power of reason and of scientific analysis in the age of rationalism and deism. Reason united all in a consensus of right and wrong and could create a human society essentially similar everywhere. Bolingbroke's *Letters on the Study and Use of History* explained that there were "certain general principles and rules of life and conduct, which always must be true, because they are conformable to the invariable nature of things." The study of history will "soon distinguish and collect them, and by doing so will soon form . . . a general system of ethics and politics on the surest foundation, on the trial of these principles and rules in all ages, and on the confirmation of them by universal experience." [92] From this concept he derived his famous definition of history as "philosophy teaching by examples." [93] Hume made the same observation. "Mankind are so much the same, in all times and places, that history informs us of nothing new or strange. . . Its chief use is only to discover the constant and universal principles of human nature." [94]

True, writers like Lord Kames accounted for the diversity of human civilization by the hypothesis of distinct races of men differing widely in their natures. [95] But the degree to which the idea of the basic unity of mankind had become axiomatic was indicated by the misgivings and uncertainty of Jefferson's judgment concerning the Negroes. Though he was unwilling to commit himself in a definite statement to the Negroes' inferiority as a race, [96] he was encouraged by Lord Kames's *Sketches of the History of Man* to suggest the hypothesis of the existence of different species of the same genus or of varieties of the same species. [97] To pacify his general convictions he conceded the Negroes' equality in emotional and affective traits, yet thought them intellectually, as well as physically, inferior to the whites. [98]

Jefferson's attitude to the problem of unity of the human race was, from the European point of view, the result of exceptionally trying circumstances. Environmental and historical factors generally accounted for the differentiation within the basic framework of the unity of human nature. Locke's epistemology and psychology proved man's mind to be plastic, changeable, and yet capable of finding verifiable truth relevant to his life and nature. Shaftesbury, Hutcheson, and others, by discovering the decisive role of society in the development of the individual and civilization, added another element of identity which, while plastic, yet remained constant. And the immense influence of Leibnitz's idea of the cosmic urge toward individuality and perfection, elaborated by Christian Wolff, seemed capable of harmonizing the individual and society, unity and diversity, change and persistence, in the idea of the progress of mankind through history and civilization. [99] The concept of mankind was given concrete form by the realization of the mutual dependence and interrelation of all men. The progress of reason and civilization was the work of all generations and led through more or less uniform stages from primitive society to the age of reason. By the eighteenth century man was capable of reshaping himself and his social life according to the dictates of reason and could reflect in his society the harmony of the laws which maintained the universe.

In spite of great variations and differences, this scheme pervaded the religion of humanity and the Enlightenment and formed the basis of the philosophy of progress and of the early sociology of the nineteenth century.[100] Progress, according to Christian Wolff, was achieved only through society, the mutual exchange of services, knowledge, and experience. It followed that each was called to aid the common good since all had the duty of recognizing the individual's right to self-preservation, self-perfection and the pursuit of happiness. The natural-rights theory was therefore adjusted without difficulty to the sociological scheme of the primary importance of society. This was the ideological framework accepted by all the social philosophers, by Hutcheson, Quesnay, Mercier de la Rivière, Marquis de Mirabeau, DuPont de Nemours, Ferguson, Price, Priestley, and Adam Smith.

Property and the exchange of goods and service constituted the point of intersection between the individual and society. Freedom and cooperation, self-interest and the common good, were achieved through the division of work. Civilization and the growth of an economy were social phenomena ruled by their own inherent laws; and political or coercive authority was needed only in marginal cases.

The great deviation from this liberal pattern of thought was that of Rousseau, who erased the sharper distinction created by the Age of Enlightenment between society and state, between individual rights and needs and those of political authority. On the surface Rousseau's social philosophy was part of the Enlightenment the premises of which he utilized in the *Discours* and the *Contrat social*. Yet underneath this surface there existed a deeper level of inspiration which endowed those works with the force of a revolutionary revelation. The Rousseauan scheme was actually a secular, quasi-scientific translation of the Christian-Augustinian concept of the fall and redemption of man. The same despair and hatred of the existing world, the same distrust of civilization and of reason, which motivated the Augustinian and Calvinist condemnation of the world motivated Rousseau's evaluation of society and history. The social contract was a rebirth of mankind which eradicated the sins derived from the fall of man. It returned, on a different level, to the beginning of a state of innocence. This revolutionary outlook gave coherence to a historical and social scheme, but it lacked the confidence in reason and in the responsibility of free men which characterized the outlook of the Age of Enlightenment. In its own way Rousseau's transition from the state of civilization to that of the social contract, from slavery to freedom, was as inexplicable as that of Hobbes from the state of nature to that of society.

Edmund Burke, in his first major publication, *A Vindication of Natural Society,* reached significantly different conclusions from the same criticism of the state and civil society.[101] The *Vindication* made a distinction between *natural society* and *political society,* the one "founded in natural appetites, and instincts, and not in any positive institution" and the other a union of society established by laws.[102] The one was maintained by mutual interests and a sense of natural justice, the other by force and for the purpose of exploiting the subjects of the state. The state perpetuated the evils it claimed to destroy and added new ones—those of oppression, exploitation, and the glorification of war and force as patriotic duties.[103] Justice and security were set aside by positive law which served the purposes of a ruling class in defending their status. "In a state of nature, it is an invariable law, that a man's acquisitions are in proportion to his labors. In a state of artificial society, it is a law as constant and as invariable, that those who labor most enjoy the fewest things; and that those who labor not at all have the greatest number of enjoyments."[104] The *Vindication* appealed to men to trust in reason, to throw off the shackles they had forged for themselves and to depend on the voluntary principle of mutual interest to regulate human affairs.[105] The *Vindication* was a forerunner of European anarchism and of liberal democracy.[106] Burke rightly divined that the concept of a natural society implied an inversion of the relation between state and society. The state was a purely functional framework which society established for the common good. The wider the circumference of society's activities, the smaller the scope of the functions delegated to the state.

There was a gap between this functional analysis of the relations between state and society and the factual development of human communities. Some theory had to account for the gap and justify the confidence in a radical limitation of the state. British Whiggism, whether of the "Tory" Bolingbroke or of the "Whig" Shaftesbury, was committed to such theory: and that supplied the context for the work of Adam Ferguson.

Society and the historical process were the primary data of Ferguson's analysis. The uniqueness of human society consisted in its progressiveness and plasticity. It was only with man that "the species has a progress as well as the individual; they build in every subsequent age on foundations formerly laid." [107] In man, art and nature were not opposed, for the spontaneity of the mind was uniquely his own. "He is in some measure the artificer of his own frame, as well as his fortune, and is destined . . . to invent and contrive." [108] This explained his almost unlimited changeability. His very nature was activity and progress and therefore became history. [109] Yet men's behavior was at the same time motivated by constant instincts, those of self-preservation and self-interest on the one hand, and of sociability and sympathy on the other. His reason was applied to knowledge or to action as approbation or as censure. He craved happiness; yet the contents of his instincts and of his reason were variable and determined by his total, ever-changing situation no less than by experience, reflection, and passion. Self-preservation led to property, and the accumulation of wealth, unless regulated, became an overpowering and destructive egotism. [110] Yet this passion was balanced by friendship, sociability, and benevolence, which derived their strength from the basic fact that man was born and had his being in society, which was a primary and underived datum of human existence. [111] The instincts of self-preservation and sociability explained the double morality of man, his identification with his own society, and his aggressiveness toward the stranger. Virtue and self-sacrifice went hand in hand with hatred, prejudice, and pugnacity toward others. [112]

Like Rousseau, Ferguson traced change and progress through the development of the modes of economic life. Mankind passed through savagery, barbarism, and civilization—stages marked by an increase in productive power and an ever-widening scope for private property. In the process, social ties became ever more intricate and interdependence increased. Social institutions became stabilized and differentiated, and social authority became defined.

Primitive societies were equalitarian; their social functions were derived from the community as a whole and were exercised according to age, talent, and disposition.[113] Their members were conscious of equality and tenacious of their rights. Subordination was voluntary and yet mutual fidelity and sacrifice were at their highest. Every individual was independent, yet cooperation was perfect without government.[114] This cohesive power arising from equality and independence was so strong that primitive societies were capable of federating without having recourse to formal government.[115]

Like his contemporaries, Ferguson was fascinated by primitive society, which seemed not only to bear the true impress of nature[116] but also to be an image of the life of the ancient Germans, Saxons, and Goths who had laid the foundation of the European and British-American liberty. The North American Indians seemed to prove Montesquieu's dictum that liberty was born in the German forests and also to vindicate the social ideals of the Enlightenment. The preoccupation of Jefferson with the Indians, his defense of their virtues and capacities, stemmed from his interest in the workings of this natural prepolitical society.[117] For the same reason, Ferguson grew eloquent in their description:

> It was their favourite maxim, That no man is naturally indebted to another; that he is not, therefore, obliged to bear with any imposition, or unequal treatment. Thus . . . they have discovered the foundation of justice, and observe its rules, with a steadiness and candour which no cultivation has been found to improve. . .[118]
>
> The love of equality, and the love of justice, were originally the same. . . He who has forgotten that men were originally equal, easily degenerates into a slave. . . This happy principle gives to the mind its sense of independence, renders it indifferent to the favours which are in the power of other men, checks it in the commission of injuries, and leaves the heart open to the affections of generosity and kindness.[119]

For such men property was no temptation. The love of society, friendship, and virtue, eloquence and courage, the original qualities of men, ruled yet uncorrupted.[120]

Ferguson described the emergence of property through the introduction of new modes of economic life in almost identical terms with Rousseau. While savages lived in an absolute democracy, barbarians inclined toward monarchy. Yet even then mankind were "generous and hospitable to strangers, as well as kind, affectionate, and gentle, in their domestic society."[121] States, especially monarchies, arose mostly through conquest, as the warrior band made itself king and aristocracy over those it conquered. The new aristocracy preserved the freedom and equality of the earlier bands.[122]

Whatever the actual course of development, the authority of the state and the happiness and prosperity of its society rested on laws beyond the contingencies of history. All authority ultimately rested on consent, and no society prospered which disregarded the laws inherent in the nature of human behavior. The progress of society was limited by its capacity to produce means of subsistence, and that depended on the security and the satisfaction which labor and inventiveness brought. "Men are tempted to labour, and to practise lucrative arts, by motives of interest. Secure to the workman the fruit of his labour, give him the prospects of independence and freedom, the public has found a faithful minister in the acquisition of wealth, and a faithful steward in hoarding what he has gained."[123] Liberty and personal security were the foundations of both national wealth and power. Public utility and social strength coincided in this way with individual freedom and interest. Man's natural rights and social needs were inseparably intertwined. Individual liberty rightly understood was the key to social happiness.[124] This formulation marked the true dividing line between liberal thought and radical or conservative *étatisme*. The liberal thesis maintained that society was built on reciprocity and mutuality among free individuals, that freedom based on equality of status and rights was the optimal condition for social welfare.

5. THE NATURAL SYSTEM OF LIBERTY—LAISSEZ FAIRE

"Man is, by nature, the member of a community," wrote Ferguson, "and when considered in this capacity, the individual appears to be no longer made for himself."[125] Yet it did not follow that society, incorporated as state, should determine the actions of the individual. "The happiness of individuals is the great end of civil society. . . That is the most happy state, which is most beloved by its subjects; and they are the most happy men, whose hearts are engaged to a community, in which they find every object of generosity and zeal, and a scope to the exercise of every talent, and of every virtuous disposition."[126]

Happiness consisted in the blessings of a candid, strenuous, and

active mind. The smaller the self-governing community, the greater the amount of freedom, consent, mutuality, and spontaneous
cooperation, and therefore of happiness. In words almost literally
to be repeated by Emerson, Ferguson described the living and
spontaneous organism which developed wherever men lived together:

> Prior to any political institution whatever, men are qualified by a great
> diversity of talents, by a different tone of soul, and ardour of the passions, to
> act a variety of parts. Bring them together, each will find his place. They
> censure or applaud in a body, they consult and deliberate in more select
> parties, they take or give . . . and numbers are by this means fitted to act
> in company, and to preserve their communities, before any formal distribu-
> tion of office is made.[127]

Individual rights and social cooperation were both necessary parts
of moral theory as they were of actual life. Natural rights were
derived from reason itself no less than from the purpose of social
cooperation. Morality had its basis in the primacy of society no
less than in individual reason. The sense of unity with mankind
informed morality and endowed people with the knowledge of
right and wrong.

It is in the light of the English-Scottish moral philosophy that
Blackstone's words are understandable: that the creator has "so
intimately connected . . . the laws of eternal justice with the happiness of each individual, that the latter cannot be attained but by
observing the former; and if the former be punctually obeyed, it
cannot but induce the latter. In consequence of which . . . [He
had] graciously reduced the rule of obedience to this one paternal
precept: 'that man should pursue his own happiness.' "[128] Blackstone qualified immediately the term "his own happiness" by the
adjectives "true" and "substantial." True happiness was that consonant with the happiness of each indivdual or the happiness of
society.

Like Blackstone, his most formidable critic, Joseph Priestley,
saw no contradiction between the greatest-happiness principle as
the criterion of social action and that of individual liberty and
natural rights.[129] "All people live in society for their mutual advantage," wrote Priestley in a treatise which Jefferson considered
a classic statement of the American standpoint, "so that the good
and happiness of the members, that is the majority . . . is the great

standard by which everything to that statement can finally be determined." [130]

"Each" and "all" were united and in their claims reconciled through society, which, as a dynamic complex of reciprocal relations, created a unity through which mankind achieved ever higher levels of power and perfection. Society, seen as a system of labor division and of exchange of goods and services, united individual liberty and spontaneity with social cooperation and cohesion. It reflected the cosmic order in its balance of dependence and autonomy, of unifying law and individuality. Here, the eighteenth century discovered the rational order for which it had vainly looked in history. Given these assumptions, the quest for liberty led to laissez faire. That theory as developed by the physiocrats and Turgot, by Adam Smith, Franklin, and Jefferson, as well as by Thomas Paine and Condorcet, was not a philosophy of individual rights but of social justice and social rationality. "Man is subject to wants, and he has faculties to provide for them," wrote Condorcet in his *Outlines of an Historical View of the Progress of the Human Mind*, "and from the application of these faculties, differently modified and distributed, a mass of wealth is derived, destined to supply the wants of the community." The apparent chaos of individual efforts and strivings led, by a general law of the moral world, to the good of the whole and "notwithstanding the open conflict of inimical interests," the public welfare requiring that each should understand his own interest, and be able to pursue it freely.[131]

The laissez-faire philosophy of a natural and free society envisioned a radical breakdown of all privileges, the equalization of opportunities, and the liberation of human energies for the mutual maximum benefit of all its members. "It is easy to prove," continued Condorcet,

that fortunes naturally tend to equality, and that their extreme disproportion either could not exist, or would quickly cease, if positive law had not introduced factitious means of amassing and perpetuating them; if an entire freedom of commerce and industry were brought forward to supersede the advantages which prohibitory laws and fiscal rights necessarily give to the rich over the poor . . . if political institutions had not laid certain prolific sources of opulence open to a few, and shut them against the many.[132]

For the ideologists of the Enlightenment of the second half of the eighteenth century the newly discovered self-directing mechanism of the economic order was the protoytpe of a free society. Property, instead of being the cause of injustice and enslavement, became in a natural economic order the foundation of freedom and social cooperation. For in a society in which all economic activity was subjected to the principle of the general utility of a free market, property became the greatest stimulant for social exertion so long as the state maintained natural justice.

'It was thus," wrote Adam Smith, "that man, who can subsist only in society, was fitted by nature to that situation for which he was made. All the members of human society stand in need of each other's assistance, and are likewise exposed to mutual injuries. Where the necessary assistance is reciprocally afforded . . . the society flourishes and is happy. . . Society, however, cannot subsist among those who are at all times ready to hurt and injure one another. . . Society may subsist, though not in the most comfortable state, without beneficence; but the prevalence of injustice must utterly destroy it." [133] In the field of economic activity self-interest and the general welfare were identical; liberty and social cooperation went hand in hand. Here it could be proved that society could satisfy its own needs by a mutuality of services without coercion and compulsive interference of the state. The discovery of the economic society and its self-regulating mechanism made the physiocrats famous.

For Mercier de la Rivière, one of the first to formulate the full implications of the physiocratic doctrine, man was by nature sociable and dependent on society, which in turn was ruled by the laws of nature and reason. Self-preservation and justice were the basis of all property rights. Property united man to society though it was also the foundation of his independence and liberty. [134] "Voulez-vous, qu'une société parvienne à son plus haut degré possible de richesse, de population, et conséquemment de puissance? Confiez ses intérêts à la liberté." [135] The universality of property rights, its twofold nature of being individually owned and socially produced made social liberty the condition of material well-being and wealth. The freer the play of economic activities and appetites, the stronger was social interdependence. [136] Left to free competition and cooperation, the natural order of social life reached its optimal state of efficiency and natural justice. The laws of the social order were, for Du Pont de Nemours, like those of the living organism. Where natural order could not develop freely there existed neither proper moral nor physical order. "Il y a donc *un ordre* naturel, essentiel et général, qui renforme les lois constitutives et fondamentales de toutes les sociétés." [137]

The same concepts, but stated more lucidly and worked out on a scientific scale, dominated the work of Adam Smith. The reciprocal relations between the individual and society acted as much in the moral as in the economic sphere. As the market regulated the activities of the individual through the laws of demand and supply, so public opinion determined his moral behavior. "Nature, accordingly, has endowed him, not only with a desire of being approved of, but with a desire of being what ought to be approved of; or of being what he himself approves of in other men." [138] Though man's native sympathy and his sense of justice might not be strong enough to determine his actions, morality became powerful through public opinion as manners, customs, and mores.[139]

Adam Smith was attracted to the doctrine of the French "economists" because it was the "obvious and simple system of natural liberty" which, left to itself, would establish social harmony. "Every system which endeavours, either by extraordinary encouragements . . . or by extraordinary restraints, [to] force from a particular species of industry some share of the capital which would otherwise be employed in it, is in reality subversive of the great purpose which it means to promote. It retards, instead of accelerating, the progress of the society towards real wealth and greatness. . . All systems either of preference or of restraint, therefore, being thus completely taken away, the obvious and simple system of natural liberty establishes itself of its own accord." [140]

Under the general, simple, and natural rule of laissez faire, "every man, as long as he does not violate the laws of justice, is left perfectly free to pursue his own interest his own way, and to bring both his industry and capital into competition with those of any other man, or order of men." Within that system the sovereign had only three duties: "that of ensuring external and internal security, of protecting society from injustice and oppression, and finally, the duty of erecting and maintaining certain public works and certain public institutions which it can never be for the interest of any individual . . . to erect and maintain." [141]

The division of work and the absolute dependence of the individual on the collective effort of production compelled him to adjust himself completely to society even though he labored for his own interest only. This coincidence between public and private goals existed only within a system of absolutely free competition and cooperation. Real exertion and productivity would always result from self-interest only. For every man is "by nature, first and principally recommended to his own care; and . . . he is fitter to take care of himself, than of any other person." [142] Nature maintained itself only by letting each strive for self-preservation and self-perfection. Yet this same force, through the cunning device of nature, became a force for social improvement and wealth. A natural and competitive free play of economic forces compelled each individual to the greatest exertion in order to compete successfully with all others, and his own benefit depended entirely on that the public would draw from it. True competition therefore developed all the powers of the individual, spurred industry and economy, distributed and spread talents where they were needed, and created harmony between the individual and the public.[143]

The fundamental concept of Adam Smith was that of the *social system*. Man lived and had his being in society and was molded by its forces. The generality of the system of relations, interdependence, public opinion, the market economy, social institutions, as well as habits and traditions, compelled man to conform. For every individual was subject and object at the same time. He was consumer and producer, purchaser and salesman, the judge and the judged, the public and the individual. He was subjective toward his own ends and objective toward those of others. As a member of society, he disciplined the individual; as individual, he strove for independence, yet had to conform. Honesty, peacefulness, and virtue were laws of reason which ruled the public, and became private morality through membership in society. Knowledge and civilization, created by society, developed with increasing complexity and with the accumulation of wealth and experience. Commerce and industry undermined the feudal system and stimulated public order, good government, and personal liberty.[144] Only such a system realized the natural rules of equity and of free individual exertions. The natural market economy, therefore, was the rule of justice and public utility. "The natural effort of every individual to better his own condition, when suffered to exert itself with freedom and security, is so powerful a principle that it is alone, and without any assistance, not only capable of carrying on the society to wealth and prosperity, but of surmounting a hundred impertinent obstructions with which the folly of human laws too often encumbers its operations." [145]

Adam Smith was far from underestimating the functional importance of the state for society. Without it a free and natural economy could not function. Yet the sphere of the state was strictly limited to what society could achieve for itself through the individual action of its members. Any interference by the state with the impersonal laws of society was harmful, for all such intervention was for the particular ends of groups, classes, or individuals, while the laws which ruled the society were general, and for the benefit of the whole.[146] This was the fault of mercantilism.[147] Power led to exploitation.[148] Companies and corporations, especially when legitimized by the state, destroyed the competitive market economy and endangered economic justice as well as progress. Impersonal corporations, where there was no relation between exertion and reward, lacked inventiveness, industry, and forethought. Only where property was secure and personal and stood in direct relation to man's labor, did it become a source of productive energy. For these reasons Adam Smith, like most British moralists, considered the unlimited increase of property, especially landed property, as socially harmful.[149] Hutcheson advocated the right of the state to limit the size of holdings through legislation and taxation.[150] Smith believed that the revocation of all restrictions on its disposal would equalize the distribution of property.[151]

The natural social system was, then, that of perfect liberty and justice. Liberty required the abstention of the state from interference with the social process; justice, the abstention of the individual from interference with the order of equity. Order in this context implied the creation of conditions of general utility such as the protection of the quality of money and other important goods, the restriction of interest, the regulation of the monetary system and of public health, and the provision of an education and such public services as roads, channels, bridges, and harbors.[152]

The concept of society had completely changed in the course of the eighteenth century. The state, or the political society, now was conceived as a superstructure which rested on the natural order of social life. The growing domination of that natural order by reason and experience and the steady growth of the sphere of voluntary cooperation and mutual service were signs of civilization and progress. The contractual theory of government and its foundation on the rights of man were feasible because man was naturally sociable and society was a natural order of human life.

It is easy to understand why the concept of society was usually identified by later historians with that of political society. From the time of the great debate with England over the rights of the colonists to the final victory of political democracy in the nineteenth century, the American people were preoccupied with political debates and theories. In this context the term "society" referred exclusively to political society; the state, the government, and man's attitude toward society were defined by the theory of natural rights and of the contractual origin of political authority. James Harrington, Algernon Sidney, John Locke, and the English post-Revolutionary constitutionalists were the obvious sources for the republican ideology in America. Yet this concept of a natural political order was based on that of a natural social order. The synthesis between the two created the ideal of society which the Jeffersonians considered as the "American system."

VII

Free Society — The Formulation of the Jeffersonian Social Ideal

The idea of the natural order of social life elucidates the meaning of the American ideal of a natural order of liberty to which the concept of a natural political society was, from its inception, wedded. The innate sociability and morality of man explained the belief that a political society, based on natural rights and limited in authority, resolved the apparent conflict between individual rights and the needs of society. Social thought after Shaftesbury largely rejected Locke's concept of society in order to save his political ideals.

Historical speculation, political economy, sociological and anthropological thought, gave new insights into the nature of human society and often led to a belief that history was subject to the laws of growth and could not be dictated by human reason. Hume, Burke, and even Adam Smith, though liberal in their views on the limits of the legitimate authority of the state, were conservative when it came to changes in political institutions and were skeptical in regard to the powers of individual reason. Others, like the disciples of Rousseau or those influenced by Helvétius' and Condillac's theories of morals, turned to social engineering to create a new society with the aid of the state and legislation.

The uniqueness of the American ideology lay in the fact that the equalitarian and libertarian political doctrine of natural rights was grafted onto the ideal of a natural order of social life to yield a new concept of a natural order of freedom, or the ideal of a "free society." In France the tendency to delegate sovereign power over society to the revolutionary citizen-state became increasingly strong: in America the ideal of a natural social order strengthened that of a natural political order and created a concept of a new society.

1. FREEDOM AND SOCIAL JUSTICE

Only America achieved a true synthesis of the philosophy of the Enlightenment.[1] The belief in the perfectibility of man and the progressive nature of voluntary social cooperation reconciled nature and history, individual rights and social justice. The theory of laissez faire became the framework of a constitutional equalitarian democracy which envisioned a radical breakup of economic, social, and political privileges, an equalization of opportunities, and a liberation of all human activities in a free and noninstitutionalized society. The Lockian concept of the purpose of political association was not supplanted but was supported by the idea of a natural free society and was radicalized by the equalitarian implications of the natural-rights theory.

The integration of these concepts was achieved first by Thomas Paine, whose writings made explicit the radical implications of the theory of a natural social order. Paine's social philosophy foreshadowed that anarchism which remained the Utopia of American thought.[2] His proposals for social reform in the *Rights of Man* and in *Agrarian Justice* were prophetic of the radical tradition of American democracy.[3]

Paine's concept was dynamic and comprehensive enough to include the idea of progress toward civilization and social justice. Democracy was to correct the damage and injustice that resulted from institutions which impeded the rule of natural justice. His "Letter to the Abbé Raynal on the Affairs of North America" and his *Rights of Man* included much of the material in Condorcet's *Outlines of an Historical View of the Progress of the Human Mind,* although Condorcet acknowledged as his masters Turgot, Price, and Priestley.[4] In Paine's theories natural justice remained the permanent criterion of civilization. Men associated as equals in the community, which remained stable only so long as the rules of equity were preserved. Justice, as a permanent self-correcting principle of social cooperation, was not based on the ideal of equality, or on the notion of society as an indivisible unity, but rather on the motives of human association, of the nature of property, and the rights to which free and equal individuals were entitled.

Basic was the assumption that natural wealth—land and resources—belonged to the community and could not be permanently alienated without compensation for the loss of social opportunity. "Land . . . is the free gift of the Creator in common to the human race. Personal property is the *effect of society;* and it is as impossible for an individual to acquire personal property without the aid of society, as it is for him to make land originally. . . All accumulation, therefore, of personal property, beyond what a man's own hands produce, is derived to him by living in society." [5]

Poverty was a product of civilization. It did not exist in primitive societies. Its main cause was the permanent alienation of the natural sources of wealth to individuals. Property was a necessary means of producing goods, but the rights to it extended only to the improvement of what existed naturally. It followed that every proprietor owed a social rent to the community which it could use to benefit those without the means to maintain their independence. Paine therefore suggested an old-age pension and a patrimony to be paid to all who reached maturity. [6] "It is not charity but right, not bounty but justice, that I am pleading for. The present state of civilization is as odious as it is unjust. It is absolutely the opposite of what it should be and it is necessary that a revolution be made in it." [7] A revolution in the state of civilization was the necessary accompaniment of a revolution in government. Only when private property benefited the whole society and accumulation increased the security of all would property rest "on the permanent basis of national interest and protection." [8]

Paine's proposals for an equalization of economic opportunities were evidently addressed to France and Europe, where the extremes of exploitation and poverty threatened class war. His proposals were the answers of a liberal democrat to the rising communism of the followers of F. N. Babeuf. [9] Yet the general attitude was valid for American democracy as well. There, a civilization based on natural justice had preceded the political and national revolution. There, the ideal of a natural order of a free society could be perfected and studied.

This had been done by Crèvecœur in his *Letters,* [10] in which he attempted to describe American society as a way of life or a social system, "the most perfect society now existing in the world." [11] His thought was pervaded by the sociological perspective. The key word of the American social system was "natural." The forces which regenerated the European in America, the new mode of life, the new laws were those of a natural order.[12]

Several chapters in the *Letters* studied the problem of how far natural society could prosper without government or when government was completely absorbed by society through a self-governing community. The analysis of the manners, customs, policy, and trade of the inhabitants of Nantucket and of Martha's Vineyard was a sociological inquiry into the workings of a natural society. These chapters dealt with society as a whole. "This happy settlement," he wrote of Nantucket,

was not founded on intrusion, forcible entries, or blood. . . It drew its origin from necessity on the one side, and from good will on the other; and ever since, all has been a scene of uninterrupted harmony. Neither political nor religious broils . . . have in the least agitated . . . its detached society. . . This singular establishment has been effected by means of that native industry and perseverance common to all men, when they are protected by a government which demands but little for its protection; when they are permitted to enjoy a system of rational laws founded on perfect freedom.[13]

The description and analysis of the communities of these islands followed several lines of inquiry guided by Rousseau's *Discours sur l'inégalité*, Montesquieu's *L'Ésprit des lois* and Abbé Raynal's *Histoire philosophique*. Yet the main intent of these chapters was to explain a society without social ills in which general comfort and equality of conditions prevailed and in which all public concerns were regulated by a communal coordination of activities. "What has happened here," observed Crèvecœur, "has and will happen everywhere else. Give mankind the full rewards of their industry; allow them to enjoy the fruits of their labor . . . leave their native activity unshackled and free, like a fair stream without dams or other obstacles; the first will fertilize the very sand on which they tread, the other exhibits a navigable river, spreading plenty and cheerfulness wherever the declivity of ground leads it."[14]

Crèvecœur emphasized the power of an enlightened morality and of a natural, simple religion for the maintenance of such society. The simple and free religious tenets of the Quakers were important elements in the social mores of those happy islands. This natural morality, comprising the Protestant and the classical virtues of simplicity, honesty, frugality, and sobriety, created a free, uncorrupted society of healthy individuals who united in their communal relations utmost liberty with maximum cooperation. A strong communal tradition was integrated with self-reliance, independence of mind, and a spirit of enterprise. These islands were a social laboratory in which the main tenets of the Enlightenment were proved feasible. "They have all, from the highest to the lowest, a singular keenness of judgment, unassisted by any academical light; they all possess a large share of good sense, improved upon the experience of their fathers; and this is the surest and best guide to lead us through the path of life, because it approaches nearest the infallibility of instinct." [15] Like the whole American experience, the society of the islands proved the basic fitness and equality of man's nature, his power to govern himself according to the rule of reason and morality.

Rousseau's *Discours sur l'inégalité* was confirmed, yet its conclusions were disproved. Though Crèvecœur accepted Rousseau's estimate of the corrupting influence of civilization and luxury, he showed that they were not necessarily the consequence of a civilized society. For Rousseau, primitive liberty was the original condition in the happiness of man; and progress toward mutual dependence, property rights and division of work was the cause of human misery. For Crèvecœur, social cooperation and individual liberty, civilization, and well-being were compatible. "Here, happily, unoppressed with any civil bondage, this society of fishermen and merchants live, without any military establishments, without governors or any masters but the laws; and their civil code is so light, that it is never felt. A man may pass . . . through the various scenes of a long life . . . and never in that long interval, apply to the law either for redress or assistance." [16] This image of a natural order of social life dominated American democracy in the Jeffersonian tradition. The ideal of the natural identity of. interest, of man's natural sociability and morality, of a spontaneous growth of social order, explained the relations between individual rights and political authority, between the distrust of political power and the concept of political democracy.

The ideals of a free and natural society and of a free and natural government created in their interaction and interpenetration a system which became the framework of national identification. American nationalism rested on identification with this system, in the name of which it followed its course of "manifest destiny" toward its own society and the outside world. Nowhere was this functional relationship between an aggressively national consciousness and the vision of a new social order more clearly revealed than in the thinking of Thomas Jefferson.

2. NATIONAL ISOLATION AS A DUTY TO HUMANITY

Jefferson was intensely conscious of the uniqueness and separateness of the American people, of their manifest destiny and mission, and convinced of the need for enlarging the borders of the United States by all means to their utmost limits. Yet his Americanism did not exclude a cosmopolitan outlook nor was it motivated by isolationism.[17] His nationalism was guided by his social and political ideals, by the need to secure the American people against the outside world, and by the desire to guarantee the maximum benefits which would ensure the survival of their social system.[18]

The ideological nature of Jefferson's nationalism explained his attitude toward the French Revolution and toward England and South America as well as his policy of annexation and conquest of contiguous territory. Toward the French Revolution his attitude was that of unflinching support even at the cost of his own popularity; his role in the preliminary phases of the Revolution was considerable.[19] Though he was in the beginning in favor of conservative reform, modeled on the English pattern, he quickly accepted the course of the Revolution as logical and correct[20] and identified himself with the regime of the republic.[21] The French Revolution had a decisive influence on the enlargement of the ideological concept of American republicanism, which only then displayed the consciousness that it was a world-wide movement.[22]

"I look with great anxiety for the firm establishment of the new government in France," Jefferson wrote to Colonel Mason in February 1791, "being perfectly convinced that if it takes place there, it will spread sooner or later all over Europe. On the contrary, a check there would retard the revival of liberty in other countries. I consider the establishment and success of their government as necessary to stay up our own, and to prevent it from falling back to that kind of half-way house, the English constitution."[23] This passionate indentification with the French republican movement led Jefferson even to excuse the reign of terror. "A failure there would be a powerful argument to prove there must be a failure here." [24] He therefore felt compelled also to justify the destruction of his own former associates, the Constitutionalists, by the Jacobins. Certainly, in the unavoidable struggle, many guilty persons fell without the forms of trial, and with them some who were innocent. "These I deplore as much as any body, and shall deplore some of them to the day of my death. But I deplore them as I should have done had they fallen in battle. . . My own affections have been deeply wounded by some of the martyrs to this cause, but rather than it should have failed I would have seen half of the earth desolated; were there but an Adam and an Eve left in every country, and left free, it would be better than as it now is." [25]

Nothing could shake this fidelity to republicanism as the principle of a new and just world order. Even when Napoleon had become a dictator and had overthrown the remnants of republican institutions, Jefferson refused to admit that republicanism had failed but only blamed the movement for not having yet learned to protect itself. [26] Yet the downfall of constitutional republicanism in France and its slow and violent deterioration under the Convention and the Directorate changed Jefferson's attitude toward the relations of America with the outside world and his general historical perspective in regard to the progress of mankind. Though he continued to believe, with Condorcet, in the indefinite progress of mankind toward freedom, knowledge, and moral perfection, he came to realize that this progress would be slow, acquired by painful experience, and conditioned by the mores and general traditions of various societies. [27] In the memorable dialogue in which Jefferson and John Adams tried to sum up their distinct beliefs and their common work toward the eve of their lives, Jefferson reaffirmed his faith in mankind and its perfectibility. "It has failed in its first effort, because the mobs of the cities, the instrument used for its accomplishment, debased by ignorance, poverty, and vice, could not be restrained to rational action. But the world will recover. . . Science is progressive, and talents and enterprise on the alert." [28] Yet freedom and human dignity, eternally self-evident truths, could not be realized unless the society which sought them was prepared in its mores and traditions to be ruled by reason. [29]

The immediate consequence of this hard-won realism was a

growing isolationism derived from the conviction that only an absolute disengagement from diseased and corrupted Europe could safeguard the hard-won achievements of the American Republic. The failure of the French Revolution, its embroilment in unceasing wars with monarchal Europe, its final destruction through the forces it had let loose, and the final victory and restoration of a reactionary and tyrannical regime, all these strengthened and fortified the tendency to isolate the American continent completely from the remainder of the world and to make it strong, independent, and self-sufficient.

This tendency was not motivated by the ordinary rules of power politics. The Hamiltonians and the New England Federalists were for alliances. But the continental isolationism of the Jeffersonians had ideological roots. America was left as the bulwark of the rights of humanity, the sanctuary, the asylum and stronghold, of human liberty and human decency. It was "the world's best hope," a "signal of arousing men to burst the chains under which monkish ignorance and superstition had persuaded them to bind themselves, and to assume the blessings and security of self-government." [30] National egoism was a sacred duty for the good of mankind and the establishment of the rights of man. America had to rely on its own strength and to fortify its achievements to increase its power until it would be strong enough to face the whole world. [31] The central obligation of Jeffersonian isolationism was to defend and to strengthen the American system.

In Jeffersonian nationalism two distinct aims combined easily with one another, though they served different purposes. The one reached its first official expression under Monroe as the Monroe Doctrine. It aimed at safeguarding republicanism by a geographical demarcation in which the Atlantic Ocean divided Europe from America, and the United States became the guardian of continental independence. The first fruit of this policy was the acquisition of Louisiana, the purchase of which was as much motivated by the fear that a European strong power, France, might become the master of the main western line of communication as by the necessity to insure the right of navigation for the West. [32] Yet the acquisition of Louisiana also revealed the second aim of this nationalism. The annexation of this huge reserve of virgin land created conditions that insured the prosperity and tranquillity of the American people for a long time. It stabilized and strengthened its social order by the sheer weight and number of its ever-increasing population. The Franklinian concepts of out-numbering the adversary and of the land reserve as the first requirement for an equalitarian republican society became an integral part of Jeffersonian nationalism.[33]

Writing to James Monroe in 1801, Jefferson stressed this aspect of his nationalism. "However our present interests may restrain us within our own limits, it is impossible not to look forward to distant times, when our rapid multiplication will expand itself beyond those limits, and cover the whole northern, if not the southern continent, with a people speaking the same language, governed in similar forms, and by similar laws; nor can we contemplate with satisfaction either blot or mixture on that surface."[34] Increasing the strength of the American nation and the durability of its system by colonizing the continent with its people and planting the American way of life wherever they settled was one way of increasing the dominion "for the blessing of freedom and equal laws."[35] "At the end of that period we shall be twenty millions in number, and forty in energy, when encountering the starved and rickety paupers and dwarfs of English workshops." By that time, he wrote to DuPont de Nemours, "your grandson will . . . bear distinguished part in retorting the wrongs of both his countries on the most implacable and cruel of their enemies."[36]

With sufficient strength, Europe and its system of exploitation and permanent warfare could be contained and freedom become the rule for the whole American continent. Then the "meridian of the mid-Atlantic should be the line of demarkation between war and peace."[37] This idea, first expressed by Thomas Paine in his *Common Sense*, repeated in *The Federalist*, and in Washington's "Farewell Address," became the lodestar of Jeffersonian nationalism and the guiding principle of American policy in the nineteenth century. It was a national and international policy guided by a social ideal.

"The day is not distant," Jefferson wrote to William Short, "when we may formally require a meridian of partition . . . which separates the two hemispheres . . . and when, during the rage of the eternal wars of Europe, the lion and the lamb, within our regions, shall lie down together in peace. . . The principles of society there and here, then, are radically different, and I hope no American patriot will ever lose sight of the essential policy of interdicting in the seas and territories of both Americas, the ferocious and sanguinary contests of Europe." [38]

Jefferson had earlier formulated the same idea, in geopolitical terms, to Baron Alexander von Humboldt, and in environmental and historical terms to Correa De Serra, and eventually he proposed it to President Monroe as official doctrine of the United States regarding international relations. Such doctrine would be "the most momentous since . . . Independence" as it would ensure that the principles of the Declaration of Independence would become the recognized system for the whole continent. As Europe was the domicile of despotism, "our endeavor should surely be, to make our hemisphere that of freedom." [39] The ideological character of this doctrine also justified annexation and conquest which would ultimately benefit humanity. Conquest and annexation did not mean the subjection of one society by another but rather the expansion of a way of life, the extension of liberty, self-government, and of the sphere of a free and natural society. [40] Unlike European nationalism since the French Revolution, in which expansionism went hand in hand with the glorification of the state and the justification of its increased power, the Jeffersonians believed that the great American empire could be built on the principles of self-government and freedom. Jefferson denied the validity of the prevailing theory, propounded especially by Montesquieu, that the greater the territory the stronger and more autocratic the state had to be. On the contrary, he maintained, the principle of self-government and of representative democracy was the only form of government which was applicable to indefinite expansion as it was built on an infinite number of self-governing units related to each other by contractual and natural relations of common utility and the exchange of services. [41]

3. THE IDEAL OF SELF-GOVERNMENT

For Jefferson the concept of self-government was the core of the American system and the good society. Self-government held together and integrated the natural social and political orders; it coordinated individual liberty with social cooperation; and it achieved human dignity and social justice. The term itself contained two interrelated meanings. It connoted the power and the right of the individual to guide his own destiny according to his own reason and his innate morality, to pursue happiness without impinging on the same right of others. From this point of view it comprised all the inalienable individual rights of men.[42] Yet the same term referred to the structure in which individuals managed their own affairs and met their common needs either directly in the economic, social, and religious spheres, or indirectly through their representatives in the political sphere.

Such an ideal was based on assumptions which were seldom made explicit—that men were capable of living in society without coercion and that in such a society a natural identity of interests made compulsion and extraneous authority a marginal necessity. Yet this assumption was true only if society was ruled by absolute justice or the rule of equity—in other words, if social equality was perfect. Demanding the ceaseless judgment and participation of its members, such a society required a high standard of enlightenment and knowledge. Even then, it could function successfully only if the political task of administering its needs and executing its desires was simple enough to be performed by its members and representatives and was restricted to those concerns which applied equally to all. The severe restriction and the purely functional definition of the tasks of the state implied that all other activities which served the needs of the society would be performed outside the political framework through the spontaneous activity of its members. Yet these requirements could be met only when all the individuals in society enjoyed basically equal opportunities in their pursuit of happiness. In other words, the idea of self-government implied the idea of social equality and justice.

The Jeffersonians found the philosophical and ideological framework for these assumptions in the philosophy of enlightenment as developed by the English and Scottish moralists, and the physiocrats.[43] This was especially evident in the Jeffersonian insistence on the inborn morality and sociability of man, without which the ideal of self-government was a chimera. Jefferson himself considered this the crucial question which divided him from the Federalists and from Washington and John Adams. He had, as he wrote, "more confidence than . . . [Washington] . . . in the natural integrity and discretion of the people, and in the safety and extent to which they might trust themselves with a control over their government." [44]

In his *Commonplace Book* Jefferson had excerpted from Lord Kames ideas about the new moral philosophy of a natural society. "Man, by his nature is fitted for society, and society by it's conveniences, is fitted for man. The perfection of human society, consists in that just degree of union among individuals, which to each reserves freedom and independency, as far as it is consistent with peace and good order." [45] The idea of the natural fitness of man for society and of society for the needs of man was an ever-recurring theme of Jefferson, who had to postulate the innateness of the moral sense and of its independence of education, religion, state, and even of reasoning. Otherwise, society had to rest on force and the guidance of an elite.

> Man was destined for society. His morality, therefore, was to be formed to this object. He was endowed with a sense of right and wrong, merely relative to this. This sense is as much a part of his nature, as the sense of hearing . . . it is the true foundation of morality, and not . . . truth, &c. . . It is given to all human beings in a stronger or weaker degree. It may be strengthened by exercise. . . This sense is submitted, indeed, in some degree, to the guidance of reason; but it is a small stock which is required for this: even a less one than what we call common sense . . . lose no occasion of exercising your dispositions to be grateful, to be generous, to be charitable, to be humane, to be true, just, firm, orderly, courageous, &c.[46]

Unlike such moralists as Bolingbroke, Helvétius, and the Utilitarians, Jefferson held fast to the position that sociability and morality were not based on selfishness and interest but rather on innate sociability, instinctive justice and virtue. "Nature hath implanted in our breasts a love of others, a sense of duty to them, a moral instinct. . . The Creator would indeed have been a bungling artist, had he intended man for a social animal, without planting in him social dispositions." [47]

Only by assuming that sociability and morality were innate could the natural rights of man be preserved in society as mutuality of rights and duties without external authority. "Man was created for social intercourse; but social intercourse cannot be maintained without a sense of justice; then man must have been created with a sense of justice." [48]

Like many of his contemporaries, Jefferson proved the existence of a prepolitical society by the example of the Indian societies.[49] They had passed the stage of single families; they lived in perfect cooperation and formed a tightly knit community. Yet they knew of no government. Every man was perfectly free to follow his own inclinations. "Their leaders conduct them by the influence of their character only; and they follow . . . him of whose character for wisdom or war they have the highest opinion."[50] The Indians also proved that the transition from a natural to a political society created a representative democracy akin to natural association rather than patriarchal or monarchal forms.[51] Republicanism, or direct democracy, was then actually a return to natural society on a higher level. A society was natural to the degree that it approached complete self-government.[52]

The Indians validated the Jeffersonian theory of society. They demonstrated the compatibility of sociability and independence, of liberty and social cooperation; their self-sacrificing love for the natural community developed without coercion and rested solely on the identity of the personal and the communal interest.[53] They showed that not property or civilization, but the need for mutual aid and intercourse, was the basis of society. It had been said that they were averse to social life. Could anything be more inapplicable than this to a people "who always live in towns or clans?" Or could they be said to have no "republic" who conducted all their affairs in national councils, who prided themselves on the national character, who considered an "insult or injury done to an individual . . . as done to the whole, and resent it accordingly?"[54] True, only small societies could rest on absolute freedom and the sway of the natural harmony of interests and feelings. Yet the Indians preferred the blessings of self-government to all the advantages of power. "Their only controls are their manners, and that moral sense of right and wrong, which . . . makes a part of his nature. An offence against these is punished by contempt, by exclusion from society, or . . . by the individuals whom it concerns . . . crimes are very rare among them, insomuch that were it made a question, whether no law, as among the savage Americans, or too much law, as among the civilized Europeans, submits man to the greatest evil, one who has seen both . . . would pronounce it to be the last; and that the sheep are happier of themselves, than under care of the wolves."[55] Nor could it be said that these evils were necessary in all great societies. The Indians proved that a natural society could be infinitely extended by the principle of federation in which each sphere was circumscribed in its function and based on direct or representative action.[56] "It will be said, that great societies cannot exist without government. The savages, therefore, break them into small ones."[57]

The idea of self-government based on the innate morality of man and exercised in a natural confederation of societies was the cardinal element of difference between the Jeffersonians and the Federalists, especially those, like John Adams, who were influenced by Puritanism. Adams had little faith in human nature; self-interest and self-love were the mainsprings of human action. While Jefferson looked toward nature and the American experience as a guide, Adams appealed to history as proof of his pessimistic outlook. Like other conservative thinkers, Adams inclined to identify historical reality with nature and to accept it as the true key to man's being.[58] He therefore relied more on the European experience and on its realistic interpreters, Harrington, Montesquieu, Hume, and Adam Smith than on the deistic, moral sense philosophy.

Men, wrote John Adams in his *Discourses on Davila,* "continue to be social, not only in every stage of civilization, but in every possible situation in which they can be placed. As nature intended them for society, she has furnished them with passions, appetites, and propensities, as well as a variety of faculties, calculated both for their individual enjoyment, and to render them useful to each other in their social connections."[59] Among these attributes none was "more essential or remarkable, than the *passion for disinction.*"[60] Emulation, ambition, jealousy, envy, vanity, were the driving forces and the history of mankind was little more "than a simple narration of its operation and effects."[61] Just as nature maintained self-preservation through rewards and punishment, so it promoted the good of mankind by rewards of esteem, or punishment by neglect and contempt. By regulating and utilizing these passions, government turned them into instruments of the public good, imposing order, subordination, and obedience on society.[62]

The implications were far-reaching. They amounted to a rejection of democracy and of the idea of self-government. If the desire for distinction, power, and self-enjoyment were the mainsprings of social action, the structure of political society had to satisfy these urges and yet prevent their destructive tendencies. It had to utilize men of birth, wealth, and talent and, by allowing them a dominant part in the government, interest them in the general welfare of the community. It had to balance their influence at the same time by a system of checks. The state became an intricate system of social and economic orders, checking each other to permit individual freedom to survive.[63] "Experience concurs with religion in pronouncing . . . that this world is not the region of virtue and happiness; both are here at school, and their struggles with ambition, avarice, and the desire of fame, appears to be their discipline and exercise."[64]

Inequities in power, talent, and riches were fundamental facts of human nature; they could not be changed but had to be utilized. They could cause either social progress or misery. In a rational system of politics they were the basis of liberty and stability. Their abolition would lead to anarchy and despotism. "The increase and dissemination of knowledge, instead of rendering unnecessary the checks of emulation and the balances of rivalry in the orders of society and constitution of government, augment the necessity of both. It becomes the more indispensable that every man should know his place, and be made to keep it."[65] The assumption of the equality and morality of man was a dangerous illusion. "Remember, democracy never lasts long. It soon wastes, exhausts and murders itself."[66]

Progress was limited, and self-preservation as well as emulation would forever remain the mainsprings of human action. The vast majority of mankind were doomed to poverty and intellectual and moral inferiority.[67] "The modern improvers of society,—ameliorators of the condition of mankind, instructors of the human species,—have assumed too much. They have . . . undertaken to build a new universe."[68] The balance of a well-ordered government alone could prevent ambition and emulation from degenerating into conspiracy and rivalry, destructive factions, sedition, and civil war.[69]

The views of John Adams and the Federalists were no less pervaded by the climate of the Enlightenment than those of their opponents, the Jeffersonians. They too believed in the progressive movement of history, in the power of reason to learn from the

collective experiences of mankind, and in the progress of science.[70]
They believed in the supreme value of liberty and self-determination which they aimed to secure by creating a political structure
the mechanisms of which would mark out a sphere of individual
liberty. Yet they were realists. The qualities and conditions productive of liberty and reasonableness were rare and were found
only in highly civilized societies and in an elite. Adams and his
followers therefore held a view of the relation between the state
and society, between liberty and authority, different from that of
the Jeffersonians. The concept of a free society based on self-
government rested on illusory premises. There could be no integration of society and government. Reasonableness and freedom
could only be achieved through the state as their guardian. The
political order was supreme in all society. "The great art of law-
giving" consisted in "balancing the poor against the rich in the
legislature," and in constituting the legislature a perfect balance
against the executive power, at the same time that no individual
or party could become its rival. The essence of free government
consisted in "an effectual control of rivalries." [71]

John Adams' views, shared by most of the northern Federalists,
were steeped in fears created by centuries of political experience.[72]
Society had to be mastered by the state so that liberty could be
safeguarded without destroying the social order.[73] "I am not
often satisfied," Adams wrote, "with the opinions of Hume; but in
this he seems well founded, that all projects of government founded in the supposition . . . of extraordinary degrees of virtue, are
evidently chimerical. Nor do I believe it possible . . . that men
should ever be greatly improved in knowledge or benevolence,
without assistance from the principles and systems of government." [74] True, there was less cause to fear democracy in America
because most of the population were landholders and property
owners. Poverty was not yet widespread, and the average level of
morality and education was exceptionally high. "They are not
subject to those panics and transports, those contagions of madness
and folly which are seen in countries where large numbers live . . .
in dayly fear of perishing for want. We know, therefore, that the
people can live and increase under almost any kind of government,
or without any government at all. But it is of great importance to
begin well. . . All nations, under all governments, must have

parties; the great secret is to control them . . . either by a monarchy and standing army, or by balance in the constitution. Where the people have a voice, and there is no balance, there will be . . . fluctuations, revolutions, and horrors, until a standing army, with a general at its head, commands the peace." [75] Yet though the American people were predestined by geography, history, and their inheritance to become a free nation, the torch-bearer of liberty and representative government, their political structure was conditioned by exceptional circumstances which would not last forever; their social stability and individual liberty rested on the diffusion of property. Society had developed in the wake of the growth of property rights which it was the main task of the polity to secure. The "stake in society" theory dominated the thinking of the conservatives. They accepted as axiomatic Locke's view that political society was created for the defense of property.

Jefferson, on the other hand, discarded the older concept and defined the right to property as a civil, not a natural, right, one which had to give way to the superior claims of life, liberty, and happiness. The right to the pursuit of happiness was more than a "glittering generality." [76] Jefferson reduced the generally accepted right to property to a convention circumscribed by man's natural rights and the needs created by society. [77] It was true that individual property was a necessary condition for all advance in civilization and the irreplaceable motive inciting men to exertion, industry, and foresight. It was the basis of individual security and liberty and a social convention without which neither the individual nor society could develop or live in order. Yet, the right to property was, unlike natural rights, of a strictly functional character and could be treated as a corollary rather than as a primary right. The great general principle on which property rights were based was the right of man to the free exercise of his faculties which were the real property of man. The labor principle which underlay Locke's explanation of property rights was only the application of the general principle that man had a natural right to the exercise of his faculties and the fruit of his exertions. This principle was identical with that of liberty and happiness and was the core of the idea of self-government. Destutt de Tracy, whom Jefferson considered the greatest of all social philosophers and whose *Commentary and Review* he published, had clearly revealed the political implications which resulted from this theory of property and wealth. "There is nothing besides the exercise of the human faculties, which can procure subsistence for man, and without this there is nothing; but all useful things, which are at our disposal, must be considered as well the fruit of our intellectual as our manual labor, of our knowledge, as well as our industry, and the surplus wealth of society consists of what remains after all are adequately subsisted." The happiness and power of a society increase through all these means; and "the multiplication of useful productions by labor . . . render it as productive as possible," and also diminish "superfluous consumption." [78] It followed from this view that as all who participated in the production of wealth were necessary for the well-being of society, no special right could be granted to owners of property. [79]

The substitution of the right to pursue happiness for the right to property changed the nature of the political society and the character of citizenship in two ways. If property was no longer the basic principle of political association, then political society coincided with natural society. It was created and maintained for the good life of all its members, and citizenship was universal. [80] Yet the right to pursue happiness, set in the context of the social contract, defined the purpose of political society in a new way. Its purpose was to achieve the happiness of each and all—in short, to create a good society in which members could attain happiness. The American society was not only built on justice and equity but aimed at the good life and created thereby a social order. "The equal rights of man, and the happiness of every individual, are now acknowledged to be the only legitimate objects of government." [81]

The implications of these differing views on property rights were clear to both sides. While conservatives aimed to secure an existing social order, characterized by stratification and inequalities of opportunity, through a complicated structure of political authority independent and distinct from society, the Jeffersonians aimed to create a society in which equality of rights and natural justice resulted in social well-being and happiness and in which a natural social order absorbed political society.

The relation between state and society found its classical expression in Jefferson's First Inaugural Address which was a defense of the republican creed of self-government as well as of its vision of the good society. The aim of good government was justice in its widest sense, which was guided by man's equal right to liberty, the exertion of his faculties, and the use of equal opportunities created by nature and society. The chosen country "with room enough for our descendants to the hundredth and thousandth generation" presented the natural guaranty for such society. The sense of "our equal rights to the use of our own faculties, to the acquisition of our industry, to honour and confidence from our fellow citizens, resulting not from birth but from our actions" represented the moral principles which guided men in their mutual relations as members of a free and natural society. The sum of good government consisted in equity and in the provision of those needs which could be secured neither through individual nor voluntary exertions. All the rest would be done by society itself when men were left free "to regulate their own pursuits" and when they could enjoy the fruit of their labor.[82] The natural and the political society were fused in the idea of a free society ruling itself through self-government.

Conservatism, tending to preserve the historically grown structure of property rights and social status, required a strong and independent government to maintain the status quo. It also required force as an ultimate weapon. "You never felt the terrorism of Shays' Rebellion in Massachusetts," wrote John Adams to Jefferson in defense of his Discourses on Davila. "I believe you never felt the terrorism of Gallatin's insurrection in Pennsylvania. You certainly never realized the terrorism of Tries's most outrageous riot and rescue, as I call it. . . You certainly never felt the terrorism excited by Genet in 1793. . . Nothing but the yellow fever . . . could have saved the United States from a total revolution of government."[83]

Yet Jefferson had already at the time of Shays' Rebellion observed, "I hold it, that a little rebellion, now and then, is a good thing, and as necessary in the political world as storms in the physical."[84] Rebellion, anarchy, and class war were never the results of a true republican society but always of social injustice. They were "the agonizing spasms of infuriated man, seeking through blood and slaughter his long-lost liberty."[85] There was no truth in the belief "that nature has formed man insusceptible of any other government than that of force." Experience and reason showed that there existed three forms of society: that of natural society "without government as among our Indians"; a society under representative government; and society ruled by force "as is the case in all other monarchies, and in most of the other republics. . . To have an idea of the curse of existence under these last, they must be seen. It is a government of wolves over sheep. It is a problem, not clear in my mind, that the first condition is not the best. But I believe it to be inconsistent with any great degree of population. The second state has a great deal of good in it. The mass of mankind under that, enjoys a precious degree of liberty and happiness." [86]

The question for Jefferson, then, was to form a system of government that approached the first model of society and, while capable of ruling a country as large as the United States, would yet prevent political power from becoming an instrument of oppression and exploitation. The answer lay in the blending of the concept of the natural political society which preserved men's individual rights and social cooperation with the concept of the natural society characterized by freedom and spontaneous social cooperation. The polity was to be strictly defined in its functions to be forever dependent on the will of society and subservient to its true ends—the rights of men, their liberty and happiness. "What has destroyed liberty and the rights of man in every government which has ever existed under the sun? The generalizing and concentrating all cares and powers into one body." [87]

Human freedom required man to make himself "the depository of the powers respecting himself, so far as he is competent to them, and delegating only what is beyond his competence by a synthetical process, to higher and higher orders of functionaries, so as to trust fewer and fewer powers in proportion as the trustees become more and more oligarchical." [88] Only by dividing and subdividing political power, and distributing to every sphere the functions for which it was set up, could a great society remain free. This federalism was fundamentally different from that of the Federalists. The latter aimed at the concentration of power in the national government, safeguarding liberty by checks and balances and by the growing independence of the federal government from the tryannical will of the majority. Jefferson, on the other hand, aimed to limit severely the political unity expressed by the federal government. "Let the national government be entrusted with the defence of the nation, and its foreign and federal relations; the State governments with the civil rights, laws, police, and administration of what concerns the State generally; the counties with the local concerns . . . and each ward direct the interests within itself." [89] Unity was not to be achieved through the state but through the social order and its ideals. This federative republican unity created by the principles of self-government and citizenship would be the "strongest government on earth . . . the only one where every man, at the call of the laws, would fly to the standard of the law, and would meet invasions of the public order as his own personal concern." [90]

This polity, resting on the ideal of self-government, was immune to the danger that its liberties might succumb to the power of those at the helm of the state. "Where every man is a sharer in the direction of his ward-republic, or of some of the higher ones, and feels that he is a participant in the government of affairs, not merely at an election . . . but every day; when there shall not be a man in the State who will not be a member of some one of its councils . . . he will let the heart be torn out of his body sooner than his power be wrested from him by a Caesar or a Bonaparte." [91] This was the core of Jefferson's states'-rights philosophy; the ideal natural society, in which government was absorbed by the self-governing social association, was through its very nature limited in size and strength. The only way to approximate it and to create a truly free society on a national scope was to divide and subdivide political power. [92] The federal government was, by its very structure, its composition and the modes of the election of its officers, twice removed and partly independent from society, and therefore less representative and less dependent on the people. It should therefore be strictly limited in its scope to deal only with those concerns which were strictly national. [93] The state, on the other hand, more nearly represented self-government and direct representation. As early as 1791 Jefferson wrote: "It is easy to foresee, from the nature of things, that the encroachments of the State governments will tend to an excess of liberty which will correct itself . . . while those of the General Government will tend to monarchy, which will fortify itself from day to day, instead of working its own cure." [94]

This criticism explained Jefferson's insistence on states' rights and strict construction of the Constitution. "We both consider the people as our children, & love them with parental affection," he wrote Du Pont de Nemours. "But you love them as infants whom you are afraid to trust without nurses; and I as adults whom I freely leave to self-government."[95] "We consider society as one of the natural wants with which man has been created; that he has been endowed with faculties and qualities to effect it's satisfaction by concurrence of others having the same want; that when, by the exercise of these faculties, he has procured a state of society, it is one of his acquisitions which he has a right to regulate and controul, jointly indeed with all those who have concurred in the procurement. . . We think experience has proved it safer, for the mass of individuals composing the society, to reserve to themselves personally the exercise of all rightful powers to which they are competent, and to delegate those to which they are not competent to deputies named, and removable for unfaithful conduct, by themselves immediately."[96]

The Jeffersonian preference for state over federal authority was conditional, however. Only the fully representative and democratic state could claim the confidence of society.[97] The indictment of the federal government in the Kentucky Resolution—"Free Government is founded in jealousy, and not in confidence; it is jealousy and not confidence which prescribes limited constitutions, to bind down those whom we are obliged to trust with power"— was valid against all independent power whether that of Virginia or of the United States.[98] It was in regard to the former that Jefferson wrote:

> Mankind soon learn to make interested uses of every right and power which they possess, or may assume. The public money and public liberty . . . will soon be discovered to be sources of wealth and dominion to those who hold them. . . Nor should our assembly be deluded . . . and conclude that these unlimited powers will never be abused. . . Human nature is the same on every side of the Atlantic. . . The time to guard against corruption and tryanny, is before they shall have gotten hold of us.[99]

States' rights thus had meaning to Jefferson in the general context of his ideal of self-government and in the perspective of his insistence on subdividing the polity into ever smaller units.

4. THE SOCIAL STRUCTURE OF THE FREE SOCIETY

The Jeffersonian vision, not the conservative theory, won out and became the American ideology. John Adams himself testified that his own views were out of harmony with public opinion.[100] Though "he had the courage to oppose . . . his own opinions to the universal opinions of America, and, indeed, of all mankind . . . the work [*Discourses on Davila*] . . . powerfully operated to destroy his popularity."[101] For Jefferson and most Americans these views were heresy. John Adams saw the truth clearly when he wrote with wry irony, "Your steady defense of democratic principles, and your invariable favorable opinion of the French revolution, laid the foundation of your unbounded popularity. *Sic transit gloria mundi!*"[102]

The paradox of the situation was that the two leaders were both wrong and both right. If Adams could claim that history proved his judgment of the course of the French Revolution to be prophetic, Jefferson could do the same for his evaluation of the course of American democracy. The one interpreted the American democratic movement in the light of the European past; the other, the European present in the light of the American experience. Only at a later period did Jefferson realize that the structure of social institutions, popular attitudes, and the maturity of the people conditioned the capacity to effect change without destroying the foundations of free society. The fatal illusion of the French radicals was their belief that the transition from a traditional to an ideal society could be achieved by the fiat of a revolutionary and idealistic leadership which, though able to destroy the old order, could not fashion a new one.

Condorcet, in the face of death, trying to gain a clearer perspective on his life's work, rose above despair to reaffirm his faith in humanity. He compared the American and French revolutions to find the reasons for the apparent success of the one and the failure of the other. Of the American Revolution he said:

Then was observed, for the first time, the example of a great people throwing off at once every species of chains and peaceably framing for itself the form of government and the laws which it judged would be most conducive to its happiness; and as, from its geographical position, and its former political state, it was obliged to become a federal nation, thirteen republican constitutions were seen to grow up in its bosom, having for their basis a solemn recognition of the rights of man.[103]

Yet the American Revolution was less equalitarian than the French. While it aimed to realize the same ideals, it stopped short of their full application. Instead of equality of rights it emphasized man's individual rights and relied on the system of checks and balances to insure freedom and justice. Its great contribution to political theory was in the distinction between legislative and constitutional action and the self-amendment of the Constitution.[104]

The Revolution in France, Condorcet wrote, "was more complete, more entire than that of America, and of consequence was attended with greater convulsions . . .

because the Americans, satisfied with the code of civil and criminal legislation which they had derived from England, having no corrupt system of finance to reform, no feudal tyrannies, no hereditary distinctions, no privileges of rich and powerful corporations, no system of religious intolerance to destroy, had only to direct their attention to the establishment of new powers to be substituted in the place of those hitherto exercised. . . In these innovations there was nothing that extended to the mass of the people, nothing that altered the subsisting relations formed between individuals; whereas the French Revolution, for reasons exactly reverse, had to embrace the whole economy of society, to change every social relation, to penetrate to the smallest link of the political chain.[105]

With this estimate and comparison Jefferson entirely agreed. "Our Revolution commenced on more favorable ground. It presented us an album on which we were free to write what we pleased. . . We appealed to those [laws] of nature, and found them engraved on our hearts."[106] Having been reared on the freest tradition of the English Constitution, inheriting the democratic traditions of the Anglo-Saxon society, American society was ready to proceed to establish its rules according to the laws of nature and reason.[107] It was the fatal mistake of the French idealists to have disregarded the tremendous obstacles to radical change posed by the accumulated past and the unpreparedness of their society. The mass of illiterate and unenlightened Frenchmen, unaccustomed to the rights of person and property and unable to understand the principles of liberty, were not ready to be free. Therefore the Revolution became a tyranny of the many, then of the few, and eventually of one. The Constitution of 1791 reached the limits of viable reform and the idealists should have been satisfied then. "They did not weigh the hazards of a transition from one form of government to another, the value of what they had already rescued from those hazards, and might hold in security . . . nor the imprudence of giving up the certainty of such a degree of liberty, under a limited monarch, for the uncertainty of a little more under the form of a republic." With the defeat of the Constitutionalists the Revolution was lost.[108] Moreover, by overthrowing their own Constitution, by destroying all safeguards for liberty, and by consolidating all power in the hands of one government, the Revolution had itself established tryanny over France. "The republican government of France was lost without a struggle, because the party of the '*un et indivisible*' had prevailed. . . But with us, sixteen out of the seventeen States rising in mass, under regular organizations, under legal commanders, united in object and action by their Congress, or, if that be in *duresse,* by a special convention, present such obstacles to an usurper as forever to stifle ambition in the first conception of that object." [109]

Another lesson could be drawn from the two revolutions. Liberty and self-government could not exist where men lived in such abject conditions as to be incapable of rational thought. The *canaille* of France had destroyed the Revolution even as the rabble and mobs in all history had turned liberty into lawlessness and class war and had always supported the tyrant and the despot who promised them bread and pleasure.[110] On this all were agreed in America as well as in Europe, that history had proved beyond doubt that liberty and self-government were forever threatened by the propertyless who had no stake in the existing order of society. All agreed also that the wide diffusion of property, the general standard of well-being, the unlimited opportunities of America, made a republican society feasible and liberty safe.[111] Tyranny, despotism, and political subjection went hand in hand with exploitation, pauperism, ignorance, and moral degradation. They were part of a vicious circle in which each maintained and caused the other. "The mobs of great cities add just so much to the support of pure government, as sores do to the strength of the human body. It is the manners and spirit of a people which preserve a republic in vigour." [112]

The manners and spirit depended on economic conditions. Economic independence and security were basic to the love of liberty and the condition of independence. "Dependance begets subservience and venality, suffocates the germ of virtue, and prepares fit tools for the designs of ambition." [113] The French Revolution showed that this circle could not be broken by a change in the political structure. Yet without such change how could the total situation be altered?[114]

Here agreement ceased and ways parted. Conservatives, claiming with Harrington and Locke that power always followed property, which was the main reason for the emergence and maintenance of the state, found the solution in making the propertied classes the chief support of government and in limiting the powers of the state. Liberty and the gradual progress of enlightenment would steadily increase the number of those to whom government could be safely entrusted.

For the Jeffersonians this position was unacceptable because society was "one of the natural wants with which man has been created," one of the acquisitions which he had a right to regulate and to control. Property, the legitimacy of which derived from the exercise of man's faculties, could not become the foundation of citizenship nor could a democratic society exist without a general and equal opportunity to acquire material independence. The concentration of wealth, poverty, and indigence was a perversion of natural justice. A free society built on self-government could not persist where the greatest number of its members were paupers, and poverty and material subjection could not endure where the rights of man were realized. Europe proved that poverty, landless pauperism, a downtrodden peasantry, and an impoverished middle class were created by the alliance of political force and class rule. America, on the other hand, proved that man, urged on by his natural faculties and needs became, through the free application of labor, industry, and intelligence, a property-owner and rose to economic security and material comfort.

The proposition that the state had been throughout history an instrument of class rule was not the discovery of Marx. The relation of political and economic power had become a commonplace of political theory after the seventeenth century and pervaded the thinking of liberals as well as of conservatives in the eighteenth and early nineteenth centuries. But while Marxians and many conservatives believed that property rights and political power were eternally correlated, the liberals maintained that it was political power, independent of society, which became the center of all exploitation. When society ruled itself by self-governing and representative institutions, class exploitation and social injustice disintegrated and natural justice was re-established with the equal rights of men. A new form of society appeared, guided by the principle of social happiness.

The evidence of the old regimes of Europe finally crystallized Jefferson's democratic views and taught him the dangers of all consolidated power. European misery was created by the "curse of bad government," their "kings, nobles or priests" which formed an "abandoned confederacy against the happiness of the mass of the people" and which had divided the nations into "wolves and sheep."[115] It was not a question of more or less democracy. "A mixed constitution" was as dangerous to society as a monarchy since both were governments by "force" which maintained a system of exploitation. Thus, since 1714 "the vital principle of the English constitution" had been corruption and the subsequent consequence, "a pampered aristocracy, annihilation of the substantial middle class, a degraded populace, oppressive taxes, general pauperism, and national bankruptcy."[116] The English government was a coalition of the nobility, the wealthy commoners, the higher clergy, and the politician for the exploitation of the laboring classes. Its paupers were the recruits for its navy and army and a weapon to keep the working classes down and their labor cheap. The government had no meaning for the majority of the people. What should such a society defend? "The pauperism of the lowest class, the abject oppression of the laboring, and the luxury, the riot, the domination and the vicious happiness of the aristocracy."[117]

The difference between such a government by force and the American government was that between social justice and happiness and exploitation and misery. The one was preserved by violence, the other was a "model of government, securing to man his rights and the fruits of his labor, by an organization constantly subject to his own will."[118] The Jeffersonian view on the relationship between the social order and the political system in Europe and America was expressed in its final form by Jefferson in a letter to Judge William Johnson.

The doctrines of Europe were, that men in numerous associations cannot be restrained within the limits of order and justice, but by forces physical and moral, wielded over them by authorities independent of their will. Hence their organization of kings, hereditary nobles, and priests. Still further to constrain the brute force of the people, they deem it necessary to keep them down by hard labor, poverty and ignorance, and to take from them, as from bees, so much of their earnings, as that unremitting labor shall be necessary to obtain a sufficient surplus barely to sustain a scanty and miserable life. And these earnings they apply to maintain their privileged orders in splendor and idleness, to fascinate the eyes of the people. . .[119]

We believed . . . that man was a rational animal, endowed by nature with rights, and with an innate sense of justice; and that he could be restrained from wrong and protected in right, by moderate powers, confided to persons of his own choice, and held to their duties by dependence on his own will. . . We believed that men, enjoying in ease and security the full fruits of their own industry, enlisted by all their interests on the side of law and order, habituated to think for themselves, and to follow their reason as their guide, would be more easily and safely governed, than with minds nourished in error, and vitiated and debased, as in Europe, by ignorance, indigence and oppression.[120]

The accretion of institutions, laws, beliefs, and habits tends to destroy this harmony. But the natural order of freedom and justice can re-establish itself through self-government. Political power may, in the last resort, become the instrument to break down artificial institutions and laws. The state can be used to abolish itself.

Here was the core of the peculiar Jeffersonian view that no generation had a right to bind the generations to come. This view, following strictly from the premise that man had a right to regulate and control the polity, appeared relatively early in Jeffersonian thought and was explicitly stated in a letter to James Madison in September 1790. It rested on the conviction that in a free and just society all political decisions emanated from consent. The state and its institutions had no existence independent of the society. Its institutional form, its laws and decrees, ended with those who created them. They could not bind posterity for that would undermine the rights of man and the contractual character of all government.[121]

This principle is valid not only with respect to constitutions and laws, but also with respect to contractual obligations and economic institutions. "The earth belongs always to the living generation: they may manage it, then, and what proceeds from it, as they please, during their usufruct. They are masters, too, of their own persons, and consequently may govern them as they please. But persons and property make the sum of the objects of government.

The constitution and the laws of their predecessors are extinguished then, in their natural course, with those whose will gave them being." [122] The limitation of the validity of all institutional, legal, and contractual obligations halted the process of attrition and accretion by which the accumulated past destroyed the natural order of society. The rule of reason was thus preserved and the way to progress kept open. "Laws and institutions must go hand in hand with the progress of the human mind. As that becomes more developed, more enlightened, as new discoveries are made, new truths disclosed, and manners and opinions change with the change of circumstances, institutions must advance also and keep pace with the times." [123] Yet such principles seemed to strengthen immensely the power of society—or the majority of it—over its members and thereby to endanger individual liberty. Moreover, they seemed open to a radical interpretation of the right to a periodic redistribution of property.

Jefferson's reply to both questions was that the authority through which each generation was entitled to refashion society was the same as that which set limits to all political action—the rights of nature and the rule of justice. Society had the right "to declare and enforce only our natural rights and duties, and to take none of them from us. No man has a natural right to commit aggression on the equal right of another; and this is all from which the laws ought to restrain him; every man is under the natural duty of contributing to the necessities of the society; and this is all the laws should enforce on him." [124] Since society rested on the mutuality of needs and satisfactions and was limited in its scope by the natural rights of men, its powers were restricted to those which could not be achieved by the individuals alone. It remained stable because most of its activities were outside the sphere of political action and occurred in spontaneous and voluntary activity.

The first principle of any social association was "the *guarantee* to every one of a free exercise of his industry, and the fruits acquired by it." Property rights were derivative from other primary rights, yet they were none the less necessary and could therefore be claimed by all. "I believe . . . that a right to property is founded in our natural wants, in the means with which we are endowed to satisfy these wants, and the right to what we acquire by these

means without violating similar rights of other sensible beings." [125]
Therefore the ownership of natural wealth or the utilization of
public needs and social wealth stood apart from possessions acquired by labor. The former categories belonged to society by the
right of nature, and the individual could appropriate them in
usufruct only. The exclusive and permanent ownership of sources
of income was therefore under the jurisdiction of both natural justice and social utility. "The laws of civil society indeed for the
encouragement of industry, give the property of the parent to his
family on his death, and in most civilized countries permit him
even to give it, by testament, to whom he pleases. . . But this does
not lessen the right of that majority to repeal whenever a change
of circumstances or of will calls for it. Habit alone confounds what
is civil practice with natural right." [126]

As long as the pattern of property-holding satisfied both justice
and public utility, society retained it. A revolution in the distribution of property occurred when inequality grew to such measure
that society lost its stability. Then it was the duty of society to re-
establish natural justice by destroying the inequality which arose
from the permanent alienation of what nature had given. Such
was the case in France. [127] Undoubtedly Jefferson agreed with the
dictum of Thomas Paine that "a revolution in the state of civilization is the necessary companion of revolutions in the system of
government"; [128] and that "the present state of civilization is as
odious as it is unjust." [129] Most of the inequalities in property had
been the result of the expropriation of the people by an aristocracy
using force and brute power. This was the origin of the feudal
system, of the great monopolistic corporations and of the great
capitalistic fortunes. Whether landed or moneyed, the aristocracy
had attained its status with the aid of the armed power of the
parasitic state. [130]

As early as 1774 Jefferson had attacked the system whereby
land was arbitrarily held and sold by the Crown. [131] The theory of
natural rights and of natural justice compelled him to postulate
the equal right of men to the use of the natural sources of sustenance. [132] "It is agreed . . . that no individual has, of natural
right, a separate property in an acre of land. . . By an universal
law, indeed, whatever . . . belongs to all men equally and in
common, is the property for the moment of him who occupies it,
but when he relinquishes the occupation, the property goes with

it. Stable ownership is the gift of social law, and is given late in the progress of society." [133] It followed that if alienation of the sources of natural wealth infringed on the equal rights of men and deprived some members of the opportunities which nature had given to all, then society had to re-establish those opportunities either by limiting the rights of property or by retrieving part of the wealth derived from this monopoly for the benefit of those deprived. [134]

The accumulation of wealth in the hands of a few and the pauperization of the many endangered liberty and self-government. No viable republic had ever existed in which economic inequality was permanently established. America could maintain a new social order only by preventing the growth of inequality and maintaining social justice. Destutt de Tracy had shown that the flourishing and decline of all Empires was in direct relation to the growth of inequality. [135] "Declaimers have maintained," he wrote in his *Treatise on Political Economy,* "that *inequality* in general is useful, and that it is a benefit for which we ought to thank Providence... Every inequality of means, and of faculties, is at bottom an inequality of power... The object of the social organization is to combat the inequality of power; and most frequently it causes it to cease, or at least diminishes it." [136] Economic inequality subverted society and hampered economic growth by the creation of great fortunes. "The more there are great fortunes, the more national riches tend to decay and population to diminish... The perfection of society, then would be to increase our riches greatly, avoiding their extreme inequality." [137]

A free society created to realize the rights of man and to aim at social happiness was therefore constrained to maintain a minimal equality of opportunities and standard of living which insured personal independence. This was an absolute and necessary condition for its survival. For self-government and liberty were not only based upon equity and justice but also upon equality of individual power and enlightened morality. [138]

The French Revolution had failed because the mobs of the cities, debased by ignorance, poverty, and vice, could not be restrained to rational action. [139] America alone was in a position to create a middling equality of conditions for all its citizens without resort to political means.

Jefferson was not a physiocrat. [140] Having endorsed the prin-

ciples of Adam Smith and later of Jean Baptiste Say and Destutt
de Tracy, he differed from the physiocrats on the source of natural
wealth and the nature of productive work as well as on the theory
of taxation.[141] They attracted him by their role in propagating the
"obvious and simple system of natural liberty," and by their
preoccupation with agriculture as the source of all wealth and
social stability which made their teachings particularly important
to the United States.[142]

Yet the decisive element that drew Jefferson to the physiocrats
was their view of the moral and social merits of the agricultural,
as compared to the urban and industrial, sectors of the population.
In the eighteenth century it was a well-nigh universally accepted
opinion that "those who labor in the earth are the chosen people
of God . . . whose breasts he has made his peculiar deposit for substantial and genuine virtue"; that "cultivators of the earth are the
most valuable citizens . . . the most vigorous, the most independent,
the most virtuous, and . . . are tied to their country, and wedded to
its liberty and interest, by the most lasting bond." [143] Not only was
theirs the good and happy life, being in communion with nature,
but it bred liberty, independence, patriotism, and virtue. Such
views had been transmitted in an unbroken tradition of classical
republicanism since the seventeenth century.[144] The manifold
meanings of the word "nature" seemed to be focused on the
farmer, his work, and his virtues and to bridge the chasm between
the cosmos and man, between physics and morality. The beneficence of the cosmos was daily revealed in the life-giving forces
of the earth which gave sustenance to all who worked it.[145] Men's
natural rights to life, liberty, and the pursuit of happiness were
based on the bounty of nature which enabled them to live together in justice without losing their independence; to gain sustenance by the fruit of their labor without violating the equal
rights of others to enjoy theirs. Here alone property was grounded
in honest work and "mine" was divided from "thine" through the
clear division of spatial boundaries. Through the land alone was
security attained, and only here man could start with the capacities
God had given him, gain a livelihood, raise a family, and become
a useful and equal member of society.

Benjamin Franklin, whose views closely resembled those of the
"economists," had already shown that the greatness and happiness

of the Americans lay in their immense land reserve, which made for the astonishing increase of its population, for early marriages, pure morals, and independent minds.[146] Because of this, "labour will never be cheap here, where no man continues long a journeyman to a trade, but goes amongst the new settlers and sets up a trade for himself."[147] Earlier than Jefferson he had rejected the industrialization of America as incompatible with the freedom and equality of its society.

Manufactures were always founded in poverty. The multitude of poor without land who had to "work for others at low wages or starve" enabled "undertakers to carry on a manufacture. . . But no man, who can have a piece of land of his own, sufficient by his labor to subsist his family in plenty, is poor enough to be a manufacturer, and work for a master."[148] Only in agriculture did man receive "a real increase of the seed thrown into the ground, in a kind of continual miracle, wrought by the hand of God in his favor, as reward for his innocent life and his virtuous industry."[149]

The views of Jefferson were similar. "In Europe the lands are either cultivated, or locked up against the cultivator. Manufacture must therefore be resorted to, of necessity, not of choice, to support the surplus of their people. But we have an immensity of land courting the industry of the husbandman. . . It is the mark set on those, who not looking up to heaven, to their own soil and industry, as does the husbandman, for their subsistence, depend for it on casualties and caprice of customers.[150]

Jefferson, nevertheless, was not a physiocrat. He accepted no basic distinction between the mode of production in agriculture and in other spheres of the economy.[151] All labor which produced more than it consumed created wealth to the degree that these products possessed social utility. Society was "a continual series of exchanges. It is never anything else in any epoch of its duration. . . Exchange is an admirable transaction, in which the two contracting parties always both gain; consequently society is an uninterrupted succession of advantages, unceasingly renewed for all its members."[152] It followed that all useful work was productive and that the laborious, whatever their occupation, merited equally the name of productive classes. "The truly sterile class is that of the idle, who do nothing but live . . . on the products of labor executed before their time."[153] Jefferson's distinct agrarian philosophy was therefore inspired by his social ideal of a self-governing democratic society composed of free, economically independent, and basically equal citizens.

Self-government could function only if all the members of the community were nearly equal in status and power, and independent as individuals. Self-government, moreover, depended on the simplicity of the relations between the members of society and the limited scope of the tasks which the government had to perform. Self-government also depended on the social happiness of society and the maintenance of social justice. All these conditions were met in a predominantly agricultural society; there, a simple pattern of individual independence and social cooperation rewarded industry and met the needs of its members by a fair exchange of goods and services. Both economic exploitation and political tyranny were thus avoided. Such a society could escape the landlessness that forced the paupers of Europe to sell their labor at the cheapest price and permitted the aristocracy to feed themselves on the labor of the productive classes and maintain its rule by a government which shared in its spoils.[154]

There were no paupers in America. Workers made up the great mass of the population; few were idle rich. Most of the laboring classes possessed property, cultivated their own land, or worked with sufficient wages, living in moderate decency. "They were not driven to the ultimate resources of dexterity and skill, because their wares will sell." [155] This social happiness made unnecessary a standing army or the immense expenses and taxation needed to maintain a huge bureaucratic machine.[156] "The agricultural capacities of our country constitute its distinguishing feature; and the adapting our policy and pursuits to that, is more likely to make us a numerous and happy people than the mimicry of an Amsterdam, a Hamburg, or a city of London." [157] The one brought peace and happiness, the other misery, pauperism, and disastrous wars.[158]

Equality, material competence, social happiness, and natural justice, based on widely diffused individual ownership, were the basic features of the social structure of a free society which were provided by the immense reserve of public land in the United States. As long as these conditions existed, society would rule itself according to the laws of justice, reason, and nature.

This was the Jeffersonian concept of a free and natural society.

Liberated from all oppression by political force, from all artificial distinctions of social status and special rights, ruled for its own interests by its own will in the limits set by inalienable individual rights, the natural order of social life was left undisturbed to its own laws of rewards and punishment, to create an identity of interests between the individual and the society. It was the function of the state to safeguard this social order. The political system was the instrument to destroy the artificial order and create the conditions of a free and equitable society.

VIII

The Jeffersonian Ideal – Social and Political Democracy

1. THE ECONOMIC POLICY OF A FREE SOCIETY

Self-government aimed to realize freedom through the creation of the conditions for a natural order of social life. Political democracy existed to defend society against the attempts of individuals and classes to impose upon it a fixed structure of rights, privileges, and economic powers for their own benefit. This belief animated the land policy of the federal government, as expressed in westward expansion and the policy of acquisition, annexation, and conquest.[1] The acquisition of Louisiana insured the future diffusion of the blessings of freedom and equality.[2] The same motives prompted the continuous expansion toward the West. Jefferson's hope for the endurance of the American Republic rested "much on the enlargement of the resources of life going hand in hand with the enlargement of territory, and the belief that men are disposed to live honestly, if the means of doing so are open to them."[3]

This land policy was to create as large a class of property owners as possible. It followed that the state had the duty of putting still unoccupied land at the disposal of the landless citizens who were in greatest need of it. Jefferson's suggestions with regard to land distribution in his "Proposed Constitution of Virginia" remained representative of his thought. "Every person of full age neither owning nor having owned [50] acres of land, shall be entitled to an appropriation of [50] acres . . . in full and absolute dominion. And no other person shall be capable of taking an appropriation."[4] For the same reasons he at first opposed the suggestion that Congress should have the power to sell land for the payment of the Continental debt and upheld the right of the bona fide settler. To the Reverend James Madison he expressed the opinion that "whenever there are in any country uncultivated lands and unemployed poor, it is clear that the laws of property have been so far extended as to violate natural right." [5]

The state's role in creating material competence was not limited to the policy of agrarian settlement and expansion. It was the duty of the government also to improve the general well-being by performing those tasks which individuals would not or could not perform. The opposition of the Jeffersonians to national improvements was not based on the principles of laissez faire but on the fear of granting too much power to a government which was not strictly representative and might thereby become even more powerful and independent. At the same time Jefferson upheld, like the physiocrats and Adam Smith, the right and duty of the state to increase the wealth of the country by the initiation and maintenance of public works and public utilities. This included a scientific survey of the geography and nature of the country as well as that of its resources; the improvement of rivers and harbors, the construction of roads and canals; the development of the arts, invention and manufacture, and the setting up of a general system of education.[6] "Our revenues once liberated by the discharge of the public debt, & it's surplus applied to canals, roads, schools, &c., and the farmer will see his government supported, his children educated, & the face of his country made a paradise by the contributions of the rich alone."[7]

In his Second Inaugural Address Jefferson had sought to solve the dilemma posed by the need for internal improvements and the fear of increasing the powers of the general government by an amendment to the Constitution to permit a just repartition of federal revenue among the states for the express purpose of financing enterprises of public utility.[8] He was even willing to allow the federal government to undertake these works under such limitations as "to secure us against its partial exercise. Without this caution, intrigue, negotiation, and the barter of votes might become . . . habitual in Congress."[9]

The social and political philosophy of the Jeffersonians thus could not be subsumed, without decisive qualification, under the concept of laissez faire as understood in the second half of the nineteenth century. Its guiding principles implied positive interference by the state for the creation of economic opportunities, "the enlargement of resources" by political action. Its concept of the equality of power of all the members of society also required the state to obstruct the increase of economic inequality through manipulation of political power.[10] Thus Jefferson initiated legislation to abolish entail and primogeniture in Virginia to prevent the perpetuation of accumulated wealth in the same hands and to destroy thereby the causes which created "a Patrician order" and new aristocracies.[11]

The Jeffersonian scheme for a comprehensive system of education maintained by the state illustrated clearly the conceptual relation between the political and the natural society, between liberty and equality.[12] Its aim was not only to open to all opportunities to develop their powers but also to create the conditions for a natural aristocracy of virtue and ability. A democracy could not exist without leadership. Yet, unless the elite was selected by the criteria of virtue, knowledge, and ability, its functions would be taken over by the "pseudo aristocracy" of wealth, birth, and power which would transform government into an instrument of power and exploitation. It was, then, the duty of society to provide the conditions under which a natural aristocracy could be formed "from every condition of life."[13]

The same rule applied to society as a whole. Natural justice and the free, spontaneous activities of the natural society could express themelves only if the state created a general framework of equity and equality as well as the conditions of social well-being.

Such a society, republican in form and equalitarian in rights, was threatened mainly by two forces—consolidated political power and consolidated economic wealth. In a free society, wealth was gained by personal ability and tended to disappear with the change of generations;[14] the accumulation of wealth was subject to the law of the exchange of services. Commerce, as Destutt de Tracy observed, "is not only the foundation and basis of society, but . . . is in effect the fabric itself; for society is nothing more than a continual exchange of mutual succours, which occasion the concurrence of the powers of all for the more effectual gratification of the wants of each."[15] Mutual utility, then, in the exchange of services, was the principle which ruled society. Only then was exchange "an admirable transaction, in which the two contracting parties always gain." [16] It followed that in a society ruled by free competition, by a steady increase of knowledge, division of labor, and the exchange of its products according to the laws of common utility, the increase of individual wealth depended on the increase of the general wealth of society, and that individual inequalities of wealth were in the long run equalized. The fundamental principle of laissez faire as Jeffersonians understood it was to achieve through free competition and the free exchange of services the optimal gratification of social wants. In a truly self-governing society, natural justice, individual freedom, and industry were identical with social utility and social happiness. For natural justice meant essentially in the economic field "the *guarantee* to every one of a free exercise of his industry, and the fruits acquired by it." [17]

The sum of good government was essentially to establish this justice, which "shall restrain men from injuring one another, which shall leave them otherwise free to regulate their own pursuits of industry and improvement, and shall not take from the mouth of labor the bread it has earned." [18] This state could be achieved only by the rule of free exchange or free trade and the nonintervention of the state in the workings of economic processes. The remarks of Jefferson in regard to international free trade were applicable to the general principles of economic society. "Instead of embarrassing commerce under piles of regulating laws, duties and prohibitions, could it be relieved from all its shackles in all parts of the world, could every country be employed in producing that which nature has best fitted it to produce, and each be free to exchange with others mutual surplusses for mutual wants, the greatest mass possible would then be produced of those things which contribute to human life and human happiness; the numbers of mankind would be increased, and their condition bettered." [19]

The only valid and legitimate qualification of this rule arose when the free play of economic forces endangered society. The impact of the Revolutionary and Napoleonic Wars, the continental system, the English blockade, converted Jefferson to a qualified economic protectionism. [20] The survival of the American system required its independence not only from the world's diplomatic entanglements but from its economic power. [21] Both experience and his changed views on political economy taught him that self-imposed isolation would avail little if America was unable to supply her own needs. The United States was, after all, sufficiently extended and its natural wealth variegated enough to aim at a closed economic system of production and exchange. "Experience has taught me that manufactures are now as necessary to our independence as to our comfort; and if those who quote me as of a different opinion, will keep pace with me in purchasing nothing foreign where an equivalent of domestic fabric can be obtained, without regard to difference of price, it will not be our fault if we do not soon have a supply at home equal to our demand, and wrest that weapon of distress from the hand which has wielded it." [22]

The principle of laissez faire in itself was not sacrosanct, but was subject to higher values and dependent on circumstances. Natural justice, equality of rights, and democratic self-government could be defended best under the general policy of laissez faire, which averted the chief danger to free society—a consolidated political power exploiting society for its own purposes and a consolidated economic aristocracy supported by the state. Economic inequality had always resulted from the use of state power to redistribute wealth through taxation, monopolies, and outright expropriation for the benefit of favored individuals and classes. Hence Jefferson opposed the Hamiltonian scheme for the enlargement of the federal power and its arrogation of economic functions. Hamilton's Federalism illustrated the connection between the monarchical principles and class rule. His open contempt for the masses and his cynical view of the nature of man led him to seek the support of the state in furthering the acquisitive instinct of the propertied classes, especially the merchants. [23] The federal assumption of the total nominal debt and the funding system as proposed by Hamilton were steps in the exploitation of society through a coalition of private interests and the state.

The crowning achievement of the "mercenary Phalanx" was the establishment of the Bank of the United States and the utilization of the import revenue for the protection and financing of industry. [24] "A system had there been contrived, for deluging the States with paper money instead of gold and silver, for withdrawing our citizens from the pursuits of commerce, manufactures, buildings, and other branches of useful industry, to occupy themselves and their capitals in a species of gambling, destructive of morality, and which had introduced its poison into the government itself." [25] Hamilton succeeded thereby in creating a mutual dependence between the capitalistic classes and the federal government and in purchasing the support of enlarged and consolidated power by the favors and privileges it granted to them.[26] His adoption of the English system of a permanent funded debt coupled to a governmental banking system which was ruled by private interests made the whole nation permanent debtors to special interests which impoverished society by hoisting upon its back a permanent tax burden in the double disguise of direct taxes and paper money.[27] "The truth is, that capital may be produced by industry, and accumulated by economy; but jugglers only will propose to create it by legerdemain tricks with paper." The only object of giving the bank the right to put notes into circulation was "to enrich swindlers at the expense of the honest and industrious part of the nation." [28] The bank not only received a virtual monopoly of the circulation medium, but also diverted capital from productive investment into speculative channels, retarding thereby the development of the economy and demoralizing the nation.[29]

Jefferson distrusted the mercantile, and later the manufacturing, interest for the same reasons. The former was based on the exploitation of the world market, was highly speculative, and demanded the permanent protection of federal power. Being in constant need of capital, it was allied to the banking interest and it flourished on wasteful consumption which impoverished the country.[30] Its ideal was England, with its corruption, pauperism, and dominance by the mercantile interest. Supporters of the New England separatist movement during the War of 1812 sufficiently proved their lack of patriotism and hatred of democracy.[31] Their interest lay in "licentious commerce and gambling speculations for a few, with eternal war for the many." Their income was derived from satisfying the appetites for luxury and their enterprises involved the states in permanent war.[32]

The manufacturing interest, as soon as it obtained the aid of the state for protection against competition and gained thereby the power of a monopoly became no less exploitative and parasitic. Though Jefferson advocated its protection during the years of war he changed his estimate with the increasing pressure of manufacturers for protection against foreign competition. Their alliance with the banking interest made them in his eyes sharers of the national plunder and exploitation. Their successful coalition with the western farmer, and the formulation of the "American system" threatened the overturn of the country's political and economic structure, and by consolidating the federal government to turn it into an instrument for economic power.

A whole people, mainly agricultural, became subject to the monopoly of the few.[33] The chief danger lay in the consolidation of the powers of the federal government. Without its aid, commerce, banking, and manufactures would be compelled to adapt to the laws of fair exchange and would become productive forces. But in alliance with a centralized government they became parasitic forces which threatened to destroy the free society.[34] Any centralized government was corrupt, venal, and oppressive; America was in danger of becoming like Europe, "where every man must be either pike or gudgeon, hammer or anvil." [35]

After the downfall of the Federalist party in 1801 and after the defeat of their separatist schemes in the War of 1812, the chief danger for republicanism, Jefferson thought, lay in the growing power of the judiciary and its persistent encroachment on representative government. Irremovable and therefore independent of popular favor, the judges became the stronghold of Federalism, laboring to increase the powers of centralized government and to fortify privileges by an adroit construction of the Constitution.[36] After Marbury v. Madison, Jefferson suspected that the judiciary was determined to achieve the Federalist aim of setting up a monarchical government by making itself the sole interpreter of the Constitution.

The case of McCulloch v. Maryland strengthened this opinion. The decision gave legal validity to the doctrine of implied power, vindicated the Bank and its monopoly, and established the Supreme Court as arbiter of the relative powers of the state and federal governments, upholding de facto the superiority of the latter over the former.[37] So, too, the decision of the Court in the case of Fletcher v. Peck set aside the sovereign rights of the people. The right of the state to annul a fraudulent grant was denied by an appeal to the sanctity of contracts under the Constitution. The decision in the Dartmouth College case limited even further the power of the state to interfere with corporations whose title derived from a voluntary act of the state and which served public purposes. The very fact that this decision was later nullified justified Jefferson's view that Chief Justice Marshall had consciously turned the judiciary into an instrument of Federalist conservatism.[38]

The constitutional nationalism of the Supreme Court was best expressed by the words of Marshall in the case of Cohens *v.* Virginia:

. . . That the United States form for many, and for most important purposes, a single nation has not yet been denied. In war, we are one people. In making peace, we are one people. . . In many other respects, the American people are one; and the government which is alone capable of controlling and managing their interest in all these respects, is the government of the union . . . and laws of a state, so far as they are repugnant to the Constitution and laws of the United States, are absolutely void. These states are constituent parts of the United States. They are members of one great empire—for some purposes sovereign, for some purposes subordinate.[39]

Joseph Story, Marshall's colleague and in many respects his intellectual guide, reflected accurately the conservative tendency of the Judiciary in his eulogy of the Chief Justice.

He became enamored not of a wild and visionary Republic, formed only in the imaginations of mere enthusiasts as to human perfection, or tricked out in false colors by the selfish to flatter the prejudices or cheat the vanity of the people; but of that well-balanced Republic, adapted to human wants and human infirmities, in which power is to be held in check by countervailing power; and life, liberty and property are to be secured by a real and substantial independence, as well as division of the . . . departments. . . He was in the original genuine sense of the word, a Federalist.[40]

Jefferson was therefore increasingly hostile toward the arrogated authority of the Supreme Court. He pointed out the incompatibility of the legal philosophy derived from Blackstone and the neo-Toryism of England with that of American democracy.[41] The constitutionalism which underlay the Jeffersonian outlook limited the sphere of governmental action, without infringing upon the right to democratic self-determination in the field allotted to it. The constitutionalism of the Judiciary created a fixed structure of property rights and institutional power impervious to the social will. While Jefferson emphasized the right of each generation to self-determination, the Judiciary bound the present and the future to the dead hand of the past, erecting a structure of positive rights which slowed down all progress. Above all, by setting itself up as supreme authority in the state, it put the fate of the Republic in the hands of a body which was unresponsive to the needs of society, arbitrary in its action, and likely to become the agent of minority interests and special privilege. The judges were "the subtle corps of sappers and miners." [42] "Like a thief" stepping "over the field of jurisdiction," they worked "until all shall be usurped from the States, and the government of all be consolidated into one." [43] Their double work of transferring authority from the states to a consolidated central government and of subjecting the latter's representative branches to the fiat of judicial interpretation was instrumental in the transformation of the American government into one resembling closely that of England with its centralized, irresponsible, and corrupt class rule,[44] that would destroy the Union by causing either Revolution or secession. "If ever this vast country is brought under a single government, it will be one of the most extensive corruption, indifferent and incapable of a wholesome care over so wide a spread of surface. This will not be borne." [45]

The Jeffersonian answer to the combined threat of centralizing economic and political forces was twofold. There was immediate emphasis on the separate and equal authority of the states and the federal government and the strict definition of the powers of each. Yet the ultimate solution could come only through a democratization of the total institutional framework of the Union, and the dispersion of political power downward from the federal government to the self-governing community of the ward and the township. In a letter addressed to Samuel Kercheval, Jefferson outlined this larger program in which he anticipated the whole program of the Jacksonian period. Advising his friend not to be afraid of the "croakings of wealth against the ascendency of the people" he summed up his proposals in seven points: 1) general suffrage; 2) equal representation in the legislative; 3) direct election of the Chief Executive; 4) the election or removability of the judges; 5) the election of all justices, jurors, and sheriffs; 6) the decentralization of the state in self-governing units; and 7) the periodic amendment of the Constitution, as "laws and institutions must go hand in hand with the progress of the human mind" and as every generation was capable of taking care of itself. National unity would be the product not of consolidation of political power but of the idea of self-government and the social promise of a free society, aiming at the realization of the good life and natural justice. The Constitution had not created national unity but the spirit of the people had fostered true republicanism. "Owing to this spirit, and to nothing in the form of our Constitution, all things have gone well. But this fact . . . is not the fruit of our Constitution, but has prevailed in spite of it."[46]

The conflict, then, of the Jeffersonians and the conservatives was in the last analysis based on a difference in the concepts of society and the nation. For the Jeffersonian, society was a free association of equal and self-determining individuals who continued in a natural society for their common happiness and the satisfaction of their common needs. Political society was strictly contractual, limited to safeguarding the rights of its members and to realizing their common ends and interests. The American nation was the great association of all these societies, and its members were united by its common purpose of realizing the good life and defending it against the outside world. Its unity lay in its social system and not in the integral unity of the sovereign state.

For the Federalist or Whig, society was a natural state created by history, a factual structure rather than a value system or a moral end. Its main purpose was to avoid anarchy and to establish security for the person and his property. This purpose was achieved by the state, which, through its system of power, kept society at peace and secured the rights of the person and his property. For this reason it had to be independent from society in force and in institutional structure. The state created the unity of society and embodied the unity of the nation. The more centralized and powerful the state, the more unified and powerful the nation. Its rational aim was to enlarge the equal liberty of all and to afford all equal security to life and property. Yet this aim could be achieved best by aiding those who had a stake in society and in the nation as a whole. Federalist nationalism held to a vision of a rational and free life established through guidance of an elite, by those whose interests, social status, and achievements insured responsibility, virtue, and respectability. The stronger their influence and the more the national government utilized their services and furthered their interests, the greater would be the happiness and well-being of the whole.

For both sides there existed an American system of values derived from universal experience and justified by universal standards.[47] Orderly liberty was the highest good, and arbitrary government the source of all evil. "The fundamental article of my political creed," wrote John Adams, "is, that despotism, or unlimited sovereignty, or absolute power, is the same in a majority of a popular assembly, an aristocratic council, an oligarchical junto, and a single emperor; equally arbitrary, cruel, bloody, and in every respect diabolical."[48] Yet while liberty was, for Jeffersonians, part of the whole structure of man's equality of rights and the rule of natural justice, it was for the Federalist an achievement which had carefully to be built into the complicated structure of government. While historical experience had taught the Jeffersonian that all independent power corrupted and exploited and that all consolidated power was inimical to the rights of man, the Federalist had learned that man untamed by the state was vicious and that only the balance of all interests could civilize and socialize him. The one appealed to the identity of interests in a natural, free, and equalitarian society; the other to the permanent conflict of interests between men who were by nature unequal in powers and capacity, unless subjected to the political order.

2. INDIVIDUALITY AND SOVEREIGNTY

This fundamental conflict between concepts, interests, and ideologies gained its clearest—though somewhat distorted—expression in the writings of John Taylor of Caroline. Taylor did not integrate all the elements of the Jeffersonian ideology but rather emphasized some of them and neglected others.[49] He was, far more than Jefferson, committed to the priority of states' rights. His concept of society was always related to the contractual association of men, and the relevant distinction between natural and political society existed only as a consequence of his laissez-faire philosophy. More important, the aims of society were far more strictly construed and were subservient to the theory of individual rights. Jefferson's tendency to envision in society an instrument for social happiness as well as his distinction between

natural and civil rights was neve   tings.[50]
Unlike Jefferson, Taylor regarde   erty as
basic rights and by substituting p   happiness gave less emphasis to the o   lement
of social justice and improvement.   vritings
throw into high relief some of the   rsonian
ideology.

The main issues of Taylor's ar   nerican
Revolution did not exchange one form of government for another,
nor transfer political sovereignty from the English to the American
people, but rather reduced the political framework to contractual
forms of self-government.[52] "Before the American Revolution,"
he wrote, "the natural right of self-government was never plainly
asserted, nor practically enforced; nor was it previously discovered, that a sovereign power in any government . . . was inconsistent with this right, and destructive of its value."[53] The
concept of the sovereignty of the state was subversive of the
principles of American government, for it presupposed undefined
and unlimited power. The fundamental idea of the American
government was the limitation of all power and its distribution
for strictly defined purposes.[54] The true purpose of the Revolution
and the aim of America's civil society was to liberate man from
dependence on an alien will and from his servitude to force and
exploitation which had existed under all previous forms of government, whether democracy, aristocracy, monarchy, or mixed. It
aimed at the realization of the rights of man by creating a system
of social liberty and self-government. "The political society created
by a constitution, is the only existing society, and the government
is its agent; but under the natural individual right of self government, this political society itself may be dissolved. Until dissolved,
it is the master of the government, or the real political sovereignty;
but the natural right of self government, is superior to any political
sovereignty."[55] For these reasons the American system was not
political at all but a new order of human life, and its policy "is
rooted in moral or intellectual principles, and not in orders, clans
or [castes], natural or factitious."[56]

With this description, John Taylor defined the basic distinction
between the Jeffersonian idea of the society and the nation and

that of the conservatives. "Mr. Adams's political system, deduces government from a natural fate; the policy of the United States deduces it from moral liberty." [57]

> The constitutions [of the States] build their policy upon the basis of human equality . . . and erect the artificial inequalities of civil government, with a view of preserving and defending the natural equality of individuals. Mr. Adams builds his policy upon the basis of human inequality by nature . . . and proposes to produce an artificial level of equality, not of individuals, but of orders, composed of individuals naturally unequal. . .
>
> The constitutions consider a nation as made of individuals; Mr. Adams's system, as made of orders. Nature, by the constitutions, is considered as the creator of men; by the system, of orders. The first idea suggests the sovereignty of people, and the second refutes it. . .
>
> In short, Mr. Adams's system is bottomed upon a classification of men; our constitutions, upon an application of moral principles to human nature.[58]

The reason for this difference, John Taylor thought, lay in the evaluation of the forces which brought man into society. Governments founded on fraud, ambition, avarice, or superstition produced effects unlike those founded on honesty, self-government, justice, and knowledge.[59] Both sets of attitudes existed in man, who, striving to do good to himself, had a propensity to do evil to others. In order to preserve his life and pursue his own happiness he had to live in society. Yet he could achieve the benefits of social life either through the acknowledgment of mutual needs and equality of rights and duties or through force, fraud, ambition, and avarice.[60] Only the first means was truly natural. Any other being beneficial to a minority only, would be resisted by the majority and could be maintained only by injustice and force. Its defense was based on the claim "that man is naturally vicious, and his own worst enemy; and that this self-malignity disqualifies him for self-government and can only be restrained by force or fraud." [61]

The fundamental question was whether or not natural sociability was the logical condition for the realization of the equality of rights in society. "Much contention and ingenuity has arisen out of the question, whether society is natural or factitious. If society is natural, then natural rights may exist in, and be improved and secured by a state of society. Payne [sic] contends for the natural rights of man; Adams for the natural rights of aristocracy. If society is factitious, those who make it, can regulate rights." [62] Society is thus abstracted from the individuals who compose it;

and the privileged represent the whole. "So by the magick of avarice and ambition, the word society is severed from a nation, and converted into a metaphysical spectre, auspicious only to the tyrants of society." [63]

The organic concept of society or the nation or the state, conceived as a higher unity independent of the actual individuals in it, was, then, an ideological ruse to disguise the actual mechanism by which inequality was maintained and privileges perpetuated. Yet all society was built on the multiple relations among the individuals who composed it and when this fact was bared the true quality of the society was revealed. The question then arose how a society deteriorated from its true natural purpose into the forms of force, fraud, and inequality.

Taylor's answer was less naïve than that of his contemporary democratic ideologists. The history of society was shaped by the potentialities of man for good and evil. Given the opportunity, he was inclined to gain power, wealth, and material enjoyment by exploitation and against the will of society. The task of political science was to restrain man's selfish inclinations and yet satisfy his inherent drive for self-preservation and happiness. "The analysis contended for, admits that human nature is compounded of good and evil qualities, and hence it is not merely allowed, but strenuously contended . . . that government ought to be modelled with a view to the preservation of the good and the control of the evil." [64]

In the past, self-seeking groups had endeavored to gain economic power and wealth through an alliance with the compulsive authority of the state. Such a coalition could be created only if political power, supported by physical force, was independent of the will of society. Then the state became an instrument for the attainment of unearned wealth, social and economic monopolies, and privileges. [65] Society remained a battlefield of classes warring with each other for control.

In this chain of causes and effects, inequality, injustice, and exploitation were the effects rather than the causes. Monopoly could not exist without the aid of coercive political power, but the latter could develop without the former and through its own force create social and economic exploitation. Here was the fundamental difference between American democratic thought and the later Socialist theory of the relation between the exploiting classes and the state.[66] While the Socialists maintained that the economic exploitation created the state as an instrument, the Jeffersonians explained economic exploitation and inequality as the product of political power used to subject society. Absolute power alone created special privilege and was the universal cause of oppression.[67] The American polity had liberated mankind by destroying the power of the state and thus its control of property. The political life of the United States thus activated the good inclinations of man and restrained his negative and evil appetites.[68]

The American government, having been established on absolute equality of rights preserved by the social contract, was unlike any other; it never surrendered to the state the capacity for self-government of all its members. It alone withheld sovereign power from the state. The very word "sovereignty" had been struck from its constitutions. "The language of all these sacred, civil authorities, is carefully chastened of a word, at discord with their purpose of imposing restrictions upon governments, by the natural rights of mankind to establish societies for themselves."[69] The American people had eradicated consolidated political power by investing governments with specified and limited powers and by preserving all others to themselves.[70] Only with the American Revolution had the truth been discovered "that a sovereign power in any government was . . . destructive" of the rights of self-government.[71]

These rights were secured by treating the state as distinct from society, which was considered an association of individuals who possessed equal rights and agreed to associate for specific purposes under a constitution.[72] The constitutions enumerated the conditions under which certain individual rights were surrendered for the preservation of other rights.[73] Sovereignty, then, rested only with the people, who preserved for themselves the unlimited rights of self-government.[74] "The more power is condensed, the more pernicious it becomes. . . The more it is divided, the farther it recedes from the class of evil moral beings. By a vast number of divisions, applied to that portion of power, bestowed on their governments by the people of the United States; and by retaining in their own hands a great portion unbestowed, with a power of controlling the portion given; the coalescence of political power, always fatal to civil liberty, is obstructed."[75]

John Taylor drew far-reaching conclusions from these premises. The American nation was a free association of individuals who maintained the union for the better preservation of their individual rights and for the achievement of mutual benefits and common happiness. This Union had no powers other than those which its members delegated to it for specific purposes. It was not formed by an incorporation of all its members into one society through the Constitution, but was rather created by a free association of the people of the several states who were in the true sense political societies.[76] Only in the states had there been a contract among the members and a direct delegation of powers through direct elections. Therefore the power of the federal government was in the last resort based on mutual agreements and its scope was determined by the contract of the federating societies or the people of the states.[77] Yet if the United States was only a union of peoples, what then united it or gave its members a common bond of unity and identification?

Taylor's answer was that nations are united by a united will, emanating from common interest created by the principles of self-government, equal rights, natural justice and social happiness.[78] These created unity through the will of all to maintain a society in which each could achieve the good life. National identification was, then, the product of a just society in which the equal rights of the individual determined the social structure. *"Individuality is the substratum of our policy."* [79]

This definition was itself not new; it expressed the spirit which had created the revolutionary states and had been embodied in Jeffersonian democracy. Yet the effort of John Taylor to differentiate American democracy from all other forms of social and political organizations gave a new meaning to the social order which in the nineteenth century would be accepted as individualism.

Taylor used the term "individuality" connoting the basic principle of "American polity" to emphasize the Jeffersonian contention that society was forever subject to the will of its members and had no personality of its own. "The sovereignty of the people arises, and representation flows out of each man's right to govern himself." [80] All power was therefore delegated power, never independent of the wishes of the individuals from whom it emanated. Taylor

introduced the term "individuality" to strike down the contention
of nationalists like Marshall, that the federal state held sovereign
power in its own sphere. The principle of individuality signified
that all political and social organization remained subservient to
the interests of its members and never represented a superpersonal
interest or personality. All was delegated and representative only
and could never contradict the principles of self-government.[81]

But the term "individuality" indicated also the basic difference
between American democracy and all the others where sovereign
power was vested in the people assembled directly or represented
by a national government. Sovereign power, being undefined and
unlimited, was independent of the will of its members and bound
by no other principle than that of expressing the collective will.
It recognized no individual rights and no limitations. American
democracy on the other hand remained forever a contractual association of the individuals which bestowed on society only those
powers which were consonant with the equal rights of each.
Though American democracy was government by the people, the
term "people" did not mean a collective mass, but always individuals associated and retaining their distinctiveness.[82] Those
distinctions broke the vicious circle in which classes and rulers
exploited society in the name of the interest of the whole and the
masses plundered and suppressed minorities in the name of the
sovereign will.

The term "individuality" connoted, then, a social organization
which realized and secured the equal rights to individual self-
expression and self-government, destroyed independent consolidated power and achieved thereby natural justice, the rule of
liberty and social happiness. "It was reserved for the United States
to discover, that by balancing man with man, and by avoiding
the artificial combinations of exclusive privileges, no individual of
these equipoised millions, would be incited by a probability of
success, to assail the rest, and that thus the concessions of powerful combinations, and the subversion of liberty and happiness,
following a victory on the part of one, would be avoided." [83]

In Taylor's work, even more than in that of Thomas Paine and
Jefferson, the American system of policy was motivated by the
quest for natural and social justice through securing the equal
rights of men. Among these rights, Taylor included as central that

of the inviolability of property. That right was a basic protection against social injustice and economic exploitation because Taylor had narrowed it to such possessions or acquisitions as were the fruit of individual exertion. "I do not include under the idea of property," he wrote, "any artificial establishment, which subsists by taking away property; such as hierarchical, kingly, noble, official and corporate possessions, incomes and privileges. . . I consider those possessions as property, which are fairly gained by talents and industry, or are capable of subsisting, without taking property from others by law." [84] Property, then, was legitimate only to the degree that it derived from the principle of individuality and from man's equal rights of self-government and self-expression. Social justice was achieved if every member enjoyed the same rights and opportunities to acquire property. Social injustice existed when those rights and opportunities were limited and when property was acquired by force, fraud, or by political authority.

All earlier societies had been poisoned by the power of the sovereign state to dispose of the property rights and the liberty of its members for its own benefit and for that of the social classes allied to it. Monopoly of power and privileges had gone hand in hand.[85] Representative government had destroyed the privileges of aristocracy, the monopoly of income and knowledge of the state church, and the parasitism of bureaucratic classes. Yet as long as government, by taxation and legislation, could transfer the property of society to groups and individuals, aristocracies of paper and patronage could emerge which would eventually destroy the whole structure of equal rights and representative government. This had happened in England.[86] "Sinecure, armies, navies, offices, war, anticipation and taxes, make up an outline of that vast political combination, concentrated under the denomination of paper and patronage. These, and its other means, completely enable it to take from the nation as much power and as much wealth, as its conscience . . . will allow it to receive." [87]

The Americans had destroyed the aristocracy of force but had completely overlooked the dangers from an aristocracy of paper fed on the public debt, on the monopoly of banking, and on protective tariffs.[88] "Monopoly is the leading principle of their political, religious, and mercantile systems; every thing the reverse of monopoly, constitutes our political, religious and mercantile systems." [89]

The natural right of property was the criterion for economic justice and also abrogated the legality of all property rights derived from monopoly or from acquisition without fair equivalents. It followed that the accumulation of wealth through a monopoly of banking, through charters received by fraud and corruption, through bounties, subsidies, and protective tariffs, and through a public funding system or taxation were based on fraud or force and therefore invalid. Hamilton's and Clay's system of a national economy was a conspiracy against the equal rights of man for the benefit of a new plutocracy. The nation had to void this system of property and take back by law what law had illegally donated.

There was thus a conflict between "the principles of equity" which annulled contracts that defrauded an individual and the justice that required "law charters which defraud a nation, to exist and have their effect." Every such charter, therefore, was a "standing temptation to governments to do evil, and an invitation to individuals to become their accessories; by its help, a predominant party may use temporary power, to enact corporate or individual emoluments for itself, at the national expense... Under the sanction of law charters, governments now buy a faction, rob the nations of enormous wealth, and soar beyond responsibility. . . Thus a nation, which won self-government . . . may lose it again in the modern law charter dogma; and thus a nation, which thought it morally wrong to suffer slavery from troops . . . may be persuaded that it is morally right to suffer slavery from troops hired by dividends, interest upon stock, and protecting duty bounties." [90]

The conclusions drawn from the philosophy of the inviolability of property rights strengthened the Jeffersonian point of view that society had a right to regulate property. John Taylor explained that "property was only made a common stock, so far as the social safety and happiness required." [91] Yet as such cases were of marginal character and open to abuse, the only sure rule of good government was to limit public expenditure to the maintenance of public and social order and to leave property free from any political interference. [92]

John Taylor thus advocated a policy of absolute laissez faire on grounds extraneous to economic considerations. It was a corollary of the analysis on the causes of social injustice and was derived from the axiomatic belief in the rights of man to self-government, to liberty and to the earnings of his labor.[93] These were all aspects of the idea of individuality or self-government. Labor, he explained "is a natural faculty, like that of seeing, given to all men, that each might provide for his own individual happiness. . . Workers upon the land, or upon the ocean, who give to things new forms or new places, are all manufacturers; and being comprised in one essential character, are entitled to the same freedom in free societies. It is this equality of rights, and nothing else, which constitutes a free, fair and mild government." [94]

This statement reveals the strong influence of the free-trade school and above all of Destutt de Tracy, whose idea of the unity of all economic processes enabled Taylor to connect freedom and the rights of man with the specific theory of the self-regulating mechanism of the economic society. As Destutt de Tracy had shown, liberty and happiness were the same as the freedom of man to exert and dispose of the products of his faculties. Where the latter were free, general productivity increased.

A strict "separation of the state and market" that reduced government to its natural scope, permitted the harmonious workings of society and enabled it to progress through an infinite exchange of services toward higher levels of prosperity and happiness. Only through liberty and equality could value be collected wherever it was found and energies liberated for the highest effort.[95] "All, or most intellectual improvements, are referable to the free exercise of each man's will, in procuring his own happiness. It unfolds his understanding, increases his knowledge, and animates his virtue. By mutiplying the relations between the individuals of the human family, the blessings of society are also multiplied. . . These relations are called commerce; and all obstacles thrown in its way are diminutions of an intercourse, from which men have derived their accomplishments, and a capacity for happiness." [96]

The theory of laissez faire, then, was absolutely necessary to maintain the vision of a society created for the realization of man's individual rights and of the common benefits derived from social intercourse. The natural social order of freedom which united all individuals in a common bond of mutuality of wants and needs made such ideals feasible and remained, therefore, a permanent and central element of the American ideology. This element also provided the program of a revolutionary policy which aimed to destroy social injustice and economic exploitation through the utilization of political power for economic benefits. It provided standards for the ideal of social justice, equality of opportunities and social happiness.

Since Jefferson and Paine, this "collective individualism" has signified for the American people the essence of their social system, of their national identification, and of their mission to the world.[97] The declaration of Orestes A. Brownson that the Democratic party was the American party because it aimed to establish and develop "the sovereignty of man" summed up the basic idea of this ideological attitude.

Almost all significant American political thought in the nineteenth century centered on the radical concept of laissez faire as the natural order of society which harmoniously fused social justice and liberty. It animated the reform movements of the Jacksonian era—the Free Soilers, the Loco-Foco, and the "Barnburners"—no less than those of the Greenbackers, the Single-Taxers, the Populists, and Bryan's and Wilson's democracy. Its Utopia was the anarchism of Godwin which was for the first time fully spelled out as a scheme of social salvation by Josiah Warren's doctrine of the "Sovereignty of the individual."[98]

Yet the social implications of Jeffersonian democracy had already been contained in the writings of the Founding Fathers. The vision of a new society fashioned on the natural order of freedom was the center of the national ideal. Its full implications became apparent with the broad Jacksonian coalition of the "producer classes" against the influence of consolidated capital.[99] Martin Van Buren, its spokesman, expressed confidence in the natural free order of society when he stated: "Left to itself, and free from the blighting influence of political legislation, monopolies, congregated wealth and interested combinations, the compensation of labor will always preserve this salutary relation. It is only when the natural order of the society is disturbed by one or the other of these causes, that the wages of labor become inadequate."[100]

In October 1838 a new magazine, *The United States Magazine and Democratic Review,* made its debut. The declared aim of its editor, John L. O'Sullivan, was to make it the advocate of the democratic principle and of the new social and political system created by "the American experiment." [101] John O'Sullivan was eager to represent the cause of Jackson and Van Buren on a level which would appeal to the northern intelligentsia and to defend their policy in the disturbed atmosphere that resulted from abolition of the Second Bank of the United States and the panic of 1837. [102]

Sullivan attempted to prove that the Jacksonian economic policy and its political measures were neither motivated by agrarianism nor by the radical Jacobinian concept of the unlimited power of the sovereign people over society. [103] American democracy was not a political regime at all but rather a social and moral order which was centered in the belief in the capacity of men for self-government. The dangers in other democracies did not apply to America for its ideal was not sovereign power but limited government. Not the Democrats but their opponents were attempting to fortify the state and to use it for economic rule over society. The ideal of democracy was to establish a free and natural society ruled by the voluntary principle which would liberate man from all compulsion and educate him in the art of self-government until morality, and the power of rational self-determination would be supreme. [104]

Understood as a central consolidated power, managing and directing the various general interests of the society, all government is evil, and the parent of evil. A strong and active democratic *government* in the common sense of the term, is an evil, differing only in degree and mode of operation, and not in nature, from a strong despotism. . . The best government is that which governs least. No human depositories can, with safety, be trusted with the power of legislation upon the general interests of society, so as to operate directly . . . on the industry and property of the community. . . Legislation has been the fruitful parent of nine-tenths of all evil, moral and physical, by which mankind . . . since the creation of the world . . . has been self-degraded, fettered and oppressed. . . Its domestic action should be confined to the administration of justice, for the protection of the natural equal rights of the citizen, and the preservation of social order. In all other respects, the *voluntary principle,* the principle of freedom . . . affords the true golden rule. The natural laws which will establish themselves and find their own level are the best laws. . . This is the fundamental principle of the philosophy of democracy, to furnish a system of administration of justice, and then leave all the business and interests of society to themselves, to free competition and association—in a word, to the *voluntary principle*.[105]

This, then, was the meaning of the American nationality, the structure of its identity, and its mission to the world—to make freedom and the voluntary principle of social cooperation the rule of society and a nation. Such a concept of the nation was altogether compatible with ardent and expansionist nationalism. O'Sullivan himself became an active member of "Young America," and preached its fervent nationalism under the slogan he had coined of America's "Manifest Destiny." [106]

Part Two

Individualism and the Free Society
— the American Quest for Utopia

IX

A European Concept
Crosses the Atlantic

Our inquiry has repeatedly dealt with changes in the meaning of ideological concepts brought from Europe to the New World. The transforming power of America was revealed not only in the people and institutions which crossed the Atlantic but also in such ideas, concepts, and terms as constitutionalism, natural rights, state and society.

The comparison between the Jacobin and the Jeffersonian traditions disclosed a broad divergence of outlook between the French and American concept of the state, society, and the individual. The former was collectivistic, unitary, and étatist; the latter was inspired by an attitude of pluralism, voluntarism, and the quest for individual liberty.

The growing awareness of the uniqueness of American democracy and its way of life created a need to define this pattern through terms which would indicate its peculiar character. That need was enhanced by the confrontation with the European revolutionary movements of the nineteenth century and the shift of emphasis from the political regime to the social order, which occurred in the Jacksonian period. As soon as political democracy was securely established the question of its meaning and relevance to the social order became predominant. For a growing number of Americans the answer was found in the concept of "individualism."

Yet this concept and the term that described it were of foreign origin and part of an ideology which stood in direct opposition to the system of values accepted in America. It was therefore necessary to transform the concept of individualism from one loaded with a negative meaning into one which meant more and more an ideal and principle of the American way of life.

1. THE NATURE OF THE DEMOCRATIC CONSENSUS

The election of Jackson to the presidency doomed all open resistance to political democracy. Neither Daniel Webster nor James Kent would dare again openly to oppose its extension, or to obstruct the will of the majority. Even the Supreme Court, that fortress of conservatism, yielded with the appointment of Roger B. Taney. The defeat and dissolution of the Second Bank of the United States, the "Specie Circular," and President Van Buren's Independent Treasury Bill were proofs that no group could afford to flout public opinion. The nomination and election of the hero of Tippecanoe to the presidency and Henry Clay's "distribution scheme of the public lands" which heralded the Pre-emption Act of 1841 showed that the Whigs had thoroughly grasped the situation and were ready to challenge the hegemony of the Democrats on their own grounds.[1]

In the beginning of the 1830's Tocqueville had already observed that all circles accepted the power of democracy as invincible.[2] "What strikes me," he wrote, " is that the immense majority of spirits join together in certain *common opinions*. . . The great majority understand republican principles in the most democratic sense. . . It is an opinion so general and so little disputed . . . that one might almost call it a faith."[3] All recognized the sovereignty of the people interpreted in the sense of the unlimited power of society to determine the structure, the personnel, and the policy of the state. The numerical majority held undisputed sway, and its will was recognized as sole ground of legitimate authority.[4] Republican government was as deeply rooted in America as the monarchy had been at the time of Louis XIV in France. It existed there "without contention or opposition, without proofs or arguments, by tacit agreement, a sort of *consensus universalis*."

Yet creation of a common consensus involved a subtle transformation which adjusted the meaning of democracy to the outlook, attitudes, and interests of all the parties involved. Tocqueville mirrored the process of the interpenetration and reconciliation. Like his New England contemporaries he held liberty and a stable social order to be the supreme good and was haunted by fear of the despotism and the anarchy which had usually come in the wake of democracy. Moreover, he regarded democracy with the "holy terror" of one beholding the onrush of providential or irresistible forces. The question which confronted the nineteenth century was not whether to reject or accept democracy. The choice "now lay between a democracy without poetry or elevation indeed, but with order and morality; and an undisciplined and depraved democracy, subject to sudden frenzies, or to a yoke heavier than any that has galled mankind since the fall of the Roman Empire." [5] Like his American Whig friends, he recognized that American democracy was a political and social system *sui generis* whose strength and stability had to be explained by principles different from those of popular sovereignty. Unlike the classical and the French republics, the United States feared centralization of power in the hand of the state and "there is no surer means of courting the majority than by inveighing against the encroachments of the central power." [6] The reason was that the Americans never constituted a single political entity but were federated as a nation for limited and clearly defined purposes. [7] The union was only an "accident" and the principle of national unity which usually favored concentration of power was not a natural part of American political consciousness. [8]

True national unity arose from a common origin, mode of life, outlook and habits, and above all from a consciousness of uniqueness. [9] "Not only are the Anglo-Americans united by these common opinions, but they are separated from all other nations by a feeling of pride. For the last fifty years no pains have been spared to convince the inhabitants of the United States that they are the only religious, enlightened, and free people. They perceive that, for the present, their own democratic institutions prosper, while those of other countries fail; hence they conceive a high opinion of their superiority, and are not very remote from believing themselves to be a distinct species of mankind." [10]

The great paradox of the American nation was that its unity existed in spite—or rather because—of the absence of the traditional attributes of union embodied in the consolidated and unlimited authority of the state. "The new society in which we are . . . has no prototype anywhere," wrote Gustave de Beaumont, Tocqueville's companion, on his first impressions of America. "It's quite a remarkable phenomenon, a great people which has no army, a country full of activity and vigor where the action of the government is hardly perceived!" [11] And Tocqueville observed the same phenomenon with astonishment. "Here freedom is unrestrained, and subsists by being useful to every one without injuring anybody... The fact is that this society is proceeding all alone and is lucky ... to encounter no obstacles." [12] The Frenchmen, accustomed to thinking in terms of political unity and to explaining national cohesion by the force of traditions, ethnic and religious unity, and permanent residence, were puzzled at the absence of all these elements in American society, where only change was permanent. [13]

Tocqueville resolved the paradox by explaining that the national union of the American people was created by the pattern of social and political life and that their national consciousness was maintained by a social and political ideology. "The observer who examines what is passing in the United States upon this principle will readily discover that their inhabitants, though divided into twenty-four distinct sovereignties, still constitute a single people; and he may perhaps be led to think that the Anglo-American union is more truly a united society than some nations of Europe which live under the same legislation and the same prince." [14]

It was difficult to define properly the principle which underlay the structure of American society and ideology. [15] "Democracy" was an ambiguous term. As a principle of social relations aiming at equality of conditions and rights, it surely had reached perfection in America where it had permeated every aspect of life. [16] Yet to define democracy as equality of conditions was not altogether satisfactory. It fell short of explaining that which was usually connected with this term—the American idea of the relations among the individual, society, and the state. For, quite unlike the European democrat, the American narrowly circumscribed the sphere of the state and exalted that of the individual. The dichotomy and tension which elsewhere existed between liberty and equality disappeared in America. If one could believe such New England leaders as George Ticknor, Jared Sparks, Franz Lieber, the Quincys, Daniel Webster, the Adamses, the Everetts, and William Ellery Channing it was political liberty, the spirit of republican self-government rather than that of democracy, which had shaped American history. [17] The unrestricted liberty of action, beliefs, and association which Josiah Quincy insisted was the recognized principle of the American society could hardly be described as "democracy." This spirit of freedom explained the unbounded energy of the American, his self-confidence, his capacity to cooperate in voluntary enterprises, and his tendency to restrict governmental action to its narrowest limit. America seemed to confirm the truth and practicability of the credo of liberals that society left alone to the satisfaction of its mutual wants and needs was perfectly capable of taking care of itself. From this point of view "a republican government . . . is the slow and quiet action of society upon itself. It is a regular state of things really founded upon the enlightened will of the people." [18]

Tocqueville's diary recorded the lesson:

> Note one of the happiest consequences of the absence of government (when a people is so fortunate as to be able to get on without it, a rare thing) is the development of individual power which never fails to result. Each man learns to think, to act for himself, without counting on the aid of an outside power which, however vigilant one suppose it, is never able to respond to all social needs. The man, thus accustomed to seeking for his well-being only from his own effort, rises in his own opinion, as in the estimation of others, his spirit expands and grows strong at the same time.[19]

Voluntary association could solve all social needs better than government. From this observation Tocqueville proceeded to another. "The greatest care of a good government should be to habituate people little by little to doing without it." [20]

There were then in American society at least two principles equally active and fundamental which in their interaction had created the peculiar structure of American society and its national ideals—liberty and democracy. The one meant self-government of the individual, of the town, of the nation, or of society in their appointed fields. The other implied the principle of the equal rights of citizenship, of popular sovereignty, and the binding power of the popular will, the moral as well as political obligation to conform to the decision of the majority.[21] In this balanced system, liberty had inspired the fundamental pattern of society by creating equality and by shaping the philosophy of life of the American people.[22] Men and institutions in the United States had been molded by the quest for liberty.[23] This was the essence of the Republic.[24]

In America a republican government was based on enlightened

judgment and conciliation of opposing interests and opinions.[25] "They profess to think that a people ought to be moral, religious, and temperate, in proportion as it is free." The "tranquil rule of the majority" was ever tempered by countervailing constitutional balances. It rejected the idea of sovereignty of the will of the majority. "Above it in the moral world are humanity, justice, and reason; and in the political world, vested rights."[26]

Here was the unique element in the American polity. Other democratic republics accepted the sovereign power of the state based on the equal rights of citizenship. They never attempted to legitimize their actions on moral grounds as long as democracy legitimized sovereignty itself. "Until our time, it had been supposed that despotism was odious, under whatever form it appeared. But it is a discovery of modern days that there are such things as legitimate tyranny and holy injustice, provided they are exercised in the name of the people."[27] In the United States, on the other hand, sovereign power was strictly defined by a moral structure and was actually only the idea of self-government applied in those fields where the nation was entitled to act. It was not isolated but rather the "last link of a chain of opinions which binds the whole Anglo-American world."[28]

Yet, as Tocqueville quickly discerned, the idea of self-government itself had an ideological structure. It presupposed faith in the wisdom and good sense of men and in human perfectibility, and a general belief in the necessity of making knowledge general and spreading enlightenment to the utmost.[29] "The majority of them believe that a man by following his own interest, rightly understood, will be led to do what is just and good. They hold that every man is born in possession of the right of self-government, and that no one has the right of constraining his fellow creatures to be happy. They have all a lively faith in the perfectibility of man . . . they all consider society as a body in a state of improvement, humanity as a changing scene, in which nothing is, or ought to be, permanent."[30] This, then, was the ideological structure of American democracy and, with it, of the American national consciousness.

Had Tocqueville really captured the meaning of the universal consensus of the Americans concerning their own society? There is little doubt that much of his interpretation was guided by the

New England intellectual elite which received him so warmly and attempted to impress on him the central position of their region in the evolution of the American mind.[31] His work was the outcome of a great intellectual effort to examine and grasp "as scientifically as possible, all the mechanism . . . of that vast American society which everyone talks of and no one knows." [32] Yet, though the first part of his *Democracy* captured a great deal of what was intrinsic to the American society, the synthesis between liberty and equality which he recognized as the secret soul of the Republic was a fusion of mutually antagonistic and exclusive principles rather than two aspects of the one idea.[33] And indeed the second part of his book was dominated by the idea of the incompatibility of the two elements and by the fear that the inevitable spread of the principles of equality would subject all other factors to its own laws and eventually destroy the republican framework itself.[34]

Tocqueville discovered the reasons for this development in the democratic tendency to create a mass society, to destroy the organic forms and the leadership rooted in the aristocratic and corporate structure of traditional society. The growing isolation of the modern individual, his exclusive concern with his own circle and his consequent selfishness, together with his dependence on an impersonal government, created patterns of centralized and consolidated political power. The mass of isolated individuals, beyond their striving for personal independence and social equality, were incapable of acting as members of a commonwealth. Liberty, in order to survive, had to be institutionalized in the very structure of society. It lived only by unceasing social activity and civic responsibility and by constantly counteracting the influence of the featureless and masterless mass.

In olden society everything was different; unity and uniformity were nowhere to be met with. In modern society everything threatens to become so much alike, that the peculiar characteristics of each individual will soon be entirely lost in the general aspect of the world. Our forefathers were always prone to make an improper use of the notion that private rights ought to be respected; and we are naturally prone, on the other hand, to exaggerate the idea that the interest of a private individual ought always to bend to the interest of the many. The political world is metamorphosed; new remedies must henceforth be sought for new disorders. To lay down extensive but distinct and settled limits to the action of the government; to confer certain rights on private persons, and to secure to them the undisputed enjoyment of those rights; to enable individual man to maintain whatever independence, strength, and original power he still possesses; to raise him by the side of society at large, and uphold him in that position; these appear to me the main objects of legislators in the ages upon which we are now entering.[35]

And yet the dichotomy between equality and liberty, between the individual and society, between self-interest and public good, was never conceded to be natural or inevitable by American democracy, which on the contrary held that in a free and natural society they went hand in hand.

The peculiar blindness of Tocqueville when it came to the quest for that social justice and equality of opportunity which motivated the Jacksonians and to the social implications of the philosophy of laissez faire showed that he fell short in his understanding of the American concept of a free society. Though he elaborated on the American belief in the perfectibility of man and the progressive character of history, the driving force behind this faith escaped him. His analysis of democracy revealed that an increasing number of intellectuals felt it necessary to define more concisely the general, generic principle of American democracy, beyond its political implications. The economic and social questions raised by the Jacksonians, the Loco Foco party, the Free Soilers and Barnburners, the moral questions raised by the emerging controversy over slavery, and the political and national problems raised by the southern states' rights theory made such a clarification ever more urgent.

2. INDIVIDUALISM AND DEMOCRACY

John Taylor was the first, in defining basic Jeffersonian principles, to go beyond the natural theory, by giving the *principle of individuality* a central position in the ideological system. The individual's right to self-government and to pursue happiness explained American democracy.[36] Limitation of the political sphere, equal rights in a contractual society, and natural justice as well as equality of opportunity were corollaries of this view. The same idea was taken up in the pages of the newly founded *Democratic Review*. Its concept of a free and natural society, maintained by "free competition" and association—in a word, by "the *voluntary* principle"— aimed at social justice no less than at individual freedom. The focus of a self-governing society was the free and self-governing individual, liberated from subjection and exploitation and able to develop in cooperation with others the powers which nature gave man. The full implications of the doctrine of individuality emerged in an article in the *Democratic Review* a year later. (1839)

Democracy, according to the author of "The Course of Civilization," did not mean simply popular sovereignty. It implied "the supremacy of the people, restrained by a just regard to individual rights—that condition of society which secures the full and inviolable use of every faculty. Its foundation is the fact of perfect equality of rights among men. It recognizes the distinct existence of individual man in himself as an independent end. . . His instinctive convictions, . . . his boundless capacity for improvement, conspire with all the indications of Providence, with all the teachings of history . . . to make the doctrine of individual rights the greatest of political truths. Clearly to define and religiously to respect those rights, is the highest, almost the only duty of government." [37] Democracy created a framework for voluntary social cooperation and for the development of man in the utmost freedom. "It is true, a long time must elapse before the point of ultimate perfection is attained; though, meanwhile, the duty of Democracy is to correct abuses, one after another, until the nature of individual man is thoroughly emancipated." [38]

The total past of mankind was a preparation for his liberation, for the right to self-government, and for the full development of his capacities; and American democracy was the final stage. [39] The free self-governing society closed the circle in which man had moved from the state of original freedom and savage independence to re-establish his freedom and dignity on the highest level of civilization.

The concept which summed up this philosophy of progress and liberty and which gave meaning to its ideology was that of "individualism." The *Democratic Review* used the term in this sense for the first time in order to describe the motive force and the direction of history and to relate American democracy to progress. "The history of humanity is the record of a grand march . . . at all times tending to one point—the ultimate perfection of man. The course of civilization is the progress of man from a state of savage individualism to that of an individualism more elevated, moral,

separation and independence were the be-
be the end, of the great progressive move-
erence—that in its last and more perfectly
the sense of justice shall have supreme con-
al will." All history was subject to the law of
added another and necessary element for the
man. "The last order of civilization, which
is democratic, received its first permanent existence in this country. . . The peculiar duty of this country has been to exemplify
and embody a civilization in which the rights, freedom, and mental
and moral growth of individual man should be made the highest
end of all social restrictions and laws." [40]

The concept of individualism was closely related to the Jeffersonian ideas of self-government, free society, and the rights of
man. At the same time the term bore connotations of its own and
referred to new elements which, though long latent in American
thought, only now became explicit. It endowed democracy with
a philosophic dimension, closely related to religion and to the
philosophy of history. It was intimately connected with the theory
of laissez faire and described as well the patterns of behavior
typical of the American way of life. Moreover, individualism
repudiated the concept of popular sovereignty and by robbing
democracy of its terrors, made it acceptable to all. Once this concept had captured the public mind it was increasingly accepted as
a basic characteristic of American society. By the end of the Civil
War the term, with growing frequency, described the unique
character of the nation.

Although the connotations and definitions of individualism
varied with the point of observation and the data under consideration, there was a general assumption that it was a fundamental
characteristic of American life. Both the apologists and the critics
of the concept agreed that it described adequately the peculiar
nature of the American national consciousness, yet did so without
examining the historical significance of its unique prestige in
American public opinion.

That significance lay in the identification of national values and
ideals with individualism as a system of social and ethical values,
which demonstrated even in a higher degree than the idea of the
natural and free society that social and moral ideals and norms

determined the American national consciousness. It revealed the paradoxical nature of American nationalism, its universalistic orientation, its utter rejection of natural or historically molded frameworks of collective identification, and its suspicion of political power and of the sovereign state. Like the idea of "free society," from which it arose, individualism as national ideal implied that America was a social system which became significant for humanity as a whole.

This concept was virtually of purely American origin and represented the original contribution of American thought to the general stock of Utopias and social ideals. For, although individualism as a historical and sociological concept was elaborated in Europe, its value-content changed completely with its transplantation to America. The term, which in the Old World was almost synonymous with selfishness, social anarchy, and individual self-assertion, connoted in America self-determination, moral freedom, the rule of liberty, and the dignity of man. Instead of signifying a period of transition toward a higher level of social harmony and unity, it came to mean the final stage of human progress.

This transformation of the meaning of the concept in the course of its transplantation was highly significant. It revealed the profound differences between the major European ideological developments and those of America. For European nationalism and socialism, individualism was a concept of negative value. Democracy, caught between these two movements, would for the same reasons reject its implications. Only a relatively small group of liberals and Protestant humanists accepted the idea of individualism as an integral part of their own orientation in Europe.

The history of the transplantation of the concept to America and of the transformation of the meaning of the term as its popularity grew thus offers a clue to the understanding of important social and ideological trends on both sides of the ocean.[41]

3. LIBERTY AND INDIVIDUALISM

The term and concept of individualism were introduced to the American public by various European Socialists and non-Socialist writers. For the former, the word referred to the basic principle of the modern uprooted society; the latter used the term in a narrower sense; for Tocqueville, Michel Chevalier, and Friedrich

List it characterized the forces which corroded the bonds of social, national, and political unity and created instability and anarchy.

Most writers who have dealt with the history of the term in the English language have credited Tocqueville with its introduction and have accepted the publication of Henry Reeve's translation of the second part of *De la démocratie en Amérique* in 1840 as its birth date.[42] This notion was founded less upon the examination of the contemporary literature than upon the fact that Henry Reeve found it necessary to explain the term by the following footnote: "I adopt the expression of the original [individualism], however strange it may seem to an English ear, partly because it illustrates the remark on the introduction of general terms into the democratic language . . . and partly because I know of no English word exactly equivalent to the expression."[43]

Yet the Americans attributed to the concept a meaning different from that of Tocqueville and utilized other sources in their discussion of it. The contemporary literature reveals that the term was introduced by various other writers who preferred different connotations from that of Tocqueville. In October 1839 the author of "The Course of Civilization" had already treated the concept as the central force of human progress and the core of American democracy. Michel Chevalier, in his *Lettres sur l'Amérique de Nord*, written first as a series in the *Journal des debats* published in Paris in 1836 and in 1840 in America as *Society, Manners and Politics of the United States*, also used the word.[44] Albert Brisbane's *Social Destiny of Man*, which inaugurated the American Fourierist movement in 1840 gave a different meaning to the term.[45] And Friedrich List's *Das Nationale System der Politischen Ökonomie*, which discussed economic individualism, although unavailable to the American reader until some years later, was relevant to the situation.[46] All these writers utilized a term which had been coined in the school of Saint-Simon to sum up their criticism of the structure and character of contemporary society.

Tocqueville's treatment was without doubt the most significant and most influential. Not only was the author already world-famous, but the concept itself held central place in his historical and sociological analyses.[47] Moreover, he alone among the nineteenth-century historians had pondered on the significance of such general concepts and had, anticipating a true sociology of knowl-

Emersonian

edge, considered them as the results of processes which shaped modern society.[48]

The context in which Tocqueville introduced the word individualism was the modern mass society which destroyed all distinctions and all organic forms of communal life and loyalty, and created free, masterless individuals who desired absolute independence and absolute equality of status and rights. In the general instability and mobility, society recognized no traditions, no group opinions, no authority. What remained was the self-sufficiency of the individual, his faith in his own reason, and his preoccupation with his own appetites and needs. In this atomized condition the only common bonds which survived were the state and the ever-changing economic nexus. Individualism was the attitude toward such a society and toward political obligations in general. It arose out of the feeling of modern man, and in particular of the new bourgeosie, that they "owe nothing to any man, they expect nothing from any man; they acquire the habit of always considering themselves as standing alone, and they are apt to imagine that their whole destiny is in their own hands." Equality of conditions made man "forget his ancestors," hid from him his descendants, and separated him from his contemporaries. Thrown back forever upon himself alone, in the end he was confined "entirely within the solitude of his own heart." [49] *Tocqueville*

Individualism was not identical with egotism, a moral and personal character trait found at all times. It was a passionate and exaggerated love of self which determined all relations. "Individualism is a mature and calm feeling, which disposes each member of the community to sever himself from the mass of his fellows and to draw apart with his family and his friends, so that after he has thus formed a little circle of his own, he willingly leaves society at large to itself." [50] Its opposite was virtue, or the dedication to the common weal. "Individualism, at first, only saps the virtue of public life; but in the long run it attacks and destroys all others and is at length absorbed in downright selfishness." [51]

The profound significance of this attitude lay in its relation to political liberty and democratic equality. In itself, individualism expressed the objectively imposed isolation of each person reflected in his striving to achieve subjective independence. Yet in the framework of a mass society the individual became powerless.

centrifugal
centripetal force

Being passionately jealous of his equal status which he could not influence except through the state, each man transferred to the government greater and greater power while he himself retreated more and more into himself. "Our contemporaries are constantly excited by two conflicting passions: they want to be led, and they wish to remain free. . . They combine the principle of centralization and that of popular sovereignty; this gives them a respite; they console themselves for being in tutelage by the reflection that they have chosen their own guardians."[52] Political liberty which demands the personal participation in the affairs of the state by active citizens was destroyed by the desire for subjective liberty and a general equality of conditions.

The consequence was an ever-increasing consolidation of political power and authority and a steady weakening of society. At the end of this process all powers of decision would be transferred to the omnipotent state.[53]

For Tocqueville the term individualism did not connote the elevation of the individual over and against society.[54] It referred rather to the attitude which arose from the isolation of the individual and the atomization of society. A remark written many years later in *L'Ancien régime et la revolution,* elucidated the real meaning of the term: "Our fathers lacked the term individualism which we have created for our own use, because in their time, there was not, in effect, an individual who did not belong to a group and who could be considered absolutely alone."[55] Tocqueville distinguished between individuality and individualism. The former inspired man to shape his own destiny, his capacities and faculties, as an active member of society with which he identified himself and thus jealously maintained his own liberty. The latter involved a withdrawal from society, and therefore a loss of strength and character; it created apathy toward the public weal and left uprooted man only the enjoyment of the feeble pleasures of privacy.[56] Individualism was the attitude of the masses who thought always in terms of generalization, of progress, society, the state, but never in the concrete terms of the true dignity of men.[57]

There existed, then, a paradox in Tocqueville's formulation. Individualism in its indifference toward society destroyed the individual, who could retain his liberty only through unceasing public virtue.[58] Two contradictory concepts thus confronted each other. Individuality, involving public virtue, aimed at strengthening the social body, limiting the state, and preserving liberty. Individualism, on the other hand, involving private liberty and equality of rights and status, aimed at strengthening the sovereign state, atomizing society, and destroying political liberty. Yet Tocqueville never explicitly stated these alternatives, though they had already been formulated in 1831 by the Swiss theologian Alexandre Vinet.[59] Tocqueville's supreme concern was to safeguard liberty against the despotism created by the leveling process of the democratic era.

Only American society had the answer, for in the United States social and political democracy had evolved to their utmost limit, and civil and political liberty was securely established. The explanation was that Americans had found the means of successfully combating the corrosive influences of individualism.[60] Individualism could be kept from becoming despotism even under democratic conditions through the establishment of free institutions which compelled each citizen to take part in public affairs. A commonwealth built on the principles of self-government and federation impeded the concentration of political power and authority and encouraged the active citizenship of all.[61]

Yet Tocqueville had introduced here, unconsciously perhaps, a *deus ex machina* to solve a difficulty he had himself created. How did it happen that in the land in which democracy was the sole principle of society, atomization had not destroyed citizenship in spite of the equalization of social conditions? [62] Though he noted that individualism was kept within bounds by the inveterate habit of Americans of solving most of their problems by voluntary association, he could only explain that phenomenon by the necessities of self-government and by the realization that private interest could be served best by serving the public good. In short, the principle of enlightened self-interest (*l'intérêt bien entendu*), he thought, was generally accepted in America. The idea that enlightened self-interest was the sole basis for public virtue in a modern democratic society dawned upon Tocqueville almost as soon as he became acquainted with the United States.[63] Representative government and the direct participation of all in the affairs of the country were the only means of arousing patriotism and interesting each in the welfare of all.[64]

A "refined and intelligent egoism" had created the republican structure in America, which in turn compelled the inhabitants to serve the public in order to serve themselves.[65]

> The American moralists do not profess that men ought to sacrifice themselves for their fellow creatures *because* it is noble . . . but they boldly aver that such sacrifices are as necessary to him who imposes them upon himself, as to him for whose sake they are made. They have found out that, in their country and their age, man is brought home to himself by an irresistible force; and, losing all hope of stopping that force, they turn all their thoughts to the direction of it. They therefore do not deny that every man may follow his own interest, but they endeavor to prove that it is the interest of every man to be virtuous.[66]

Yet the proposition that selfishness and self-interest alone were the sole motivating forces of modern society was gratuitous or at best a projection of the spirit of Guizot's bourgeosie upon society as a whole. As a matter of fact it was exactly the "love of liberty and the dignity of man" which had inspired the American theory of society.[67] Enlightened self-interest was a means to an end which was not self-interest but a free society. Because he failed to understand this, Tocqueville's use of the term individualism meant little to the American reader who shared neither his apprehensions nor his estimate on the true basis of self-government and who could hardly sympathize with the clearly expressed aristocratic leanings of the second part of *Democracy in America*.[68]

The connotation given the term by Tocqueville left its mark more on the dictionaries than on the minds of men. Webster's *American Dictionary* defined individualism in 1847 as "an excessive or exclusive regard to one's personal interest, self-interest; selfishness." [69] And other dictionaries also made the term synonymous with self-seeking egotism.[70] A good word had been spoiled and thrown away. Few reviewers noticed Tocqueville's remarks on individualism at the time of first publication or in the 1860's when a new edition, revised and annotated by Francis Bowen soon after the death of its famous author, gave rise to a considerable amount of comment. And none who dealt with Tocqueville's concept of individualism accepted the meaning he had given to it. The comment on Tocqueville's analysis of individualism revealed significant trends in American ideological development.

4. FIRST REACTIONS TO A NEW CONCEPT

The first American comment on Tocqueville's concept of individualism was in the *Boston Quarterly Review.*[71] The article focused on Tocqueville's observation that Catholicism was in the ascendancy in the United States because of the increasing similarity between the members of society, and asserted, "His acute powers of observation convince him [Tocqueville] that in the midst of the extreme 'individualism,' the isolated efforts at personal ascendancy in society, there is at the same time an active tendency among us towards a general assimilation of character and belief."[72]

Though the reviewer intended to sum up the meaning of Tocqueville's concept of individualism, he unconsciously enlarged it by characterizing the whole modern situation and position of man in society, his isolation and his drive for power, with that term. Moreover, the evaluation of this phenomenon was absolutely different. It was described as "that strong confidence in self, or reliance upon one's own exertion and resources," as "the strife of all our citizens for wealth and distinction of *their own,* and their contempt of reflected honors."[73] The idea of self-government which had created a new society out of the spirit of freedom and individual independence also created a new faith in man. "That incessant recurrence of the individual to the inherent and profound resources of his own mysterious being, which De Tocqueville repeatedly certifies to be a prominent characteristic of the American citizen, and by which we have lost faith in all traditionary institutions, and mere hereditary and transmitted worth, has, while urging 'individualism' rapidly towards the extreme refinement, nigh driven it into an organic unity of the collective race."[74]

The destructive and negative phenomenon thus became positive and constructive. " 'Individualism' has its immutable laws . . . which . . . when allowed to operate without let or hindrance,— however at first . . . their effects may appear destructive and anarchical,—must, in the end assimilate the species, and evolve all the glorious phenomena of original and eternal *order;*—that order which exists in man himself, and alone vivifies and sustains him."[75]

Individualism, according to the reviewer, by destroying traditions and conventions, by isolating man and throwing him upon himself, liberated him. As against Tocqueville's description of the fragmentation of modern society, the reviewer depicted the emergence of a new order based on the spontaneous relationship of free and authentic personalities. Moreover, the reviewer saw individualism in the context of another concept, conspicuously absent in Tocqueville—that of the progressive movement of history, whose goal was the liberation of individuality. The voice of New England Transcendentalism, modified by the accents of Swedenborg, echoed through these lines and endowed the term with a new and positive significance.   1865 ?

Another review, written twenty-four years later by E. L. Godkin, editor of *The Nation,* submitted the relationship between democracy and individualism to a searching analysis.[76] Godkin's essay on "Aristocratic Opinions of Democracy" criticized Tocqueville's views, his methodology, and his deductive reasoning which attempted to reduce the explanation of complicated phenomena to a single force. An ardent student of John Stuart Mill's *Logic,* Godkin emphasized the plurality of all historical causation and accused Tocqueville of having confused cause and effect.[77]

Godkin explained the peculiarities of American society by the "frontier life" through which it had passed, rather than by the equality of conditions.[78] Life on the frontier had fostered the idea of equality and of individualism.[79] Godkin thus not only overturned Tocqueville's views but changed the character and historical significance of individualism in general. Unlike Tocqueville, he stressed its strength. It was not the vice and apathy of a society of long standing, but the primordial energy which conquered an empty and wild continent and built a new society, and it reflected the pioneer's lonely fight for survival and the character this mode of life developed. "The settler gets into the habit of looking at himself as an individual, of contemplating himself and his career separate and apart from the social organization. We do not say that this breeds selfishness—far from it; but it breeds individualism."[80]

The difference between the views of the two authors lay not only in the causal relationship between individualism and democracy, but in Godkin's emphatic statement that individualism was a fundamental character trait of the American. It expressed itself in self-reliance, abundant energy of action, ideals of unrestrained individual freedom, the capacity for organization and daring enterprise, and the belief in a free competitive economy.[81] As against Tocqueville's view that its free institutions and enlightened self-interest had defeated individualism in America, Godkin concluded that both rested on the vigor of American individualism. Godkin's evaluation revealed the degree to which Americans had accepted the concept of individualism as a basic character trait of their society in the years since Tocqueville's analysis. Godkin lacked also the fervent quasi-religious attitude of the transcendentalist reviewer of the Boston Quarterly Review. Unable to accept the existence of individualism on its own premises, as a humanistic interpretation of democracy, he related it instead to the peculiar conditions in which American society had developed.

Another reviewer presented the attitudes of liberal protestantism. John Williamson Nevin of Marshall College shared Tocqueville's fears of the anarchic and disruptive effects of modern libertarian equalitarianism. Yet he could not wholly accept Tocqueville's negative evaluation of individualism, some of the attributes of which were inherent in the Protestant contribution to America.[82] The undue assertion of the prerogatives of individual life over and against the idea of authority "as something absolute and universal," threatened the true balance of liberty and authority and might lead to a licentiousness which could end in despotism. True freedom was voluntary obedience to law by the autonomous will. But it was not possible, on the other hand, "to fall in with the views of those who would persuade us that the only remedy for the evils of a licentious individualism is to be found in casting ourselves once more blindly in the arms of mere outward authority. This were to fall backward to the period which preceded the Reformation, when we should seek rather to make our own period the means of advancing to one that may be superior to both."[83] The danger to the survival of a stable social order lay not in the ideal of freedom, but in the theory of natural rights with its denial of binding moral and civil authority. Not individualism, but "licentious" individualism, created the danger.

Individualism itself was an offspring of the Reformation. While Nevin admitted that "the principle of individual liberty has been, in fact . . . carried to an extreme, at least in some cases, in the progress of the Protestant era," he stressed its abiding value for humanity inherent in this historical development. "A new stadium is in progress, for the universal life of the world; having for its object now the full assertion of what may be styled the subjective pole of freedom." Protestantism was thus the fountain of all modern religious and political liberty. It had broken the chains of authority and had engaged the human mind "to a bold vindication of its own rights in opposition to all blind obedience of whatever kind." [84] Individualism, then, was not a social vice but the very soul of progress.

Yet individualism was not the sovereignty of the individual over himself and the abrogation of all authority. True freedom required the individual to subject his will to the universal law of truth. Moral freedom recognized order as the true law of reason to which it subjected itself. [85]

Nevin revealed the dilemma forced by Tocqueville's concept of individualism upon the Protestant liberal clergy in general and upon the northern Whigs in particular. Individual freedom, based on the primacy of conscience and reason was, as Tocqueville himself had stressed, closely connected with the Puritan tradition. It had become almost axiomatic with Protestant historians that republican liberty was the product of the Reformation. Yet they were at the same time aware of the fact that equal liberty had been made a weapon of radicalism and that only a conservation of the institutional framework of society, a reverence for the authority of the state, the church, and the law could impede a general deterioration toward anarchy and Caesarism. Moreover, the Federalist legacy, the idea of an active national government, made them suspicious of individualism as a social philosophy. They therefore hesitated to use a term which, though related to their central values, had become tainted through the displeasure of so august a writer as Tocqueville.

The dilemma was further illustrated in a declaration of the Whig principles in *The American Review*. The Whigs proclaimed with greater emphasis than the Democrats the principle of the absolute rights and liberties of the individual as the guiding idea of the American Republic in order to offset the claim of the majority to govern society. Yet in the same breath the Whigs defended the organic unity of the nation and the duty of the government to legislate for the protection, development, and welfare of the whole society irrespective of the particular interests of its constituent parts.

This nationalism was limited, however, to economic and institutional matters; it did not extend to the internal affairs of society.[86] Furthermore, the idea of the national will as superior to that of the states was to be strictly limited by the Constitution of which the judiciary was the sole legitimate interpreter. "The doctrine . . . that the whole people, as sole and sovereign source of power, established the Constitution for a guarantee of individual freedom, and a source of all authority, is the doctrine of liberty. . . Ultrademocratic doctrine, on the contrary, indulges men in a perpetual revolution, cutting off the past from the present, and the present from the future; making its own decrees utterly forceless and contemptible, by deriving their authority from acclamation, instead of placing it where it belongs, under the Constitution of the whole people. . . They [the Whig Party] would have no man or body of men, majorities or minorities, exert a shadow of real power over their neighbors; and they refer all power and authority whatsoever back to its original source, the will of the nation as a whole, expressed in the Constitution. This is the real sovereignty of the people."[87]

Here then was the dilemma. Under the pressure of adjustment to democracy, Whig theory had established the principle of the absolute and equal liberty of the individual as the main characteristic of the American Republic and as the guiding spirit of its Constitution. "For, your Whig refers all rights and liberties back to their original source in the individual, and holds that society is established for the protection of these rights and liberties. . . The one side holds, that this very decision by majorities is not established by any merely natural law, but by a constitutional regulation; while the other side contends, that the majority . . . can assume power over individuals—to govern the few by the many—to keep each one in fear of a multitude, and to make rights and wrong by acclamation."[88] No word would better fit such ideology than "individualism." And yet the predominant conservative attitudes of the New England leadership, its deeply rooted sense of its own tradition and its English roots, as well as its economic and constitutional nationalism, prevented it from using a term which answered many of its requirements for a broader ideological definition of its idea of American nationality.

5. INDIVIDUALISM AS AN AMERICAN CHARACTER TRAIT— MICHEL CHEVALIER

Another book, which had, prior to Tocqueville, described *Society, Manners and Politics of the United States* in terms of the concept of individualism, apparently aroused little interest and only a faint response in America. And yet Michel Chevalier's *Lettres sur L'Amérique de Nord* were hardly less famous or less celebrated in France than Tocqueville's *Democracy in America.*

Unlike Tocqueville, Chevalier had already been the focus of public attention in France before his visit to America.[89] His book made a sensation.[90] In America, Gallatin valued it as the best and truest picture of the social situation in the United States, and the famous Humboldt considered it a new and original treatise on the civilization of the Western people.[91] The *Lettres* established Chevalier's fame and earned him decorations and office. In 1840 he was appointed to the chair of Political Economy of the Collège de France; a year later he became Chief Engineer of Mines and in 1845 he was elected to the Chamber of Deputies.

Though Chevalier had broken with the Saint-Simonians, their views permeated his ideas and terminology. No one who passed through Saint-Simonianism, or even came into close touch with it, did so with impunity.[92] It was the source of Chevalier's historical generalization, of the idea of the dialectical progression of history through the clash and synthesis of antithetical forces, and of his sociological orientation.

There were also similarities to Tocqueville.[93] Yet the conceptual framework and the attitudes toward America were absolutely different. Tocqueville's work was analytical; it attempted to discover what distinguished America from other societies and thereby to arrive at a general law of the development of democratic civilizations. As a true liberal he approached democracy with scientific detachment despite his passionate partisanship.

To Chevalier democracy was only a passing stage in the evolution of humanity toward its unification into one economic, religious, and political society.[94] He was skeptical and antagonistic toward the liberal system of values. The world needed an order of social justice and well-being, a new elite with complete authority to be recruited from science, industry, and new organic aristocracies. It needed a new faith and unity of belief to create principles of hierarchy, subordination, and social cooperation based on a new economic, industrial, and scientific civilization.[95] Within this general framework were embedded a number of eclectic historical generalizations. He assumed that there was a relation between the inherited qualities of racial groups and their beliefs and social structure. Protestantism was the natural religious expression of the Teutonic peoples; Catholicism of the Latin. The former were republicans, the latter monarchical. Yet the forces of civilization had a historic dialectic of their own which would mold the world into one great community.[96] At that moment Western civilization was the carrier of universal progress through its achievements in religion, philosophy, science, technology, and economy.[97] Within it, the dynamic energy, mobility, liberty, private enterprise, and inventiveness of the Teutonic, Anglo-Saxon, Protestant people had, more than any other force, generated progress. This process of creative uprootedness had been driven to its utmost limit in the absolutely new society of the North Americans. An incredible mixture of wisdom, energy, and daring, an admirable aptitude for business, an indefatigable love of work, and above all the broad rights of the laboring classes, made them superior to the rest of the human family.[98] The conquest of the human spirit, of which the Reformation was the point of departure, and the attendant development of industry and science, in Europe benefited only an elite, but in America benefited all.[99]

Into this general context Chevalier introduced the concept of individualism, which he considered the general characteristic of modern society, closely bound up with the revolt of reason against authority in religion, politics, and society. Individualism was a creative and liberating force because of its power to dissolve tradition and authority and to liberate energies. This element had reached its utmost limit in the United States, which was an offspring of the Protestant revolution.[100] The values of man shaped by Protestantism and republicanism, and the pattern of his relations to society, are the content of individualism.

For Chevalier individualism was not wholly a negative force, as it was for Tocqueville.[101] It was an historic phenomenon which, though inimical to all authority created from above, was yet capable of creating new forms of social life through individual self-determination.[102] American republicanism was its product.

> The American Republic subdivides itself indefinitely into independent republics on various levels. The states are republics in the Union; the cities are republics in the states; a farm is a republic in the county. The banking and canal . . . companies are also distinct republics. The family is an inviolable republic . . . and each individual is himself a little republic in the family. The only effective militia consists of voluntary companies which have no connection among themselves. The religious organization is like the civil and political. Various sects are independent of each other.[103]

Individualism elevated the principle of voluntary and contractual association to the primary form of social organization by destroying the indivisible unity of the hierarchic structure of authority prevalent in the monarchical and Catholic traditions.[104] For this reason, the American had hesitated to use the potential powers of the democratic Republic. Centralization, though necessary to commerce and manufacturing, had been impeded and the field left wide open to individualism.[105]

Within this general pattern Chevalier distinguished between the northern and southern types of civilization. The Virginian exhibited many of the traits of the European gentleman-aristocrat; but the Yankee was the absolute opposite. Dominated by the spirit of modern times—of secularism, rationalism, utilitarian motivation, and pragmatism—he was serious, graceless, practical, industrious, sober, and frugal. Logical and disciplined, he was the born entrepreneur and a good administrator—the progressive element in the country's economy. These characteristics derived from the Puritan inheritance, belief in the morality of work and the hatred of pleasure. The same heritage also explained the reforming impulse and missionary activities. The New Englander was individualism incarnate.[106]

Chevalier made individualism compatible with patriotism and the direct cause of the unique American forms of self-government and voluntary association. It explained the active participation of the citizens in the affairs of the community and it was set in the context of Protestantism and the heritage of the English political tradition, the forces which molded American national character.

6. FREE TRADE AND INDIVIDUALISM—FRIEDRICH LIST

The negative meaning of individualism was more prominent in a work which dealt with the problem of free trade and laissez faire as against economic nationalism or neo-mercantilism. Friedrich List's *Das Nationale System der Politischen Ökonomie* (*The National System of Political Economy*) was an outstanding criticism of the classical free-trade doctrine, a pioneering work in the historical school of economics, and probably the first great defense of economic nationalism.[107] List introduced the term individualism to characterize and to stigmatize the theories of the free-trade school. The term helped to prove that the free traders and classical economists had not dealt with political economy but rather with the workings of private, isolated economics, and had completely ignored the historical and national framework of all economic activity. The school was therefore accused of abysmal "Kosmopolitismus," of deadening "Materialismus," disorganizing "Partikularismus," and lastly of "Individualismus" which sacrificed the welfare of the nation to individual wealth acquisition.[108] The free-trade system wrongly elevated individuality to the sole source of productive power. It falsified the relationship between economy and nationality by denying to the state all economic functions and thereby robbed the nation of the advantages of political organization.[109]

All the major conclusions and part of the terminology of *The National System* had already appeared in an earlier work by List, written to defend the American protectionists. *The National System* only developed fully those ideas which he had first formulated in his twelve "Letters," printed as a pamphlet under the name "Outlines of a New System of Political Economy" on the occasion of the national convention of the Protectionists at Harrisburg, Pennsylvania in 1827.[110]

The "Outlines" marshaled the arguments against free trade in exactly the same way as *The National System*. Adam Smith and Jean-Baptiste Say had thought only in terms of individual economy which they had confused with political economy. Their cosmopolitical and atomistic views of society and states explained their failure to value correctly the creative power of the state in the development of national wealth.[111] The "Outlines" also coupled the terms cosmopolitanism, individualism, and materalism.[112]

List's appeal to the Americans to develop their country's unlimited natural resources and its productive power through a true national policy of protectionism and internal improvements was well known to American politicians and publicists.[113] His arguments, based on those of Alexander Hamilton, Hezekiah Niles, the Protectionist Mathew Carey, and especially Daniel Raymond, had been widely read and utilized by advocates of the "American system." [114] Undoubtedly the economist Henry Charles Carey early became acquainted with List's thought; Stephen Colwell, his friend, edited and sponsored the American edition of *The National System*.

The negative evaluation of the laissez faire philosophy, expressed in the term individualism, revealed the tension between economic nationalism and the system of freedom and equal rights. Yet, after all, List was a liberal by conviction who had not altogether discarded the ideal of free trade. Free enterprise, as much as political liberty and a republican government, was an axiomatic value. The derogative meaning of individualism was therefore narrowly defined and equated with materialism and particularism and contrasted with "union and liberty," the true nationalism.

The limited meaning of List's nationalism and individualism emerges from a comparison with that infused into the concepts by Stephen Colwell, the editor of his work in America. Colwell perceived the connection between the claims of social justice and national unity. Endowing the idea of national protection and improvement with the spirit of Christian social ethics, he gained a higher vantage point for a comprehensive assault not only on the theory of free trade but on the system of laissez faire in general.[115]

Colwell's *New Themes for the Protestant Clergy* (1851) attacked the concept of the purely formal state that left the economy to work out its own needs through free competition regulated solely by the laws of the market. Government was not only to aid in the development of wealth but was also to be responsible for a fair and equitable distribution. Protection defended the rights of labor as well as those of property and industry. Singling out Spencer's *Social Statics* as representative of the extreme laissez-faire philosophy, he wrote: "It forbids the thought of charity, or brotherhood, or sacrifice; it consecrates selfishness and individualism as the prime feature of society. . . Its principle is the least possible restriction, the fewest possible enactments; the weak must be left to their weakness, the strong must be trusted with their strength, the unprotected man must not look for favor, and government must resolve itself into the lowest possible agent for non-intervention." [116]

To List's criticism of the free-trade school Colwell added the socialist's criticism of the anarchy and cruelty of capitalist economy; the term individualism stood, therefore, for the whole system of laissez faire. The concept of the state as an instrument of social justice was contrasted with the concept of individualism.

> The social, political and commercial institutions of the present day, founded upon, and sustained by, a selfishness heretofore unequalled, are the great barriers to the progress of Christianity. . . Followed out to the utmost, the spirit of political economy leads to the fatal conclusion—that the conduct of the social life should be left entirely to the spontaneous operation of laws which have their seat of action in the minds of individuals, without any attempt on the part of society, as such, to exert a controlling influence; in other words, without allowing the State . . . any higher function than that of protecting *individual* freedom.[117]

Colwell's rejection of individualism was prophetic of the social gospel movement which grappled with the problem of social order in an industrial society, and upheld the decisive role of the state in the solution of this question.[118]

The absence of such conclusions and the similarity of the ideas in his earlier writing with those in *The National System* proved that List had arrived at his negative evaluation of individualism before he left his homeland—under the influence of the German *Polizei-und-Kameralwissenschaft,* through the impact of Napoleon's continental economic policy, and through the inner logic of the European idea of the nation-state.[119] At the same time it is evident that he borrowed the term individualism from the Saint-Simonian and socialist literature which had first coined the word in its negative sense.

As introduced to the American public by Tocqueville, Chevalier, and Friedrich List, the term individualism connoted various aspects of modern society which in the opinion of the authors corroded traditional bonds of social, national, and political unity and, by elevating unduly the status of the individual, created social instability and anarchy. All three authors more or less accepted the social and economic pattern of society as inevitable and natural;

none extended their critical attitude to modern society as a totality. Yet it was precisely in that sense that the Saint-Simonians had coined the term individualism. And only their comprehensive meaning implied in the socialist criticism of modern society gave the concept of individualism the importance it acquired in America.

It is, then, to the Saint-Simonian concept that we must retrace our steps if we are to understand the true significance of the term individualism.

X

Individualism and Socialism:
The Birth of Two New Concepts

The term "individualism" was coined by the Saint-Simonians to characterize the condition of men in nineteenth-century society—their uprootedness, their lack of ideals and common beliefs, their social fragmentation, and their ruthless competitive and exploitative attitudes which evolved from this legitimized anarchy. This concept was part of the comprehensive social criticism which the Saint-Simonians, together with socialists and conservatives, leveled against liberal and democratic tenets, the natural-rights theory, laissez faire, and the quest for utmost individual liberty.

The negative and destructive character of individualism was set against the ideal of an organic and unitary social order, held together by traditions, common purpose, and functional interdependence. In such comparisons, collectivism and authoritarian social order were favorably evaluated, regardless of whether individualism was contrasted with socialism or with the Catholic ideal of the corporate state, or with the organic unity of the "folk state." Such criticism involved the elaboration of a new theory of history and society. The rise of modern sociology and of historicism was intimately connected with this counterrevolution against the ideals of the Enlightenment.

The Saint-Simonian school was the most important of these sources of criticism. It fused sociology and historicism into a theory of social criticism and planning and contrasted individualism with the ideal of a regenerated society—in other words, with socialism. By challenging the ideals accepted in America, which had its own romantic Utopia, this school popularized the term individualism.

1. THE GREAT CHALLENGE; THE RISE OF ROMANTIC UTOPIANISM

The Saint-Simonian school had an extraordinary impact on the European mind. The ideas it created, reformulated, or popularized spread rapidly among the intellectual elite and permeated the thought and action of the most divergent groups. The school itself disappeared but the seeds it spread in all directions took root.[1]

Socialism bore the indelible imprint of Saint-Simonian influence. The ideals of "young Europe," with its democratic yet collectivistic nationalism and its vision of a fraternal confederation of the reborn nations, were kindled by the Religion of Humanity.[2] Yet no less permanent was the Saint-Simonian impact on the entrepreneurial ideology of a planned economy, guided by a technocratic, scientific, and capitalistic elite, as it was partly realized by the *Crédit mobilier* in France, the Darmstadter Bank in Germany, and later by the German industrialist, Walter Rathenau.[3] The Bonapartism of Louis Napoleon, no less than the social monarchy of Bismarck and Wilhelm II, showed signs of the new insights of the school. The hero concept of Carlyle and the groping for the charismatic leader were direct offsprings of Enfantin's self-enthroned Messianic lawgiver.[4] Auguste Comte's Positivism and the humanitarian social sensitivity of John Stuart Mill both reflected some of the ideas of Saint-Simon. The diversity and variety of its influences made the school a powerful factor in the history of the nineteenth century.

The doctrine of Saint-Simon was more than a "counterrevolution" against the liberal Enlightenment of the eighteenth century.[5] It was a conscious attempt to create a new synthesis from the revolutionary elements of the Enlightenment and the conservative reaction. By utilizing the truth in both and rejecting their mistakes, it hoped to lead humanity to a peaceful, stable, and just social order. "We have come to bring peace between these two armies by announcing a doctrine that inveighs not only against the horror of bloodshed but also against the horror of struggle, under whatever name the latter may be disguised—be it as *antagonism* between a spiritual and a temporal power, as *opposition* for the sake of political liberty, or as *competition* for the greatest welfare of all. We do not believe in the eternal necessity of any of these engines of war. Nor do we acknowledge any natural law of civilized mankind that obliges and condemns it to commit suicide." [6]

Such a synthesis could only be reached by a re-examination of historic experience. A new methodology and a new conceptual framework would grasp historic reality, discover its laws, and so recognize the basic needs and aims of man.[7] The basic data with which all reflection had to deal was the turbulent period through which the world had passed since the French Revolution. The obvious failure of the Revolution to achieve its postulated aim had revealed the inadequacy of the rationalistic and liberal approach either to organize a state or to account for history. The revolutionary era had discredited liberalism in particular and political ideologies in general. History had its own laws which could not be understood in these terms.[8]

Yet the revolutionary era had not been sterile. A return to the *ancien régime* was unthinkable. The law of progress in the history of humanity made each period the heir of its predecessor. This law manifested itself not in the political annals of mankind but in its intellectual, religious, and social fate. The final result of progress was the integration of men into one humanity. "The golden age, which blind tradition has hitherto placed in the past, lies before us. . . The earthly paradise is within sight." [9] All history moved toward the unity of mankind, in knowledge, in faith, and in fraternal and universal association.[10]

The universal association of the future would bring about a state of absolute social and economic cooperation in which exploitation would disappear. The dominion over nature would become absolute, and the fully developed harmony between man's spiritual and physical being would be mirrored in the unity of faith and of spiritual and secular rule.

Mankind, once it has reached this state . . . will march faster than ever towards perfection. But this epoch will be final for mankind in the sense that it will have realized the political combination most favorable to progress. Man will always have to love and to know more and more and to assimilate the outside world more completely to himself. The fields of science and industry will gather daily more abundant harvests and will furnish man with new ways to express his love even more nobly. He will broaden the sphere of his intelligence, that of his physical power, and that of his sympathies, for the course of his progress is unlimited. But the social combination that will be most favorable to his moral, intellectual, and physical development, and in which every individual, whatever his birth, will be loved, honored, and rewarded according to . . . his efforts to improve the moral, intellectual, and physical existence of the masses, and consequently his own . . . is not susceptible of perfection. In other words, the organization of the future will be final because only then will society be formed directly for progress.[11]

This new vision of the future had absorbed all the Messianic and millennial impulses of Jewish and Christian eschatological thought and translated them into secular terms of planned social and scientific action.[12]

This ideal of progress was linked to that of liberal democracy. Saint-Simon himself fully acknowledged his debt to Turgot and Condorcet.[13] The Saint-Simonians to a certain degree accepted the belief of the eighteenth-century philosophers of history—Lessing, Turgot, Kant, and Condorcet—that the law of progress could be discovered by an analysis of the human mind and that the advance of knowledge and the growth of self-determination gave a dynamic character to history. The three stages of Turgot's scheme were taken over by Comte and absorbed into the two stages of Saint-Simon.[14]

Moreover, the eighteenth-century expectation that science and technology would equip man with infinite powers over nature so that he could change his own future found its apogee in the technocratic approach of Saint-Simon and his school.[15] That approach, dominating the École Normale, the École Polytechnique, and the École de Médecine, inspired Saint-Simon to seek a new science to solve the ills of society.[16] The spirit of social planning and social organization, of union through scientific consensus, which dominated the school, plainly derived from the *Encyclopédie* and French scientific positivism.[17]

And yet Saint-Simonism also represented the antithetical and conscious rejection of the philosophy of freedom and natural rights developed by the Enlightenment. Of the great revolutionary triad of ideals—liberty, equality, and fraternity—the Saint-Simonians accepted only fraternity, which they insisted was incompatible with the other two. Saint-Simon and his disciples transformed the liberal ideal into an ideology of an all-inclusive social order through a reinterpretation of society and history, the central concepts of the liberal Enlightenment.

The Scottish moral philosophers—Francis Hutcheson, Adam Ferguson, David Hume, and Adam Smith—and the physiocrats had developed a science of society which endeavored to discover the laws that ruled social life and that determined the transition from one form of organization to another. The concept of historical process implied that impersonal and changing patterns of institutions, ideas, and social relations were the determining elements in development.[18] Yet these thinkers did not abandon the idea of the unity of mankind. Progress, the work of all generations, led mankind through more or less uniform stages of development to ever higher levels of social life and collective wisdom and power. Man thus became capable of reshaping himself and his social life according to the dictates of reason and of reflecting in his society the harmony of the laws of the universe.[19] The tension between these sociological and historical concepts and the Enlightenment's quest for freedom and individual rights had been overcome in the liberal synthesis of the philosophy of laissez faire and the idea of the free and natural society. It was this synthesis which the ideologies of conservatism and the Saint-Simonians rejected.[20]

The conservatives created an alternative snythesis by a new integration of the ideas of the historical and sociological process. They discarded the liberals' dichotomy between nature and history, reason and instinct, custom and the growth of social institutions, and between the individual and society.[21] Man's nature and the laws of reason, ruling his true course, were those of his history. The accumulated experience of his past and the slow growth of human societies revealed the true will of God and the true law of nature. The conservative counterattack made the social order the sole legitimate unit of the historical process. The historically formed nations, the great religious associations such as the Christian churches, the traditional estates of the realm, were the true products of the wisdom embodied in the collective experiences of the total human past. The medieval concept of society as the body politic, reinterpreted in the light of eighteenth-century sociological and historical thought, became the concept of society as a spiritual and functional organism. The state was not an institution created by contract but the mind and will of the social organism whose actions were determined by the spiritual unity and character which had evolved according to its own innate laws. Individual reason was powerless and blind when it acted independently of this structure of social order and spiritual unity, or set itself up in judgment against society and history.[22] History was not made, it grew; and the state could develop its own powers only when it acted in the "context of the historical-dynamical structure."[23] Unaided by the collective wisdom of the past, embodied in the living structure and beliefs of society, individual reason was unable to grasp historic reality, which could be understood only through intuitive apprehension.[24] Rationalism attempted to master reality by reducing everything to quantitative and mechanical terms and by generalizing into an artificial whole what in reality was a living entity.[25] Its very method compelled it to dissolve society into isolated individuals, to destroy the loyalty and organic cohesion of the social body through its hedonistic or utilitarian ethics, and to deride religion as unreason and superstition. Thus society became an agglomeration of equal units and the state a contract for the satisfaction of equal claims. The demands for equal rights were simply projections of purely quantitative and mechanical concepts. Yet, though rationalism could not recognize reality, it could destroy it by becoming a principle of action.[26]

Language reflected perfectly the organic and communal nature of historic and social reality. Language was not created by individuals, but was an instrument of the collective mind. The uniqueness of each language on the one hand and the analogous structure of all languages on the other revealed the relation between the uniqueness of each society and the spiritual unity of mankind.[27] Language, like society, possessed a history and was subject to permanent change. Yet neither the individual nor the group could consciously change language without destroying the possibility of communication.[28]

2. THE RISE OF HISTORICISM

After the French Revolution a new concept of history influenced the thought of all thinking Europe. Though historicism was primarily developed by conservative thinkers, its spread was due to the fact that it was a genuine scientific and philosophic discovery.[29] As against the linear and static concept of the European Enlightenment, the new image of history employed the ideas of development and of growth. The Enlightenment attempted to explain variability, change, and progress by the interaction of natural causes and human needs on the one hand and the power of reason, science, and civilization on the other. The new view perceived history as a dynamic process in which humanity expressed itself through beliefs, institutions, and collective activity and discovered ever new potentialities in collective forms. For the men of the Enlightenment society was an aggregate held together by common needs; historicism saw it as a living collectivity with an inner unity that could be understood only through an interpretative understanding of the norms and values embodied in its life, style, and institutions. Human nature and the human mind had no permanent pattern but became what they were in the process of history and were subject to the laws of growth and change.[30]

The question of truth, or rather of the correspondence of beliefs to reality, was misleading when applied to historical phenomena. The human mind was creative. Each epoch and each society lived in its own mental environment. It followed that the psychology and epistemology of Descartes and Locke were at best insufficient and at worst totally wrong, for the mind imposed its own patterns of ideas, forms, and symbols on reality. Ideas, conventions, traditions, beliefs, and symbols of emotions and affections were the stuff of history and changed with the times. It was therefore impossible to discover, as the Enlightenment sought to do, a nature and a reason apart from the historic context.

The emergence of this view preceded the French Revolution. Giambattista Vico had fully formulated the principles of the "New Science" by the 1720's. J. G. Hamann, G. E. Lessing, and J. G. Herder also enunciated similar views which were systematized by Schelling and Hegel as a philosophy of history.[31] Joseph de Maistre, Louis G. A. de Bonald, and P. Ballanche had used these ideas against the revolutionary principles of the Enlightenment.[32] Yet Augustin Thierry, Jules Michelet, Edgar Quinet, François Guizot, Théodore Jouffroy, and Victor Cousin, who also used them, were far from traditionalists or monarchists. Indeed, the consciousness of the historicity of social life had penetrated all European thought irrespective of its political or social orientation.[33]

The years between 1789 and 1815 had demonstrated that historical events followed their own pattern. The intellectual and institutional structures, customs, beliefs, and habits could not be eradicated overnight by the fiat of reason. The experience of those years made it necessary to seek anew the forces of change and stability, to speculate afresh whether general laws ruled history and if so what was their character, and to reopen the question of whether the whole process was progressive or moved toward any goal whatever.

On several tenets almost all agreed. Not individuals but nations were the true actors in history through which continuity and change were revealed. The nation was located in the higher framework of the civilization; and both the nation and the civilization were unified by their collective mind and character, expressed in institutions, norms, values, and arts. This was the "objective spirit" of Hegel, the *Volksgeist* of the Romantics, and the genius of the nations and the civilizations in French historiography. All agreed, too, that a rationalistic rejection of medievalism and supercilious attitudes toward religious culture were signs of a failure to grasp fundamental aspects of human life and were therefore entirely unhistorical.

Leopold von Ranke's statement, "Each epoch is immediate to God, and its values do not consist in that which issues out from it, but in its own existence, in its own self," summed up the new attitude toward the past.[34] The concept of history as a creative process of uniquely individual forms of life demanded a rejection of the mechanistic mathematical and naturalistic world view of Descartes and Newton and the adoption of a totally different philosophy. The methodological division introduced by the Germans between *Geisteswissenschaften* (the sciences of the mind) and *Naturwissenschaften* (sciences of nature) reflected this new orientation. History was the realm of the mind which could not be understood or explained in terms of the natural sciences. Here, in contrast to nature, the breath and power of the spirit was immediate. Nature and history were two media, as different in their structure as space and time, matter and mind, in which God expressed his purposes.

Yet beyond this consensus the views on history diverged. Liberals and conservatives differed fundamentally on the question of the nature and direction of historical progress. Their respective points of view were determined by their attitudes toward the creeds of the revolutionary period. For the liberals, the ideas of freedom and equality as well as that of permanent growth of knowledge were the true forces which, beyond all contingencies, determined the direction and course of history. This concept characterized the philosophy of Lessing, Herder, Humboldt, and Kant, no less than that of Madame de Staël, Benjamin Constant, Cousin, Guizot, and Michelet.

The conservatives rejected this view of progress, though this rejection was more categorical among Catholic and Lutheran thinkers like De Maistre, L. G. A. de Bonald, August Wilhelm Schlegel, and Friedrich J. Stahl than among Protestants like Schleiermacher, Ranke, or Hegel. For the Catholics, supreme morality was revealed in the teachings of the Church, and ultimate order was anchored in the authority of its head, the Pope. Progress could therefore be envisioned only in the growing power of its discipline over men.[35] The objective truth, morality, and authority presented in the Catholic Church demanded a parallel system of social order in the realm of secular life. Not individual liberty but a unitary social order was the seat of reason. The attempt of the individual to set himself up as ultimate judge of society led not only to anarchy and war but to the destruction of his moral and intellectual powers, his deterioration into sin, and his eventual self-destruction. Yet social unity and order could be maintained only by the concentration of power and authority in the ruler who was absolute and independent of the will of the subject. Such sovereignty does not clash with traditional orders and constitutions. The legitimacy of both had developed from the past, which was permeated by the supreme wisdom which God bestowed on all life.

The basic difference between the French authoritarian, theocratic, and traditional attitude and German Romantic conservatism lay in the question of progress and individuality. French thought was collectivistic and static. The truth was given, and salvation came from subjection to its authority. The German view was dynamic; its central concept was unity through the interaction and growth of sharply differentiated historical forces.[36]

This difference was closely related to that between the Catholic and Protestant world views. The Catholic intellectual either broke with his religious tradition to become a deist or a materialist, or accepted its unitary and authoritarian dogma; the Protestant intellectual remained within the sphere of religious influence, yet was driven to interpret the historical world through the categories of development and through the idea of the slowly transforming power of the spirit in the world. "It is from the bosom of the Protestant Church," wrote Benjamin Constant, "that Christianity, restored at once to its ancient purity and to its progressive advancement, is now presented as a doctrine contemporaneous with every age, because it keeps pace with every age; open to every access of light, because it accepts it from every quarter; enriching itself with every discovery, because it contends against none; placing itself on a level with every epoch, and thus laying aside every notion which is behind the progress that is daily made by the human mind." [37]

It was hardly a coincidence that Madame de Staël, Constant, and Guizot were Protestants and that Leibnitz, Herder, and Schleiermacher were imbued with the spirit of a Protestant pietism.[38] For such Protestants, Christianity was the progressive unfolding of the divine truth in history. Their relation to the whole Christian tradition was by nature historical; their denial of the state church, the concept of toleration, and the subjective concepts of salvation, piety, and righteousness seemed to confirm the ideas of individuality, of progress through moral growth, and of the multiplicity of forms through which Providence worked in history. These attitudes made adoption of the static and collectivistic views of the Catholic reaction impossible. The secular rationalized state, the multiplicity of nations, the progressive unfolding of truth, as well as the recognition of inner freedom as a supreme value, were permanent parts of the Protestant attitude and had to be integrated in the conservative ideology.[39]

The philosophy of Hegel was the supreme achievement of this ideological synthesis, as the world view of Ranke was in the field of history. The eighteenth-century quest for liberty and for a rationalization of society and politics was transformed by the idea of development. Reason in itself became the soul of the historic process which pervaded ever greater spheres of life and history. Yet the transposition of rationalism into the reason of history implied a fundamental difference between the individual's rationality and that of the historical process. Historic reality had its own wisdom; and only if the individual mind worked inside the framework of that reality was it in harmony with the true law of reason.

3. INDIVIDUALISM AS A TERM CRITICAL OF MODERNISM

The main object of the counterrevolution of romantic conservatism was to overcome the impact of the Enlightenment through historical exposure. All conservative thought was unanimous in the definition of the central evil of the Enlightenment as the dissolution of the historic community of life, faith, and custom and the establishment of individual interest, reason, and will as the ultimate criteria of social life. In short "individualism" was the basic evil of modern times.

The term gained general currency only in the 1830's and mainly through the Saint-Simonians. But the phenomenon had been fully discussed earlier. To Edmund Burke, for instance, the French Revolution was "not a victory of party over party," but "a destruction and decomposition of the whole society." [40] The Revolution had rejected all past history and had adopted a new dogma which could only be compared to the rise of the great religious ideas with their "proselytizing spirit." [41] The core of this doctrine was the reliance on individual reason, individual rights and interests.[42] It presumed to build society anew on its own abstractions and generalizations into an agglomeration of selfish individuals without past and without future, without piety and without dignity, without faith and without loyalty.[43] For Burke the true dignity and freedom of human life lay in the symbolism—the emotional bonds—and in the traditional respect for rank and excellence derived from the past. But the "sophisters, oeconomists, and calculators," had extinguished the glory of Europe forever.[44] "Never, never more, shall we behold that generous loyalty to rank and sex, that profound submission, that dignified obedience. . ." [45] "All the pleasing illusions, which made power gentle, and obedience liberal, which harmonized the different shades of life, and which, by a bland assimilation, incorporated into politicks the sentiments which beautify and soften private society, are to be dissolved by this new conquering empire of light and reason." [46] All was leveled to the same measure. "A king is but a man, a queen is but a woman"; the laws of government were to be supported "by the concern, which

each individual may find in them, from his own private speculations, or can spare to them from his own private interests." Institutions became a convenience and society a contract. Only interest
and force kept society together and united individuals.[47]

Thus had Burke already marshaled all the elements of romantic
conservatism with incomparable rhetorical power. The revolutionary philosophy had smashed the historic organisms which
revealed the "great primeval contract of eternal society, linking
the lower with the higher natures, connecting the visible and
invisible world."[48] It relied on the individual's "private stock of
reason," rejecting the "general bank and capital of nations and
ages."[49] Yet it was unable to create a new order. Its individualism
was sterile and suicidal. Though he did not use the term, Burke
groped for the word when he wrote: "Thus the commonwealth
itself would, in a few generations, crumble away, be disconnected
into the dust and powder of individuality, and at length dispersed
to all the winds of heaven."[50]

Burke's analysis became the prototype of the conservative
argument.[51] De Maistre, Bonald, Adam Müller, Wilhelm von
Schlegel, and even Hegel—all shared this view, though the terms
used varied and the arguments differed.[52] Moreover, Burke had
already made the romantic distinction between individuality, the
true form in which all living forces expressed themselves, and
individualism, the mechanical division of the organic forms into
equal units and the severance of all social and spiritual bonds.[53]

4. THE LIBERAL DEFENSE OF INDIVIDUALITY

For the liberals, on the other hand, historicism gave the concept
of individuality a positive significance which it lacked in the
Enlightenment. They had been compelled to discard the natural-
rights philosophy and they shared the romantic world view of
their conservative opponents. They could defend themselves only
by integrating the concept of individuality with those of liberty,
progress, and civilization, into a new ideology of liberalism and
laissez faire.[54] The principles of 1789 and of the Constitution of
1791 were still valid.[55] It was the Rousseauan concept of the state,
the idea of popular sovereignty, of the *volonté général*, which had
destroyed the Revolution. The ideology of liberalism was therefore
forged no less to oppose the Jacobin than the conservative tradi-

tion. Both were inimical to the right of man to his own life, liberty, and the free development of his powers. Both were authoritarian, collectivistic, and static. Restoration liberalism, still believing in the indefinite progress of mankind toward enlightenment, freedom, and well-being, turned therefore toward Germany, England, or the United States for guidance.[56] Benjamin Constant, Madame de Staël, Victor Cousin, and Théodore Jouffroy were among those who introduced the idealistic-romantic world of German thought into French liberalism and who looked to England for the patterns of constitutional liberty. For such republicans or democrats as Destutt de Tracy and La Fayette the American Republic remained the guide.[57]

Benjamin Constant expressed the concern of this liberal philosophy with freedom, individuality, and progress in his introduction to the *Mélanges:*

> For forty years I have maintained the same principle—freedom in everything, in religion, in philosophy, in literature, in industry, in politics; and by freedom, I understand the triumph of individuality; as well over the authority which aspires to govern by despotism, as over the masses which claim the right of subjecting the minority to the will of the majority. . . Everything which does not interfere with order; everything which belongs to the inward nature of man, like opinion; everything which in the manifestation of opinion, does not injure another . . . everything which in regard to industry, permits the free exercise of rival industry,—is individual and cannot legitimately be subjected to the power of society.[58]

The same conceptual framework underlay Guizot's *History of Civilization in Europe.* Individuality as the principle of the growth of man's mental and moral powers as well as of his capacity to live in freedom was both the hidden force and the aim of historical progress. Individuality was the dynamic principle of civilization.[59] Progress, development, and improvement were characteristic of the historical continuum which molded all individual and aggregate actions into patterns of communal life.[60] Yet the idea of progress implied spiritual power which alone was capable of spontaneous activity, experience, and learning. Two elements, then, were comprised in civilization: "the progress of society, the progress of individuals; the melioration of the social system, and the expansion of the mind and faculties of man. Wherever the exterior condition of man becomes enlarged, quickened, and improved;

wherever the intellectual nature of man distinguishes itself by its energy, brilliancy, and its grandeur . . . there man proclaims and applauds civilization." [61]

Both individual and social improvement were ultimately dependent on freedom and social order. Without freedom the mind could not improve itself and without social order, individual life could not exist. There could be no social improvement which did not rest on intellectual and moral growth nor could the individual advance without the progress of society. Moral and social progress was thus the true history of man. Each epoch had added to his well-being, freedom, and enlightenment.

Yet ultimately man stood outside nature as a spiritual being. The individual mind and soul explained his historicity and ultimately all progress was evaluated, as it was motivated, by the growth of individuality. [62] In this context Guizot quoted Royer-Collard: " 'Human societies are born, live, and die, upon the earth; there they accomplish their destinies. But they contain not the whole man. . . There still remains in him the more noble part of his nature; those high faculties by which he elevates himself to God, to a future life, and to the unknown blessings of an invisible world. We, individuals, each with a separate and distinct existence, with an identical person, we, truly beings endowed with immortality, we have *a higher destiny than that of states.*' " [63] Thus the concept of individuality became in French liberal thought, as it had in the earlier German thought of Humboldt, Schelling, and Kant, the criterion of progress. The dignity of man, his capacity for self-government, and freedom were the moral principles to which all history was subservient. [64]

Translated into the political sphere, the concepts of individuality, liberty, and progress led to the advocacy of strict constitutional limitations on power, to a policy of laissez faire, and to a pronounced preference for representative government. The second *Charte* was welcomed as a true program of French liberalism. It incorporated the spirit of 1789 within the framework of the historical experiences of Jacobin terror and Napoleonic despotism. [65] Yet the ascendancy of the ultra-royalists and ultramontane parties in 1820 raised anew the question of the basis of legitimate rule and the form of government which the *Charte* had successfully evaded. Republicanism, Bonapartism, and the doctrinaires on the one hand,

and the legitimists and traditionalists on the other, would no longer compromise on these issues.[66]

It is in this context that *individualism* as a political principle was first introduced.[67] In 1831 François de Corcelle, one of its first proponents, recalled that a major group of those who founded the French *Carbonari* called themselves "Société d'Individualistes." [68] The movement aimed to establish a federative republic by conspiratorial and revolutionary means.[69] The name "Individualists" was drawn from the main tenet of their political and social ideology. The society believed that "one should derive all the civil and political rights from the faculties and the needs of man considered as an individual." They opposed any system which subordinated individual rights to those of society or, rather, to the arbitrary action of governments.[70] Their republicanism opposed Rousseau's collectivistic concept of the general will, as much as the legitimists and the defenders of the *ancien régime*. With the failure and disintegration of the French *Carbonari* movement, its members dedicated themselves to the propagation of "individualism." [71]

The political concepts of the Individualists were a fusion of the liberal criticism of the Jacobins and of republicanism based on the absolute right of men to self-government. While liberals like Benjamin Constant saw England's Glorious Revolution as the only alternative to Jacobin democracy, the liberal republicans turned to America as the prototype. For the former, liberty and individuality were the main principles to be safeguarded, for the latter the equal rights of all individualists. Armand Marrast, criticizing the glorification of England, pointed out that the Revolution of 1688 "was certainly an energetic and honorable vindication of personal independence." But it made individuality the sole measure and the sole criterion of all truth.[72] This ideal of "personal independence" gave the protagonists of liberalism tremendous popularity among the youth.[73] Marrast, himself a democrat influenced by Saint-Simonian thought, emphasized the importance of individual freedom for the ideology of "young France" in the Carbonari movement.[74]

Yet the Individualists also demanded absolute equality of civil and political rights for all members of society, an equality derived not from the social compact but from the nature of social life itself. Each man had the right to satisfy his needs, to live, to work at a trade, to have a home, to think, and to defend himself. Since each had the same rights, all were absolutely equal. One was just when one respected that equality; one was free when one fully enjoyed it.[75]

This concept of equality was identical with that of American democratic republicanism, which decisively influenced it. The fact that Corcelle was among the founders of the *Carbonari* movement, that La Fayette was at one time elected its head, that the whole conceptual framework reflected the ideas of Destutt de Tracy, showed the impact of American ideology on the Individualists. This was the only alternative to the Jacobin democratic tradition. The Individualists aimed to substitute for the assumption of the French declaration of rights of 1789, concepts in which the state, the nation, and sovereignty were accommodated to equality of individual rights.[76]

Yet this liberalism was not destined to grow in France. The July Revolution disclosed that the regime of the doctrinaires under Louis Phillippe was only the undisguised rule of the upper middle class. Nationalism and democracy tended to become closely allied, and together they nurtured a strongly collectivistic attitude toward politics. Furthermore, the rise of Saint-Simonism and its impact on the French mind precluded the possibility of the development of a genuine liberal tradition.

5. THE SAINT-SIMONIAN CONCEPT OF INDIVIDUALISM

Many leading Carbonari, among them Saint-Amand Bazard and Philippe Buchez, attracted by the vision of true fraternity and social progress, became disciples of Saint-Simon and theoreticians of the movement. It was likely that the former revolutionary liberals transferred the term individualism into the Saint-Simonian literature but changed its positive value into a negative one. This step was all the easier because Saint-Simonism aimed at the same social ideal as the liberals—the ultimate happiness of mankind.

Saint-Simonism was tremendously attractive to the intellectual elite of Europe because it synthesized all the major intellectual movements of its time. It accepted frankly the conservatives' criticism of the Enlightenment and of liberalism, and the condemnation of destructive individualism. Yet as against the sterile ideals of a conservatism which denied the optimistic belief in the progress of mankind it upheld a utopian ideal of ultimate social salvation, to be achieved through the innate laws of progress.[77]

Though the Saint-Simonians believed they had created the science of society, they were thoroughly activistic, and this also appealed to the generation which vainly sought to discover its place in the society of the Restoration and the July Monarchy. Like Marxism and Communism, which were only further states in its development, Saint-Simonism claimed to possess the absolute truth and called upon men to gird themselves for the great work of social salvation that would establish the reign of fraternity by applying science and a new humanitarian morality to social life.[78]

Theirs was a different liberty from that of liberalism. It was the liberty of collective creativity, supported by the assurance of unity, and by the religious exhilaration which stemmed from the feeling of dedication toward the absolutely valid, the happiness of society and mankind. For these reasons Saint-Simonians at first, and Marxists later, considered themselves and became in fact the only powerful historical and ideological antagonists of liberalism.

This antagonism was revealed in theories of society, of history and progress, and of human values. The fundamental concepts of the Saint-Simonians concerned society and humanity; the individual had no existence, no powers, rights, or capacities independent of those of society. Each society had its unique characteristics, its central idea, expressed in its beliefs, institutions, economic organization, and culture.[79] Yet each was subject to the law of change which eventually disrupted and destroyed it to create a new social system at a higher level. Saint-Simon discovered that the only elements of civilization always were the sciences, the arts and industry; that the political institutions, the state of the societies, are always the result and the expression of the development of the human species in these three directions.[80] Yet these elements were in nature progressive and led not only to ever higher stages of social organization and civilization but to the disruption of the social systems which could not adjust themselves to the changes.

Thus far, Saint-Simonism was reconcilable with the eighteenth-century liberal concept of progress. The antiliberal element sprang from a hypostasis of the conceptual unity of society and mankind.

This unity was a fundamental historical tendency and the basic principle of morality and of social action. Humanity was a collective entity which had grown from generation to generation by its own law of progressive development that made man conscious of a social destiny. Political institutions applied this concept "to the establishment, preservation and progressive development of social relationships."[81]

All healthy societies, according to Saint-Simonism, aimed to safeguard their unity through systems of belief, morality, and social institutions. Otherwise, they would disintegrate and destroy the vital forces which maintained the spirit, the soul, and the body of man. Yet the nature of this unity was subject to historical change. Only when the idea of unity coincided with the truth of science and with the absolute morality of fraternity and service to humanity would history proper come to an end and the period of strifeless human cooperation begin. Then the alternation of organic and critical periods would be resolved by the age of universal association. For that alternation was a consequence of the fundamental drive toward progressively higher forms of association and acted only so long as fraternity was confined to limited areas while force, antagonism, and strife remained the chief compulsion of mankind.

The permanent confrontation of antagonism, force, and exploitation with voluntary association, of unity with disunity, was the motivating element of historical change. In all history, society was ultimately maintained by force because exploitation and warfare were predominant. Yet with each period the sphere of true association had grown. Savagery disappeared, slavery gave way to serfdom, and serfdom to the modern wage system. The tribes united into nations and then into empires. Polytheism and religious cults were defeated by monotheism, and Christianity established the brotherhood of man. The rise of science and industry and the expansion of peaceful economic activity limited the use of military force. Strife, the primordial source of social change, created the condition that would ultimately eliminate it. In the organic periods society was united and all its activities were subservient to the organic whole. In the critical periods society dissolved, and the rootless individual emerged. Only strife, class war, and economic exploitation held together the atomized society, and morality became purely utilitarian, while skepticism and rationalism destroyed the intellect.

The organic periods were the truly creative ones; and the Catholic Church was the greatest historical realization of the idea of unity of mankind and the prototype of all its future spiritual organizations.

Yet the critical periods were historically necessary. While the destruction of social authority weakened the old society, it prepared the new through the enlargement of the intellectual, moral, and emotional horizons. Thus Greek philosophy led to Christianity and the Reformation to a new faith in humanity. "Catholicism has fulfilled its destiny; another general doctrine is called upon to continue today the task for which the former has become inadequate. This doctrine, as that which preceded it, is destined to gain political power, to dominate and direct exclusively and completely . . . the social and individual activity." [82] The Saint-Simonians were to introduce the final organic period of universal association. The critical period ushered in by the Reformation had fulfilled its historical function by dissolving medieval society; but its outlook was orientated solely toward the individual and it was unable to recognize the true problems of the contemporary world, which were social and spiritual, not political. [83]

It is in this context that the Saint-Simonians introduced the term individualism. [84] Individualism was the generic principle of the critical periods and especially of modern times. It expressed itself in all aspects of life—in philosophy, science, and morality as well as in political, social, and economic institutions and activities. Liberalism, laissez-faire attitudes, atheism, materialism, skepticism, Protestantism, and utilitarianism were its intellectual and religious manifestations. The international chaos among states paralleled internal anarchy, economic parasitism, exploitation, and competitiveness. [85] Men were motivated solely by egotism and self-interest and all unity and authority disintegrated with the atomization of society. [86] The "enlightened self-interest" of Helvétius and the categorical morality of Idealism were all expressions of individualism. All "amicably join hands in matters of morality and politics." All were "defenders of individualism." [87]

Liberalism was, then, nothing but an ideological glorification of the last stage of antagonism. Its philosophy rationalized selfishness; laissez faire was a thin disguise for exploitation of the working masses by the owners of property. The limited power of government and the representative state perpetuated social anarchy and the rule of self-interest through a purely negative concept of order. It was the idealization of egotism and individualism.[88] The Saint-Simonians thus endowed the concept of individualism with a historical and sociological perspective of fundamental importance. By embodying in the term the criticism of the conservative ideologists, they gave individualism a strict meaning to destroy liberalism. Anticipating the tactics of Marxism, they related the ideology of their opponents to a stage in historical development and to group interests. But the Saint-Simonians went beyond the charge of relativism; they directly attacked the values of liberalism and denied the spiritual and moral autonomy of the individual. Personal rights and freedom were crisis phenomena, expressions of disintegration and of the loss of spiritual orientation.

On these points they agreed with the romantic reactionaries. Liberty was meaningless, human rights negative.[89] There was no need for freedom of conscience but for truth and authority.[90] The masses could not exist without certainty nor could they live in liberty.[91] They needed "faith and harmony" and found true freedom only in purposive social action.[92] The individual was "free to the extent that social action masters him increasingly to aid in developing his special aptitude, to exercise his faculties fully, and to overcome the vicious inclinations which would expose him to the vindictiveness of the laws and to infamy."[93] The salvation of mankind lay not in individualism but in universal association and brotherhood, in the full utilization of science and technique for the organization of society and the welfare of all. It lay in peace, not in strife, in planned cooperation and not in competition, in the unity of faith and morality and not in liberty and individuality. In this confrontation of individualism with associationism or, as it would soon be called, with socialism, the Saint-Simonians outlined two social systems and the two rival ideologies which would struggle for the mind of Europe in the future.[94]

The impact of the Saint-Simonian gospel on the European mind came with the July Revolution. The regime of Louis Philippe underlined the relevance of the teaching of the group and exploded the pretensions of liberals and doctrinaires.[95] Here was a new science of history and society which penetrated the basic questions of man and society. Here was a new vision of the future. Here, above all, was a program of action. Artists like Victor Hugo and Balzac, George Sand, Franz List, Chopin, Heine, and Wagner became Saint-Simonians. The Catholic writer Lamennais and his organ *L'Avenir* spread the theories. The newly founded French Protestant weekly, *Le Semeur*, started to discuss them. The *Globe*, with Sainte-Beuve, Pierre Leroux, and Michel Chevalier, became Saint-Simonian.[96] The *Doctrine Saint-Simonienne*, with the systematic theory of Saint-Simonism, was published in November 1830. *La Revue encyclopédique*, published by Hippolyte Carnot and Pierre Leroux, began with a systematic study of socialist theories. Even the leading ideologists of liberalism, Jouffroy and Cousin, accepted elements of the Saint-Simonian teachings.[97]

6. INDIVIDUALITY VERSUS INDIVIDUALISM AND SOCIALISM

In the ever-widening debate on the merits of the Saint-Simonian doctrine, the terms individualism and socialism were both accepted largely with the Saint-Simonian connotation and evaluation.[98] The earlier term, associationism, was discarded as the opposite concept to individualism because it connoted the voluntary cooperation of equal individuals. The shift in usage showed the collectivistic and communalizing aspect of Saint-Simonism.[99]

The growing dogmatism of the Saint-Simonian sect, the establishment of its priestly hierarchy and its claim to infallibility, its pseudo-mysticism and pseudo-religion, revealed the defects of its doctrines. The rejection of the traditional morality of sex relations and the last act of the tragic comedy—the communal ascetic life as the believers retired to their "houses" and split over the apostolic succession and pontifical supremacy—destroyed the sect. But certain valuable insights and basic achievements of Saint-Simonism endured.[100] Among these the sociological and economic interpretation of history, the criticism of modern society, the concept of individualism, the emphasis on economic problems and on the necessity of organization, and the vision of humanity united by brotherhood became an integral part of the revolutionary movement the world over.[101]

This, then, was the context of the debate on individualism. Almost none of the thinkers who emerged from the scattered movement accepted the hierarchic and charismatic pretensions of the Saint-Simonian church. Nor did they accept its totalitarian and antiliberal outlook. Liberty, equality, and social organization for economic justice, achieved either through the state or through free association, became the guiding principles of the social movement in France.[102] The liberation of socialist thought through the destruction of the sect was best expressed in the programmatic article published in *La Revue encyclopédique,* "De la société Saint-Simonienne." Individualism destroyed all unity of action which now had to be renewed. No revolution was valid which did not restore to the majority of the people its rights. The French Revolution had been only the precursor of the Great Revolution in which the proletariat would rise against its masters to secure equality, universal association, classification of all according to their capacity, and the liberation of the workers. Yet the article condemned "an inflexible parallelism between Catholicism and Saint-Simonism" which established as a principle the unity of absolute power.[103]

To give form to such ideas, the concept of individuality was revived with its liberal and humanitarian connotations and contrasted with individualism. Individualism stood for spiritual rootlessness, destructive rationalism, utilitarianism and hedonism, and exploitation under the disguise of laissez faire. Individuality, on the other hand, stood for human dignity, the capacity of man to grow in reason and morality, for liberty, equality, and fraternity. Individualism had to be suppressed by a reorganization of society: individuality was a valid norm of all human progress. This distinction was emphasized wherever the merits of socialism were argued. "Beware," wrote Alexandre de Saint-Cheron, "of confounding individuality with individualism, with that mean egoism, lonely and disunited, which chokes all dignity, all the elan of the soul, all faith, while the sentiment of individuality is the holy exaltation of man, conscious of the life in him and all others, in God and nature." [104] In the same sense, Joncières stated the relationship of individuality to socialism, "We don't intend to sacrifice the personality to socialism any more than socialism to the personality." [105]

Pierre Leroux, above all, aimed to arrive at a new humanitarian socialist philosophy through a systematic inquiry into the concepts

of individualism, socialism, association, and individuality. In 1832
he showed that the ideology of individualism had been developed
in the Restoration period to defend the achievements of the Revolution against theocratic and royalist reaction. Under its banner,
lovers of freedom had formed a liberal coalition. Yet individualism
was a principle of negation.[106] With the end of the Restoration,
it lost its *raison d'être*. The individualism expressed in "political
economy" was that of "everyone for himself, and . . . all for riches,
nothing for the poor."[107] That "political economy" was dead.[108]
It had been a suitable instrument only for liberating the bour-
geoisie; now it exploited the propertyless masses. The only alternative was the system of association which would realize the
equality and brotherhood of man.[109]

A year later Leroux had progressed further in the rejection of
collectivism. The only principle which completely expressed the
nature of man was "liberty and individuality."[110] The French
Revolution had not intended to organize society according to an
exclusive scheme. Society was "to give satisfaction to the individuality of all." Individualism and authoritarianism were alike dangerous. The individualism "of the English political economy . . . in
the name of liberty" made men "rapacious wolves" and reduced
society to atoms. It left to government nothing but the task of a
policeman, while property became the sole basis of society. The
result was the enslavement of twenty-five million Englishmen to
three hundred families.[111] On the other hand, the partisans of
socialism marching bravely toward their "organic epoch" threatened to extinguish all liberty and spontaneity. Individualism cut
men loose from all that had gone before or was yet to come, for
the sake of the immediate present. The socialists projected the
principles of orthodoxy and medievalism into their vision of the
future and interdicted the whole modern era, its Protestantism
and philosophy.[112] "We are," Leroux therefore concluded, "neither
individualists nor socialists. We believe in individuality, personality, liberty; but we also believe in society."[113]

The identification of the concept of individualism as synonymous with the rootlessness of the times was quickly accepted by
all those who were critical of contemporary society. The disciples
of Fourier employed the term in this way to characterize the
economic, social, and moral evils which they studied with far

greater depth and discernment than the Saint-Simonians.[114] Others followed, and individualism became part of the vocabulary of all who reflected critically on the character of modern civilization. In this more generalized sense it served Tocqueville as well as Chevalier; the antimodernist attitude of Catholic writers no less than the defenders of economic nationalism and the positive state.[115]

XI
Social Criticism in America

The impact of socialist and romantic thought evoked in Americans a new concept of individualism as the principle and ideal of social and political organization. The problems revealed by the challenge of socialism compelled a restatement of social, political, and moral values under the name of individualism.[1] The transformation of the concept involved the acceptance of the historicism and the sociological outlook which was the original contribution of socialist and romantic conservative thought.[2] The adoption by the American intellectual elite of a mode of thinking which destroyed the natural-law and natural-rights theories and which established the idea of a social order changing according to its own genetic principles, created a new awareness of the unique character of its own social system which it associated with the term individualism. The use of that word demanded a reinterpretation both of the concept structure and of the social order in the light of those principles now perceived as fundamental to American life.

The challenge of socialism in the 1830's and 1840's was not the same in America as in Europe. Though the immediate appeal of the idea was related to the growing concern with the problems of an urban industrial order revealed by the great depression of 1837, its true impact came from its messianic and idealistic promises. The Americans had been convinced since the Revolution that they were the *avant-garde* of mankind and that their social and political system was universally valid. Now they confronted an ideology which claimed these attributes for itself and which exposed the glowing injustice and shortcomings of contemporary society.

Socialism became widely known in the United States through

the associationism of Fourier, which possessed none of the objectionable characteristics of early Saint-Simonism or of later state socialism. Its practical proposals for a reorganization of society and its rejection of revolutionary methods appealed to many Americans. Fourierism was easily coordinated with the numerous reform movements which agitated the northern states in the 1830's. Albert Brisbane, Parke Godwin, Horace Greeley, and William Henry Channing considered associationism to be in complete harmony with the deepest aspirations of Christianity and of their own country; and they were in close contact with the radical wing of the democratic movement and with the no less radical intellectual elite of New England, the Transcendentalists. Those connections led to widespread discussion of socialist thought. Although their response was to a large degree negative, Americans were stimulated to social and historical inquiry and compelled to find new ideological answers to newly discovered problems.

1. ALBERT BRISBANE

Albert Brisbane used the term individualism in his *Social Destiny of Man* to characterize contemporary civilization.[3] In the period which commenced with the Reformation, anarchy, waste, and the conflict of opposing interests marked the economic and social order.[4] There was "a miserable application of all the great sources and means of production, such as labor, capital, soil and natural advantages."[5] Since government action was excluded from the sphere of industry, the means of production were left in the hands of individuals who employed them blindly.[6] Individualism, the underlying spirit of this epoch, was synonymous with chaotic social relations, antagonism, and egotism. Its ideology was that of individual liberty, but it led to the pauperization of the middle classes, the growing concentration of capital in fewer and fewer hands, and ultimately to a new commercial and industrial feudalism. As long as modern industrial society was divided into individual households and the means of production were monopolized as private property, the masses were absolutely subservient to the rulers of the economy.[7]

A review of Brisbane's book, in the November 1840 *United States Magazine and Democratic Review*, summarized the implication of the individualistic social system.[8] The article emphasized the revolutionary meaning of Fourier's theory which aimed at the reorganization of society on totally new principles.[9] False competition among the laborers, caused by sheer necessity, led to the steady reduction of wages and the creation of a multitude of wage slaves entirely dependent on their employers. The same system created periodic excesses and permanent fluctuations of production and caused stagnation, depressions, and starvation although society could create abundance for all. So long as commerce and industry were conducted by isolated individuals with conflicting interests instead of by large associations, there was no possibility of guarding against disaster.[10]

Individualism was the spirit of the members of such a society. It enabled them to fight for survival and to gain status and wealth. Its suppression was necessary to prepare for the reorganization of society on the basis of associationism. "Free competition and individual action" engendered "such spirit of selfishness and individualism in men that a secret antipathy to association and unity of action" existed.[11] Individualism, then, was the conceptual antithesis of associationism or socialism, a term which was immediately applied to the Fourierist movement in the United States. Brisbane had concluded, "We must introduce into society, *Unity of Interests, Combined Action,* and the principle of *Association,* and replace by them the conflict of all interests, the incoherent action, and the universal individualism, and the antagonism, that now reign."[12]

The Fourierist critique which defined and correlated the generic traits of American society through the concept of individualism evoked an immediate response, evident in the experiments in associationist settlement in the 1840's.[13] Brook Farm became for some time almost the center of the New England intellectual movement. The peculiar amalgamation of congregationalist tradition with transcendentalist and socialist thought was expressed in its *Articles of Agreement and Association between the Members of the Institute for Agriculture and Education.* Its members came together "in order more effectually to promote the great purpose of human culture; to establish the external relations of life on a basis of wisdom and purity; to apply the principles of justice and love to our social organization in accordance with the laws of Divine Providence; to substitute a system of brotherly cooperation

for one of selfish competition . . . to institute an attractive, efficient
and productive system of industry; to prevent the exercise of
worldly anxiety by the competent supply of our necessary wants;
to diminish the desire of excessive accumulation by making the
acquisition of individual property subservient to upright and dis-
interested uses; to guarantee to each other the means of physical
support and of spiritual progress." [14] The support of Americans of
such high standing as Albert Brisbane, Horace Greeley, Parke
Godwin, George Ripley, and Charles Dana gave the new concepts
a profound influence on American thought. [15]

2. ORESTES A. BROWNSON

Albert Brisbane had introduced into the general intellectual
ferment of reform a new plan for the reorganization of society
which involved not only a comprehensive critique of the existing
social and economic pattern of life, but a new outlook on history
and society. Yet associationism was not a political movement and it
refused to consider government as a lever for social change. The
state was to be superseded by the ever-broadening network of
groups. [16]

To Orestes A. Brownson, who had fought for the transformation
of political into social democracy, such schemes seemed not only
impracticable but immoral. They evaded the main question, which
was the liberation of the working classes from poverty and wage
slavery.

Brownson was one of the first American writers to be preoccupied with the economic and social reorganization of American society. Unlike Brisbane, whose outlook had been formed by
the intellectual climate of Western Europe, [17] Brownson strove
consciously to develop a true American culture and to solve social
problems in harmony with basic American traditions. Yet in spite
of his varied activities and his close contact with the New England Transcendentalists and other intellectuals, Brownson remained a lonely man. While he devoted a great part of his earlier
literary career to the defense and elucidation of the aims of radical
democracy, he fought the ideology of laissez faire and of the
negative state which its leaders advocated. He considered himself
a member of the Loco-Foco wing of the Democratic party; yet his
definition of the aim of the party as "social Democracy, as distin-

guished from political" was not accepted by most Democrats.[18] He conceived of democracy as a permanent revolutionizing force— "the most profound and comprehensive spirit that has ever claimed or obtained the control of society."[19] Yet he also envisioned the state as the supreme instrument for the realization of a social republic. Independent in outlook, Orestes Brownson was a man whom few could love but many esteemed. As founder and editor of the *Boston Quarterly Review,* as regular contributor to the *Democratic Review,* and as editor of *Brownson's Quarterly Review,* he was widely known.[20] Bronson Alcott thought the *Boston Quarterly* "the best journal now current on this side of the Atlantic," and George Ripley considered it "the best indication of the culture of philosophy in this country," while Theodore Parker preferred it to the *Dial.*[21]

Persevering only in the search after spiritual truth and faith, he had in quick succession abandoned the Calvinistic faith, and embraced Universalism, Unitarianism, and finally ended by accepting the doctrine, precepts, and discipline of the Roman Catholic Church.[22]

Brownson sought to relate the social order to a system of religious values that would save the individual from social and spiritual isolation. His quest for social justice, order, and dignity drew him to the socialist thought of Europe in the 1830's.[23] Pierre Leroux's post-Saint-Simonian concepts of the unity and solidarity of humanity revealed to him the esoteric meaning of Catholicism and thus gave him the courage to enter the Catholic Church.[24]

The Saint-Simonian influence was also discernible in Brownson's idea of progress. The future would develop new forms of social life permeated by human solidarity and sustained by a new faith in moral unity, a renewed, indivisible Catholic Church. Saint-Simonism increased his understanding of the problems of urbanization and industrialization and riveted his attention on the position of the American worker. In words which revealed the influence of Lamennais, he denounced the wage system as modern slavery.[25] "Wages is a cunning device of the devil, for the benefit of tender consciences, who would retain all the advantages of the slave system, without the expense, trouble, and odium of being slaveholders."[26] This attitude, which anticipated the pro-slavery arguments of the southern literati, enabled him to accept the leadership of John Calhoun in a coalition between the southern democracy and the northern working men against the Whigs, the party of finance and industrial capitalism.[27] Like Calhoun, Brownson considered the social question the fundamental problem of the age.[28] Yet, unlike Calhoun, he saw the solution in the realization of a just social order through an active and positive state, not in states' rights.[29]

The fundamental idea of democracy was not the sovereignty of the individual but "the supremacy of man." The Democratic party was "the American party" because it embodied that idea which it was "the mission of American institutions to realize." "The order of civilization, which it is ours to develop, is an order . . . in which things are subordinate, and subservient to Humanity. Humanity, in all its integrity, is in every individual man." [30]

The concept of humanity endowed the individual with dignity and demanded not only social justice but also solidarity. This idea Brownson later developed in terms of Pierre Leroux's philosophy.[31] In the past, individuality and community had been two opposing terms. "Community without individuality is *tyranny*, the fruits of which are oppression, degradation and immobility, the synonym of death. Individuality without community is *individualism*, the fruits of which are dissolution, isolation, selfishness, disorder, anarchy, confusion, war. . . What we need, then is . . . communalism and individuality harmonized . . . atoned." [32] Socialism and individualism, attempting to build society exclusively on partial truths and needs, were both destructive. All individuality had its roots in the community, and the community realized itself only in its individual members. Both were reconciled through property, the family, and the state, all of which related the individual to society and humanity.[33] The social state which secured to each the right of property and civil liberty would realize the ideal of the oneness and dignity of humanity. It would provide for both aspects of man; his individuality, which when abused became selfishness, yet which was the basis of liberty and progress; and his social nature, which implied sympathy, cooperation, and mutual assistance, yet which when dominant "cannot fail to degenerate into practical tyranny." [34] Therefore Brownson attacked both the individualism and the associationism which preoccupied his New England Transcendentalist friends. His articles between

1838 and 1843 reflected the endless arguments with Emerson, George Ripley, William Henry Channing, and Bronson Alcott, while Thoreau silently listened.

Brownson had Emerson in mind when he described the philanthropist's attitude toward the social question—"self-trust, self-reliance, self-control, self-culture." Man was sufficient unto himself, and would work out his own salvation by isolated, unaided effort. That position implied idealism in philosophy, egoism in morals, individualism in politics, and naturalism in religion, and was necessarily atheistic in spirit and tendency.[35] Brownson rejected this moral and philosophical individualism as untrue and immoral. Man was a social being dependent on the collective past of humanity. Society was not an aggregate, but an organic whole; and self-improvement could not alter basic social facts which were impersonal and intrapersonal. Society could be changed only by the state.[36] Individualism made the isolated man the sole carrier of responsibility and creativity; and limiting democracy to purely political categories could not deal with the real problems, which were social. The belief that a free and unrestrained economy would ultimately achieve justice rested on the false assumptions of the political economists.[37] It presupposed that *"free competition* between individuals will regulate everything, produce justice, harmony, universal well-being."[38] No greater calamity could befall a people than seriously to contemplate carrying this principle out in practice.[39] Laissez-faire liberalism presupposed an equality of conditions and powers of all the members of society. Yet only the state, to which liberalism denied any creative function, could assure that equality. Not less but better and wiser government was required.

Brownson rejected the various systems of communism and socialism on the grounds that no scheme of social reorganization could succeed which denied the basic necessity of individual property, civil law, the state and religion, and also because the two systems were inconsistent and self-contradictory. In all matters except property Owen's communism was "a system of pure individualism; in property it was the denial of all individualism. Individualism cannot co-exist with a community of property. Either individualism will triumph and dissolve the community, or the community will triumph and absorb the individual."[40]

For Brownson, individualism had become the fundamental characteristic of America, which explained its predominant ideologies and its ethical, religious, political, and economic behavior.[41] It meant the self-sufficiency which cut man loose from the ties uniting the individual with mankind and God. The result was that politics, religion, morals, and economics became dissociated from each other and were conceived solely in the light of individual reason, utility, and appetites.[42]

Brownson, like Bazard, the Saint-Simonians, de Maistre, and Bonald, considered individualism the end result of the historical development which, starting with the Reformation, destroyed all common faith and dissolved the man in the individual and humanity in society. Advocates of the modern ideas had "no conception of society as an organism—no conception of the unity of humanity as the generative principle of individuals." They lost sight of "the diversity of individual function," and tried "to compress all individuals into one, with one and the same individual, and social, function."[43] The nearer Brownson came to Catholic philosophy, the more comprehensive became his criticism of individualism and the more he saw in it the generic principle and vice of modern society. Individualism and communism were two aspects of that fall from grace, introduced by Protestantism, which had cut man loose from the creative and sustaining forces of the universe.[44]

Brownson's conversion was the last act in his protest against that individualism which meant for him the increasing loneliness of man. Saint-Simonism was for him, as for others, the bridge between the democratic radicalism of his Protestant origin and the sanctified and unified order of Catholicism. His philosophy of history showed a surprising similarity to that which Louis Blanc developed a few years later in *Histoire de la révolution française*. Yet their relation was that of two intersecting trains of thought which met and then proceeded in opposite directions. For Louis Blanc progress lay in the synthesis of the principles of individuality, equality, and fraternity. Individualism had introduced the first two, and socialism would realize the third. For Brownson, on the other hand, individualism was a cul-de-sac into which mankind strayed and from which it had to retrace its steps.

Brownson stimulated the New England intellectuals, with whom he was in close contact for many years. His opinions were rarely accepted but they could not be ignored, for they challenged the American pattern of values. His criticism illuminated the deeper meaning of the American way of life to which it gave the common denominator of "individualism." [45] His direct and positive influence was greater in Europe than in America,[46] but his original and fearless analysis of modern society deeply disturbed his contemporaries in the United States.[47]

3. WILLIAM HENRY CHANNING AND SOCIAL PERFECTIONISM

William Henry Channing was one of the New England Transcendentalists. Disciple of his uncle's Christian humanism, he also belonged to the group of associationists who propagated Fourier's schemes for the reorganization of society. His Christian socialism, though preoccupied with the social and economic ills of American society, stemmed from an optimistic faith that the hour had arrived to realize the aspirations of mankind and to approach perfection in its individuals as well as in its social organization. He participated in most of the reform movements. In women's rights, antislavery, temperance, associationism, and Swedenborgian spiritualism he found the means to express his belief that the millennium was drawing near and that each individual was called upon to change himself and to dedicate his life for the salvation of humanity.[48]

Channing believed that it was necessary to change the existing social environment and institutions. But this change could ultimately be effected only through the perfection of the individual man and through voluntary action. Industrial cooperation based on individual liberty and responsibility was the future form of social organization. A wandering minister, writer, and lecturer, he founded several papers to proclaim his gospel of Christian socialism.[49] His periodicals gave prominent space to the ideas of French socialism and of American Fourierists.[50] Channing's views were an eclectic synthesis of the French liberal version of the romantic philosophy of progress, of the Saint-Simonian concept of social harmony, of the economic criticism of Fourier, and of his own religious humanitarian evangelism.[51]

This composite outlook explained Channing's ambivalent evaluation of individualism. "The evil of evils," he wrote, was "disunited interest." *"Mankind are one,"* he asserted, "and until we admit this principle . . . we must reap the penalty of folly in prisons and batteries, in armies and polices, in rapine and murder, private and public. . . This age [must] answer the question, 'how can we have community with individuality . . . and so love our neighbors as ourselves'. . . The error of the modern doctrine of liberty, has been its tone of selfish independence; its idol has been individualism; its sin, lawlessness; it tendencies, to anarchy." [52] Yet, unlike Brownson and the Fourierists, Channing considered individualism a necessary stage through which man was liberated from the bonds of authority and his individuality developed. Now, however, the age of "composite reunion," "hierarchy and individuality," having been tried, society was ready for "collective mediation." [53]

The new society would preserve its individualistic, Protestant heritage and would consist of a multiple network of associations. The Protestantism, or rather congregationalism, of this socialism was reflected in the movement for the cooperatives and the phalansteries of the Fourierists. Individualism had drawn men out of the traditional Church, professions, and other institutions, but would now give way to sympathy, to harmony. Individualism was thus not antagonism, anarchy, or self-seeking, but the realization of the moral autonomy of the self in religion as in other activities. [54]

The influence of the religious attitude changed the connotation and evaluation of the sociological and historical concept. Individualism was related to Protestantism, not as the desertion of the collective framework of faith, but as an effort to reach the truth through the growth of maturity and spirituality. Individual liberty was not license but moral responsibility; individuality was not the development of man's natural gifts but the formation of character by the rational will. "Protestantism, or Individualism," was "the miracle worker, that . . . rejects effete material and assimilates vitalized elements, slowly organizing every filament of Humanity." [55]

In this new philosophy of history, individualism since the Reformation was the driving power of human progress toward self-determination and moral autonomy. [56] This view did not deny the Saint-Simonian correlation of Protestantism and individualism but changed its evaluation. [57] What the Saint-Simonians and the Catholic philosophers regarded as destructive and purely negative became positive and constructive. Protestant humanism thus reinterpreted history and society in the light of its own secularized values. It made out two antagonistic tendencies in historic Christianity. The Catholics believed in self-surrender, blind faith, and authority; the Protestants believed that God was present only as the ever-creative, renewing, and progressive force in the individual will, heart, and reason.[58] "The final cause of human society," stated a writer in the *Dial*, "is the unfolding of the individual man, into every form of perfection, without let or hindrance, according to the inward nature of each."[59] Brownson's criticism of Tocqueville expressed a similar view. Individualism would in the end evolve an order which existed in man himself.[60]

Such a reinterpretation of the term individualism could not be made by orthodox Protestantism; it demanded a humanistic approach which detached the moral and ethical values of Christianity from the question of dogmatic truth and transferred the scheme of salvation to the historical dimension. Only a religious movement which had fully accepted the relevance of modern science, philosophy, and history could make such a re-evaluation.

Through the concept of individualism as the essence of human progress the separatist and congregationalist religious tradition summed up the meaning of its own history and of the social patterns which it believed it had created. It thus projected the values of its heritage, transmuted by the process of enlightenment, into the past as well as into the future as a general philosophy of history, society, and man.

XII

Foundations of the American Ideal of Individualism

Individualism demanded a reinterpretation of the American ideology. Its relationship to the Jeffersonian tradition was similar to that of continental liberalism to the great French Revolution. Both reformulated the *a priori* natural-rights concepts without rejecting the achievements of the revolutionary period. In this process of selection European liberalism had a freer hand than its American counterpart. The French Revolution had destroyed itself with its radicalism; it was therefore easy to select the ideals of liberty, civil equality, and free enterprise and to reject Jacobin democracy. The principles of the American Revolution, on the other hand, had become the foundation of national existence. The range of selection and rejection was therefore extremely narrow. American liberalism could counter implications dangerous to social stability by reinterpreting democracy in such a way as to avoid the revolutionary consequences of the principle of popular sovereignty.

1. PURITANISM AND THE AMERICAN WAY OF LIFE

Attempts at such a reinterpretation were made systematically by the Federalists and their successors, the Whigs. Ever since John Adams, the center of this ideological tendency had lain in the New England leadership of these parties.[1] New England claimed to have been the fountainhead of American republicanism and to have developed first the pattern of constitutional republicanism, self-government, and ordered liberty.[2] With the rise of revolutionary democracy the intellectual leaders had more and more emphasized the unique, historical origins of the ideal of American

liberty. Their reinterpretation of republicanism had paralleled
Burke's reinterpretation of the English Whig tradition. A strong
sense of historic continuity, of the unconscious growth of social
traditions, embodying the collective wisdom of the race, and of the
all-important function of religious, moral, and juridical elements
in the development of civil and political liberty dominated this
outlook. Both emphasized the role of a historical leadership and of
social stratification and differentiation of society in maintaining
the health and stability of the body politic.[3] Yet the New Englanders were committed axiomatically to certain principles and
ideas which made the emergence of a genuine American counterpart of European conservatism impossible.

Self-government and civil liberty, constitutionalism and republicanism, were derived not from the philosophy of natural rights
but from the civil and religious traditions of the colonists.[4] The
polity of New England was the offspring of the Puritan way of
life. New England Calvinism thus developed a political philosophy
no less than a religious creed.[5] It therefore successfully resisted
the movement for the separation of church and state until far
into the nineteenth century though conceding equal civil rights
and the "free enjoyment of the rights of conscience."[6] The maintenance of established churches in Connecticut, New Hampshire,
and Massachusetts was defended on the grounds that laws for
maintaining public worship were "absolutely necessary for the
well-being of society." "As the happiness of a people," declared
the Massachusetts Constitution of 1780, "and the good order and
preservation of civil government, essentially depend upon piety,
religion and morality; . . . therefore . . . the people of this Commonwealth have a right to invest their legislature with power . . . to
make suitable provision . . . for the institution of the public
worship of God, and for the support . . . of public protestant
teachers of piety, religion and morality."[7] That constitution which
insisted on the natural rights of men and at the same time riveted
the civil government to piety, religion, morality, and "the worship
of the *Supreme Being*" was characteristic of the social philosophy
of eighteenth-century Puritanism.

Though Congregationalism in particular and Calvinism in general had insisted on the strict autonomy of the Church in order to
safeguard its integrity and purity they had not accepted the

sectarian concept of the relation of church and society but adhered to the great tradition of the Christian churches in striving to realize the rule of God over the whole society. "In New England," wrote Robert Baird, "the Congregational churches were for a long time the ecclesiastical establishment of the country, as much as the Presbyterian Church is now in Scotland. The whole economy of the civil state was arranged with reference to the welfare of these churches; for the state existed, and the country had been redeemed from the wilderness, for this very purpose." [8]

Civil society was the realm of the natural law as distinguished from that of grace and the divine law. But it was also the instrument of discipline and education through which God prepared men to follow his will. And it was more and more permeated by God's will until it would become a truly Christian society, a holy commonwealth of Christ. No commonwealth could prosper which did not subject itself to the leadership of those who served the will of God, for the evil and corrupt nature of man was unable to discipline itself without fear of Him. The attempt to make natural reason and morality self-sufficient, to deify nature, was bound to destroy the soul of man and society. Federalism found its strongest ideological weapons against Jeffersonian democracy in the Calvinistic concept of the perversity and corruption of the "natural" man. [9] Unless liberty and civil rights were maintained by a religious spirit, a republic could not survive. [10] "The profanation of the Sabbath," remarked Timothy Dwight, "profaneness of language, drunkenness, gambling, and lewdness, were exceedingly increased; and . . . a light, vain method of thinking, concerning sacred things, a cold, contemptuous indifference towards every moral and religious subject . . . a new and intimate correspondence with corrupted foreigners introduced a multiplicity of loose doctrines, which were greedily embraced by licentious men as the means of palliating and justifying their sins." [11] "When the restraints of religion are dissolved," declared the Reverend Uzal Ogden in his attack on Paine's *Age of Reason*, "what can be expected, but that men should *abandon* themselves to the impulse of their passions? Human laws and penalties will be *insufficient* to restrain men from licentiousness, where there is no just sense of the Deity; no regard to a future state, or to the due punishment of vice, and the rewards of virtue hereafter." [12]

The dissociation of the republican principles from the natural-rights philosophy and their reinterpretation in the spirit of religious conservatism and of the federalist concept of society and government were furthered by the theory of international conspiracy of the *Illuminati* which "secretly extended its branches through a great part of Europe, and even America." According to Jedidiah Morse and Timothy Dwight, religion, "in conformity to a deep laid plan," was to be overthrown by atheism and materialism, and with it all existing institutions and natural governments, so that democratic Jacobinism, leveling and lawlessness should prevail.[13] John Robinson's *Proofs of a Conspiracy against all the Religions and Governments of Europe* had utilized the old practice of discrediting a dangerous opponent through defamation of his character and morality and through proof that the logical implications of his views brought results hateful to his supporters. Deism and democratic radicalism were defamed by the accusation that they planned to overthrow all those values which society by common consent held sacrosanct. "A plan was formed, and to an alarming degree executed, for exterminating Christianity, Natural Religion, the belief of a God, of that immortality of the Soul, and of Moral obligation; for rooting out of the world civil and domestic government, the right of property, marriage, natural affection, chastity, and decency; and in a word for destroying whatever is virtuous, refined, or desirable, and introducing again universal savageness and brutism."[14] Religion was the sole defender of civilization and its institutions. Protestantism, civil liberty, and the social order were welded into one firm and indissoluble concept as the only admissible foundation of the American Republic.

Yet this concept of national identity had to absorb two elements, too powerful in their appeal to be left out of the framework of a national ideology. Calvinism had struggled with the Newtonian concept of nature and its Lockian application to epistemology, ethics, and politics ever since the beginning of the eighteenth century.[15] Jonathan Edwards had attempted to use these concepts to confirm Calvinistic determinism.[16] Yet Berkeley and Hume had proved the dangerous implications of that procedure. A new synthesis would have to integrate these ideas into a Puritan concept of life. Moreover, progress, natural law, and natural rights were interwoven in the American national consciousness to such degree that not even Calvinism could ignore them. These complex needs were met by the concepts developed by the Scottish philosophy of "common sense." Francis Hutcheson, Thomas Reid, Dugald Stewart, and James Beattie succeeded in reconciling Calvinistic Protestantism with science and progress.[17]

The Scottish philosophy "was apologetical philosophy, *par excellence*. And the secret of its success . . . lay in its dualism, epistemological, ontological, and cosmological. . . By a firm separation of the Creator and his creation, the Scottish thinkers preserved the orthodox notion of God's transcendence, and made revelation necessary. Dualism also made possible a synchronous affirmation of science . . . and an identification of the human intellect and the Divine Mind. . . Scottish philosophers could thus be monotonously consistent in their invocations of Bacon and Newton and at the same time certify those rational processes of men which lead towards natural theology and even contemplative piety and away from relativism and romantic excesses."[18] Through the Scottish method it seemed that a new theodicy could be devised and the plan of Jonathan Edwards be carried out. History could be interpreted as an "education of mankind."[19] The "invisible hand" turned private selfishness and self-interest into a public good. The Calvinistic view of the depravity of the natural man and the economy of sin in the general scheme of Providence seemed to receive scientific demonstration.[20] The observation of the English economist Cliffe Leslie, that theology was the backbone of American economic science, was literally true.[21]

Political economy had been taught in American universities until 1860 as a branch of moral philosophy mostly by ministers, and the earliest American textbooks on this subject were written by men trained as such—John McVicker, Francis Wayland, Francis Bowen, John Bascom, and William Graham Sumner.[22] Their economics was exclusively derived from their study of the moral philosophy of the Scottish common sense school. The understanding of the principles of political economy required only "common sense and a good knowledge of the English language." Its principles were simple: wealth was the fruit of industry and frugality. "Competition," was a "beneficial, permanent law of nature," and self-interest was "the mainspring of human exertion." The "self-regarding passions"—self-love and the desire for happiness—were

the ... f action.[23] Any denial of the "natural
righ ... reduced to a minimum all the motives
of p ... er's dictum that man's "goodness, his
grea ... nergy and industry—everything good
and ... a man—is connected with the idea of
indi ... xiomatic.[25] Consequently every in-
fring ... operty was irreligious. All social and
welf... legislation, state regulation of industry and commerce,
taxation of the rich, bore this stigma. Laissez faire was an axiomatic principle of Protestantism in nineteenth-century America.[26]
Arthur L. Perry regarded the free right to exchange of goods and
services and of free contract as the main natural right, "based on
nothing less than the solid will of God."[27] There was a fixed relation between godliness expressed in economic virtues and success
and between vice and poverty.

Puritan self-discipline had provided an invaluable support for
the survival of the settlers, a fact which was again and again reaffirmed by the revival movements which gave individuals the
energies necessary for the mastery of their hard life. American
life confirmed the identification of godliness with prosperity; and
economic activity led directly to those patterns of behavior which
were conducive to piety. In a universe without grace, in which
nature was radically divorced from Divine Love, selfishness had
to serve as the prime motive power in the order of secondary causes
for the maintenance of the creation and its improvement.

The Puritan Enlightenment, expressed in the Scottish common
sense philosophy, still maintained these views. Poverty, economic
competition, the Malthusian laws of population, were natural
reflections of the stern laws of predestination. Inevitable as the
corruption of man, they incited to success those who could and
would discipline themselves, while they eliminated the weak and
tamed the natural man. In this sense, property became the basis
of a natural morality and of civil government.

In his *Travels in New England and New York* Timothy Dwight
showed the civilizing power of acquisitiveness. The unruly and
shifty as well as the radical frontier settlers became sober, industrious citizens, merely by the securing of property, as "the love of
property to a certain degree seems indispensable to the existence
of sound morals. . . The secure possession of property demands,

every moment, the hedge of law; and reconciles a man, originally lawless, to the restraints of government. Thus situated, he sees that reputation, also, is within his reach. Ambition forces him to aim at it; and compels him to a life of sobriety, and decency. That his children may obtain this benefit, he is obliged to send them to school, and to unite with those around him in supporting a schoolmaster. His neighbors are disposed to build a church, and settle a Minister. A regard to his own character, to the character and feelings of his family . . . prompts him to contribute to both these objects; to attend . . . upon the public worship of God; and perhaps to become in the end a religious man." [28] Francis Wayland's *Elements of Political Economy* considered the Poor Laws contrary to the principles of good government. By removing the fear of want they destroyed the incitement for work, demoralized the pauper, and sapped independence. [29]

The synthesis of the "common sense" philosophy with Puritanism also provided a satisfactory explanation of progress. History was still the story of the progressive redemption of humanity in an eschatological framework of final purposes. Yet the post-Edwardian emphasis on the benevolence and goodness of Providence tamed history into a process for the education of mankind toward ultimate redemption from sin. Progress could be naturalistic within the framework of final purposes. "The true theory of development," wrote Philip Schaff, "is that of . . . a progressive understanding and application of Christianity, until Christ shall be all in all. The end will only be the complete unfolding of the beginning." [30]

American history could be considered within this conceptual framework as the highest stage of development, to which all the past had been contributory and preparatory. In such a scheme the concept of the nation and the Federal Republic was not limited by the natural-rights theory. The United States was a nation through the purpose of Providence. *A Century Sermon . . . the History of the Eighteenth Century,* published by Benjamin Trumbull in 1801, was "a sketch of the works of God in the century past, and especially His dispensations towards America, the United States, New England, and this town." Similarly, Jedidiah Morse's *Compendious History of New England* started with the Reformation as the direct source and cause of the settlement of New England. [31]

"All great eras of prosperity to the church," wrote Lyman Beecher, "have been aided by the civil conditions of the world. . . I consider the text [Isaiah 66.8] as a prediction of the rapid and universal extension of civil and religious liberty, introductory to the triumphs of universal Christianity." But only the United States was "blessed with such experimental knowledge of free institutions. . . There is not a nation upon earth which, in fifty years, can by all possible reformation place itself in circumstances so favorable as our own for the free and unembarrassed operation of physical effort and pecuniary and moral power to evangelize the world." [32]

Beecher revealed clearly the religious interpretation of civil institutions and the cultural interpretation of religious institutions characteristic of New England Congregationalism. The tendency of Calvinism to create "an organization of man's whole life, emotional and intellectual" underwent a metamorphosis during the nineteenth century.[33] American civilization was the pattern of a Christian life. To convert meant for the missionary to impose the New England institutions, attitudes, and manners. A historical and national tradition was thereby translated into the absolute terms of religious universalism. That trend led toward a purely secular interpretation of religious values or toward their transformation into purely moral ones, as in Unitarianism and in the whole religious development of post-Civil War America.

This attitude explained the effort to educate and civilize the West, which was to become the center of the American nation and which would "affect powerfully the cause of free institutions and the liberty of the world." The West was rushing to manhood and "as she rises in the majesty of her intelligence, and benevolence, and enterprise," would emancipate the world.[34]

The West had to be civilized to carry out America's manifest destiny. The missionary work was defined not in terms of dogma but of civilization. "The thing required . . . is universal education, and moral culture, by institutions commensurate to that result— the all-pervading influence of schools, and colleges, and seminaries, and pastors and churches." [35]

The evangelization of the West was not a purely religious matter. Without religion, liberty would become anarchy, and democracy turn into despotism. "The great experiment is now making . . . [to test] whether the perpetuity of our republican

institutions can be reconciled with universal suffrage." Without
the work of the ministry the West would destroy itself, the nation,
and the world.[36] With it the West could liberate the whole world
and transform its social and political institutions. The kingdom of
God, identified with the New England pattern of life, would be
attained by an evolutionary transition toward self-government and
holiness rather than by some cataclysmal cosmic event. "If this
work be done . . . the government of force will cease, and that of
intelligence and virtue will take its place; and nation after nation,
cheered by our example, will follow in our footsteps, till the whole
earth is free." [37] The secularization of religious values and spiritual-
ization of national, social, and political values remained a predominant trait of the New England character, which created a
rival ideology of American national identification.

This Protestant nationalism adopted peculiar racial theories.
The legitimation of the right to conquest and the theory of manifest destiny, wherever preached by Americans, accepted to a certain degree the idea of the superiority of the Anglo-American
"race" as a progressive force which would impose liberty on all
mankind. The New England concept of the nature of the American mission blended universalism and nationalism in an ideology
which accounted for its own achievements by a theory of race
and yet believed that its patterns of life could be imposed on
others. The Anglo-American race had the duty of transmitting the
pattern of life it had developed to the whole world in order to
promote pure Christianity. The expansion of the American nation
was the means by which Providence furthered the cause of religion and the spread of pure faith. Horace Bushnell's *Christian
Nurture* (1847) expressed this idea. "Any people that is physio-
logically advanced . . . is sure to live down and finally live out its
inferior. Nothing can save the inferior race but a ready and pliant
assimilation. . . What if it should be God's plan to people the
world with better and finer material? Certain it is . . . that there
is a tremendous overbearing surge of power in the Christian
nations, which . . . will inevitably submerge and bury . . . [the
less capable] forever." [38]

Philip Schaff, "a Swiss by birth, a German by education, and
an American by choice," pointed out: "The Anglo-Saxon and
Anglo-American, of all modern races, possess the strongest nation-

al character and the one best fitted for universal dominion, and that, too, not a dominion of despotism but one, which makes its subjects free citizens. . . In them . . . the impulse towards freedom and the sense of law and order are inseparably united, and both rest on a moral basis." [39] Schaff related the Protestant character of the Anglo-Americans to their racial instincts for liberty and truthfulness. [40] America was *the grave of all European nationalities; but a Phenix grave,* from which they shall rise to a new life and new activity." [41] This pattern of thought was fully developed only after the Civil War under the impact of Spencerian Darwinism, of a fully fledged theory of individualism, and in the wake of increasing secularization. [42]

Before the Civil War a religious orientation and political conservatism impeded a purely historical interpretation of Congregational Protestantism in terms of an ideology of individualism. Believers in an established order and a morality based on the absolute authority of revealed religion regarded individualism with mixed feelings. The attitude of the theologian John Williamson Nevin was typical. [43] He and Schaff had already felt the influence of the German historical school. [44] American republican institutions were the offspring of Puritanism. [45] It was "the great work and the divine mission of Protestantism, to place each individual soul in immediate union with Christ and his Word; to complete in each one the work of redemption, to build in each one a temple of God, a spiritual church; and to unfold and sanctify all the energies of the individual." [46] It was this principle of individuality which all the institutions of the American Republic expressed.

For Schaff and others like him all history was the great unfolding of the span of universal Redemption. "The history of the world is only the vestibule to the history of the church. . . All political events and revolutions, all discoveries and inventions, all advances in arts and sciences; in fine, all that belongs to the kingdom of the Father . . . must serve the Son . . . until the whole world is filled with his glory, and all nations walk in the light of eternal truth and love." [47] America was the future of the human race and the heir of all past ages. It liberated Christianity from medieval institutions and from the authority of the state and introduced universal liberty. "There the idea is, to actualize the genuine

Protestant principle of a congregation, independent and yet bound
to an organic whole . . . and to make each Christian a priest and a
king in the service of the universal . . . King of Kings." [48] The
dignity of the redeemed individual, of his true liberty and equality,
through his subservience to the moral law and the law of God, was
reflected in the social and political institutions of the Republic.
"With the American, freedom is . . . a rational, moral self-determination, hand in hand with law, order and authority. . . He alone
is worthy of this great blessing and capable of enjoying it, who
holds his passions in check . . . from inward impulse. . . But the
negative and hollow liberalism, or rather the radicalism, which
undermines the authority of law and sets itself against Christianity
and the church, necessarily dissolves all social ties, and ends in
anarchy; which then passes very easily into the worst and most
dangerous form of despotism." [49]

Philip Schaff then differentiated between that individuality
which was the essence of the Protestant spirit and that which was
purely negative and based on a valueless and lawless rationalism,
destructive of all true freedom and human dignity. Like Tocqueville, he criticized the latter as "selfish isolation, endless division,
confusion and licentiousness." [50]

The ambiguous attitude of New England Calvinism stemmed
from the implication of its dogmatic attitudes toward religion and
society. Only a religious movement which had fully accepted the
relevance of modern science, philosophy, and history for its own
religious concepts could accept the mature humanism implied in a
philosophy of individualism. This was the case with the Unitarian movement as expressed by William Ellery Channing and
his circle.

2. THE UNITARIAN IMPULSE AND THE RISE OF A PURITAN HUMANISM

The Unitarian movement felt no need to adjust itself to the
changing climate of ideas and attitudes that followed upon the
Enlightenment and the American Revolution. Its rejection of Calvinism and its cautious belief in the power of reason and man's
capacity for self-improvement and perfectibility destined it to
become the major interpreter of the American experience and to

integrate the optimism of the age of reason with the moralistic and Puritan tradition of New England.

Unitarianism was itself a product of that growing urbanity, self-confidence, and enlightenment which characterized the religious outlook of the wealthy and educated classes of New England's coastal towns, and especially of Boston.[51] Suspicious also of the religious enthusiasm and "vulgarity" of evangelical revivalism and of the harsh doctrinaire attitude of Calvinism, it developed more as a cultural attitude and as a religious temper than as a new dogmatic movement. The enlightened Arminianism and universalism of Ebenezer Gay and of Charles Chauncy, and even the cautious rejection of the doctrine of original sin and atonement of Jonathan Mayhew, with its emphasis on free will and the role of reason and morality, continued the Erasmanian tradition in the Age of Enlightenment. The secession from the Episcopal Church of King's Chapel, under the leadership of James Freeman, the adoption of the Unitarian liturgy compiled by the English Dissenter Samuel Clarke, and the appointment of the Unitarian Dr. Henry Ware as Hollis professor at Harvard illustrated the pervasiveness of this intellectual attitude.[52] The Unitarianism of Freeman, like that of his classmate William Bentley, pastor of the East Church in Salem, was motivated by an ethical and moralistic humanism. They judged the truth and value of the Trinitarian dogma and of Calvinism by its ethical and moral implication. Humanity was more important to them than Divinity.[53]

Unitarianism was a defense of free will and reason as indispensable conditions of moral responsibility and as the basis of the dignity of man. For Freeman, Christianity meant education to moral perfection through the belief in the saving and redeeming power of the life and teaching of Jesus, which exemplified the love of God. "The way, by which men enter into this everlasting life, is not by believing in a mediator . . . but by keeping the commandments." Christianity "has raised the character of human nature higher, than it ever was before; it has refined and ennobled men, and made them kings and priests unto God." [54]

The Unitarian movement introduced Christian humanism as it had been defined in the Renaissance by the Neoplatonism of

Marsilio Ficino and Pico della Mirandola, by Erasmus and Thomas
More, to the American scene.[55] Opposed equally to the naturalism
of the French Enlightenment and the absolutism of the Calvinistic dogma, it was pragmatic in its attitude to religion, rejecting
those elements which seemed to obstruct rather than to develop
the mental and moral powers of man.[56] The Greek and Roman
cultures, with their ideals of civic virtue and their faith in the
autonomy of morality and reason, gained a new significance. They
were a promise of the capacity of man to live in rational liberty
and to achieve greatness through the cultivation of his capacities
and his moral faculties. "However numerous our doctrines,
whether simple or mysterious; whether we receive all the dogmas
of the Church or not, let us consider that we should produce good
fruits. . . When a man is found, who does not profess much, nor
despise all, who is pure from guile, peaceable in his life, gentle
in his manners, easily dissuaded from revenge, with an heart to
pity and relieve the miserable, impartial in his judgement, and
without dissimulation, this is the man of religion." [57]

This humanism appealed particularly to the respectable,
wealthy, enlightened, and erudite citizens of Boston and its neigh-
borhood. It rejected the static concept of a natural morality of
man, with its corollaries of equality of rights and its negative
definition of liberty. Virtue and reasonableness were the result of
hard training in self-discipline, of an arduous desire for truth and
knowledge. This point of view justified the Calvinist concept of
the sinfulness and brutishness of man. Without the guidance of
the revealed truth of Divine Providence, humanity would be
unable to master itself or to educate itself toward a rational life.

Here was the great dividing line between deism and Unitarianism. Maintaining the theistic concept of the transcendence of
God and of his immediate relationship to mankind as lawgiver,
guide, redeemer, and judge, revealed in the Scriptures, the Unitarians continued the pattern of a positive morality and character
training of the Puritan orientation. Yet their anti-Trinitarian attitude with its rejection of the theory of atonement swept away the
whole structure of Calvinism. Godliness was a process of growth
and education working through history as well as through the
mind and heart of the individual. An opening was made for a truly
evolutionary concept of history and man. Appealing to reason as

the ultimate judge in the true interpretation of revealed religion, and to man's innate morality as the foundation of his possibility to grow in holiness, early Unitarianism was a halfway house which accommodated both the age of reason and the Puritan skepticism of human nature.

That attitude suited perfectly the cultured elite of New England. Unitarianism supported New England's suspicion of the masses, stressed the necessity of the leadership of the enlightened, and stabilized society by its insistence on the validity of the traditional values of Puritanism. Accepting the Scottish common sense philosophy as a valid compromise between religion and science, the Unitarians were at the same time far less restricted than the Calvinists in the application of its principles to all fields of knowledge.[58] The application of the concept of historic growth and of the natural evolution of societies explained their own relation to the heritage of Christianity and accounted for the principles of the American Republic.[59]

A philosophy of progress made clear the reasons for the diversity of historical phenomena as well as for the continuous growth of civilization. The growth of rational liberty, of self-government, and of a humane morality were the main trends of progress. History was the slow education of mankind toward liberty and moral government. The efforts of John Adams to trace the origins of the Republic in New England institutions already revealed a true historical spirit.[60] Progress in his view was neither inevitable nor imposed but proceeded by natural and historical causes, developing slowly the capacities of mankind in accordance with the spirit of the nation.[61]

Unitarianism immensely encouraged the growth of a historical consciousness and of historical studies in New England.[62] The accumulated heritage of intellectual training, the unique reverence for scholarship, the power of spiritual self-discipline and inquisitiveness, liberated by the secularization of thought from its preoccupation with theology, suddenly flowered into humanistic, historical, philosophical, and artistic creativity. National pride and the consciousness of the cultural independence further stimulated this outlook. Its conceptual framework of history was to a great degree influenced by the views of the great French and English writers of the eighteenth century—Voltaire, Montesquieu,

Bolingbroke, Hume, William Robertson, Adam Ferguson, and Edward Gibbon. Its approach was largely pragmatic and rationalistic; yet the intense nationalistic consciousness and the rejection of the doctrinaire spirit of the natural-law philosophy were expressed increasingly in a true historical spirit.

The New England historians traced the slow growth of liberty and self-government from their origins in Europe to the emergence of the Republic. They stressed the institutional character of American liberty and its foundation in English laws and tradition. They emphasized the equalitarian pattern of property distribution in colonial times and the close association between political responsibility and the universal distribution of landed property. "Though the motives and views of those who settled in the different colonies, were different," wrote the New England historian Timothy Pitkin, "their situation in their new places of abode, being, in many respects similar, naturally produced in all an energy of character, and a spirit of independence, unknown in the great mass of the people they had left in Europe. . . Every man was a freeholder, and his freehold was at his own disposal. . . This independent condition of the colonists . . . combined with that equality which existed among them, arising from an equal distribution of property, a general diffusion of knowledge, and a share which all had in the government, naturally produced a love of liberty, an independence of character, and a jealousy of power, which ultimately led, under divine Providence, to that revolution, which placed them amongst the nations of the earth." [63]

The increasing reliance on historical research and documentary evidence was exemplified in the work of the historians Abiel Holmes, Timothy Pitkin, and, most of all, of Jared Sparks. The idea of growth and evolution, of the organic character of historical change, and of the continuity of tradition, deeply ingrained in New England Federalism and its Whig philosophy, was appropriate to the historical method. Jared Sparks explained: "The more we look into the history of the colonies, the more clearly we shall see that the Revolution was not the work of a few years only, but began with the first settlement of the country; the seeds of liberty, when first planted here, were the seeds of the Revolution; they sprang forth by degrees; they came to maturity gradually; and when the great crisis took place, the whole nation were prepared to govern themselves, because they always had in reality governed themselves." [64]

To Tocqueville, Jared Sparks clearly defined this New England interpretation of American history: "I believe that our origin is the fact which best explains our government and our ways. We came here republicans and religious enthusiasts. We found ourselves abandoned to our own devices, forgotten in this corner of the world. . . Our fathers . . . founded the *town* before the *state*. . . They only united together later on, and by a voluntary act. You perceive what power such a starting point must have given to the *esprit communal* which so eminently distinguished us even among Americans and in the midst of republican principles." [65] According to Senator Francis Gray of Massachusetts, the spirit of local self-government made the republic possible. It prepared a government by persuasion rather than force and the accepted rules of majorities. "It's that habit which distinguishes New England, not only from all the countries of Europe, but even from all the other parts of America. . . We have been working for 200 years to form this spirit, and we had as a starting point the English spirit and an altogether republican religion." [66]

Josiah Quincy asserted to Tocqueville: "Massachusetts was nearly as free before the revolution as to-day. We have put the name of the people where was the name of the king; otherwise nothing has changed with us." [67] This idea was in accord with the German concept of nationality which Francis Lieber, the editor of the *Encyclopedia Americana,* had brought with him to America. He considered the principles of American republicanism expressions of the national genius of the American people, not transplantable because rooted in the mores. Thus, the New England interpretation of the nature of American nationality was close to the German concept of *Volksgeist* and the organic theory of Savigny. [68] With the deepening of a humanistic outlook and the steady enlargement of its horizon, the New England elite became steadily more susceptible to the currents of contemporary European romantic thought. For reasons similar to those which motivated French liberals, an increasing number of New England intellectuals became interested in German scholarship and philosophy, as a means of developing the consciousness of their own national personality. [69] German historiography, history, literature, and philosophy were increasingly studied in cosmopolitan Boston. John Quincy Adams, Minister Plenipotentiary to Prussia, had translated Friedrich Gentz's *The French and American Revolutions Compared;* and William Bentley, a well-known Unitarian minister in Salem, introduced C. D. Ebeling, the outstanding student of American geography and history, to the literary circle of New England.[70]

Madame de Staël's *Influence of Literature upon Society* was published in Boston in 1813, and her famous *De L'Allemagne* was reprinted from an English translation in New York in 1814.[71] In 1815 George Ticknor and Edward Everett left for Germany to acquire the true method of scholarship and erudition in German universities. Joseph Cogswell, later to become professor and librarian at Harvard College, followed in 1816. George Bancroft left for Göttingen in 1819 together with Frederick Henry Hedge. These men opened the rich world of European—and particularly German—thought to the American public. The *North American Review,* founded in 1815 by William Tudor, became the main instrument for spreading these ideas in the United States.[72] Charles Follen and Charles Beck brought with them a deeper knowledge of German idealism.[73] Yet even earlier, James Marsh had been led to German idealism by Samuel Coleridge's *Biographia Literaria,* and had "promptly set out on a career of instructing Americans on the subject of German religious and philosophical progress."[74] Marsh's election to the presidency of the University of Vermont in 1826 marked the beginning of the Vermont school of transcendentalism, which spread to Concord, Boston, and St. Louis.[75] Coleridge's *Aids to Reflection* was published in 1829, and Victor Cousin's *Introduction to the History of Philosophy,* which introduced Herder, Kant, Fichte, and Schelling, appeared in an English translation in Boston in 1832. By 1840 German thought in one way or other had penetrated most fields of studies and aided in the crystallization of a new humanistic outlook in America.[76]

Germany provided alternatives to the theories of history, nationality, state, and society of the Age of Enlightenment, the rationalistic and scientific impulses of which it reinterpreted in the spirit of romantic idealism and historical conservatism.[77] Yet more important was the service German idealism rendered those who held fast to the concept of man as a spiritual being, by denying the application of the methodology and outlook of the natural sciences to the human world.

German idealism offered some New Englanders a way of escaping traditionalism in philosophy and morality, and eclectic rationalism in the field of knowledge. The new influence divided the younger from the older generation of Unitarians. Unitarianism, until then, remarked Octavius Brooks Frothingham, had "rarely, if ever, been taught . . . by . . . a Platonist. . . The Unitarian in religion was a whig in politics, a conservative in literature, art and social ethics." [78] The Unitarians had belonged to the school of Locke, which discarded the doctrine of innate ideas and its kindred beliefs. Now, German idealism and the Scottish philosophy of the moral sense supported each other in a common protest against Locke's naturalism and Hume's skepticism. It was thus that William Ellery Channing liberated himself from the epistemology of Locke and the dry rationalism of the Scotch common-sense school. [79]

3. ON THE PERFECTION OF THE SOUL

German idealism set freedom and the dignity of man in a framework of philosophy which accounted for science, for the belief in God, and for the self-determination of the human soul. The *Entfremdung*—the alienation of man from nature and God—was ended. Progress became the law of the universe, and history was the growth of liberty toward the brotherhood of man.

Lessing, Herder, Kant, and Wilhelm von Humboldt all believed that the universal emancipation of men from force, fear, inequality, and ignorance and the revelation of his true nature were the aims of the historical process. [80] Humboldt's ideal resembled in an astonishing degree that of the Jeffersonian tradition: "The true end of man" was "the highest and most harmonious development of his powers to a complete and whole existence," for which freedom was the indispensable condition. But there was also another essential—"a variety of situations," or diversity. Each human being, according to Humboldt, could act with only one force at a time. But the mutual cooperation of its members in society enabled each "to participate in the rich collective resources of all the others." Freedom of action, and diversity, stimulated and were stimulated by individuality. Therefore "*reason cannot desire for man any other condition than that in which each individual not only enjoys the most absolute freedom of developing himself by his own energies, in his perfect individuality, but in which external nature even is left unfashioned by any human agency, but only receives the impress given to it by each individual of himself and his own free will, according to the measure of his wants and instincts, and restricted only by the limits of his powers and his rights. . .* It must therefore be the basis of every political system, and must especially constitute the starting point of *the inquiry which at present claims attention.*" [81]

Humboldt's ideal resembled Jefferson's. Yet there was one basic difference between them. Humboldt's demand for the absorption of the state in a free society was not based on a contractual theory of personal rights but on the belief that the full expression of individuality was the end of all human existence. Such a philosophy had radical equalitarian implications and it penetrated the various modes of socialism in Germany, France, Italy, and Russia.[82]

The impact of Idealism on the concept of history and on formal philosophy was also profound. Fichte's scheme of historical development revealed the radical implications of German Idealism.[83] Kant seemed to legitimize the slogans of the French Revolution. The *Critique of Pure Reason,* wrote Heine, began "an intellectual revolution, which offers the most wonderful analogies to the material revolution in France." [84]

German Idealism was also the instrument through which the New England intellectual, reared in the Whig tradition and in the atmosphere of Protestantism, broke through to an affirmation of democracy and disengaged his religious concept of the dignity of man from that of Puritanism. This philosophy vindicated the spiritual nature of the soul and the existence of God in a purposive universe. It did not support the dogma of a church but rather reinterpreted Christianity in the light of history and of the idea of progress in order to rescue its ethics and its concept of the spiritual destiny of man. Having discarded the Trinitarian doctrine, Idealism could speak for all denominations on the broad grounds of its own faith in the greatness of the soul.

For this reason its influence spread in America, particularly among Unitarians who were groping for a religion of humanity outside the established sects. They, too, seeking to legitimize natural human reason, enlightened morality and liberty, relied on a theory of human progress through history. The question between the Protestants and the Unitarians, said Channing, was "whether the 17th century can return, or whether it is past without return. They opened the road, and have the pretension to stop precisely at the point where the first innovator himself stopped. We, we claim to go ahead, we maintain that if human reason is steadily perfecting itself, what it believed in a century still gross and corrupted cannot altogether suit the enlightened century in which we live." [85]

For most foreign observers and for many Americans the new Unitarianism, as preached by Channing, was the true religion of American democracy.[86] Miss Martineau, Frederick Marryat, Charles Dickens, and Basil Hall, no less than Beaumont and Tocqueville, believed that Channing was the true representative of American religious thought.[87] This was also the opinion of Thomas Jefferson, who had hoped that Unitarianism would unite the Americans in a common belief suitable to the spirit of self-government.[88]

Yet Beaumont and Tocqueville were wrong when they doubted the truly religious nature of Unitarianism, which they compared with Saint-Simonism.[89] Channing's Unitarianism was deeply religious and stemmed from a spiritual confrontation of the problems of his times. The intensity of his religious feelings was nearer to the attitudes of evangelism than to those of the other Boston Unitarians who preached to the well-to-do.[90] "The Unitarians of New England, good scholars, careful reasoners, clear and exact thinkers, accomplished men of letters, humane in sentiment, sincere in moral intentions, belonged . . . to the class which looked without for knowledge, rather than within for inspiration." [91]

On the other hand, Channing moved away from the historical doctrines of Christianity and proclaimed the gospel of the inner light, striving toward the "universal church of all good and holy men." [92] In doing so he was motivated by recognition of the latent divine spark in the soul of all men.

Here was a new kind of evangelism, seeking to liberate man's soul from darkness by recovering the hidden God in each. "I believe that Christianity has ONE GREAT PRINCIPLE . . . the doctrine, that 'God purposes, in His unbounded Fatherly Love, to PERFECT

THE HUMAN SOUL; to purify it from all sin; to create it after His own image; to fill it with His own spirit; to unfold it for ever; to raise it to Life and Immortality in Heaven;—that is, to communicate to it from Himself a Life of Celestial Power, Virtue and Joy. . . I do not mean to claim for Christianity the exclusive honour of discovering to us God's purpose of perfecting the human soul. The Soul itself—in its powers and affections, in its unquenchable thirst and aspiration for unattained good—gives signs of a Nature made for an interminable progress, such as cannot be now conceived. When, too, I contemplate the immensity and wonderful order of the Material Creation, and the beautiful structure of its minutest parts, I feel sure that Mind, the yet nobler work of God, must be destined to a more enlarged and harmonious existence than I now experience or behold." [93]

Channing's credo differed both from conservative Unitarianism and German idealism. While the conservative Unitarians held fast to the supernatural as evidence of the truth, he based his belief on the indwelling reality of the spirit of man. [94] There could be no metaphysical certainty, according to Andrews Norton, "of the facts on which religion" was founded except that derived from the Christian revelation. [95] The older Unitarianism refused to make the leap from authority to the belief in moral perfection and spiritual freedom. [96] The perfection of man was strictly confined to the religious and moral spheres as prescribed by Revelation and interpreted by logic and a Lockian reasonableness. Religion and life were separate.

How far Unitarianism would move under Channing's influence from its former position was revealed years later in the declaration of principles of the Western Unitarian Conference. "The general faith is hinted . . . in such words as these: 'Unitarianism is a religion of love to God and love to man.' It is that free and progressive development of historic Christianity which aspires to be synonymous with universal ethics and universal religion. . . We believe in the growing nobility of man. We trust the unfolding universe as beautiful, beneficent, unchanging Order; to know this order is truth; to obey it is right and liberty and stronger life." [97]

This concept of a universal ethic and universal religion, which had been mediated by Channing and the transcendental movement, constituted the difference between the American religion of humanity and German idealism. The latter either supplanted the traditional religious beliefs or, leaving them undisturbed, reinterpreted them philosophically. American idealism maintained fully the Puritan religious impulse to express itself in action and to translate its message into a pattern of life.[98] Never discarding theistic religion, as the Germans did, Americans made idealism an instrument for changing reality. Their faith in the dignity and unity of mankind transformed the philosophy of democracy. The affirmation of the rights of man, of liberty, equality, and self-government now rested on the capacity of the individual soul for spiritual growth and perfectibility. The creative power of God dwelled only in the individual, and social and historical change could be achieved only through his perfection. "The dignity of a human being . . . consists, first, in that spiritual principle, called sometimes the Reason, sometimes the Conscience, which rising above what is local and temporary, discerns immutable truth and everlasting right. . . This principle is a rare Divinity in man. . . He is a Free being; created to act from a spring in his own breast; to form himself, and to decide his own destiny; connected intimately with nature, but not enslaved to it; connected still more strongly with God, yet not even enslaved to the Divinity." [99]

The religious foundation of the concept of democracy as the realization of the spiritual destiny of man made suspect all external power over man. All social organization was subservient to the perfection of the soul. "Society is chiefly important as it ministers to, and calls forth, intellectual and moral energy and freedom. Its action on the individual is beneficial in proportion as it awakens in him a power to act on himself, and to control or withstand the social influences to which he is at first subjected. . . Inward creative energy is the highest good which accrues to us from our social principles and connections. . . Our social nature and connections are means. Inward power is the end; a power which is to triumph over and control the influence of society." [100]

Channing opposed the imposition of an organization and a creed on the Unitarian movement, always conceiving it as a free and voluntary association of individuals.[101] Democracy, too, was such an association. The American Republic made man, formed in the likeness of God, the end of its institutions. "In Europe political and artificial distinctions have . . . triumphed over and obscured our common nature. In Europe we meet kings, nobles, priests, peasants. How much rarer it is to meet *men;* by which we mean human beings conscious of their own nature, and conscious of the utter worthlessness of all outward distinctions compared with what is treasured in their own souls. . . Our position favors a juster and profounder estimate of human nature. . . The essential equality of all human beings, founded on the possession of a spiritual, progressive, immortal nature, is, we hope, better understood; and nothing more than this single conviction is needed to work the mightiest changes in every province of human life and of human thought." [102]

All political institutions were to be judged by the criterion of the growth of the individual soul and its right to self-expression and self-determination. Liberty itself was valuable only to further dignity and moral self-determination. "The only freedom worth possessing is that which gives enlargement to a people's energy, intellect, and virtues. . . Progress, the growth of power, is the end and boon of liberty; and, without this, a people may have the name but want the substance and spirit of freedom." [103]

A society is improved in proportion as individuals judge for themselves, and from their own experience and feeling, and not according to general opinion. . . A society is well organized, whose government recognizes the claims and rights of *all* . . . and aims to direct the pursuits of *each to the general good.* . . Liberty is the great social good,—exemption from unjust restraints,—freedom to act, to exert powers of usefulness. Does a government advance this simply by establishing equal *laws?* The very protection of property may crush a large mass of the community, may give the rich a monopoly in land, may take from the poor all means of action. Liberty is a blessing only by setting man's powers at large, exciting, quickening them. A poor man, in the present state of society, may be a slave, by his entire dependence. [104]

The idea of the infinite worth of the human soul, of the dignity of the individual man, capable of spiritual growth through self-perfection, became for the radical Unitarians the central doctrine of American democracy and the idea of the American nation. Through this concept the universalism which was inherent in the American Jeffersonian ideology and which was resisted by New Englanders of Federalist and Whig orientation was reborn in the form of a romantic, idealistic interpretation of the Christian view of the nature of man. It is in this idea of the infinite worth of the human soul, its perfectibility, and the expectation that the kingdom of God on earth can be realized, that the radical Unitarian movement of Channing and his disciples met halfway the perfectionism of the evangelical movement which gained in strength during the same period.

4. THE KINGDOM OF GOD IN AMERICA: A RELIGIOUS AND A SECULARIZED VERSION

The Messianic and millennial impulse, the idea of the kingdom of God in the United States, blended in the evangelical movement with pride in political liberty and the greatness of the country's future, to become a powerful concept of American nationality.[105] Lyman Beecher's *Plea for the West* was characteristic of this sense of mission and the religious interpretation of American history. The state of society predicted by the Gospels could not appear under an arbitrary despotism or under feudal institutions and usages. Revolutions and distress among the nations would precede the introduction of the peaceful reign of Jesus Christ on earth. Every sign pointed to the fact that "the millenium would commence in America." None could "place itself in circumstances so favorable as our own for the free unembarrassed application of physical effort and pecuniary and moral power to evangelize the world."[106] This sense of mission was universalistic, as the revolutionary concept of the American nation had been. Yet its frame of reference was religious and moral, and this fact shaped its interpretation of the achievement and prospects of the American Republic.[107] The American Revolution could, in this context, be described as a majestic religious revival which had "the astounding fortune to succeed."[108]

The "godlessness" of the French Revolution and the demoralizing effects of frontier life had rallied the Protestant clergy to reconquer the nation for Christian life and discipline.[109] But revivalism itself strengthened rather than weakened the democratic outlook, attitudes, and convictions of the masses.[110] "The Methodist Church and her adherents were Republicans," wrote Orestes Brownson, the saddlebag preacher. "Every convert to Methodism, in those times . . . became a Republican if he was not one before."[111] Frontier preachers "brought home to the pioneers the fact that they were masters of their own destiny, an emphasis that fitted in exactly with the new democracy rising in the West, for both emphasized the actual equality of men."[112] In the great evangelical upsurge the patterns of pietism and congregationalism were fused into a new form of Christian voluntaristic society.

The pietistic outlook made religion emotional and personal, emphasizing sanctification and perfection through the individual's life and works and treating the church as a voluntary union of believers. The emphasis upon practice and experience and the rejection of dogma tended toward universalism. The revival appealed to all men and held out salvation to all. "From the Awakening the principles of religious individualism and religious voluntarism became ever more solidly entrenched in the American scheme of things, and the transference of these principles to the political order was the inevitable concomitant."[113] The frontier environment and the revolutionary ideology of equality and self-government fitted perfectly into the evolving religious pattern. "The revivalists placed stress on the doctrine that all men are equal in the sight of God. When this doctrine is preached to humble people, it inevitably develops self-respect and a desire to have a part in the management of their own affairs."[114] The result was a growing consciousness of a national religious destiny.

The influence of the Baptists, Methodists, Disciples, and Cumberland Presbyterians corroded the Calvinist concepts of grace, election, predestination, and total depravity,[115] because American society as a whole was also subject to the impact of rationalistic and equalitarian concepts of the nature of society and government. "The Revolution was again and again presented as having been itself a majestic revival," because revivalism had accommodated itself to Jeffersonian ideas.[116] The ascendancy of the Republican party began exactly when the "Second Great Awakening" did; and the strength of Jacksonian democracy grew through the period of increasing revivalism.

The correspondence of the spiritual message of the revival movement with the secular message of Jeffersonian ideology explained the interpenetration of Christian evangelism and democracy. The concept of political and social equality fitted perfectly well that of the equality of true believers; the concept of the free society fitted that of voluntary church membership; and the concept of inalienable natural rights was derived from the religious view of the relation of man to the Creator.[117]

Self-government based on universal citizenship was feasible to the degree that people were guided by Christian ethics. The

French Revolution seemed to have proved that democracy could not endure unless secured firmly in religious morality. The challenge of liberty was, then, one of the motive forces for the immense effort of the Protestant clergy to "Christianize" the people through the reform impulse and religious perfectionism.[118]

The revival movement, however, was too pietistic and personal to evolve a political and social philosophy of its own. It generally reduced social to moral questions and was instrumental in reform only where the former could be explained in terms of the latter, as in abolition and temperance. The fact that revivalism in the first half of the nineteenth century was almost purely a rural phenomenon strengthened that tendency. American farmers, swayed by the Jeffersonian image of them as the "chosen people," received the economic, social, and political relations of society in simple moral terms acceptable to the religious and democratic mentality.[119] And indeed religious sentiment, expressed in moral self-discipline, created those virtues with which economic security and success could be achieved. Prosperity followed godliness as surely as vice created poverty.

Yet the assumptions of evangelical revivalism could not be defined in terms of the social concept of individualism. Revivalism lacked a humanistic and historical concept of man and society. Nor did it examine critically its own values, norms, and culture. Like the Jeffersonian ideology, it created attitudes which would later be understood in terms of individualism.[120] But the concept of individualism could be developed only by men who had cut themselves loose from the dogmatic creed of Christianity and reinterpreted its meaning in the spirit of humanism. This was the achievement of Channing and his circle.

For Channing, Christianity had discovered the immanence of the divine spark in the soul.[121] It had founded the worth of human nature on this metaphysical relation to the infinite and had traced the brotherhood of men to their common relationship to God. Channing's gospel of "the greatness of the soul, its divinity, its union with God by spiritual likeness, its receptivity of his spirit, to self-forming power, its destination to ineffable glory," could be easily detached by the transcendentalists from its Christian context.[122] His concept of American nationality and of its destiny in the scheme of history was broad enough to absorb the Jeffersonian ideology, the ideas of Rousseau, Condorcet, and Godwin, as well as German Idealism, in order to reformulate the faith in the universal character of its mission. America was destined to frame new social institutions, to release new human powers, to reap a new spiritual harvest, as a result of which man would rise to his full stature.[123] For the Unitarian minister Edwin H. Chapin, in 1861, the American mission was "to carry out the great ideas of a new dispensation, to elevate and improve the individual, to establish on the highest degree of the scale of human progress the standard of national greatness."[124]

The same idealistic reinterpretation of American democracy dominated the concept of history. Individuality, liberty, and self-government were the main vehicles in the progress toward perfection. Channing explained: "We were made to grow. Our faculties are germs, and given for an expansion to which nothing authorises us to set bounds. . . I no longer see aught to prevent our becoming whatever was good and great in Jesus on earth. . . Add but that element, eternity, to man's progress, and the results of his existence surpass not only human but angelic thought."[125]

History was the growing perfection of humanity toward the image of God living in its spirit.[126] "We delight to believe that God, in the fulness of time, has brought a new continent to light, in order that the human mind should move here with a new freedom, should frame new social institutions, should explore new paths, and reap new harvests."[127] Bancroft expressed the general philosophy: "In the fulness of time a republic rose up in the wilderness of America. Thousands of years had passed away before the child of the ages could be born. From whatever there was good in the systems of former centuries she drew her nourishment; the wrecks of the past were her warnings. . . The fame of this only daughter of freedom went out into all lands of the earth; from her the human race drew new hope."[128] The significance of America for mankind lay in the realization that "first in the history of mankind [it had] established mutual freedom by mutual acknowledgement of individual equality."[129]

History was the self-realization of the spiritual and the universal. The rights of man and democracy were the political expressions of religious and philosophical truth. They aimed at the vindication of the greatness of man in each individual.[130] "Democracy," wrote Henry James, is not so much a new form of political life, as a dissolution or disorganization of old forms. . . Democracy everywhere proclaims the superiority of man to institutions, allowing the latter no respect, however consecrated by past worth, save in so far as they also reflect the present interests of humanity. . . I look upon Democracy as heralding the moral perfection of man, as inaugurating the existence of perfectly just relations between man and man, and as consequently preparing the way for the reign of infinite Love.[131]

Democracy thus meant the equality of individual rights to self-development, and the Declaration of Independence could be traced through the Reformation back to the founder of Christianity in direct continuity. All were steps toward the realization, in the spiritual as in the political spheres, of the truth that man "should be left to the individual action of his own will and conscience." [132]

The term "Western civilization" was used as early as 1843 to characterize institutions which had risen on the foundations of the Roman Empire. "For fifteen hundred years, Western Civilization, with the luster of Christianity superadded, has been struggling to perfection, an ideal perfection of its own," an article in *The Dial* noted. The Magna Charta, the Bill of Rights, trial by jury, parliamentary government, democracy, separation of church and state, universal suffrage and education, progress on technique and science were the stages through which Western civilization reached toward the ideal of a society of free individuals.[133]

The reinterpretation of American democracy and republicanism through the concept of individuality created a new type of national identification in the North which was even more universalistic and more inimical to an organic concept of the nation and the state than the older Jeffersonian concept of the free society, and was no less dynamic and radical in its application to existing institutions. This moralistic humanism motivated the movement for universal reform. Abolition, education, temperance, women's rights, the elevation of the working classes, experiments in the reorganization of society and the foundation of communities, were all the legitimate offspring of radical Unitarian and transcendentalist perfectionism.[134] This perfectionism and that of the later developments of evangelical Protestantism, as exemplified by the revivalist Charles G. Finney, merged in the reform movement. Brook Farm, Bronson Alcott's Fruitlands, and even Thoreau's Walden, were no less Utopian than John Humphrey Noyes's

Oneida Community.[135] In both ideological streams, which eventually coalesced in the abolition movement, the idea of America as the kingdom of God, as the realization of absolutely valid ethical, spiritual, and social values, was predominant. Such ideals of national identification were incompatible with the acknowledgment of historically formed rights and the sovereignty of a state based on popular consent.

"I have subscribed my name to an instrument similar to the Declaration of '76, renouncing all allegiance to the government of the United States and asserting the title of Jesus Christ to the throne of the world," wrote Noyes to the abolitionist, William Lloyd Garrison, in 1837. "The Son of God has manifestly, to me, chosen this country for the theatre of such an assault—a country which, by its boasting hypocrisy, has become the laughing-stock of the world, and by its lawlessness has fully proved the incapacity of man for self-government. . . Allow me to suggest that you will set Anti-slavery in the sunshine only by making it tributary to Holiness." [136] In the same spirit Garrison burned the Constitution as "a covenant with death and an agreement with hell." [137] "Human governments" were the result of disobedience to the requirements of heaven. "Shall we, as *Christians*, applaud and do homage to human government? or shall we not rather lay the axe at the root of the tree, and attempt to destroy both cause and effect together?" [138]

"How does it become a man to behave towards this American Government today?" asked Henry Thoreau. "I answer, that he cannot without disgrace be associated with it. I cannot for an instant recognize that political organization as *my* government which is the *slave's* government also. . . If the law is of such a nature that it requires you to be an agent of injustice to another, then I say, break the law. Let your life be a counter friction to stop the machine." [139]

Thoreau's words, "I would remind my countrymen that they are men first, and Americans at a late and convenient hour" expressed the spirit of perfectionism which revolutionized the concept of American nationality in the North. Identifying the Christian and idealistic concept of the dignity of the human soul with the ideas underlying American institutions, democracy could be turned against the formal framework of the nation. The revolt in the name of the higher law was a revolt of the American ideal against

American reality. Even the gentle Channing could say: "We will not become partners in your wars with Mexico and Europe, in your schemes of spreading and perpetuating slavery, in your hopes of conquest, in your unrighteous spoils. . . I shrink from that contamination. I shrink from an act which is to pledge us, as a people, to robbery and war, to the work of upholding and extending slavery without limitation or end. I do not desire . . . to live under the laws of a Government adopting such a policy, and swayed by such a spirit." [140] The American ideal as formulated by Unitarian humanism and evangelical perfectionism involved a dynamic interpretation of democracy as a means for the free development of the human personality. Democracy was the basis of a growing perfection of the whole society through the self-education of the individual in responsibility and in spiritual and moral power.

This ideal was neither political nor national in the sense of identification with state power. It was moral-religious and social. Yet this ideal was challenged by the problem of justice and economic security created by industrialization and by the consolidation and spread of slavery. Both problems threatened the stability of the political institutions of self-government. Both developed ethical and social ideologies which contradicted the fundamental tenets of the humanistic and religious interpretation. While the slavery argument only deepened and fortified the convictions held by the Northern humanists, the social question challenged the validity of their ideas and undermined their optimism. The emergence of a radical group among Jacksonian Democrats and of a labor movement, the great depression of 1837, the European revolutionary upheavals of 1848, not only frightened conservatives but also preoccupied radical Unitarians and transcendentalists, who were compelled to re-examine the relation of American democracy to the social question. [141]

Such periodicals as the *American Review,* the *North American Review, Hunt's Merchants' Magazine,* the *Princeton Review,* and the *Church Review,* stressed the basic differences between the ideas underlying European and American radicalism. [142] Conservative Whigs insisted on the incompatibility between constitutional government and the French concept of popular sovereignty. They emphasized the American distrust of the concentration of power; the system of checks and balances, and the supremacy of the judiciary, which safeguarded the stability of self-government. The diffusion of property, the influence of religion, and the virtues of thrift and industry made Americans conservative.[143] "Surely the American ideas . . . that every able-bodied man is capable of providing his own necessities and his own luxuries—that every honest man is capable of governing himself, too, with comparatively little aid of legislators . . . that the individual man, in short, is entitled to many rights, and the government to few privileges—these views have not taken . . . root in the soil of France."[144] Here, in the reliance on the individual and the restriction of the powers of government, were the safest guarantees for maintenance of a stable social order.[145]

The conservative defense was therefore compelled to prove the difference between the American and the European democratic movements in terms of the individualistic basis of society.[146] Yet this defense could hardly serve the radical humanitarian, the transcendentalist, the radical Unitarian, whose concepts of man demanded social justice and the liberation of the masses from poverty and dependence. Such people had to take an interest in European experiments in social reform; Channing himself had been alert to the labor question since the 1820's.[147] Their question was how to harmonize schemes for social justice with the claims of individuality, "which with all the evils accompanying it, is a fundamental law of our nature."[148] From the beginning Channing rejected the French and English socialism which only showed "that the monstrous inequalities of conditions must be redressed."[149] Socialism was essentially a new human form of slavery, and improvement could come only "by increasing the power of the individual."[150] In Channing's view property was so intimately bound up with the structure of personality, character, and individuality that any system which destroyed the one would also destroy the other. Only growing enlightenment would change the structure of property ownership and develop the principle of individuality in terms of social justice.[151]

Through the confrontation of socialist theory the radical Unitarians and transcendentalists clarified their own concept of the relation between the ideal of individuality and the problem of social organization. In this process of clarification none was more important than Ralph Waldo Emerson.

XIII

Utopian Individualism
Theory and Practice

1. EMERSON: "INDIVIDUALISM HAS NEVER BEEN TRIED"

"Individualism," Emerson confided to his journal, "has never been tried. All history, all poetry deal with it only, and because now it was in the minds of men to go alone, and now, before it was tried, now, when a few began to think of the celestial enterprise, sounds this tin trumpet of a French phalanstery, and the newsboys throw up their caps and cry, Egotism is exploded; now for Communism!" [1]

In these words, written in 1847, Emerson summed up his judgment of all reform schemes that aimed to improve mankind through a change of institutions and social environment. Individualism, not socialism, he thought, alone could liberate man. Seven years earlier he had said of Brook Farm, "This was a hint borrowed from the Tremont House and the United States Hotel ... a prudent forecast on the probable issue of the great questions of Pauperism and Poverty. . . I do not wish to remove from my present prison to a prison a little larger. I wish to break all prisons." [2] The fundamental need of man was to regain selfhood; to break through conventions, creeds, institutions, and habits. The only quest worth living and dying for was that of discovering in oneself the hidden power and the hidden truth—"the word made flesh." "All the fine *aperçus* are for Individualism; the Spartan broth, the hermit's cell, the lonely farmer's life are poetic: the Phalanstery, the 'Self-supporting Village' (Owen) are culinary and mean." [3]

Emerson's rejection of the schemes of association stemmed from a system of values and a concept of life which were, for him, incompatible with socialism. Its source was a religious concept of reality and the nature and destiny of man. Emerson's world view, like that of other transcendentalists, was moralistic—a philosophy of living and acting, like Stoicism, Epicureanism, and Gnosticism. His central conception was an affirmation of the freedom, autonomy, creativity, and divinity of the human soul which could be realized through an uncompromising self-reliance and through the discipline of truthful living and acting. Emerson's gospel of the living God, realizable in the self, was rationalized by the integration of post-Kantian philosophic elements from Coleridge, Fichte, and Schelling with the Goethe-Herder-Schleiermacher concept of individuality and with elements of Neoplatonism.[4] In this philosophical synthesis, the only permanent element was the will to maintain and vindicate the freedom and creativity of the soul and its consubstantiality with ultimate reality—with God. Through the moral philosophy of Richard Price and the Scottish common sense school he extricated himself from the psychology and epistemology of Locke. The moral sense was, for Emerson, the primary evidence of the autonomy and spiritual unity of the inner man.[5]

In September 1833 Emerson was able to formulate his characteristic philosophic outlook. "A man contains all that is needful to his government within himself. He is made a law unto himself. . . Good or evil that can [befall] him must be from himself. . . Nothing can be given to him or taken from him but always there is a compensation[6]. . . The purpose of life seems to be to acquaint a man with himself. He is not to live to the future as described to him, but to live to the real future by living in the real present. The highest revelation is that God is in every man."[7]

Emerson's beliefs, though nurtured by them, were markedly different from German Idealism and transcendentalism. Strictly speaking, he was not a philosopher at all.[8] His mind was preponderantly practical, religious, and pragmatic. Emerson instinctively avoided those conclusions of post-Kantian idealistic philosophy which were inimical to the concept of individuality. He did not accept the Fichtean ego which reached true sovereignty and freedom only by subjecting itself to an absolute and universally valid reason. For Emerson, freedom and creativity were as effectively frozen to death by objective reason as by subjection to the all-compassing law of nature or to the will of God.

The idea of the infinite in the finite, of the relation of the individual to the universe as that of microcosm to macrocosm, left more room for self-determination without sacrificing the possibility of gaining knowledge from absolute reality. "Each particle is a microcosm, and faithfully renders the likeness of the world." Unity and plurality coexisted. The source and its emanations were parts of a whole, kept together by the force radiating from the inmost core. The transcendence and immanence of the divine, whether depicted in the relation of the Oversoul toward the souls or as the "Urgrund" of all being, left room enough for divinity and humanity, individuality and universality.[9] "We learn . . . that . . . the Supreme Being, does not build up nature around us, but puts it forth through us, as the life of the tree puts forth new branches and leaves through the pores of the old. As a plant upon the earth, so a man rests upon the bosom of God; he is nourished by unfailing fountains, and draws at his needs inexhaustible power. Who can set bounds to the possibilities of man? . . Man has access to the entire mind of the Creator, is himself creator in the finite. . . The world proceeds from the same spirit as the body of man. It is a remoter and inferior incarnation of God, a projection of God in the unconscious."[10]

The two permanent centers of reality were the Oversoul, God, or the Universal spirit, and the soul, the self, or individuality. The latent divinity in man, the hidden powers of creative energy, could be liberated only through uncompromising self-reliance, through the development of all the higher faculties, and the inward listening to the voice of one's conscience and intuition—in short, through uncompromising truthful living. This was individualism.[11] Individualism had for Emerson a moral, religious, and metaphysical significance. It was the principle of divine immanence in the universe which maintained the living exchange of power between the many and the one. It was the principle which alone expressed the vital, dynamic, and creative aspects of the infinite.[12] True religious worship demanded that each individual read the divine handwriting within himself and thus reach back to the ground and source of all existence. This was the

meaning of Emerson's warning against conformity, "the tendency
. . . to make all men alike; to extinguish individualism and choke
up all the channels of inspiration from God in man." [13]

A new morality based on these views gave the Puritan discipline
of life a new, fresh significance. The paramount duty of man was
"self-reliance," and "private integrity." [14] Since self-existence was
the attribute of reality and divinity, the measure of good in all
lower forms was the degree to which they possessed independence or self-determination. [15]

Humanism and the immanence of the divine created a new
basis for nonconformity and a new interpretation of Christianity
in the spirit of seventeenth-century antinomianism. "The true
Christianity,—a faith like Christ's in the infinitude of man,—is lost.
None believe in the soul of man, but only in some man or person
old and departed. Ah me! No man goeth alone. All men go in
flocks . . . avoiding the God who seeth in secret. . . They think
society wiser than their soul, and know not that one soul, and
their soul, is wiser than the whole world. . . Let me admonish you,
first of all, to go alone; to refuse the good models . . . and dare to
love God without mediator or veil. . . Yourself a newborn bard of
the Holy Ghost, cast behind you all conformity and acquaint men
at first hand with Deity." [16] "Whoso would be a man, must be a
non-conformist." [17] This emphasis on self-reliance and "character"
saved Emerson from eclecticism and gave his teaching a value
pattern peculiarly American and Protestant.

"Character" was not the German ideal of individuality only, but
rather that of the powerful and self-sufficient man, able to resist
circumstances by the integrity of his own nature. "Character is
centrality, the impossibility of being displaced or overset. . . The
uncivil, unavailable man, who is a problem and a threat to society
whom it cannot let pass in silence, but must either worship or
hate . . . destroys the scepticism which says, 'Man is a doll, let us
eat and drink, 'tis the best we can do,' by illuminating the untried
and unknown . . . Fountains, the self-moved, the absorbed, the
commander because he is commanded, the assured, the primary,—
they are good, for they announce the instant presence of supreme
power." [18]

When Emerson said that individualism had never been tried he
spoke of a universal breakthrough of creativity; when he said that

all history, all poetry, dealt only with it, he spoke of the great individuals of the past who had shaped humanity. Like Carlyle, he saw history as the biography of true individuals.[19] Yet, unlike Carlyle, his attitude was inclusive. Every man was capable of becoming a true prophet and the incarnation of the divine. The law of development in nature and history made the past a foreshadowing of the future; what was at first the power of the few became in time the possession of the many. "The ages are opening this moral force. . . What greatness has yet appeared is the beginnings and encouragements to us in this direction."[20] There were no heroes but "representative men," guides to the greatness and reality which existed in all.

Individualism was the only way to perfection, the only route of progress which history could take. Men had become "timorous, desponding whimperers. . . Our age yields no great and perfect persons. We want men and women who shall renovate life and our social state, but we see that most natures are insolvent. . . A greater self-reliance must work a revolution in all the offices and relations of men; in their religion; in their education; in their pursuits; their modes of living; their association; in their property; in their speculative views."[21]

In the ideal of individualism Emerson established a philosophy and ethics which justified democracy by setting its ideals and values on the greatness and full development of the single man. By giving freedom and self-government a higher significance it could serve as guide to a definition of the American ideal and American nationality. In 1834 Emerson had written in his journal: "The root and seed of democracy is the doctrine, Judge for yourself. Reverence thyself. It is the inevitable effect of the doctrine, where it has any effect (which is rare), to insulate the partisan, to make each man a state. At the same time it replaces the dead with a living check in a true, delicate reverence for superior, congenial minds."[22] And somewhat later he noted: "Democracy, freedom, has its roots in the sacred truth that every man hath in him the divine reason, or that . . . all men are created capable of so doing. That is the equality and the only equality of all men. To this truth we look when we say, Reverence thyself; Be true to thyself."[23]

Individualism became the sole basis of democracy as Emerson defined it. The creative autonomy of the human spirit and man's

unity with ultimate reality set li ial institutions, and prescriptive rights. cedence
over the claims of the sovereign the law
and property. It was the basis ctibility.
Socialism, abolition, the tempera s rights,
reform in criminal laws, trade un ms, and
the numerous experiments and " were, in
that light, expressions of man's g What is
man born for but to be a Reformer, a Remaker of what man has
made, a renouncer of lies. . . Let him renounce everything which
is not true to him, and put all his practices back on their first
thoughts." [24]

Yet this radicalism was inimical to change achieved by political
means and social institutions. Improvement was "the renouncing
of some impediment," the growth of liberty and not of restraint. [25]
Men must be trusted to live without crutches and to organize their
relations with each other spontaneously, as the need arose. While
reforms had "their high origin in an ideal justice" and were "sacred
in its origin," their real force derived from their "reliance on the
sentiment of man, which will work best the more it is trusted,"
and in their faith "in the private self-supplied powers of the
individual." [26]

Confronted by the social question of his times, and aware of the
justice of the criticism of the status quo, his answer was that
individualism, not socialism, would answer the needs of mankind.
"I do not wonder at the interests these projects inspire," he
wrote of the communal settlements. "The world is awaking to
the idea of union, and these experiments show what it is thinking
of. . . Men will live and communicate, and plough, and reap, and
govern, as by added ethereal power, when once they are united. . .
But this union must be inward, and not one of covenants, and is
to be reached by a reverse of the method they use. The union is
only perfect when all the uniters are isolated. . . Each man, if he
attempts to join himself to others, is on all sides cramped and
diminished . . . and the stricter the union, the smaller and more
pitiful he is. But leave him alone, to recognize in every hour and
every place, the secret soul; he will go up and down doing the
works of a true member, and, to the astonishment of all, the work
will be done with concert, though no man spoke. Government will

be adamantine without any governor. The Union must be ideal in actual individualism." [27] Here, for the first time, the term individualism designated a regulative ideal of social organization. The realization of this ideal, though it lay in the future, was rooted in the nature of man and was prepared by the tendencies of the times and by historic progress.

Emerson gave the concept of individualism no systematic treatment in spite of its fundamental importance to his teachings. It was more a prophecy than a theory. Yet it designated the positive opposite, or real alternative, to socialism. Both the term and the connotations were taken from socialist theory but were totally re-evaluated. Individualism in the Emersonian sense described a society dedicated to the free development of individuality in a pattern which permitted utmost individual self-determination and freedom of growth for all.

The political concept nearest to Emerson's "ideal union in actual individualism" was the equally American anarchism propounded by Josiah Warren, Stephen Pearl Andrews, and Benjamin Tucker. [28] Their ideas also were inimical to the state and its prerogatives and aimed at its complete absorption into the voluntary processes of society. They also objected to all forms of social organization which diminished the autonomy and the freedom of the individual; the "natural laws" of a purely economic society were sufficient for the harmonious cooperation of its members. Yet while Emerson thought that the state should wither away with the full moral development of man, the anarchists wished to abolish it because it was an instrument of exploitation and oppression. The point of departure for Josiah Warren was Jefferson's natural-rights theory and his concept of a free and natural society applied to the question of economic justice. That of Emerson was the conviction that man, grown to full intellectual and moral stature, was a law unto himself, while state compulsion was incompatible with freedom. Emerson was therefore a gradualist. Individualism would be the result of the growing self-reliance of men, made possible by their intellectual and moral development.

The basic similarity between Emerson's individualism and Warren's anarchism sprang from their reinterpretation of American reality. Both concepts were formulated under the impact of the social question and through a confrontation with socialism.

Both were attempts to establish principles to guide the country along a way consistent with its traditions and genius.

Emerson's belief in the resourcefulness of man, in the efficacy of natural law, and in the correspondence between nature and spirit was saturated with the experiences of contemporary America. "It seems so easy for America to inspire and express the most expansive and humane spirit; new born, free, healthful, strong, the land of the laborer, of the democrat, of the philanthropist, of the believer, of the saint, she should speak for the human race. It is the country of the Future. . . It is a country of beginnings, of projects, of designs, of expectations." [29] America was significant for mankind not in its achievements, or natural wealth, or even political institutions, but in its concept of human life. It was "a nation of individuals," "the home of man," "another word for opportunity." [30] Only here could man prove his powers and his selfhood, his capacity to create and maintain a society, to conquer a continent through individual effort and voluntary association. Necessity and freedom were sufficient to develop man's highest powers. "The new conditions of mankind in America are really favorable to progress, the removal of absurd restrictions and antique inequalities. The mind is always better the more it is used, and here it is kept in practice. The humblest is dayly challenged to give his opinion on practical questions, and while civil and social freedom exists, nonsense even has a favorable effect." [31] Freedom, by developing responsibilities and intelligence, by undermining vested power, classes, and artificial institutions, by producing new ideas and by testing the worth of everything, created a natural order which, while permanently changing, redressed itself ever anew and found its own balance.[32] Freedom, even that wild freedom akin to anarchy, was the source of all progress.[33]

Freedom became for Emerson the generic principle of democracy. With individuality, it characterized the American ideal of society and made it significant for all mankind. It is in the context of Emerson's political views that his cosmic optimism, his concept of "compensations, circles," his philosophy of identity and parallelism between the moral and the natural law, between the forces of history and the forces of the soul, are useful. The laissez-faire ideology that served individual liberty demanded as justification a

pre-established cosmic order through which mutual freedom resulted in harmony and not in anarchy.[34] Emerson's philosophy of
the Oversoul and of the parallelism of nature and spirit supplied
the need.

Yet his cosmic optimism involved a certain blindness toward
the reality of misery and social suffering. In this respect he was
inferior to his teacher Channing and to his contemporaries such
as Theodore Parker, the abolitionists, and the Christian Socialists.
There was never a true balance between the moralistic critique in
his philosophy of life and truthfulness and his rather quietistic
acceptance of social reality as part of "nature." This cosmic optimism applied to the social scene, and a rather devitalized version
of his concept of individualism and self-reliance were eagerly
taken up by contemporaries as apologies for the status quo and
became part of the accepted version of American individualism.
Emerson's opinion that all government rested basically on dominion and that hence "the less government we have the better,
—the fewer laws, and the less confided power," was particularly
well received.[35] Though far from original, it summed up the whole
gamut of opinion from the radical democracy of the editor William
Legget to the absolute negation of Henry Thoreau and Josiah
Warren. Here Emerson came into broad contact with the vital
traditions of his country and, by uniting them in the concept of
individualism, gave them a new perspective and unity. A truly
sane and perfect government existed only in the self-government
of the wise man and in the relations between two friends.[36] All
other regulations of human behavior based on compulsion were
at best contrivances. Real understanding of the needs of others
could only be based on love and wisdom. It followed that with
the appearance of men wise and of true character "the state
expires." [37]

This reasoning, which showed a close relationship to the religious perfectionism and the Christian anarchism of Garrison, was
supplemented in the typical Emersonian philosophy of corre-
spondences and analogies by the utilitarian and historical argument.[38] Government meant essentially that the decision of one
man bound another. There could be no representation in a true
sense. Individual interests and needs could only be satisfied by
direct negotiation and exchange. "All public ends look vague and

quixotic
was not
himself
he shou
the stat
. . . and
by the

The security of life and property
r government; "a man should be
ealth and life, for his behavior . . .
protection; should ask nothing of
gdom and a state; fearing no man
government, law and order went
sure of himself."[40] But this argu-

ment w by Emerson's explicit faith that nature and history were working toward the same ends. For nature implanted life with "the instinct of self-help, perpetual struggle to be, to resist opposition, to attain to freedom, to attain to mastery, and the security of a permanent self-defended being."[41]

Yet nature secured balance and harmony by the law which ruled human relations, that attached property to merit and exertion, and raised natural leaders to sway their fellow men.[42] "Things have their laws, as well as men. . . Under any forms, persons and property must and will have their just sway. They exert their power, as steadily as matter its attraction."[43] Therefore all regulations concerning property and other rights were either superfluous or dangerous, whether they were animated by the spirit of benevolence or by that of selfishness. As soon as they clashed with the law and reason inherent in the natural relations of men and things they became ineffective and were swept away. "The basis of political economy is non-interference. The only safe rule is found in the self-adjusting meter of demand and supply. Do not legislate . . . Give no bounties, make equal laws, secure life and property, and you need not give alms. Open the door of opportunity to talent and virtue and they will . . . not be in bad hands. In a free and just commonwealth, property rushes from the idle and imbecile to the industrious, brave and persevering."[44]

This complacent attitude, which grew increasingly callous and naïve, revealed the affinity of Emerson's individualism with the moral philosophy from which he had sought to extricate himself. That affinity could only be explained by the fact that absolute freedom and laissez faire were for him axiomatic affirmations which dictated, rather than followed from, the development of his philosophy. Later, when Spencerian and Darwinian influences supplanted his idealism, his concept of individualism was simply identified with laissez faire. The process was facilitated by Emerson's supreme confidence in the ultimate wisdom of nature. "We devise sumptuary and relief laws, but the principle of population is always reducing wages to the lowest pittance. . . We legislate against forestalling and monopoly . . . but the selfishness which hoards corn for high prices is the preventive of famine; and the law of self-preservation is surer policy than any legislation can be."[45]

Emerson also supported the theory of laissez faire by an argument based on the nature of progress. Self-government and free trade were voluntary substitutes for force; and they made for freedom restrained by responsibility and morality. From this point of view the modern order is the last product of the historic evolution of humanity through the growth of man's power and the replacement of the natural order by a moral one. Individualism was the end result, the rule of the laws of the spirit over mankind.

Progress was achieved both by great individuals, the teachers of mankind, and by imperceptible changes through the collective experience of trial and error. Philosophy, science, religion, government, and material conditions showed the same steady ascent. Feudalism, which had supplanted patriarchal rule and despotism, was itself destroyed by commerce. Then the rise of transport, technology, and science created a new society, based on a community of interest, division of work, and association for common ends, and supplanted force by agreement. By putting everything on the market, it became the principal agent of liberty, destroying the traditional institutions of power and inherited rights.[46] In this age, the state became an anachronism. "Trade goes to make the governments insignificant, and to bring every kind of faculty of every individual that can in any manner serve any person, *on sale.* . . It converts Government into an Intelligence Office, where every man may find what he wishes to buy, and expose what he has to sell."[47] The numerous reform movements, associations of workers and capital, the socialist community villages—all showed the general contempt for government. All usurped functions which the government once claimed as its prerogatives. "There really seems a progress towards such a state of things in which this work shall be done by these natural workmen; and this, not . . . through any increased disposition shown by the citizens at elections, but by the gradual contempt into which official government falls, and

Sklansky / Gilmore
on ambivalence re. market

the increasing disposition of private adventurers to assume its fallen functions." [48]

The tendencies of the time thus prepared "the ideal union in actual individualism." For while these forces seemed at first merely to disintegrate society, they created a system of an entirely new character which based all association on voluntary and mutual service and cemented solidarity with individual freedom and personal self-determination. It was in this context that the reviewers of Tocqueville's *Democracy in America* explained that individualism, though it might appear at first destructive and anarchical, "must in the end, assimilate the species, and evolve all the glorious phenomena of original . . . *order;*—that order which exists in man himself, and alone vivifies and sustains him." [49]

That explanation bore the imprint of Emerson's thought. [50] The individualism of the present prepared that of the future. The Utopia of transcendent humanism would emerge through the combined action of history and necessity.

Thus, Emerson's social philosophy only restated one of the central ideals of American democracy—the concept of the natural society of free individuals, a dynamic society perfecting itself through free and voluntary adjustment and through the moral growth of all its members. The concept of individualism gave to the idea of a free society moral and philosophical principles, depth, and a criterion of decision. Emerson was fully aware that his teaching was an interpretation of the American experience which would provide Americans with a guide to their destiny. [51] Holding before them in lectures and addresses, as in a mirror, the deeds, thoughts, and achievements of mankind, examining all aspects of human life in the light of his peculiar philosophy, he intended them to become the inheritors of all that was valuable and permanent in past ages. For the significance of America was that it should become "the home of man" and that "she should speak for the human race." Her identity lay in a moral idea and not in ethnic, racial, or historical unity. [52]

To be American was to achieve the dignity of manhood through opportunity for all. The nation's past was made of the dreams and hopes of mankind, and its future was their realization. Its beginnings were a new epoch in the evolution of liberty. "There have been revolutions which were not in the interest of feudalism and barbarism, but in that of society. . . . Now the culmination of these triumphs of humanity . . . is the planting of America. At every moment some one country more than any other represents . . . the future of mankind. None will doubt that America occupies this place in the opinion of nations." [53] This historical perspective endowed the national consciousness with a missionary character and endowed its way of life with universal significance. America alone was a "nation of men," identified by its ideals and by its loyalty to a vision of "exalted manhood." Its common bonds were the product of the opportunities it granted to all. "The genius of the country has marked out our true policy,—opportunity. Opportunity of civil rights, of education, of personal power, and not less of wealth; doors wide open. If I could have it,—free trade with all the world without toll or custom houses, invitation as we now make to every nation, to every race and skin, white men, red men, black men; hospitality of fair field and equal laws to all. Let them compete, and success to the strongest, the wisest and the best." [54] Yet these ideas showed the crystallization of a concept of the American nation in which individualism was of crucial importance. Individualism was an ideal which spoke to humanity as a whole. It was a theory of progress and a philosophy of universally valid ethics. And yet it was particularly American. Through the concept of individualism the Puritan New England elite integrated Jeffersonian ideology into its own outlook and thereby shaped a truly national ideology.

2. INDIVIDUALISM TURNS ANARCHISM—JOSIAH WARREN

In his *Autobiography* John Stuart Mill mentioned, in addition to Wilhelm von Humboldt, William Maccall's *Elements of Individualism* and Josiah Warren's "sovereignty of the individual" as precursors of his own doctrine of individuality. [55] Maccall's book was greatly influenced by both the German *Bildungs ideal* and by American transcendentalism. Josiah Warren's doctrine, on the other hand, was an original American amalgamation of the natural-rights philosophy and New England congregationalism. Warren stood at the left of Jeffersonian democracy and opposed transcendental individualism, to which he was nevertheless related in his concept of society.

The question of social justice and equality, raised by the growth of the laboring class and the emergence of an industrial economy, had loomed large in political discussion after the 1820's. Transcendentalists shared with radical democrats the opinion that the only title to property was labor and that the bounties of nature belonged to the living in usufruct only. Fourierism appealed to New England intellectuals because it promised to distribute wealth in accordance with the ideal of a liberated humanity. Yet the fight against monopolies and protection, for a more generous public land policy, for the workingman's right to organization, and for universal education seemed for most radicals sufficient to create equal opportunities and to restore natural justice.

Between these views and those of Josiah Warren, the first American anarchist, there was only a difference of degree. In quest of economic justice and taking as his point of departure the Jeffersonian ideology as developed by John Taylor and others, Warren pushed the concept of a natural society to its ultimate consequence—the abolition of the state. The emergence of anarchistic individualism revealed the impact of socialism and the inherent tendency of the Jeffersonian ideals toward individualism. William Bailie, who defined anarchism as individualism fused with the quest for social justice, considered Josiah Warren the first of those anarchists who were represented by Emerson, Thoreau, Whitman, Herbert Spencer, and Tolstoy.[56] Yet Peter Kropotkin, with greater discernment, referred to Warren as an individualist-anarchist and pointed out that this movement was mainly, if not exclusively, an American phenomenon.[57] Like the transcendentalists, but at an earlier date, Warren had arrived at his ideology of "the sovereignty of the individual" through the contact and the challenge of socialism as formulated by Robert Owen. Of old New England stock, Josiah Warren had moved in the 1820's to Cincinnati, Ohio, and had joined Owen's communist settlement at New Harmony.[58] He left after two years, having had ample time to ponder the reason for Owen's failure to establish a viable community. Through the confrontation with the first form of modern socialism Warren arrived at his characteristic system. He explained the bankruptcy of Owen's scheme by its failure to account for the individuality of men. Any system of community of goods suppressed the vital energies of man's individuality. It deadened personal responsibility and initiative and led eventually to authoritarian government.[59] "It seemed that the difference of opinion, tastes and purposes *increased* just in proportion to the demand of conformity," wrote Warren in retrospect. "We had tried every conceivable form of organization and government. We had a world in miniature.—we had enacted the French revolution over again. . . It appeared that it was nature's own inherent law of diversity that had conquered us . . . our 'united interests' were directly at war with the individualities of persons and circumstances and the instinct of self-preservation." [60]

Warren's social philosophy was based on the incommensurability and partial incommunicability of each individual, for each was a system within himself.[61] "Everyone must feel that he is the supreme arbiter of his own [destiny], that no power on earth shall rise over him, that he is and always shall be sovereign of himself and all relating to his individuality." [62]

This principle, which Warren thought was implicit in the Declaration of Independence, was the sole basis of a just social order.[63] The deplorable condition of society was the consequence of the failure of the American people to preserve the principles of the Revolution and of democracy. The natural rights, as enumerated in the Preamble to the Declaration, were the limits and the end of all society and of all government. They established for each person an absolute claim to his own time and property and to responsibility for his own life and action.[64] Society came into being to satisfy man's needs and had no fixed character and no authority other than that given it by its members.

Warren's ideal was the concurrent sovereignty of all men and women, limited only by the fact that "the sovereignty of the individual was to be exercised at his own cost." [65] It was only by individualizing each case—detaching it from all others—and by leaving everyone free to cooperate or not in the particular case at hand, "that one could secure cooperation." [66] Yet Warren recognized that, even in a society entirely built on the exchange of services, the accumulation of property and of economic power would soon enslave some of the members. Without economic equality, the whole system would collapse. Throughout his life Warren tried to solve the question of how men could unite in the economic processes of modern society and yet preserve the absolute sovereignty of the individual and the independence of all. The "equity store" in Cincinnati, the settlement in Tuscarawa County, the "time store at New Harmony," the villages of "Utopia" and "Modern Times," were all experiments to prove the practicability of individualist anarchism.[67]

Thirteen years before Proudhon, Warren conceived that social justice could be realized solely by a change in the nature of money and by the solution of the question of credit. Maintaining that the sole legitimate source of the right to property was in labor, he concluded that all wealth gained through possession and dominion—such as rent, interest, and profit—was theft. It followed that a just economy would rest on the exchange of services measured by the labor invested in them. Such economy could function through barter or through labor notes, the use of which Warren explained on those he printed in Cincinnati in May 1827: "You never will find any satisfactory solution of the great problem now up between *labor* and *capital,* or *slavery* and *liberty,* until you understand what justice *is,* and what a circulating medium, or money, ought to be. The above [a print of a labor note] is a specimen of what money ought to be. It should be used by those . . . who perform some useful service, but by *nobody* else. It should command *labor* for *labor* in equal quantities, and the most disagreeable should be highest paid." It was only confusing to pass off "metals or any other natural products . . . as pay for labor. . . This is the origin of all forms of slavery . . . and of all poverty and crime, *the insecurity of condition,* the worship of money, the antagonism of classes, and the crisis of these times. Whereas if labor were equitably rewarded (with an equal amount of labor), the hardest worker would be the richest man, and all would choose a portion of labor as a means of health and pleasure."[68] The present system of exchange, based on the market value and in which the price was fixed by competition and the quest for profit, would thereby disappear. This "civilized cannibalism" not only compelled all producers to underbid each other but robbed labor of its reward.[69]

Warren's principles of equitable commerce, first formulated in 1827, were based on "cost the limit of price," the cost being measured by hours of labor expended in production and merchandizing. Though the factual measurement was later variously modified, Warren maintained throughout his life that the principle of "cost the limit of price" and labor notes were the only means to introduce an equitable economy.[70] His reform avoided the pitfalls of socialism, which tried to impose equality of conditions either by the authority of the state or by association, without taking into account that true economic justice called for appropriate rewards for work done. Unlike socialism, it left each individual in full possession of his independence and made him responsible for the consequences of his conduct. It created at the same time a true harmony of interest and a sense of community as society became an honest framework of cooperation in which all members shared the benefits of mutual services.[71]

The proper sphere of society was to secure to labor its legitimate reward, to give security to person and property, to ensure economy in production, to let all members share equally in the utilization of land and natural resources, while leaving each individual the greatest amount of freedom. Warren believed that his settlements proved that society could be reconstructed on such principles. "We build on Individuality," he wrote. "It is only when the rights of persons or property are actually invaded that collisions arise. These rights being clearly defined and sanctioned by public opinion, and temptations to encroachments being withdrawn, we may then consider our great problem practically solved. With regard to mere difference of opinion in taste . . . or even right and wrong, good and bad, sanity and insanity,—all must be left to the supreme decision of each *individual,* whenever he can take on himself the *cost* of his decisions." [72]

"Individuality, division, disconnection, disunion" was therefore "the principle of order, harmony and progress." [73] A society in which the concurrent sovereignty of the individual included the right to the full reward of labor would eliminate exploitation and injustice and increase the cohesive force of cooperation for mutual benefit. Warren's doctrine carried out the full implications of the Jeffersonian concept of a free and natural society; like John Taylor's theory of the economic society, individuality became at the same time the basis of justice and of social cooperation.

This critic of property had thus transformed the older theories of laissez faire into the principle of the functional interdependence of all members of society united solely by the division of work. The basic concepts of American democracy—individual rights, contractual social and political obligations, the distrust of all political power, and the ideal of a natural free society—were all drawn to their logical conclusions. This Utopia embodied a conception of social justice similar to that of socialism. Yet Jeffersonian ideals, pushed to their limit in Warren's anarchism, also showed the incompatibility that existed between American individualism and socialism. For socialism dealt with aggregates, systems, and social wholes, while individualism dealt with disparate individual associates, voluntary joiners and cooperators. Warren considered all government an instrument for economic exploitation and the subjugation of one part of society by another. "Experience has proved *that power cannot be delegated to rulers of states and nations, in sufficient quantities for the management of business without its becoming an indefinite quantity,* and in this indefiniteness have mankind been cheated out of their legitimate liberty." [74]

With the disappearance of the state, society would manage its affairs on an entirely mutual basis. Free competition would lead to the adoption of the principle of "cost the limit of price." Though Warren refused to join parties and organizations, he supported the Jacksonian radicals who, he thought, moved in the right direction. Unlike European socialists and anarchists, Warren did not consider himself a revolutionary nor did he reject the past of his society. The "sovereignty of the individual" was the historical realization of that principle which had brought forth the Reformation and raised the American Republic. [75] Writing in opposition to the theories of Robert Owen and of the French socialists, Warren, like the transcendentalists, adopted their collectivist historic-sociological speculations without accepting the corollary value system or scheme of historical progress. [76] Stephen Pearl Andrews, Warren's chief literary follower, revealed the relationship in the subtitle of his *Science of Society: The True Constitution of Government in the Sovereignty of the Individual as the Final Development of Protestantism, Democracy and Socialism.* [77] Andrews, who was a former Fourierist and was well acquainted with contemporary sociological theory, believed that Warren's individualism was basic to "every manifestation of that universal unrest and revolution, which is known technically in this age as 'Progress.'" [78] By contrast, socialism was "unfit for the habitation of anything else than despotism" and was therefore strongly resisted by those "who are most thoroughly imbued with the Protestant and Democratic idea of Individuality."[79] Andrews' writings were permeated with the consciousness that American history pointed toward a doctrine which was the logical development of the human-rights philosophy.[80]

To some degree Warren's principles were identified with those of a general theory of individualism. He had used the phrase "sovereignty of the individual" in the late 1820's. When the term individualism was later introduced to America, he saw little reason to change his own exact expression; and his conception was soon regarded as a radical version of individualism.[81] Comte, writing to a disciple who resided in Warren's "Modern Times" village, said that the settlement was a "full development of Occidental anarchy. . . Like you, I prefer the complete and systematic individualism of your village to vague socialism."[82]

The doctrines of Warren and Andrews were also widely discussed in the 1850's by those who opposed them.[83] George Frederick Holmes, an apologist for slavery, analyzed these theories in 1857.[84] He considered political individualism as representative of the northern reform movement in general.[85] All the philanthropic schemes of the North were symptoms of a rapidly decaying society. Socialism, having lost its appeal everywhere, had been supplanted by political individualism as preached by Herbert Spencer, Proudhon, and Andrews, which was indeed the logical offspring of Protestantism, democracy, and socialism.[86]

Warren's concept of labor notes, of a bank of labor, and of an "equitable commerce" in the context of an individualistic philosophy had a fairly wide appeal. William Beck elaborated this theory in his *Money and Banking, or their Nature and Effects Considered together with a Plan for the Universal Diffusion of the Legitimate Benefits without their Evils,* published in 1839.[87] William Weitling, returning to America in 1849, gave up his earlier socialist theories and accepted those of Proudhon and Warren as the solution of the social question.[88] Warren's *Periodical Letter,* started in 1854, was widely read in America, England, and Ireland. Stephen Pearl Andrews' book *The Science of Society* was instrumental in creating a loose association of scientific anarchists who maintained contact with Warren until his death in 1873.[89] Keith and Robinson, influenced by Warren, set up a "House of Equity" based on the "cost the limit of price" principle. According to J. H. Noyes,

Warren was also well known to Robert Owen and influenced the latter in his attempt to establish a center of "Equitable Commerce." [90] Robert Dale Owen, the editor of the *Free Enquirer,* also came under Warren's influence and publicized his ideas in his newspaper.

Yet more important was the fact that Warren's connections with Stephen Pearl Andrews, Ezra Hayward, William Greene, J. K. Ingalls, and Lysander Spooner, who founded the New England Labor Reform League in 1869, brought his view directly to bear on the labor movement. Consciously based on the main tradition of American thought and embodying a producer philosophy, Warren's individualism remained an "ideal type" for those who rebelled in the name of American tradition against what they considered a growing exploitation of the working masses of the nation by a parasitic minority.

XIV

The Great Debate on the Nature of the American Ideal

The Missouri question aroused and filled me with alarm. The old schism of federal and republican threatened nothing, because it existed in every State, and united them together by the fraternism of the party. But the coincidence of a marked principle, moral and political, with a geographical line, once conceived, I feared would never more be obliterated from the mind; that it would be recurring on every occasion and renewing irritations, until it would kindle such mutual and mortal hatred, as to render separation preferable to eternal discord.

Thomas Jefferson to William Short, April 13, 1820[1]

The great struggle for hegemony over the Union revealed the degree to which social and ethical concepts had become embedded in the national consciousness. Attempts in the 1850's to avoid the conflict were inevitably directed toward the creation of a new type of nationalism. The Know-Nothing, or American, party thus labored to unite discordant political factions by making ethnic and religious loyalties the basis of national identification. It sought to substitute for traditional American values a nationalism of the Old World type based on common descent and religion, and thus to divert against the "foreigners" the antagonisms that existed among the native-born.[2] Similarly, the theory of race which justified Negro slavery also aimed to create an identity between North and South on the basis of a common belief in white superiority and through territorial expansion. Yet the historical situation and the national tradition frustrated these efforts and turned the conflict between free and slaveholding states into a gigantic struggle over the nature of American social ideals.

By the end of the 1840's Protestant humanitarianism and democratic radicalism were increasingly absorbed by the conflict be-

tween North and South. In the controversy over the further
extension of slavery, intellectuals on both sides justified their respective positions in the name of ultimate social and moral ideals
and proceeded to reinterpret American history and nationality in
accordance with their own ideological position.

With the dissolution of the old parties and of the national
organization of the denominations and their realignment on a
regional basis, ideologies were more often concerned with social
and ethical ideals than with political institutions and rights. The
North reinterpreted the Preamble to the Declaration of Independence as a higher law of the Union which permitted it to
attack positive laws that recognized slavery. In the name of the
rights of man it proceeded to destroy the precarious balance
established by the federal Constitution. At the same time the
South abandoned the strict constitutional interpretation and the
democratic philosophy which underlay its own states-rights philosophy and its doctrines of nullification, and formulated an ideology
consistent with the maintenance and the extension of slavery.

The attack of the southern slavery apologists on "free society"
compelled northern intellectuals to redefine their own institutions
and attitudes in terms of a humanistic ideal, the outlines of which
had been prepared by the Protestant and humanitarian philosophy
of Unitarians, transcendentalists, and by evangelism and democratic radicalism. The southern challenge, which criticized the
social system of the North with arguments drawn from socialism
and aristocratic conservatism, made transcendentalists and radical
individualists aware of their common ground, which they increasingly defined in the concept of a "free society" interpreted by
the ideal of individualism. Therefore two social ideologies faced
each other, both claiming to represent the fundamental concept
of American nationality. With the defeat of the South the northern concept became the common denominator of all those who
welcomed the establishment of an integrated national government. The concepts of individualism and of a "free society" thereby became organic parts of a new national consciousness.

1. THE SOUTHERN HERESY—"FREE SOCIETY" UNDER ATTACK

The southern apology for slavery aimed to unite the white
population through an ideology which appealed to the poor as

well as to the slaveholding planters. It set the conscience of the South at peace by proving that the northern economy exploited and degraded the white laborer to a level worse than that of the slave. For this purpose the southerners drew on all the arguments advanced by critics of competitive capitalism—on the socialists, on Thomas Carlyle, Auguste Comte—and on reports on the industrial population of Europe, especially of England. Yet the idealization of southern society which interpreted its pattern of life in terms of the aristocratic concepts of ancient republicanism rejected the premises of American democracy. The contractual theory of government was shorn of its equalitarian natural-rights theory, and with it fell the Jeffersonian concept of society. As defenders of aristocratic republicanism, the southerners appealed to northern conservatives to unite in defense of white civilization against radicalism. The true aim of abolition, as described by the South, was the abrogation of all prescriptive rights and the establishment of complete economic equality, which would lead to revolution, anarchy, and despotism.

George Frederick Holmes of the University of Virginia illustrated the twofold aspect of the southern apology. The abolitionist movement was only one aspect of the "political individualism" which permeated the reform movement and the recently founded Republican party. The reformers' attack on the historical rights and traditions which clashed with their own concept of "the higher law" would reduce society to barbarism. Holmes, like John Calhoun, did not reject free competitive capitalism, but he stressed the necessity for establishing social and political authority through an elite which alone could safeguard social order and civil liberty. He thus reconciled a slaveholding economy with free government.[3]

Yet side by side with these arguments, he leaned heavily on Carlyle's and Auguste Comte's indictment of modern society in order to prove the ethical superiority of southern institutions. As early as 1851 Holmes improved upon the tactics of Calhoun by attacking northern society with the arguments of the contemporary critics of capitalism. The authoritarian and paternalistic ideology of "Tory Socialists," of Carlyle and also of Comte, seemed particularly relevant to this purpose. Their arguments could be used to prove that the reconciliation of capital and labor could occur only in an organic and paternalistic social order. In the South, according to Holmes, the rule of mammon and ruthless competition had been supplanted by a system of social obligations and duties that had created a willing and reciprocal dependence among all classes for the common good.[4] Elsewhere society was "utter anarchy and confusion, the government of the states reduced to a mere scramble for offices . . . and the whole code of morality supplanted by a system of individual expediency." Such tendencies would lead to agrarianism, social insurrection, and Caesarism.[5]

Holmes had only followed a road which others had laid out before him. Since the 1820's southern intellectuals and politicians had been engaged in redefining their basic political and social views.[6] Thomas Dew, professor of political economy at the College of William and Mary, had defended slavery not only on historical grounds, but as an ideal of civilization. Greece and Rome, with their free citizens, their ideal of public virtue and excellence, their sense of responsibility fostered by their dominion over their clients, bondsmen, and slaves, were the examples the South was to imitate.[7] Gone was the despair of Jefferson and the older generation, who had feared that they held a "wolf by the ears, and we can neither hold him, nor safely let him go."[8] In 1838 Calhoun declared:

Many in the South once believed that it [slavery] was a moral and political evil. That folly and delusion are gone. We see it now in its true light, and regard it as the most safe and stable basis for free institutions in the world. It is impossible with us that the conflict can take place between labor and capital, which makes it so difficult to establish and maintain free institutions in all wealthy and highly civilized nations where such institutions as ours do not exist. The Southern States are an aggregate, in fact, of communities, not of individuals. Every plantation is a little community, with the master at its head, who concentrates in himself the united interests of capital and labor, of which he is the common representative. The small communities aggregated make the State in all, whose action, labor, and capital is equally represented and perfectly harmonized.[9]

It was largely under Calhoun's leadership that the South became fully conscious of its distinct character and articulated its growing fear of encirclement not only in a theory of militant isolationism but in the elaboration of its own ideology, stripped of the universalistic and humanistic outlook of the Jeffersonian tradition. The old distrust of the industrial and financial capitalism of the North and the suspicion of federal consolidation were incorporated into the southern ideology so that it was easy to continue the coalition of southern planter, northern laborer and mechanic, and western farmer. Yet this alliance no longer influenced the social outlook of the South. For the distrust of northern capitalism and federal consolidation did not now stem from an equalitarian orientation but rather from the growing realization of the divergence of interests between North and South and from the awareness that the radical democratic outlook of the eastern laborer and the western farmer endangered the social system of the South. Behind the Jeffersonian façade of states' rights and free trade a curious reversal of ideologies took place in which the South more and more accepted the social philosophy of the Federalists and of the conservative Whigs, adapting to its own peculiar situation the rejection of the natural-rights theory.[10]

Increasingly, the outlook of the South became an historically oriented conservative philosophy of ruling elites and a concomitant pessimism about human nature. "Man is born to subjection. Not only during infancy is he dependent, and under the control of others; at all ages, it is the very bias of his nature, that the strong and the wise should control the weak and the ignorant. . . The existence of some form of slavery in all ages and countries, is proof enough of this. He is born to subjection as he is born in sin and ignorance. . . Of all things, the existence of civil liberty is most the result of artificial institutions. The proclivity of the natural man is to domineer or to be subservient."[11] While the Calvinism of the North was steadily transformed into an evangelical or liberal humanitarianism, it was revived in all its stern fundamentalism in the South. Calhoun's defense of liberty and his ceaseless struggle against the consolidation of the power of the federal government stemmed from the belief that the will to power was the permanent element in all government and that economic interests were the main conditioning factors in political struggle. He thought in terms of societies and economic groups rather than in terms of individual rights.[12] Freedom was a rare achievement which could be maintained only by an elaborate structure of checks and balances as well as by confining it to those who could be trusted with it.[13] "Liberty, then, when forced on a people unfit for it, would instead of a blessing, be a curse; as it would, in its reaction, lead directly to anarchy,—the greatest of all curses. . . It is a great and dangerous error to suppose that all people are equally entitled to liberty. It is a reward to be earned, not a blessing to be gratuitously lavished on all alike; a reward reserved for the intelligent, the patriotic, the virtuous and deserving; and not a boon to be bestowed on a people too ignorant, degraded and vicious, to be capable either of appreciating or of enjoying it."[14]

In a federal structure, individual freedom could only be maintained by defending the rights and interests of the group, the community and state to which the individual belonged. Representative government resting on the suffrage of those entitled and prepared to be citizens was only one way to secure the rights of the ruled against the rulers. The doctrine of the concurrent majority was a means of protecting the minority against the majority and of reconciling order with liberty.[15] The optimistic universalism of Jefferson gave way to a pessimistic Hobbesian view of human nature.[16] Government and authority were the necessary conditions of civilization. "Each . . . has a greater regard for his own safety or happiness, than for the safety or happiness of others. . . And hence, the tendency of a universal state of conflict, between individual and individual; accompanied by the connected passions of suspicion, jealousy, anger and revenge,—followed by insolence, fraud and cruelty;—and if not prevented by some controlling power, ending in a state of universal discord and confusion."[17]

Democracy, as much as liberty, was based on conditions which could only rarely be realized. For political equality was not a human right but the outcome of factual equality. It was rather a partnership of equals as among the peers of aristocratic regimes or the citizens of the Greek *polis*. It was the rule of masters and not of servants.[18]

Abolitionism drove Calhoun to accept unconditionally the structure of the southern society as ideal and to shape his concept of liberty and democracy according to its pattern. Having become convinced that both the capitalist federalism of the northern Whigs and the democratic radicalism of its laboring and farming classes would destroy or dominate southern society, Calhoun proceeded to forge the South into a community aware of its common fate and common ideals and capable of defending its rights in the Union.[19]

By the 1850's the South had become a region highly conscious of its unity and its fundamental antagonism toward the North. A younger generation of intellectuals took the lead in violent denunciation of northern pretensions, in attacks upon the social system of the North and in the glorification of its own. The political wisdom and the profound loyalty to the Union which characterized Calhoun's activities and his theory of federalism and unity could no longer restrain the spokesmen of the 1850's.[20] In *DeBow's Review, The Southern Literary Messenger,* the *Richmond Examiner* and the *Richmond Enquirer,* ambitious writers like Senator James H. Hammond of South Carolina, George Fitzhugh, George Frederick Holmes, William Grayson, Albert T. Bledsoe, and William G. Simms systematically defended southern institutions. They proved the impossibility of emancipation by citing the catastrophes of the West Indies and the natural incapacity of the Negroes for self-rule and liberty.[21] The latent inclination to consider the Negroes as an inferior race, which had been cautiously expressed earlier, developed into an articulate scientific theory of the division of mankind into inferior and superior races that enabled the latter to become historical nations participating in the upward spiral of progress and civilization and entitled them as master races to rule the others.[22]

Almost all the southern spokesmen also attacked the social system of their opponents. They compared the happy lot of the slave with the permanent insecurity of the ruthlessly exploited wage-earner in the free society. Abolition was not only hypocrisy but a maneuver to divert the attention of the masses from their legitimate grievances.[23] "Ye capitalists, ye merchant princes, ye master manufacturers, you may excite to frenzy your Jacobin clubs, you may demoralize their minds of all ideas of right and wrong, but remember ! the guillotine is suspended over your own necks!! The agrarian doctrines will ere long be applied to yourselves, for with whatsoever measure ye mete, it shall be measured to you again." [24] Through the fusion of the arguments of a conservatism—romantic and cynical at the same time—advocating a corporate feudal society, with those of racism and socialism, a new and sinister philosophy took shape. It postulated a social ideal of a static economic order, of a hierarchy of social and political classes, powers, and rights knit together into an organic whole by the mutual obligations of masters and bondsmen.[25] The focus of the southern attack became the concept of free society and the literati of the South rejected it root and branch. "It is quite time, that this destructive and radical philosophy, beginning with the reformation, and culminating with Adam Smith, should decline, and be succeeded by an opposite system, that of conservatism," wrote George Fitzhugh.[26] Locke, Jefferson, Blackstone, and Adam Smith were the originators of that subversive doctrine of the sovereignty of the individual which had revolutionized the North.[27] "An equality of conditions, of political powers and privileges, which has no solid basis in an equality of capacity or fitness, is one of the wildest and most impracticable of all Utopian dreams. If . . . such an equality should prevail . . . all order would be overthrown, all justice extinguished, and utter confusion would reign." [28]

Abolition was only one aspect of the revolt against authority and social order implied in the natural-rights doctrine. For the moment the empty spaces of the West still provided a safety valve, but soon the conjunction of free labor, free competition, free capital, and free government would, as in Europe, produce pauperism, crime, and social radicalism.[29] The "sovereignty of the individual," Fourierism, and "free love" were the true aims of the northern radicalism. "The whole *active* intellect of Christendom, headed by such men as Proudhon and Andrews . . . [are] directly assailing every existing governmental arrangement." [30] The defense of slavery was therefore the defense of all civilization. All attempts to abolish slavery by substituting "slavery to capital for slavery to human masters" only strengthened infidelity and agrarianism.[31] The Republican party was the instrument of the social reform movement. With its victory, the slaves would be emancipated, peonage introduced, and through them the staples of the helpless South, of Mexico, and Central America would be exploited.[32]

George Fitzhugh's *Sociology for the South* proved that free society was doomed. The belief that "individual well-being and social and national wealth and prosperity will be best promoted by each man's eagerly pursuing his own selfish welfare unfettered and unrestricted by legal regulations, or governmental prohibitions," Fitzhugh argued, would lead to disaster.[33] The abstract natural-rights philosophy had, ever since the Reformation, convulsed the world in blood and hatred.[34] Socialism, its natural heir, would spread. Trade unions, phalansteries communistic settlements, and Mormonism were all forms of slavery, save that they lacked masters. Fitzhugh's only quarrel with socialism was that "it will not honestly admit that it owes its recent revival to the failure of universal liberty, and is seeking to bring about slavery again in some form."[35] Fitzhugh then vindicated domestic slavery as the ultimate form of social order and higher civilizations. Unlike the free society which rested upon universal liberty and free competition and threw the whole burden of society upon the poor, "slavery relieves our slaves of those cares altogether, and slavery is . . . the very best form of socialism."[36]

Advocating the repeal of all social and political legislation since 1776, Fitzhugh warned that the North would have to "recur to domestic slavery, the oldest, the best and most common form of socialism."[37] In words which show the impact of Catholic conservatism, he argued that sin and the love of liberty were akin. Liberty emphasized the natural inequality among men, while slavery protected the helpless and obligated the strong.[38]

In *Cannibals All!* Fitzhugh further developed the proslavery argument.[39] The growing clamor of southerners for the reopening of the slave trade made it even more incumbent upon the apologists to prove the superiority of the southern social system. "We are all, North and South, engaged in the white Slave Trade, [immigration] and he who succeeds best, is esteemed most respectable. It is far more cruel than the black slave trade, because it exacts more of its slaves, and neither protects nor governs them."[40] Fitzhugh devaluated the ideals of liberty by disclosing the underlying class interest in a manner remarkably similar to the Marxian.[41] Only the return to feudalism with its functional concepts of society and classes, its ideal of service and of fixed status, could save civilization.[42]

To the abolitionist and radical North, George Fitzhugh became the representative of the southern threat to the American ideal.[43] For the antislavery movement his books and articles were heaven-sent ammunition to be skillfully employed to prove that the time had come to unite against a South that threatened to destroy the northern way of life.[44]

The contents of *Cannibals All!* became known to innumerable northerners through Garrison's *Liberator* and Maria Lydia Child's pamphlet, *The Patriarchical Institution as Described by Members of Its Own Family.* Abel Stevens, a leading Methodist minister and the editor of the *National Magazine* and the *Christian Advocate and Journal,* impressed upon his readers the image of a sinister threat to American Christianity when he called the book "the great American Apostacy."

To many it became clear that the South had declared war on the philosophy of human rights and democracy. Had not Senator James H. Hammond, in his famous speech "Cotton is King," declared that "in all social sytems, there must be a class to do the menial duties. . . It constitutes the very *mudsill of society* and of political government. . . *Your whole Class of manual hireling laborers at the North, and your 'operatives,' as you call them, are essentially slaves."* Governor George McDuffie of South Carolina explained that slavery was "the cornerstone of our Republican edifice." Free society had failed, said Senator Mason of Virginia, and "that which is *not* free must be substituted." [45]

The North could not ignore the warnings that the South was determined to impose its social system on the whole country.[46] As early as 1856 Fitzhugh had pointed out that the United States would be either free or slave but could not continue divided.[47] And *DeBow's Review* had expressed the incompatibility of the two social systems in even clearer language. "Social forms, so widely different as those of domestic slavery, and . . . universal freedom, cannot long co-exist in the great Republic of Christendom. . . The war between the two systems rages everywhere, and will continue till the one conquers. . . We do not hope, nor wish to see slavery like ours introduced at the North. . . But we do hope, and expect, and believe that conservative men everywhere are about to adopt the principle that men should be governed, not 'let alone,' and that each one should be governed according to his wants, and morals and intellectual capacity." [48]

It was in this light that the North interpreted the events in Kansas, the federal measures to execute the Fugitve Slave Act and the Dred Scott decision. The question ceased to be constitutional, political, or ethical. A competing social ideology and social system challenged the survival of free society. Fitzhugh's statement directly inspired Lincoln's declaration at the Republican Convention in Springfield, Illinois: " 'A house divided against itself cannot stand.' I believe this government cannot endure permanently half slave and half free. . . It will become all one thing, or all the other." [49] Seward, too, came to believe that the antagonistic systems of free labor and slavery created an "irrepressible conflict" which meant that "the United States must and will, sooner or later, become either entirely a slaveholding nation, or entirely a free-labor nation." [50]

Lincoln's own views on slavery were decisively influenced by the new southern philosophy. At Peoria in 1854 he explained, "Little by little, but steadily as man's march to the grave, we have been giving up the OLD for the NEW faith. Near eighty years ago we began by declaring that all men are created equal; but now from that beginning we have run down to the other declaration, that for SOME men to enslave OTHERS is a 'sacred right of self-government.' These principles can not stand together. They are as opposite as God and mammon; and whoever holds to the one, must despise the other." [51]

The South had succeeded, through its rejection of Jeffersonian democratic ideals and through its violent attack on the free social system, in focusing the attention of northerners on their own ideals and institutions, which they thought embodied the major values of America. Lincoln concluded his Peoria speech: "To deny these things is to deny our national axioms, or dogmas, at least; and it puts an end to all argument." [52] He thus identified the principles of nationality with those of the free society, self-government, and human liberty. He made the connection even more clearly in 1859, in answer to an invitation to a Jefferson birthday celebration. With irony and insight he stressed the reversal of the ideological attitudes of the North and South and revealed the significance of the Preamble to the Declaration of Independence.

Bearing in mind that about seventy years ago, two great political parties were first formed in this country, that Thomas Jefferson was the head of one of them, and Boston the head-quarters of the other, it is both curious and interesting that those supposed to descend politically from the party opposed to Jefferson, should now be celebrating his birthday in their own original seat of empire, while those claiming political descent from him have nearly ceased to breathe his name everywhere.

Remembering too, that the Jefferson party was formed upon their supposed superior devotion to the *personal* rights of men, holding the rights of

property to be secondary only, and greatly inferior, and then assuming that
the so-called democracy of to-day, are the Jefferson, and their opponents,
the anti-Jefferson parties, it will be equally interesting to note how completely the two have changed hands as to the principle upon which they
were originally supposed to be divided. . . It is now no child's play to save
the principles of Jefferson from total overthrow in this nation. . . The
principles of Jefferson are the definitions and axioms of free society. And yet
they are denied, and evaded, with no small show of success. One dashingly
calls them "glittering generalities"; another bluntly calls them "self-evident
lies"; and still others insidiously argue that they apply only to "superior
races."

These expressions, differing in form, are identical in object and effect—the
supplanting the principles of free government, and restoring those of classification, caste, and legitimacy. . . They are the van-guard—the miners, and
sappers—of returning despotism. We must repulse them, or they will sub-
jugate us.[53]

The same effect can be observed in the utterances of most of
the prominent northern spokesmen. The writings of Fitzhugh and
the *Richmond Enquirer* were continually quoted by the congres-
sional representatives of Massachusetts, Illinois, Wisconsin, Michigan, Ohio, and Minnesota to prove the sinister intentions of the
South.[54] The frequent references by Republicans to the southern
philosophy showed how it crystallized a northern sectional party.
The South provided the radical North with immensely popular
slogans through which laborer and farmer, the small entrepreneur
and the merchant, could be drawn away from the existing parties
and aligned with the antislavery camp through the consciousness
of common values.[55]

The keystone of this new ideological awareness was the concept
central to the Jeffersonian tradition and implicit in transcendental
and radical individualism—the concept of a "free society." The
Declaration of Independence was now interpreted in terms of
social rather than political ideals; and that enabled the Republican
party to take possession of the Preamble.[56] The ridicule and scorn
heaped on the idea of a free society united large sections of the
North against the South. These words of the *Muscogee Herald* of
Alabama, reprinted by the northern *Independent* in 1856, were
duly utilized by the Republicans: "*Free* society! We sicken of the
name. What is it but a conglomoration of *greasy mechanics, filthy
operatives, small-fisted farmers,* and moon-struck theorists?"[57] In
the debate between Douglas and Lincoln, the Republican sup-

porters carried a huge banner reading, "Small fisted-farmers, mud-sills of society, greasy mechanics for A. Lincoln." [58]

The southern attack fused the idealistic and humanitarian aspects of transcendentalism and the Protestant reform movement with radical democracy and thereby legitimized the system of competitive economics and private property. A coherent system of ethical, social, economic, and political values had been created. The actual economic and social structure was set in the framework of absolute and universal ideals, those of human dignity and personal freedom. The national and the social ideal coalesced.

2. FORMATIVE FORCES IN THE RISE OF A RADICAL NORTHERN NATIONALISM

The Republican party emerged between 1854 and 1856 as a coalition of most of the radical movements of the North. Their common denominator was less a militant abolitionism than the extension of the rights of the common man toward equality of economic and social opportunities. The fusion of Jacksonian Democrats, Conscience Whigs, political abolitionists, and New England humanitarians into the Free Soil party was the result of the disintegration of old parties and the formation of new ones around social ideologies.

A typcial expression of that radicalism which split both the Democratic and Whig parties was the proposed constitution of the Barnburner wing of the Democratic party of New York, which entered the Free Soil party in 1848. It held that "man's natural rights are, his right to exist, and to enjoy his existence; and the right to exercise those physical and mental faculties with which nature has endowed him. Man's natural rights in relation to things are, his right to things produced by the exercise of his personal endowments, and his right to participate in those bounties which nature has equally given to all." [59] These ideas, incessantly propagated by William Cullen Bryant and William Leggett of the *Evening Post,* by Senator Thomas Hart Benton and labor editor George Evans, became part and parcel of the Free Soil movement and through it of the young Republican party.

The growing tension between the North and the militant South united New England transcendentalists, reformers and humanitarians, radical abolitionists and left-wing Democrats. Free-trade concepts, agrarianism, antimonopolism, and equalitarianism, as well as the distrust of the state an an instrument of economic exploitation, were among the elements which characterized the movement.[60]

Yet in the actual definition of the aims of the Republican party and the formation of its ideology the influence of New England radicals and of the Greeley circle in New York was quite out of proportion to their numerical strength. They had developed an ideology which, by interpreting American democracy in terms of a Protestant humanism, was able to express the aspirations of northern democracy through the almost synonymous terms of "individualism" and "free society." Their doctrine of the infinite worth of the human personality, of its capacity for growth and self-government, and the priority they gave to liberty over all other values made their theory particularly relevant to the question of reform and slavery and furnished a valid answer to southern attacks on the wage slavery in the North.

Emerson had given his support to the Free Soil movement. He even overcame his aloofness and aversion to politics and spoke on behalf of John G. Palfrey, an abolitionist candidate for the governorship of Massachusetts on the Free Soil ticket. Ever since Daniel Webster had supported the Compromise of 1850, Emerson had turned his back on the Whigs. He supported the abolitionist movement not for ethical reasons alone; he realized that the conflict with the South involved the survival of the fundamental value pattern of America and that of human progress in general. The criterion of any social system was whether it favored the greatest liberty for each individual and the highest elevation of human dignity in all. Appealing to this standard as the higher law, Emerson boldly favored the individual and collective nullification of the positive law which supported slavery and extended its powers over the Union.

Emerson's position was characteristic. Many, like him, were not Garrisonians but became abolitionists because slavery was incompatible with a free society, with man's self-realization through liberty. Thoreau, Theodore Parker, Charles Sumner, Gerrit Smith, Wendell Phillips, William Cullen Bryant, and Horace Greeley all spoke the same language. Their national and ethical social ideals coincided. The emphasis on the higher law as superior to all human law and the abolitionists' demand to remove ethnic or racial conditions from national and civil rights made the American concept of nationality truly universal. In the enlargement of the Unitarian and transcendentalist position to embrace all men, none was more influential than Theodore Parker. William Seward, Salmon P. Chase, Charles Sumner, Henry Wilson, and John P. Hale all testified to his role in the foundation of the Republican movement. Lincoln's law partner, William Herndon, spread Parker's fame in Illinois.[61]

Parker's passionate hatred of slavery sprang from his ethical-religious interpretation of American democracy, which at the same time drove him to a radical criticism of contemporary American institutions.[62] "Our laws degrade, at the beginning, one-half the human race, and sacrifice them to the other and perhaps worser half." [63] He visualized a reformed Christianity through which it would be possible to "build up a great state where there was an honorable work for every hand, bread for all mouths . . . culture for every mind, and love and faith in every heart." [64] In his social interpretation of Christian ethics he formed a link between transcendentalism and radical democracy. He opposed the conflict with England over the Oregon Territory and the war against Mexico as serving the cause of slavery; and the enactment of the Fugitive Slave Act made him one of the leaders of the antislavery movement. Earlier than most, he realized that the conflict between slavery and freedom was irrepressible and could not be solved by compromise and legal subterfuge. The Kansas-Nebraska Act convinced him that only organized political power and, if need be, force, could halt the extension of slavery over the whole union. In May 1854 he suggested to William Seward a convention at Buffalo of all the representatives of the free states to take council against the establishment of despotism. On the side of slavery were arrayed the banking and industrial interests, power politicians, and the profiteers of the spoils system.[65] Fully realizing the trend of the southern mind,[66] he described the conflict between North and South as one between democracy, or the rights of man, and despotism—a despotism that stood for "bondage for poor whites," "slavery for greasy mechanics," "no free schools," "no free press," "no free pulpit," "no free speech," "no free man." [67] Parker's transcendentalism was an admirable basis for that fundamentalism which repealed the positive in the name of the higher law and justified revolution on ethical grounds. Here was the Jeffersonian legitimation of revolution readopted through a dynamic concept of the rights of man. "A State *has no right to enact wrong*. . . Rights and duties are anterior to all laws or institutions, and always superior to them." [68]

Parker's appeal to the higher law derived from his transcendental philosophy of individualism and its interpretation of congregationalism as the historic expression of the spirit of independence. "We are a rebellious nation," he wrote. "Our creeds are infidelity to the mother church, our constitution treason to our fatherland. . . Though all the governors in the world bid us commit treason against man . . . let us never submit. Let God only be a master to control our conscience." [69]

The contribution of the New England radicals to the ideological development of the North lay, therefore, in the formulation of the ethical and social principles which could claim to represent the true principles of American national identity. The reform impulse which originated with this ideology led inevitably to political abolitionism and fused with democratic radicalism to form the Republican party in the 1850's.

Horace Greeley was a typical representative of the confluence of all the reform impulses with those of radical democracy. [70] The New York *Tribune*, especially its weekly edition read by hundreds of thousands in the East and West, became the propaganda vehicle of the Republican party movement. In 1854 the weekly had a circulation of 112,000, and many times that number of readers. "There being few popular magazines during this decade, the weekly newspaper, in some degree, took their place; and through this medium, Greeley and his able coadjutors spoke to the people of New York and of the West, where New England ideas predominated, with a power never before or since known in this country." [71]

After being read out of the Whig party for his anti-rent, abolitionist, Fourieristic, and "Vote-Yourself-a-Farm" doctrines, he worked ceaselessly for the formation of a new alliance of radical democracy, which was achieved through the Republican party. [72] Greeley had joined the Fourierist movement because he believed the existing economic order to be incompatible with the promise of American democracy, which he interpreted in the spirit of Protestant humanism. He held the fundamentally Jeffersonian ideal of a free society of independent and self-supporting citizens who enjoyed equality of economic and social opportunities. Such a society was to be realized by the industrial association or the producers' cooperatives and by a radical land reform which would open up the natural resources of the nation to the productive classes.[73] In the main, he adopted the theories advocated by George Henry Evans in the *Working Man's Advocate* and *Young America*. Greeley's agitation for homestead laws started in 1845, and by making Evans' "Vote Yourself a Farm"[74] the practical goal of the radical northern democracy, he helped to swell the votes of the Republican party.[75]

Evans' social views, like those of the transcendentalists and anarchists, had been shaped in a conscious attempt to solve the questions raised by the socialists' critique without accepting their solution.[76] While Evans interpreted the labor theory of wealth as the absolute right of labor to the full income of its productive work, or the equivalent of it, he maintained at the same time that socialism would destroy that liberty and personal independence which were fundamental human needs and primary conditions of progress. Social justice must be based on individuality and man's right to property. It meant an equal share in natural resources and the right to the full income of one's labor. In an absolutely free market, with the destruction of a class monopoly which was supported and maintained by political power, and with the opening up of the public land to the laboring class, equality of economic opportunity would be achieved.

Evans' principles of equality, inalienability, and individuality, derived from Jefferson and Thomas Paine, constituted, together with Warren's individualist anarchism and Kellogg's schemes for monetary reform, the typical American version of social radicalism.[77] In all three cases the decisive reason for the direction taken by social and economic radicalism was the concept of individuality, and individual rights, and of the relation between state and society as developed both by Jeffersonians and the Protestant humanists.

Greeley's incessant agitation for the limitation of the size of landed property, for the opening of the public domain, and for exemption of homesteads from seizure for debt—all based on Evans' proposals—united radical elements behind the abolitionist agitation against the extension of slavery to the western territory. Another associate of Evans, Alvan E. Bovay, organized at Ripon, Wisconsin, the first conference of Whigs, Democrats, and Free Soilers as a political party to resist the extension of slave power and suggested the name "Republican party" to Greeley.[78]

The full impact of the New England attitude was expressed in the appeal of Chase, Sumner, J. R. Giddings, Edward Wade, Gerrit Smith, and Alexander De Witt—all Independent Democrats and prominent abolitionists—to their constituencies in 1854 to oppose all compromise with the South on the extension of slavery into the territories. The question of the nature of the Union was conceived in purely ethical and social terms. The "higher law" could become either the basis of a strong Unionism—a new federalism which completely disregarded the old constitutional structure—or of a movement toward secession.

> We appeal to the people. We warn you that the dearest interests of freedom and the Union are in imminent peril. . . We tell you that the Union can only be maintained by the full recognition of the just claims of freedom and man. The Union was formed to establish justice and secure the blessings of liberty. When it fails to accomplish these ends it will be worthless. . . We entreat you to be mindful of that fundamental maxim of Democracy— EQUAL RIGHTS AND EXACT JUSTICE FOR ALL MEN. . . We shall go home to our constituents, erect anew the standard of freedom, and call on the people to come to the rescue of the country from the domination of slavery. We will not despair; for the cause of human freedom is the cause of God.[79]

This was the same social and ethical conception of federal nationalism that would inspire Lincoln's Gettysburg Address.

The consciousness of unity of purpose and ideals was strikingly expressed in the general readoption of the Jeffersonian Preamble to the Declaration of Independence as a symbol of national and social purpose.[80] The Liberty and Free Soil parties had introduced a humanitarian-social interpretation into the concept of the Preamble. Abolitionists, humanitarians, and transcendentalists had interpreted it in terms of the religious concept of the dignity of man and the idea of the higher law. The Declaration had thereby become the vehicle for maintaining that individual freedom was the ultimate and best of all social values.

This idea, which the Free Soil party had simplified in the motto,

"Free Soil, Free Speech, Free Labor and Free Men," was reflected in the incorporation of the Preamble to the Declaration into the Republican party platforms of 1856 and 1860.[81] The comments of Owen Lovejoy, abolitionist of Illinois, in the National Convention of the Republican party in 1856 were typical. The American mission, he declared, was "to maintain and illustrate the self-evident truths laid down in that Declaration of Independence"

. . . Now, what was the principle thus set up?. . . It was a reaffirmation of that Divine truth which was announced ages ago, when the Creator said: "Let us make man in our own image." As man was made in the likeness of God, every man had an aspiration after the eternal, and was conscious of there being a miniature God within himself; and that image must not be crushed, however degraded, for God was there. There was a germ of immortality there, which at some time, however remote, would emerge and shine as a star forever and ever. . . He . . . might be allowed to quote the saying of Franklin, who asserted that "he would go to the verge of the Constitution in favor of freedom." But he [the speaker] would not be satisfied with that—he would jump off the Constitution to promote the same object.[82]

3. "A NEW BIRTH OF FREEDOM"—THE CRYSTALLIZATION OF A NEW NATIONALISM

The southern attack and the actual forces which aligned themselves in the Republican party made it inevitable that social and economic questions would be uppermost in the minds of those who became the spokesmen of the free states. The term "free society" connoted not only the supreme value of individual liberty and personal independence but also the trend toward "equality of opportunity" for all in a free and competitive order of society. Such a social concept suited both the western farmer and the eastern industrial elements.

The adoption of the Preamble to the Declaration as a social and not as a political objective was a significant development of the great crisis which preceded the Civil War. The nation was pledged to the humanitarian ideal of a free society, of an order of freedom and progress. The Republican party fused Jeffersonian universalism into a new nationalism the key words of which were equal liberty, equality of opportunity, and the maintenance of a truly national government to support those ideals. "Let us readopt the Declaration of Independence," said Lincoln in Peoria, "and with it the practices and policy which harmonize with it."[83] In his message to Congress of July 4, 1861, Lincoln defined his view on the conflict. "This is essentially a People's contest. On the side of the Union, it is a struggle for maintaining in the world, that form, and substance of government, whose leading object is, to elevate the conditions of men—to lift artificial weights from all shoulders—to clear the paths of laudable pursuits for all—to afford all, an unfettered start, and a fair chance, in the race of life." [84] These words set the essential elements of the concept of free society in relation to the functions of government and the meaning of national unity. [85]

Lincoln modified the radicalism of the northern democrats and made their uncompromising ideology serviceable to a democratic national government. The rights of individuals and society were above the claims of political unity and national sovereignty, and revolution was "a most sacred right . . . which we hope and believe is to liberate the world." [86] Yet Lincoln conceived Jeffersonian democracy as the vehicle of a strong nationalism and federalism. Equality of opportunity demanded the existence of a positive state. Government as a regulative force thus became an integral part of the Jeffersonian theory. [87] In a society in which property was widely diffused and education general, social justice would be secured by furnishing sufficient opportunities for all the thrifty, the industrious, to secure the material benefits to which labor entitled them. Lincoln, as a westerner far removed from despotic power and less rooted in local traditions than southerners and easterners, could hardly imagine any contradiction between the dynamics of a free society and the role of the national government. His concept of an integral national unity dissociated the Jeffersonian idea of a free society from the political implications that had produced the states'-rights theory. Lincoln, the self-made man, conceived the social ideal of the Union largely in terms of the western experience, so that social justice for him meant the equality of opportunity to achieve material competence and independence. The metaphors "unfettered start" and "fair chance in the race of life" expressed these attitudes. The older traditions of Puritan self-reliance and of equalitarianism were thereby linked in a highly dynamic and individualized concept of social opportunities and progress.

Emerson's interpretation of Lincoln's significance was essentially accurate. Democracy was for Lincoln a natural environment which became a problem only through the challenge of the South and the growing sectional struggle. He was "a quite native, aboriginal man, as an acorn from the oak." He was representative because his life and attitudes expressed the social and personal dynamics of American democracy.[88] In Lincoln's view the equating of a fair chance of success with equality of economic opportunity was subordinate to an essentially equalitarian ideal. This was his answer to the southern challenge. Speaking before an audience of New England laborers on strike, he strove to reconcile laissez faire with equality of opportunity.

I am glad to see that a system of labor prevails in New England under which laborers can strike when they want to, where they are not obliged to work under all circumstances. . . . I take it that it is best for all to leave each man free to acquire property as fast as he can. Some will get wealthy. I don't believe in a law to prevent a man from getting rich; it would do more harm than good. So while we do not propose any war upon capital, we do wish to allow the humblest man an equal chance to get rich with everybody else. When one starts poor, as most do in the race of life, free society is such that he knows that he can better his condition; he knows there is no fixed condition of labor for his whole life . . . that is the true system.[89]

Lincoln had in mind the southern polemics against the industrial slavery of the North while formulating his concept of the true system of free society.

His answer was more relevant to the western agrarian economy than to the industrialized society of the East. He saw in the wage earner only a man in transition toward the economic independence of the self-employing farmer, the mechanic, the merchant, and the professional man.[90] Having observed everywhere in his life the process of primary capital accumulation through thrift, economy, prudence, and industry, he fused the gospel of individual success with economic opportunity and social justice. "The prudent, penniless beginner," he remarked in Milwaukee, "labors for wages awhile, saves a surplus with which to buy tools or land, for himself; then labors on his own account another while, and at length hires another new beginner to help him. This, say its advocates, is *free* labor—the just and generous, and prosperous system, which opens the way for all—gives hope to all, and energy, and progress, and improvement of conditions to all. If any continue through life in the condition of the hired laborer, it is not the fault of the system, but because of either a dependent nature . . . or improvidence, folly, or singular misfortune." [91]

Lincoln conceived this pattern of relations as a social system to which America was pledged. Yet he thought inevitably in patterns of individual careers and histories. Free society became a framework for individual efforts, for a fair chance for each to gain material competence. The concept of man's natural rights was thus applied to social theory. The Declaration of Independence became, more than the Constitution, the charter of the national idea. This concept of American identity was clearly formulated by Lincoln in his speech at Independence Hall, Philadelphia, immediately before his inauguration. "I have often inquired of myself, what great principle or idea it was that kept this Confederacy so long together. It was not the mere matter of separation from the motherland; but something in that Declaration giving liberty not alone to the people of this country, but hope to the world for all future time. It was that which gave promise that in due time the weights should be lifted from the shoulders of all men, and that *all* should have an equal chance." [92]

Walt Whitman expressed the same idea in his "Democratic Vistas." The common man fought and died for the Union to preserve democratic society and the right of each to develop his own life. The final meaning of democracy was "to bring forward and modify everything else with the idea of that something a man is . . . standing apart from all else, divine in his own right . . . sole and untouchable by any canons of authority." [93] He thus defined American democracy as a system of universal liberation of the individual, and his self-realization, in fine, as individualism. [94]

The war created a growing need to define the ideals of American democracy and nationality through a generic principle. John William Draper's *History of the American Civil War* showed the utility of the term individualism as a means of characterizing northern social institutions and ideals. [95] Written immediately after the war, it explained the conflict as the product of an increasing antagonism between two societies based on mutually exclusive principles of social organization. The governing principle of the North was that of individualism while that of the South was aristocratic feudal particularism. In the former, each pursued his own well-being and interests independently while in the latter each lived in a self-contained world.

In the North the population was in a state of unceasing activity; there was corporeal and mental restlessness. Magnificent cities in all directions were arising; the country was intersected with canals, railroads . . . companies for banking, manufacturing, commercial purposes, were often concentrating many millions of capital. There were all kinds of associations . . . churches, hospitals, schools, abounded. The foreign commerce at length rivaled that of the most powerful nations of Europe. This wonderful spectacle of social development was the result of INDIVIDUALISM, operating in an unbounded theatre of action. Everyone was seeking to do all that he could for himself.[96]

Meanwhile, the South, retrogressing into slavery, was condemned by history to be defeated.[97] Aware of the antagonism of the two societies, the South attacked the system of individualism and preferred to secede rather than to be drawn into the whirlpool of social confusion.[98]

The concept of individualism brought into a general pattern all the elements of the social system which described the national ideal of the militant North. This context accounted for the immense popularity in the United States of John Stuart Mill's *Principles of Political Economy with Some of Their Applications to Social Philosophy*. Mill confirmed rather than influenced the outlook of the North.[99] He related the competitive economic order to the ethical values of a free society and made the former the condition for the existence of human freedom, individuality, and true justice. Mill's concept of the state's function, less doctrinaire than that of most Free Traders, eminently suited the ideas of the North. The activities of the state would be limited to the increase of opportunities offered for individual action. "A good government will give all its aid in such a shape, as to encourage and nurture any rudiments it may find of a spirit of individual exertion. It will be assiduous in removing obstacles and discouragements to voluntary enterprize, and in giving whatever facilities and whatever direction and guidance may be necessary . . . in aid of private efforts rather than in suppression of them." [100]

Mill's attitude toward the distribution of wealth was strongly tinged by his humanitarian philosophy.[101] He advocated state regulation of natural monopolies, public works, and social legislation.[102] His demand for the limitation of property rights in land and its fair distribution among actual farmers, as well as his cautious schemes for land nationalization, derived from his ethical and social views rather than from purely economic considerations. While he believed that private property, freedom of contract, a general laissez-faire policy, were both just and useful, he criticized the views of Malthus, David Ricardo, and James Mill as illegitimate extensions of the mechanics of the economic process into the sphere of economic and social policy.[103] Deeply impressed by the socialistic critique of the competitive economy, John Stuart Mill endeavored to prove that the existing order of individual property contained the elements of an alternative order of social justice.

This aspect of J. S. Mill's views became particularly relevant to American intellectuals who faced the same criticism from the South. He defended private property by relating it to the values of freedom, progress, and the ideal of self-realization, in almost the same words as Emerson. "It is not the subversion of the system of individual property that should be aimed at; but the improvement of it, and the participation of every member of the community in its benefits. The principle of private property has never yet had a fair trial in any country." [104] John Stuart Mill therefore helped to clarify and systematize that ideology of individualism. Becoming the accepted authority on political economy and moral philosophy in most American colleges, he molded significantly the outlook of the post-Civil War generation.[105]

Thus a new sectional consciousness took form in the free states through the clash with a hostile southern ideology. Though this consciousness was in the main concerned with ethical, social, and economic questions it also became a new national ideology. In this manner it could claim to represent not a sectional but a national party which based its policy on the defense of the principles of a free society.

The Civil War played an important role in the growth of an integral American nationalism.[106] Yet from the beginning this nationalism crystallized around social and moral, rather than political, concepts. The questions involved in the sectional conflict were not the rights of the existing states but the fate of the national domain and the nature of the social structure of the United States. The slaveholding and the free states each charged the other side with an attempt to rule the Union in its own interest through an undue extension of federal power and a conscious misinterpretation of the Constitution. The militant North interpreted the Fugitive Slave Act, the Kansas-Nebraska Act, the endorsement of the Lecompton Constitution, and the Dred Scott decision as a conspiracy to impose slavocracy upon the whole Union. Secession was defended on the grounds that a house divided against itself could not stand. It thus involved a nationalism so identified with social ideology that both sides preferred dismemberment of the Union to concession. The northern emphasis on the maintenance of the Union by all means was expressed only after it had won control of the federal government and faced the factual secession of the South.

This fusion of social ideals with group loyalty, fanaticism, the will to political power, and the maintenance of the Union, created a new type of nationalism on the eve of the Civil War. It became the primary function of the federal government to suppress the southern threat to destroy the social system of democracy through secession and war. The appeal to patriotism and national loyalty in defence of the Union was at the same time an appeal to maintain democracy and the institutions of a free society. This changed the traditional relationship between state and society. The paramount duty of the state was to maintain in the world that form of government whose leading object it was to elevate the conditions of men.

The antagonism toward centralized power, latent in the Jeffersonian tradition, disappeared during the Civil War, at least for those actively engaged in defending the Union side. The government, having become identified with a definite social philosophy, became the trustee of its realization, and through it the focus of loyalty, the expression of the general will of the nation.

The heightened consciousness of the uniqueness of American society which emerged with nationalism during the War needed a term adequately to define and explain its character. The term supplied by the New England intellectuals was individualism. This concept "of the singleness of man, individualism," described, according to Whitman, the dynamic and progressive motive force of modern history and explained the aspiration of the American nation.[107]

Whitman's concept of individualism reflected the amalgamation of the great traditions of pre-Civil War America inside the Republican party, a synthesis which was carried over by liberals and radical Republicans into the post-Civil War period. Individualism integrated the radical democratic concept of a free society with its connotations of laissez faire, inalienable rights, and its distrust of centralized political power, with the transcendentalist-Unitarian concept of individual self-determination and self-perfectibility. Increasingly, after the Civil War, this concept described the character of the American commonwealth and its ideals, its institution and behavior pattern. The same concept was implicit in most of the writings of American intellectuals in the latter half of the nineteenth century and inspired most of the legislative, political, and judicial actions of the several branches of the federal Republic.[108]

XV
Epilogue

"There are," remarked James Bryce in *The American Commonwealth,* "certain dogmas or maxims which are in so far fundamental that they have told widely on political thought, and that one usually strikes upon them when sinking a shaft, so to speak, into an American mind." [1] Among these, Bryce thought, were the notions about man's inalienable rights, popular sovereignty, the distrust of centralized political power, and the conviction that the functions of the government must be kept at a minimum if the community and the individual were to prosper. [2] "Everything tended to make the United States in this respect more English than England, for the circumstances of colonial life, the process of settling the western wilderness, the feelings evoked by the struggle against George III, all went to intensify individualism, the love of enterprise, the pride in personal freedom. And from that day to this, individualism, the love of enterprise, and the pride in personal freedom, have been deemed by Americans not only their choicest, but their peculiar and exclusive possessions." [3]

This was indeed a far cry from Tocqueville's statement some forty years earlier that the Americans, by the use of liberty, fought and conquered the individualism that equality generated.

This striking discrepancy in the evaluation of the relationship of individualism to American life can be explained neither by a difference in the point of observation nor by a change in the scene observed. What had indeed changed in the period which had elapsed between Tocqueville and Bryce was that Americans had transformed the concept of individualism from a term of abuse to one of approval, from a remote sociological notion to one which more than any other defined Americanism.

Bryce described what Americans considered in the 1880's as

their basic attitude toward society and government on the one hand and as the traditional ideal of their personal behavior and value pattern, on the other. The first aspect was summed up in his statement that "the nation is nothing but so many individuals. The government is nothing but certain representatives and officials, agents who are here to-day and gone to-morrow."[4] This atomistic view of the social and political body was strengthened by a "common-sense notion that everybody knows his own business best, that individual enterprise has 'made America,' and will 'run America' better than the best government could do."[5] In its other aspect, individualism meant self-reliance, the love of enterprise, and fierce pride in personal independence. "So far as there can be said to be any theory on the subject," Bryce concluded, "*laissez aller* is the orthodox and accepted doctrine in the sphere both of the Federal and of State legislation."[6]

Bryce maintained these evaluations in spite of apparently contrary trends toward the growing demand for state interference into ever-widening fields.[7] He emphasized the paradox that the demand for state interference was strongest in the West, though that section prided itself as being pre-eminently the land of freedom, enterprise, and self-help, where the sentiment of individualism was strongest.[8] The apparent contradiction between the observed clamor for state interference and the no less obvious adherence to "individualism" did not, in Bryce's opinion, invalidate his observation. State interference was usually appealed to in order to protect the majority against the power of the few. Individualism as a behavior pattern was so deeply entrenched in the American that the paternalism of France and Germany was "repellent to him."[9]

Bryce's interpretation of the American concept of individualism revealed his close contacts with the New England and New York liberals, who in the late nineteenth century were America's intellectual leaders, the transatlantic counterpart of the progressive wing of British liberalism.[10] This group had elaborated the theory of individualism in the second half of the nineteenth century and applied it to the American scene. The group included practically all those who united in 1872 to found the Liberal Republican party, who supported Tilden and Cleveland, created the "Mugwump" Movement, and advocated civil service and free trade. The

"Free Religious Association" (founded in 1867), the Boston Radical Club, and the American Social Science Association expressed the aims of this liberalism in the field of philosophy, ethics, and social sciences.[11] Their organs, the *Nation, Harper's Weekly,* the *Springfield Republican,* and the *New York Evening Post* enjoyed a high prestige among educated Americans. While they wielded little organized political power, they spoke with intellectual authority. Charles Francis Adams, Jr., Henry Adams, William Cullen Bryant, Charles A. Dana, Horace Greeley, George W. Curtis, Charles Sumner, Carl Schurz, and Lyman Trumbull were all saturated with New England ideals. Their connection with the *Nation,* with the Free Religious Association, and with the Boston Radical Club showed the continuous development of a pre-Civil War New England humanism into the liberalism of the later period.

For this group the Civil War was a victory for universal freedom and social equality. The promise of America had come true and a new nation had been conceived in freedom and in the service of man's rights. It was the sole duty of the democratic state to provide the framework within which to work these aims out. Further progress would not be achieved by political means but by moral, economic, and social forces which would by voluntary association and competition, and by the spread of enlightenment, realize the highest aims to which society could aspire. The platform of the Free Religious Association, as suggested by the Unitarian philosopher Francis Ellingwood Abbot, stated: "*Whereas,* the grand end of human society is the freest, fullest, and the highest development of the individual. . . *Whereas,* the grand end of the individual soul is the realization, in itself and in the world, of the highest Ideal of Humanity, and is thus identical with the great cause of universal human progress;—*Article I* Therefore, we hereby associate ourselves into a Free Brotherhood, for the purpose of helping each other and our fellow-men in the endeavour after the perfect Spirit, Life and Truth." [12]

"For the first time in history, free personality is the sum of all purposes," wrote one member of this group.[13] C. C. Schackford defined the principle of the new civilization as "Manhood." [14] The Civil War and Reconstruction were the last acts of liberation in which the gospel of humanity achieved its final victory. It pre-

pared the road on which mankind would "rush forth on the
mighty winds' of Science, Trade, and Freedom that make one
country of the world." [15] To William B. Scott the great vehicle of
progress was free cooperation and competition which, "unfettered
by monopolies and subsidies, always elevates the superior over
the inferior, and urges on genuine improvement and progress by
the most efficient means." [16] "What we want," Scott continued, "is
freedom and justice,—that is, freedom to do all that we will,
provided that we . . . [do not] trespass . . . upon the freedom of
any other person." [17]

The characterization of laissez faire which James Bryce gave to
the liberal version of individualism was accurate, in its nineteenth-
century connotation. It stood for adherence to the theories of the
classical political economy, utilitarian morality, and progress. The
synthesis of liberty and social justice achieved in Whitman's concept of individualism, which was based on a humanistic interpretation of the natural-rights theory, was not maintained. The
Protestant Ethic prevailed over the eighteenth-century elements
of the Enlightenment that were inherent in the Jeffersonian concept of society.

John W. Draper defined individualism as the principle which
maintains "that man shall be his own master, that he shall have
liberty to form his opinions, freedom to carry into effect his resolves. He is, therefore, ever brought into competition with his
fellow men. His life is a display of energy." [18] Self-reliance and
enlightened self-interest, competition and association, were the
conditions of liberty and progress, to be preserved even though
equality of conditions should perish.

Most post-Civil War liberals still maintained that individual
liberty and social justice, meaning equality of economic opportunities, would inevitably result from a rigid application of laissez-
faire individualism. Yet the more serious and sincere among them
conceded the tension and contradictions between these concepts
and were ready to affirm the priority of individual liberty over
any other claim.

Post-Civil War liberalism, however, was haunted by the fear
that American democracy would repeat the historic pattern of
deterioration and end in class war, anarchy, and Caesarism. Macaulay's prophecy that "either some Caesar or Napoleon will seize

the reins of government with a strong hand, or your Republic will be as fearfully plundered . . . in the twentieth century as the Roman Empire was in the fifth" seemed not unfounded.[19] These were the years of the Reconstruction, of the Tilden elections, of the regime of spoilsmen and politicos, of the impeachment trial of President Andrew Johnson, of growing labor unrest, and of the revolt of the farmers.

The liberal answer to Macaulay's dictum that "institutions purely democratic must, sooner or later, destroy liberty or civilization or both," was that American democracy was more than a political regime, that it was a new social system of which individualism was the outstanding characteristic and thus exempt from the dangers of decline.[20] The classical expression of this sobered liberalism was given by William Graham Sumner, professor of political and social science at Yale.[21] "The modern jural state, at least of the Anglo-American type, by its hostility to privileges and servitudes, aims to realize . . . liberty. . . If all privileges and all servitudes are abolished, the individual finds that there are no prescriptions left either to lift him up or to hold him down. He simply has all his chances left open that he may make out of himself all there is in him. This is individualism and atomism. There is absolutely no escape from it except back into a system of privileges and servitudes."[22] Sumner emphasized the natural antagonism between liberty and democracy. Only in modern times were they "closely allied with each other, and democracy as a political form has helped and been helped by liberty in the social order. The product of liberty and democracy is individualism. Under it men have been emancipated from tradition, authority, caste, superstition . . . if we could maintain liberty and democracy long enough, we might perhaps produce individualistic results so great that men would be emancipated from delusions and from phrases."[23]

Edwin L. Godkin, editor of the *Nation* and the *New York Evening Post*, and one of the most influential writers of his generation, defined democracy as a socio-political system in which all relations were regulated by contract and not by status.[24] Social justice consisted in the creation of such conditions that each member entered into contractual relations as a perfectly free agent, with full knowledge of their nature and under no compulsion either to accept or to refuse them. Equality in education, land reform, restriction of monopolies, absolute free trade, and the right of collective bargaining were necessary conditions of contractual equality and the legitimate sphere of political action.[25]

This, then, was the mission of individualism: to liberate men from all compulsion and to make them perfectly free agents. The uniqueness of American democracy lay in the fact that individualism had become not only characteristic of the social and political organization but the source of the individual's behavior pattern and of the nation's value system.[26] "The cardinal idea of the American system . . . is . . . the development of the individual man; and that the individual man is best developed by being supplied with the means of education, and secured in the enjoyment of the fruits of his industry, and then let alone." [27]

This philosophy of laissez-faire individualism was upheld on two grounds. Laissez faire was the social framework of individual liberty and at the same time the principle of social justice and progress. This twofold aspect of competitive individualism—as a system of liberty and as a principle of justice—explained the popularity, the academic dominance, and the persuasiveness of its influence in shaping public opinion and action. For whenever the validity of one aspect of this creed was questioned, the other was invoked as sufficient ground for the maintenance of the whole. Whenever purely economic theories, as, for example, the Malthusian law of population, the wage-fund theory, or that of prices, were challenged on philosophical grounds, it was pointed out that unless the laws of the market or of the accumulation of property were left to themselves, liberty would be destroyed by governmental despotism, and vice versa.

Yet individualism was not only the ideology of the intellectual elite of the country, but a living faith of most Americans. One of the indications of the pervasiveness of this attitude is the incredible popularity and influence of the theories of Herbert Spencer in America during the last three decades of the nineteenth century. This influence affected all strata of American society. Businessmen, Protestant ministers, politicians, farmers, and workers resorted to his ideas and slogans no less than university teachers, writers, lawyers, and judges. Spencer's vogue was that of the philosopher of individualism *par excellence,* who seemed to have proved the harmony of the cosmic purposes with those of the American nation.[28] William James, who, though very critical of the merits of Spencer's *Synthetic Philosophy,* still admitted that "his politico-ethical activity in general breathes the purest English spirit of liberty, and his attacks on over-administration and criticisms on the inferiority of great centralized systems are worthy to be text-books of individualists the world over." [29]

Emile de Laveleye wrote concerning Spencer's *Man versus the State:* "The individualist theory was, I think, never expounded better or with stronger arguments based on first principles, or supported by so great a number of clearly analyzed and admirably grouped facts." [30] The same reason accounted for the attraction which Spencer held in a popularized version for the common people of the United States.[31] The social scientist John R. Commons recounted from his boyhood: "Every one of them in that Eastern section of Indiana was a Republican . . . and every one was a follower of Herbert Spencer who was then the shining light of evolution and individualism. . . I was brought up on Hoosierism, Republicanism, Presbyterianism, and Spencerism." [32]

This statement reveals the most peculiar aspect of Spencer's vogue in America, namely, his conquest of the Protestant church.[33] The initial distrust of Protestant ministers toward the philosophy of natural evolution began to wane in the 1870's. Henry Ward Beecher, the most popular of preachers, was already an admirer of Spencer in the 1860's and declared himself openly for evolution. The weekly *Independent* tried to prove the compatibility of Christianity and evolutionary natural selection and the survival of the fittest. Lyman Abbott, successor to Henry Ward Beecher at the Plymouth Church, New York, led the *Outlook* in the battle for a Christianized version of evolutionism. By 1885, when Josiah Strong published *Our Country* for the Home Missionary Society, the concept of evolution had already colored the viewpoint of many prominent Protestant ministers.

Spencer's impact was felt in legislation as well as in the decisions of the courts. The well-known dissenting opinion of Justice Holmes in the case of Lochner *v.* New York protested against decisions based on premises taken from the theory of laissez faire while denying to the majority the right to embody its opinions in law. Speaking on the peculiar interpretation the Fourteenth Amendment had received through lawyers and judges, Holmes declared: "The Fourteenth Amendment does not enact Mr. Herbert Spencer's *Social Statics*," and "a constitution is not intended to embody a particular economic theory, whether of paternalism and the organic relation of the citizen to the state or of *laissez faire*." [34]

The combined action of legislators and ministers inspired by the Spencerian version of individualism was revealed in the famous Dawes Act of 1887 which formulated the federal policy toward most Indians for the next four decades. That act attempted to civilize the Indian, teach him agriculture, and merge him with the body politic of the nation. It provided for the dissolution of all but a few of the tribes as legal entities and the division of the tribal lands among the individual members. [35] In the formulation of that policy, humanitarian and landed interests worked together. Especially influential were Lyman Abbott, the Protestant Episcopal Bishops Huntington, Hare and Whipple, the Reverend Phillips Brooks of Boston, and Merrill E. Gates, President of Rutgers College, working through the Indian Rights Annexation and the Annual Lake Mohonk Conference of the Friends of the Indians as well as through the United States Board of Indian Commissioners. [36]

As early as 1879 Lyman Abbott had advocated the destruction of the tribal system and the Indians' acculturation to Western civilization through the introduction of private property. "In this country we have tried . . . to fence around the Indian civilization (which is barbarism). . . . But God's way of making men and women is through suffering and by struggle, and there is no other way." [37] Abbott's interpretation of the ways of God and the growth of civilization was inspired less by the New Testament than by Spencer's gospel of progress through fierce competitive struggle for survival. This was also Gates's view. The Indians had to become individual citizens and be prepared for this by hard work, the acquisition of property, individual responsibility, and family life. "There is no other 'manifest destiny' for any man. . . To this we stand committed, by all the logic of two thousand years of Teutonic and Anglo-Saxon history, since Arminius . . . made a stand for liberty against the legions of Rome." [38]

The first step was the break-up of tribal organization, for community of lands and goods "cuts the nerve of all that manful effort which political economy teaches us proceeds from the desire for wealth." [39] "Individualism, the key-note of our socio-political ideas in this century, makes itself felt by sympathetic vibrations." [40] Like Abbott, Gates believed that the submission of the Indians to the discipline of competitive economy would do more good than missionary work. "It cultivates the habit of *looking to the future* and of seeking to modify the future for one's self by one's own efforts. And this habit persevered in develops . . . that power which is the highest prerogative of man . . . *will power,* intelligently and voluntarily exercised in subjection to law!" [41]

John T. Oberly, Superintendent of Indian Schools of the Department of Interior, declared to great applause at the Third Annual Meeting of the Lake Mohonk Conference, that both Senator Dawes and Lyman Abbott were in agreement "that the first essential thing in the attempt to solve the Indian problem is agreement, that the Indian is a man and that he should have individualism." [42] The American doctrine of natural right to self-determination had given vitality to the political doctrine of individualism, and this was the answer to the age-long search for a just basis of politics. "When America said to the world, 'The answer to the great political riddle of the ages is, Manhood, because all legitimate political power comes primarily from the individual,' a new truth was asserted." [43]

Senator Dawes agreed that the tribal community system was at the root of the Indians' backwardness. "It is Henry George's system, and under that there is no enterprise . . . there is no selfishness, which is at the bottom of civilization." He agreed with the view of Gates that "the desire for the acquisition of property is . . . on the whole the mainspring that daily keeps in motion the mechanism of the world's daily routine." [44] Here was a perfect example of that confluence of "Hoosierism, Republicanism, Presbyterianism, and Spencerism" into a working model of action.

The extraordinary influence of Spencer over the American mind has been explained by the fact that he supplied the new elite of industrial capitalism with a rationale appropriate to the necessities of adjustment to political democracy. [45] Spencer, by fusing Malthusianism with the laissez-faire ideology of the Manchester School, had created a formula of individualism which legitimatized American capitalism. [46] Yet such an explanation does not account

for Spencer's hold over the minds of intellectuals of radical democratic leanings, over Single-Taxers, anarchists, and such acid critics
of the Gilded Age as Hamlin Garland, Jack London, and Theodore
Dreiser. The fact is that he appealed to divergent groups and
interests—to the conservative liberalism of Free-Traders and anti-
Imperialists such as William Graham Sumner and Grover Cleveland; to the preachers of the Gospel of Wealth and Success; to the
conservative ideology of the courts; to the radical movement of
farmers and workers; and to those who carried on the intellectual
tradition of the New England Enlightenment.

The common ground of Spencer's appeal can be summed up
under five headings: his concept of individuality as the end of
cosmic and social evolution; his ethic of competitive individualism;
his unswerving suspicion of the state; his almost anarchistic doctrine of the self-sufficiency of economic society and his belief in
laissez-faire policy; all four of which led to the fifth—an optimistic
theory of cosmic progress culminating in a perfect adjustment
between the individual and society. These doctrines were identical
with those elaborated by American individualism before the arrival of Spencer's gospel in America. His success rested, to quote
Henry George, on his capacity to give "coherence and scientific
formula to opinions which already prevailed. Its wonderful spread
. . . has not been so much a conquest as an assimilation." [47]

Henry George has given in *Progress and Poverty* a résumé
of the popular version of Spencer's philosophy in America: The
present civilization was the product of the law of evolution which
ruled supreme in all realms of Nature and in the social sciences.
The law stated that the steady progress of differentiation and
growing complexity was achieved in the social as in the biological
realm through the struggle for existence and survival in the course
of which the fittest individuals and species survive. The efforts,
inventions, and habits created in this struggle were perpetuated
and transmitted biologically as well as culturally to posterity.

War, slavery, tyranny, . . . famine, . . . want and misery, which fester in
modern civilization, are the impelling causes which drive man on, by
eliminating poorer types and extending the higher . . . Thus, while this theory
is, as Herbert Spencer says, "radical to a degree beyond anything which
current radicalism conceives," inasmuch as it looks for changes in the very
nature of man; it is at the same time, "conservative to a degree beyond any-

thing conceived by current conservatism," inasmuch as it holds that no change can avail save these slow changes in man's nature.

The law of evolution drove civilization inexorably if slowly to higher and higher levels of achievement and forms of social life.[48] Henry George here described that "hopeful fatalism" which justified ruthless competition and social exploitation through the vision of a final happy end and consoled itself with Andrew Carnegie's maxim, "All is well since all grows better."

Yet there existed in Spencer's philosophy facets which had appealed to Henry George no less than to other radicals, among them Spencer's prediction that society would develop higher and higher forms of social adjustment between the individual and the community until an equilibrium of highest individualization and highest cooperation should result. At that stage the need for coercion and for the state would disappear, and each individual would spontaneously cooperate with the community.[49]

This ideal underlay Spencer's formulation of the law of evolution. "There is another form under which civilization can be generalized . . . a progress towards that constitution of man and society required for the complete manifestation of every one's individuality."[50] Spencer repeated here, only in different words, the "ideal union in actual individualism" of Emerson and the transcendentalists. Like them, he derived the rights of property from the concept of individuality.[51]

The contribution of Spencer to American thought consisted in the integration of economic, political, ethical, and philosophical individualism into an apparently consistent scientific theory of irresistible progress. At the core of his voluminous writing lay the will to prove the compatibility of absolute individual liberty with social cooperation and progress. His sociology was a deliberate attempt to demonstrate that the "tacit assumption that Individualism means the solitary life of the individual is an entire misapprehension. It may and does go along with an elaborate form of mutual dependence."[52] These were basic convictions of the Jeffersonian tradition and of the Enlightenment.

An analysis of Spencer's appeal to different segments of public opinion in America thus shows both the broad basis of common agreement and the sharp differences in the interpretation of the American concept of individualism. The radical wing of American democracy, the individualistic anarchists, Henry George and his followers, the radical transcendentalists, and labor leaders such as Samuel Gompers, were all indebted to the author of *Social Statics*. They acclaimed the earlier writings of Spencer no less than the later writings of John Stuart Mill. Yet the same qualities which made Spencer attractive to the radicals made him suspect to the conservatives before the Civil War. The evaluation changed because the concept of individualism in Spencer's later writings was suited to the temper and aspirations of American democracy, yet responded easily to the needs and interests of the new industrial and financial elite on the one hand and the fears of liberals on the other. By substituting nature and history for the organized will of the community as the instrument of progress and social well-being, Spencer fulfilled a popular demand in America. His theories could be utilized by all those who feared that the political revolution of the Civil War and Reconstruction period might develop into a social revolution. His "incongruous mixture of Natural Rights and physiological metaphor," and his theory of ruthless competition as the motive force of progress, simultaneously supplied the new economic elite with a rationale and a vocabulary which they were reluctant to abandon.[53]

Competitive economic activity was, in Spencer's opinion, not only the way to progress but the principle of natural justice. The ambiguous expression, the "survival of the fittest," which seemed to make survival the criterion of fitness and therefore of value, became more definite through Spencer's statement that throughout life "each adult gets benefits in proportion to merit, reward in proportion to desert, merit and desert being understood as ability to fulfill all the requirements of life."[54]

In adapting this theory to the needs of American democracy through the "Gospel of Wealth" and the "Cult of Success" an ideology was created which fulfilled the complex requirements of satisfying different strata of the American nation at the same time. Its main elements were the assertion that American democracy meant the equality of chances for success, the mobility of social classes, the beneficial effects of the private accumulation of wealth on the material well-being of the whole nation, and the correspondence between success and merit.[55] Moreover, to many who, like Andrew Carnegie, attempted to reconcile their positions with the rules of Christian morality and democratic principles, it provided an almost religious comfort.[56] The glorification of individual success gave democracy a new meaning by transforming equality of rights into an equality of opportunity. The popularity of the appeal was basically derived from the pioneer tradition of the moving frontier. It translated the character ideal of an earlier period, with its belief in self-reliance and faith in the identity of private and public interest into a goal of the industrial urban world.[57] "Not simply do we see," wrote Spencer, "that in the competition among individuals of the same kind, survival of the fittest has from the beginning furthered production of a higher type; but we feel that the increasing warfare between Species is mainly due both to growth and organization. Without universal conflict there would have been no development of the active powers." [58]

A typical example of the identification of the interests of private industrial enterprise with that of the nation through the Spencerian concept of individualism was the address of Senator Chauncey M. Depew given at Vanderbilt University. "The American Commonwealth is built upon the individual. It recognizes neither classes nor masses. . . We have thus become a nation of self-made men. We live under just and equal laws and all avenues for a career are open. . . Freedom of opportunity and preservation of the results of forecast, industry, thrift and honesty have made the United States the most prosperous and wealthy country in the world. Commodore Vanderbilt is a conspicuous example of the product and possibilities of our free and elastic conditions. . . He neither asked nor gave quarter. The same . . . open avenues, the same opportunities which he had before him are equally before every other man." [59]

Andrew Carnegie, the only sincere disciple of Spencer among the giants of American industry, was less inclined to flatter the democratic sentiment by illusions. "To those who propose to substitute Communism for this intense Individualism, the answer therefore is: The race has tried that. All progress from that barbarous day to the present time has resulted from its displacement. Not evil, but good, has come to the race from the accumulation of wealth by those who have had the ability and energy to produce it. But even if we admit for a moment that it might be better . . . a sufficient answer is, This is not evolution, but revolution. It necessitates the changing of human nature itself—a work of eons. . . We might as well urge the destruction of the highest existing type of man because he failed to reach our ideal as to favor the destruction of Individualism, Private Property, the Law of Accumulation of Wealth, and the Law of Competition." [60]

The fusion of this business ideology with the laissez-faire philosophy of liberals and conservatives created a theory of individualism which remained a legitimate and popular formulation of the American Way of Life. The identification of this theory of individualism with American nationality was consistent after the last third of the nineteenth century.[61] Henry Clews, author of *The Wall Street Point of View*, made this identification blandly in an address delivered in 1907. "I stand firmly in favour of the principle of competition, and that system of Individualism which guards, protects and encourages competition. . . Take away the spirit of Individualism from the people, and you at once eliminate the American Spirit—the love of freedom,—of free industry,—free and unfettered opportunity,—you take away freedom itself." [62] The same message was repeated again in 1946 in the statement of the principles of the National Association of Manufacturers, *The American Individual Enterprise System:*

Nearly every page of this book drives home the fundamental feature of our traditional enterprise system, namely its individualism. At the threshold of our national existence we solemnly asserted "the unalienable right to life, liberty, and the pursuit of happiness"; we fought the Revolutionary War for that right, and adopted a Constitution to guarantee and propagate it. We became a nation of free men not serving political masters but ourselves, free to pursue our happiness without interference from the state, with the greatest liberty of individual action ever known to man. Individuals, conscious of unbounded opportunity, inflamed by the love of achievement, inspired by the hope of profit, ambitious of the comfort, power and influence that wealth brings, turned with . . . vigor to producing and offering goods and services in freely competitive markets. The individual wanted little from the government beyond police protection while he confidently worked out his own destiny. . . Our "private enterprise system and our American form of government are inseparable and there can be no compromise between a free economy and a governmentally dictated economy without endangering our political as well as our economic freedom." [63]

This ideology of individualism was purposely propagated in the face of a reality which more and more contradicted the "Gospel of Wealth" and the "Cult of Success," in order to identify the masses with industrial and corporative capitalism.[64] The fear of a movement toward socialism, of the revolutionary organization of the industrial masses, and of the growing demand for state intervention, regulation, and protection for the benefit of the laborers and middle class had been steadily growing since the 1870's. It pervaded the minds of business leaders and of Republicans, especially in the first two decades of the twentieth century. The Progressive Movement was largely committed to an attack on the distortion of democracy and national unity by the ideology of laissez-faire individualism. The Progressives were conscious of the rapid transformation of the nation by the industrial and urban revolutions as well as by the growing immigration of non-Protestant ethnic groups from central, southern and eastern Europe. Some turned to an organic and even racist nationalism, others to a neo-Jeffersonian democracy, and still others to a pragmatic espousal of measures that would lead to a welfare state. But all agreed on the dangers of a laissez-faire concept of the state and of an individualistic philosophy of the relation between the individual and society.

Frederick Jackson Turner had shown how the earlier experience of American life had fostered both equalitarian democracy and unrestrained individualism through the conditions of life on the moving frontier and through the free lands of the virgin West.[65] He had also shown how the ideal of the self-made man was translated from the agricultural to the industrial frontier.[66] This historical analysis of the simultaneous origins of American individualism and equalitarianism disclosed the reasons why equalitarian democracy and unrestrained individualism were incompatible. Democracy had begun with competitive individualism as well as with the belief in equality. But the farmers "gradually learned that unrestrained competition and combination meant the triumph of the strongest, the seizure in the interest of a dominant class of the strategic points of the nation's life. They learned that between the ideal of individualism, unrestrained by society, and the ideal of democracy, was an innate conflict; that their very ambitions and forcefulness had endangered their democracy."[67] The question was whether a new concept of democracy could save the abiding values of individualism and yet create a "just social order that shall sustain the free, progressive, individual in a real democracy." [68] That became the central problem of the Progressive Movement.

The American Economic Association, founded in 1885, had, even earlier, made a critical examination of the laissez-faire theory. Strongly influenced by the German historical school of economics, by the founders of the *Verein für Sozialpolitik,* and by the "socialism of the chair," Richard T. Ely, Henry C. Adams, Edmund James, Simon M. Patten, John B. Clark, E. R. A. Seligman, and Richard M. Smith criticized American ideological fundamentalism. The platform for the American Economic Association, as proposed by Ely, declared:

1. We regard the state as an educational and ethical agency whose positive aid is an indispensable condition of human progress. While we recognize the necessity of individual initiative in industrial life, we hold that the doctrine of *laissez-faire* is unsafe in politics and unsound in morals; and that it suggests an inadequate explanation of the relations between the state and the citizens.

2. We do not accept the final statements which characterized the political economy of the past generation. . .

3. We hold that the conflict of labor and capital has brought to the front a vast number of social problems whose solution is impossible without the united efforts of Church, state, and science. [69]

This platform, which was actually a very conservative adaptation of the principles which Simon Patten and Edmund James had suggested, clearly showed the impact of German thought, and especially of the ideas of Adolf Wagner which demonstrated that the ever-increasing participation of the state in social and economic life was the law of evolution. [70] Thoughtful Americans who confronted the chaotic consequences of the industrial revolution found in these theories a welcome antidote both to the individualism of Spencer and to the democratic radicalism of the masses. [71] The Historical School, wrote Ely, has "placed man as man, and not wealth in the foreground, and subordinated everything to his true welfare. . . In opposition to individualism, they emphasize Aristotle's maxim . . . or, as Blackstone has it, man was formed for society." [72]

Yet most of the members of the convention opposed the socialist glorification of the state with its purely historical approach toward the ideal of individualism. William G. Sumner, F. Lawrence Laughlin, Frank W. Taussig, and A. T. Hadley refused to accept even the compromise program of the Association. Others, like Henry C. Adams, E. R. A. Seligman, John B. Clark, and E. J. James, insisted on the differentiation between a laissez-faire individualism which could not be maintained and the general philosophy of individualism which in their opinion was the backbone of modern civilization. "We ought to be careful," asserted Professor Alexander Johnston of Princeton, "while fighting the illegitimate application of the doctrine [of laissez faire] to matters properly within the domain of morals or the state, not to seem to ask the total abolition of the legitimate principles, the secret of individualism, the basis of modern society." [73]

Dealing with "The Relation of the State to Industrial Action," Adams insisted that, while laissez faire had proved untenable, no other theory could "take the place of the principle of individualism which has been forced to abdicate its seat of authority." [74] He maintained that all progress was made by "the growth of individualism and the decay of communalism; and no one who fully appreciates the opportunities thus offered . . . can seriously advocate a return to the conditions of the past." [75] Laissez faire was not intrinsic to the development of individualism but rather tended under certain conditions to destroy it. A theory of social direction must be worked out to preserve the basic achievements of individualism. "It is an intellectual blunder to say that all extensions of the functions of government are in the direction of socialism," Adams declared. [76] "The American people are obliged to choose between the principle of individualism and the principle of socialism." His own conclusions, he said, were "motivated by the theory of individualism, and not by the theory of socialism." [77]

The same, to a large extent, was true of the Social Gospel Movement which, by 1912, was the dominant creed of Protestantism in America. As in other countries, industrialization, urbanization, and the creation of a rootless working class compelled the churches to ponder upon the social implications of Christianity. The threatening chaos and the disintegration of the Protestant pattern of American civilization, as well as the challenge of socialism, necessitated an ideological reorientation which involved a criticism of the individualistic philosophy. The Social Gospel was the reaction of Protestantism to the ethics and practice of capitalism "markedly stimulated by socialism." [78]

The Protestant ministry was therefore preoccupied with the

merits of the alternative systems of socialism and individualism. The claim that socialism realized the true intent of Christianity, although departing from its religious premises, presented a serious challenge.[79] "We wrestle with the problem of socialism and individualism," declared Phillips Brooks, "and we wonder which of the two must be sacrificed to the other." [80]

The strength of the Social Gospel Movement lay in the fact that it incorporated the economic and historical views of those who had founded the American Economic Association. This enabled these Protestants not only to formulate a plan of social action but also to separate the ethical and religious values of individualism, which they wished to maintain, from its economic and social theories, which they wished to discard. The difficulty of such a separation was testified to by the Congregationalist minister Washington Gladden. "Absurd and unscientific" as was the inevitable alliance of individual freedom and laissez-faire economics, it had nevertheless "been dinned into the ears of the multitude so consistently for the last century that it is hard to get them to take any other view of social relations. Economic science is rapidly clearing itself of these errors, but the philosophy of the street . . . is still rank individualism." [81]

Yet most of the Social Gospelers, although they condemned the ruthless competitive capitalism of their times, ascribed to individualism an important historical role in the progress of humanity and maintained that it had abiding value as a regulative ideal of society and morality. John Rae, author of the immensely popular *Contemporary Socialism,* defined the attitude of progressive Americans toward the spheres of private and public action. "While opposed to the State doing anything either moral or material for individuals, which individuals could do better, or with better results, for themselves, they [English economists, philosophers, and statesmen] agreed in requiring the State, first, to undertake any individual work it had superior natural advantages for conducting successfully; and second, to protect the weaker classes effectively in the essentials of all rational and humane living . . . not only against the ravages of violence or fear or insecurity, but against those of ignorance, disease and want." [82]

It was, then, under the threefold assault of progressivism, radical democracy, and socialism that the Spencerian version of individualism combined with the Gospel of Wealth, and the Cult

of Success was formulated and propagated.[83] There was a conscious effort to create through individualism an ideological identification between the nation, democracy, and industrial enterprise. Individualism made competitive private enterprise and
American identity parts of one pattern, through which the new
elite hoped to stabilize its own position inside the framework of
democracy. This group considered individualism not only an
ideology which gave wider significance to its activities, but also a
system of values which expressed the aspirations and the sense
of identity of the American nation as a whole. This accounts for
the fact that not only the Republican party but also the Democrats
under Bryan and Wilson, the Rooseveltian Progressives, and even
the Populists, Single Taxers, and labor leaders were committed to
the concept of individualism as a national ideal.

The Republican party consistently held to this ideology. The
great depression dramatized Herbert Hoover's famous speech on
the "American System of Rugged Individualism," setting his high
confidence in the unique success of the "American System" in the
ironic context of the collapse of the economy. But Hoover's faith
in individualism as the American System was typical of the middle-
of-the-road liberals of the early twentieth century.[84] It was under
the leadership of Theodore Roosevelt that the G.O.P. declared
the "Republican Party stands for a wise and regulated individualism."[85] Roosevelt himself, in spite of his organic concept of
nationhood and state, considered individualism "the fibre of our
whole citizenship."[86] His progressivism came "not to destroy but
to save individualism" from socialism and plutocracy.[87]

By the beginning of the twentieth century members of each
party, except for Herbert Croly's *New Republic* circle and the
Socialists, felt obliged to invoke this idea in order to appear as the
national standard-bearer. The Republican platform of 1912 abandoned even the mild qualifications it had made in 1908 and defined
its concept of individualism in terms of strict constitutionalism
and laissez-faire policy.[88] Elihu Root, the intellectual power behind
the scenes at the Convention of 1912, defended the Republican
synthesis which welded laissez-faire philosophy to the Gospel of
Wealth and to Spencerian evolution, as the only system which
could maintain the "individualism which underlies the social
system of Western civilization."[89]

Yet, William Jennings Bryan, the "Tribune of the People," also justified his radical attack on the corporate structure as necessary to preserve the American system of individualism.[90] The issue between the Republican and the Democratic concepts was accurately assessed by Thomas R. Marshall, Governor of Indiana and Democratic candidate for the vice-presidency in 1912. Affirming that Wilson's New Freedom was an adaptation of the Jeffersonian ideal of social justice to changed conditions, he declared: "An individualism which teaches the right to success without emphasizing the duty of not depriving any other man of his opportunity, is as much an evil as the system which exalts our common right by depriving us of our personal rights." Rejecting the Republican version of individualism, he concluded: "Our birthright in America is the right to success, but it is not success unless thereby men attain unto collective opportunity. . . Unless the individualism of America rests upon fraternity and faith, it will crumble." [91]

The most revealing evidence for the identification of Americanism with the concept of individualism is afforded by the fact that the radical social criticism leveled against industrial capitalism by Single Taxers and Populists was also made in the name of individualism. After the Civil War all radical democratic movements defined their aims in terms of Jeffersonian philosophy. The guiding principles of the "producers' philosophy" were like those of American anarchism, a radical extension of the natural-rights philosophy. Labor was the only title to property and the measure of value; free competition, in the absolute absence of privileges and monopolies, was the ideal regulator of the production and distribution of wealth; natural wealth belonged to the community and could not be privately owned, so that public services and utilities should be under public control; and, finally, a producers' society was capable of directing its affairs by voluntary action so that the functions of the state were to be limited to purely administrative concerns or to measures which safeguarded the existence of the natural order of society. These were the axiomatic beliefs of the leaders of radical democracy, of individualist-anarchists, of the followers of George Henry Evans, Edward Kellogg, and Henry George.[92]

State socialism with its doctrine of class war, and with its immense enlargement of the authority of the state, was rejected as inimical to the spirit of American democracy and as destructive to freedom and progress. Even the socialist wing of the indigenous American Labor movements—the International Working Men's Association and the I.W.W.—were anarchistic in their ideals and rejected state socialism.[93]

The natural-rights philosophy persisted among left-wing radicals because it represented the national tradition and offered an alternative to socialism. It contained all the messianic elements of socialism, its promise of social justice, of ultimate harmony between individual and collective needs, and the perspective of material and spiritual progress. Yet, unlike socialism, these doctrines were capable of realization within American democracy, through the enlargement of the areas of liberty and equality. They were socially inclusive and affirmative of the nation, of democracy, and the present pattern of life. They required for the fulfillment of their aims no eschatological revolutionary unheaval.[94]

The adherents of the "producers' philosophy" had, however, to reinterpret the term individualism which had already been preempted by defenders of the economic status quo. The process of adaptation was revealed in the writings of Henry George and his followers.

George himself never accepted unqualifiedly the term individualism, unless it could be made to coincide with the ideal of a free society and the Jeffersonian concepts of natural rights.[95] But Hamlin Garland's "New Declaration of Rights" on behalf of the Single-Tax League was less cautious and identified individualism with the cause of Populism. "We are individualists mainly," he wrote in 1891, and he continued:

We stand unalterably opposed to the paternal idea in government. We believe in fewer laws and juster interpretation thereof. We believe in less interference with individual liberty, less protection of the rapacious demands of the few, and more freedom of action on the part of the many. . . *All men are born free and equal in opportunity, to live, to labor . . . and to enjoy the fruits of their own industry.* This is the reading which we, as single tax men put . . . upon that immortal and hollow sounding instrument. . . We mean *all* men.[96]

The past is not individualistic, but socialistic. The Age of Socialism is not coming on, but departing. . . What the Nationalists anathematize as "individualism," we, as individualists, are as ready to condemn as they, because it is not individualism at all, but the surviving and slow retreating effect of socialism, paternalism and special privilege.[97]

The attachment to the term, revealed in that reinterpretation, showed the extent to which individualism at the end of the nineteenth century had become firmly embedded in the concept of national identity.

It has been the purpose of this inquiry to study the American quest for national identity through a description and analysis of the concepts of a natural social order, "free society," and "individualism." There was a striking degree of continuity in the formation and crystallization of these concepts throughout the nineteenth century. Not all aspects of American political and social thought fitted this pattern of ideas and values, but the conclusions here reached were not the products of arbitrary selection. Though no attempt has been made to present a comprehensive history of American thought, there has been an effort to examine those ideas concerned with the meaning of American nationhood and of national identification. Assuming that the basic trend of American history was toward growth in the quality and breadth of democracy and an ever-greater national integration, this survey has sought to analyze the relation between the democratic aspiration of the American people and the contents of their national consciousness.

This analysis revealed that American democracy has meant more and less than equality of political rights and the sovereignty of the people. Both were, rather, corollaries of the concept of the rights of men which sought to express itself in the establishment of a natural social order of men as a "free society." This concept explained the peculiarity of American democracy, its distrust of state interference and of the political regimentation of society. Because of it, the idea of individualism became the symbol and ideal of its national identity.

The relationship between individualism and national identity raised the question: How could concepts, ideas, and values, universally valid, which were inimical to the idea of the sovereignty of the state, become the basis of national identification? Part of the answer lay in the English heritage—Puritanism and the Whig tradition—which, in the environment of an absolutely new beginning, constantly repeating itself through immigration and western migration, created the new contents of the national consciousness. These factors provided decisive, formative elements but were not conclusive. What was usually overlooked was the peculiar dynamic force by which American society constituted itself a nation. The revolutionary severance from the mother country that created the American nation compelled it to adopt the universal values and norms of the rights of man and of natural law, not only as the basis of independent statehood, but as the definition of its own identity. Political emancipation involved a radical break with the past that made it imperative to define the character of the new nation. Universal and rational modes of thought, which had served Americans in their struggle against England, enabled them to interpret their own pattern of life, institutions, and traditions. Though neither deliberate nor conscious of its own direction, this revolutionary élan, which had broken historical continuity, established in America a new pattern of social life explainable by the natural-rights theory. The pattern of disrupting historical continuities inherent in colonization and legitimized by the Revolution was repeated with every new wave of immigrants and with the westward movement of settlement. Successive groups of new arrivals sought national and social equality by formulating their identity in terms of the universal norms of a moral and social order which gave them equality of status, liberty of expression, and the right to consider themselves citizens.

The revolutionary heritage was therefore permanently attached to the Jeffersonian tradition, which had identified American nationality with the ideals of a natural equalitarian order. With the spread of political democracy, the concept of the American society as a system of liberty and equality became the dominant concept of national identity. The growth of nationalism and the great crisis of the Civil War made it more necessary than ever to find terms adequately to describe this national consciousness and to serve as symbols of identification. These functions were fulfilled by the concept of individualism which attempted to define the ideals of the American way of life in a generic way.

Individualism supplied the nation with a rationalization of its characteristic attitudes, behavior patterns, and aspirations. It endowed the past, the present, and the future with the perspective of unity and progress. It explained the peculiar social and political organization of the nation—unity in spite of heterogeneity—and it pointed toward an ideal of social organization in harmony with American experience. Above all, individualism expressed the universalism and idealism most characteristic of the national consciousness. This concept evolved in contradistinction to socialism, the universal and messianic character of which it shared. Both claimed to create systems of social justice and to show a way toward the perfection of the human race. This twofold aspect—universalism and the capacity to describe values peculiar to American society—made individualism a term synonymous with Americanism.

These developments help explain to some degree several phenomena peculiar to American history—the weakness of the socialist movement, the fixation of social ideologies through identification with national values, and, in recent years, the willingness to consider the United States the appointed leader of the West against world communism. The identification of Americanism with the ideals of a free society and individualism, occurring relatively early, made the socialist formulas seem not only impractical but "un-American," inimical to the traditions of democracy and the system of individual behavior in the United States. Socialism was incompatible with American nationalism because the latter was already committed to a rival ideology.

For this very reason Americans considered themselves natural leaders of the "free world" and of "Western civilization." The concept of the "free world" had the same significance and the same emotional implications as the concept of a "free society" had had during the great controversy with the slaveholding South. The struggle for freedom had only moved from the national to the international sphere. The earlier struggle had created the identification of American nationalism with "free society" and individualism. The later one involved the application of terms which would reflect the existence of a supernational unity of values and of international solidarity.

Those who have attempted to disentangle the concept of American national identity from those of individualism and of a natural order of freedom have usually followed Tocqueville in maintaining that democracy in the United States was a social rather than a political system. In the late nineteenth and early twentieth centuries the Progressive Movement attempted to postulate an American ideal of democracy which would satisfy the needs of the people, without having recourse to the ideology of individualism. To do so it was necessary to find an alternative basis of identification and loyalty. Any redefinition of the nature of American nationality could be successful only if it preserved the peculiar pattern which distinguished the United States from other nations— its claim to represent a social order in which equality, liberty, and social justice were reconciled in the framework of a political structure.

The Progressive Movement endeavored to keep within this formal structure of American national consciousness. Visualizing an immense enlargement of the functions of government in the service of social democracy, it hoped to create a new center of loyalty and identification in the state.

An alternative was to base national identification on ethnic loyalties, traditions, and common memories. Individualism, like democracy, could then be considered as embodying national, historical, or racial characteristics which could be subordinated to the higher unity of the nation as embodied in the state. This position was adopted with differing nuances and emphases by the followers of Theodore Roosevelt's organic and integral "New Nationalism."

Both of these tendencies emanating from the Progressive Movement had a permanent effect upon American national consciousness. The deliberate blocking of further mass immigration in the 1920's, the growth of the federal welfare state in the following decades, the sheer accumulation of common historical experiences, created a community of national identification which became increasingly independent of the ideological structure we have studied. Yet the repeated ·attempts to reformulate the basis of national identification in terms of purely historic, ethnic, religious, or racial loyalties have been half-hearted and, though powerful, have been unable to achieve their purpose. Only a concept which interpreted Americanism in terms of a social order aimed at the realization of universally valid ideals of humanity could serve as a basis of national identification.

Notes

CHAPTER I: INTRODUCTION

1. Alexis de Tocqueville, *Democracy in America*, Phillips Bradley, ed. (New York, 1945), I, 243.

2. Richard Koebner, "Semantics and Historiography," *The Cambridge Journal*, 7:132 (1953).

3. See Karl Mannheim, *Ideology and Utopia; An Introduction to the Sociology of Knowledge* (New York, 1936), p. 22.

4. Koebner, "Semantics and Historiography," pp. 131–32, 138–39.

5. See Harold Walsby, *The Domain of Ideologies, a Study of the Origin, Development and Structure of Ideologies* (Glasgow [1947]), p. 145; also Werner Knuth, *Ideen, Ideale, Ideologien* (Hamburg [1955]), pp. 50–51.

6. Mannheim, *Ideology and Utopia*, chap. ii; Gottfried Salomon, "Geschichte als Ideologie," *Wirtschaft und Gesellschaft* (Frankfurt, 1924), pp. 417ff; and Vilfredo Pareto, *The Mind and Society*, ed. A. Livingston (London, 1935).

7. Mannheim, *Ideology and Utopia*, pp. 192, 205.

8. This terminology is quite obviously not satisfying as it fails to establish a term which would describe both as types of the same phenomenon.

9. See Otto von Gierke, *Natural Law and the Theory of Society, 1500 to 1800 . . . with a Lecture on the Ideas of Natural Law and Humanity by Ernst Troeltsch*, trans. Ernest Barker (Boston, 1957), pp. xxxix–xlvi, 35–55; John N. Figgis, *The Divine Right of Kings* (Cambridge, 1914), chaps. v–ix, and especially chap. ix; and John N. Figgis, *Studies in Political Thought from Gerson to Grotius* (Cambridge, Eng., 1923), chaps. iii–vii; David G. Ritchie, *Natural Rights* (London, 1916), chap. i; Bertrand de Jouvenal, *Sovereignty: An Inquiry Into the Political Good*, trans. J. F. Huntington (Cambridge, Eng., 1957), pt. III.

10. For a general survey see Arthur S. P. Woodhouse, *Puritanism and Liberty, being the Army Debates (1647–9) from the Clarke Manuscripts* (London, 1938), Preface; George P. Gooch, *English Democratic Ideas in the Seventeenth Century* (Cambridge, Eng., 1954), chaps. iii–xi.

11. See Chapter IV below, on the development of the Whig theory of government and Chapter VI, below, on its theory of society.

12. On Ferguson see William C. Lehmann, *Adam Ferguson and the Beginnings of Modern Sociology* (New York, 1930); Georg Jahn, "Physiokratisches System," *Handwörterbuch der Staatswissenschaften* (Jena, 1925),

VI, 865ff; Georg Jahn, "Adam Smith," *ibid.* (Jena, 1926), VII, 490ff; Leslie
Stephen, *History of English Thought in the Eighteenth Century* (London,
1927), II, 23–33, 33–41, 57–77; Georg Simmel, *Grundfragen der Soziologie
(Individuum und Gesellschaft)* (Berlin, 1917); Werner Sombart, "Anfänge
der Soziologie," *Hauptprobleme der Sociologie Erinnerungsgabe für Max
Weber*, ed. Melchior Palyi (Munich, 1923).

13. Ernst Troeltsch, "The Idea of Natural Law and Humanity in World
Politics," in Gierke, *Natural Law*. The idealization of the group tends to
brutalize romance and to romanticize cynicism and represents "a curious
mixture of mysticism and brutality." See William Buthman, *The Rise of
Integral Nationalism* (New York, 1939); also Heinrich G. von Treitschke,
Politics, trans. B. Dugdale (London, 1916), vol. I; Boyd C. Shafer, *Nationalism, Myth and Reality* (London, 1955), chap. xi.

14. This definition of "nationalism" is different from that of Friedrich
Hertz who would define nationalism as an exclusive concern to elevate and
aggrandize the nation as national personality. See Friedrich O. Hertz,
Nationality in History and Politics (London, 1951), pp. 21, 26–27, 34–37.
It is also different from that of Carlton J. H. Hayes who defines nationalism
as an "emotional fusion and exaggeration of . . . nationality and patriotism."
See Carlton J. H. Hayes, *Essays on Nationalism* (New York, 1928), p. 6. Any
definition of nationalism has to include the four elements of state, citizenship
or other forms of political belonging, community of identification, and the
feeling of collective distinctiveness as constant variables in an ideological
system. National consciousness would then be the awareness of belonging to
a political society through a community of identification, and the nature of
the identifications with the group would determine the character of its
consciousness. This definition purposely avoids introducing the concept of
nationality into its description since nationality is the result of this identification and not a natural state.

15. On the semantic changes and different interpretations of the word
"nation," see Hertz, *Nationality in History and Politics*, pp. 5–8; Friedrich
Meinecke, *Weltbürgertum und Nationalstaat* (Munich, 1908), chaps. i, ii;
Carlton J. H. Hayes, *The Historical Evolution of Modern Nationalism* (New
York, 1931), chaps. ii, iii; see Hans Kohn, *The Idea of Nationalism, A Study
in its Origin and Background* (New York, 1951), pp. 166ff and chap. v;
also Shafer, *Nationalism*, sect. 1; and Morris Ginsberg, *Nationalism: A Re-
appraisal* (Leeds, 1961).

16. On the dichotomy of "Kratos" and "ethos" and the dialectical relation
between these elements of the state see Friedrich Meinecke, *Die Idee der
Staatsräson in der Neueren Geschichte* in *Werke* (Munich, 1957), Introduction.

17. [Henry] Spenser Wilkinson, *War and Policy, Essays* (New York,
1900), p. 368; John A. Cramb, *The Origins and Destiny of Imperial Britain*
(London, 1915); for France, see Marie, Marquis de Roux, *Charles Maurras
et le nationalisme de L'Action Française* (Paris, 1928); Maurice Barrès,
Scenes et doctrines du nationalisme (Paris, 1902), and *The Faith of France*,

trans. Elisabeth Marbury (Boston, 1918). On resurgent Russian nationalism under Soviet rule, see Royal Institute of International Affairs, *Nationalism; a Report by a Study Group* (London, 1939), pp. 75–80; Hans Kohn, *Nationalism in the Soviet Union* (New York, 1933). See also Alfred Rosenberg, *Der Mythus des 20 Jahrhunderts* (Munich, 1930), p. 591; Franz Schnabel, "Bismarck und die Nationen," in *Europa und der Nationalismus,* Bericht über das III. Internationale Historiker-Treffen in Speyer, 17. bis 20. October 1949 (Baden-Baden, 1950), pp. 95–96.

18. Alexis de Tocqueville, *Democracy in America,* ed. Phillips Bradley (New York, 1945), I, 244.

19. Walter Sulzbach, *Nationales Gemeinschaftsgefühl und wirtschaftliches Interesse* (Leipzig, 1929).

20. Jacques Droz, "Concept français et concept allemand de l'idée de nationalité," in *Europa und der Nationalismus,* pp. 112–14; Hans Kohn, *The Idea of Nationalism* (New York, 1951), chaps. iv, v, and vii; Royal Institute of International Affairs, *Nationalism,* pp. 19–34; Hayes, *Essays on Nationalism,* pp. 44–49; Shafer, *Nationalism,* pp. 105–117.

21. Anthony Ashley Cooper, 3rd Earl of Shaftesbury, *Characteristicks of Men, Manners, Opinions, Times* (London, 1737–38), III, 143n; Hertz, *Nationality in History and Politics,* pp. 310–18.

22. "Reflections on the Revolution in France," in Edmund Burke, *Works* (London, 1803), V, 184.

23. Ernest Renan, *Qu'est ce qu'une Nation? Conférence faite en Sorbonne, le 11 mars 1882* (Paris, 1882). See also John S. Mill, *Considerations on Representative Government* (London, 1861), p. 287; Giuseppe Mazzini, "Thoughts upon Democracy in Europe," in [Emilie A. Venturi], *Joseph Mazzini, A Memoir* (London, 1875), pp. 171ff.

24. See the decisive role of Rousseau in identifying the concept of popular sovereignty with that of the nation in his *De l'économie politique, Contrat social,* and *Considérations sur le gouvernement de Pologne,* in *The Political Writings of Jean Jacques Rousseau,* ed. C. E. Vaughan (Cambridge, Eng., 1915), I, 251–57, 453; II, 31–40, 427, 492.

25. For the impact of liberal thought on the formation of German national consciousness see Meinecke, *Weltbürgertum und Nationalstaat,* chaps. iii–vi; George P. Gooch, *Germany and the French Revolution,* Royal Historical Society Transactions (London, 1916), ser. 3, vol. X, pp. 51–76; and Hertz, *Nationality in History and Politics,* pp. 329–39, and Hans Kohn, *Idea of Nationalism,* chaps. vii–viii. See also Veit Valentin, *Geschichte der Deutschen Revolution von 1848–9* (Berlin, 1930–31).

26. For the integration of the concepts of history and citizenship in English national consciousness see Herbert Butterfield, *The Whig Interpretation of History* (London, 1951); and Samuel Kliger, *The Goths in England; a Study in Seventeenth and Eighteenth Century Thought* (Cambridge, 1952). See also Frederick Pollock, *The Expansion of the Common Law* (London, 1904); Herbert Butterfield, *The Englishman and His History* (Cambridge, Eng., 1944), pp. 49–55 and pt. II.

27. See Georg Jellinek on the English national consciousness in the seventeenth and eighteenth centuries in *Die Erklärung der Menschen- und Bürgerrechte* (Leipzig, 1904), pp. 36–46; also Hans Kohn, *The Idea of Nationalism*, pp. 166–83, and chap. v; also Guido de Ruggiero, *The History of European Liberalism* (Oxford, 1927), pp. 410–15.

28. See Hayes, *Essays on Nationalism*, pp. 27–33, 262; Hertz, *Nationality in History and Politics*, pp. 323–25; Jacques Droz, "Concept français et concept allemand de l'idée de nationalité"; Franz Schnabel, "Bismarck und die Nationen."

29. On the cleavage of the French national consciousness see George P. Gooch, *History and Historians in the Nineteenth Century* (London, 1920), pp. 187, 238, 258; Roger H. Soltau, *French Political Thought in the Nineteenth Century* (New York, 1959), chap. xv; and Hertz, *Nationality in History and Politics*, pp. 374–79.

30. On the rather unique pattern of Russian nationalism see Tomáš Garrigue Masaryk, *The Spirit of Russia* (London, 1919), vol. I; Nicholas Zernov, *Moscow the Third Rome* (London [1937]); and "The Rise of Russian Nationalism," in Royal Institute of International Affairs, *Nationalism*, chap. v. See also Hayes, *Essays on Nationalism*, pp. 52–55, 62–69.

31. See page 6–7 of the Introduction, above.

32. Neither Hegel nor Herder was an ideologist of nationalism in the full sense of the term as understood in this study. They were strongly oriented toward universalistic ideals and rationalistic humanitarian concepts of the Enlightenment. Yet undoubtedly their philosophical and political theories were the cornerstones of a romantic theory of nationalism. See Friedrich C. Sell, *Die Tragödie Des Deutschen Liberalismus* (Stuttgart, 1953), chaps. i–iii; also Hertz, *Nationality in History and Politics*, pp. 331–36, 353; see also Friedrich Meinecke, *Die Idee der Staatsräson*, pp. 403–80.

33. On Italian nationalism see Giuseppe Mazzini, "The Duties of Man" in [Venturi], *Joseph Mazzini, A Memoir;* Hans Kohn, *Prophets and Peoples, Studies in Nineteenth-Century Nationalism* (New York, 1946), chap. iii.

CHAPTER II: IDEOLOGY AND THE AMERICAN WAY OF LIFE

1. Bernard Faÿ, *The Revolutionary Spirit in France and America* (New York, 1927), pp. 68–262. See also Howard M. Jones, *America and French Culture, 1750–1848* (Chapel Hill, 1927); Durand Echeverria, *Mirage in the West; A History of the French Image of American Society to 1815* (Princeton, 1957), pp. 267–79; Gilbert Chinard, *The Correspondence of Jefferson and DuPont de Nemours* (Baltimore, 1931); Gilbert Chinard, *Jefferson et les idéoloques* (Baltimore, 1925); Georg Jellinek, *Die Erklärung der Menschen- und Bürgerrechte* (Leipzig, 1904), pp. 9–33; Alfred O. Aldridge, "The Debut of American Letters in France," *French American Review*, III (1950), 1–23.

2. See Jellinek, *Die Erklärung;* Benjamin F. Wright, Jr., "American Interpretations of Natural Law," *American Political Science Review*, 20:528–32 (1926), and "Natural Law in American Political Theory," unpubl. diss.,

Harvard University, 1925; Charles H. McIlwain, *The American Revolution* (New York, 1924), chap. iii.

3. For early expression of these fears see the debates of the Puritan army in A. S. P. Woodhouse, *Puritanism and Liberty* (London, 1938); Edmund Burke, "Reflections on the Revolution in France," *Works* (London, 1854–57), II, 277–518; M. C. Tyler, *The Literary History of the American Revolution, 1763–1783* (New York, 1957), I, chaps. i, ii. See also Joseph Galloway, *Political Reflections on the Late Colonial Governments* (London, 1783).

4. For a general survey of the rise of conservatism see Vernon L. Parrington, *Main Currents in American Thought* (New York [1927]), I, 148–63, 292–320, II, 20–27, III, 7–136; John Adams, "Discourses on Davila," *Works* (Boston, 1850–56), vol. VI; and "A Defence of the Constitutions of Government of the United States of America," *Works*, vol. V; "Letters of Publicola," John Quincy Adams, *Writings*, ed. W. C. Ford (New York, 1913–17), I, 65–110; and of course James Madison's *Journal of the Federal Convention*, ed. E. H. Scott (Chicago, 1893).

5. Fisher Ames, "The Dangers of American Liberty," *Works* (Boston, 1809), p. 380.

6. *Ibid.*, p. 392.

7. Quoted by Jacob P. Mayer, *Prophet of the Mass Age; A Study of Alexis de Tocqueville* (London, 1939), p. 30.

8. Alexis de Tocqueville, *Democracy in America*, ed. Phillips Bradley (New York, 1945), I, 243. See also Tocqueville's diary quoted by G. W. Pierson, *Tocqueville and Beaumont in America* (New York, 1938), p. 114.

9. Richard Koebner, "Semantics and Historiography," *The Cambridge Journal*, 7:132 (1953).

10. See Tocqueville, *Democracy in America*, especially "Why The Americans Show More Aptitude And Taste For General Ideas Than Their Forefathers, the English," II, 13ff; "The Philosophical Method of the Americans," II, 3ff; "How The American Democracy Has Modified The English Language," II, 64ff; and on individualism, II, 98ff.

11. Tocqueville, *Democracy in America*, I, 392.

12. See letter to L. de Kergolay, June 29, 1831, as quoted by Pierson, *Tocqueville and Beaumont*, p. 152.

13. *Ibid.*, p. 693.

14. Tocqueville, *Democracy in America*, I, 244. In speaking of the unity of opinions and states, he notes "the observer . . . will readily discover that their inhabitants, though divided into twenty-four distinct sovereignties, still constitute a single people. . . ," *ibid.*, pp. 392–94.

15. Though Tocqueville has been generally recognized as one of the earliest and greatest sociological historians, many have been puzzled by his equivocal use of the concept and term "democracy." See Pierson, *Tocqueville and Beaumont*, pp. 7, 165. Pierson, though realizing the sociological approach of Tocqueville, failed to grasp Tocqueville's idea that "democracy" in America referred to a new social system whose unifying principle was democ-

racy. The suggestion that the title of Tocqueville's book should have been "Concerning Equality in America" (Pierson, *Tocqueville and Beaumont*, pp. 7, 158n, 165) does not express the author's concept of the total determination of American life through its social system. See Mayer, *Prophet of the Mass Age;* Bernhard Fabian, *Alexis de Tocqueville's Amerikabild* (Heidelberg, 1957); Albert Salomon, "Tocqueville, Moralist and Sociologist," *Social Research*, 2:420–22 (1935); on the influence of sociological French thought on Tocqueville see Chapter IX below.

16. Benito Mussolini, "La Dottrina del Fascismo," *Scritti e Discorsi* (Milan, 1934), VIII, 67–96, and "Forza E Consenso," III, 77–79; see also Elie Halévy, *The World Crisis of 1914–1918* (Oxford, 1930), Lecture I.

· 17. On the spontaneous conformity of the Englishmen see Adolf Löwe, *The Price of Liberty* (London, 1937), pp. 13–25.

18. See Tocqueville, *Democracy in America*, I, 244; John Robert Godley, *Letters from America* (London, 1844), I, 19; see also James Fenimore Cooper, *Notions of the Americans* (Philadelphia, 1832), II, 108–9; also James Fenimore Cooper, *Gleanings in Europe* (New York, 1928–30), II, 316–17; also [Calvin Colton], *The Americans. By an American in London* (London, 1833), pp. 14–15; Gustav H. Blanke, *Amerikanischer Geist: Begriffs-und wortgeschichtliche Untersuchungen* (Meisenheim am Glan, Hain, 1956), pp. 18–24, 24–29, 29–33, on the concepts of Americans, American literature and American national unity, and pp. 41–42 on the "American System." See also Merle E. Curti, *The Roots of American Loyalty* (New York, 1946); on early nationalism in literature see *Cambridge History of American Literature*, ed. W. P. Trent, *et al.* (New York, 1917–21), I, 168–89; Benjamin T. Spencer, *The Quest for Nationality: an American Literary Campaign* (Syracuse, 1957); Edward H. Reisner, *Nationalism and Education since 1789* (New York, 1922); see also Albert K. Weinberg, *Manifest Destiny; a Study in Nationalist Expansionism in American History* (Baltimore, 1935).

19. Tocqueville, *Democracy in America*, I, 393–94.

20. See Friedrich O. Hertz, *Nationality in History and Politics* (London, 1951), p. 21; also Carlton J. H. Hayes, *Essays on Nationalism* (New York, 1928), pp. 86–90, 109–14, 119–23.

21. See above, Chapter I.

22. See *ibid.*, pp. 10–11.

23. See *ibid.* and Chapter I, 22–23.

24. H. S. Commager, ed., *Documents of American History* (New York, 1948), I, 170; see also Friedrich von Gentz, *The American and French Revolutions Compared* (Chicago [1955]). The classical expression of this view is given by John Adams: see "Defence of the Constitutions" and John Quincy Adams, *Letters of Publicola.*

25. See Pierson, *Tocqueville and Beaumont*, pp. 370–71.

26. *Ibid.*, pp. 377–78.

27. *Ibid.*, pp. 381–420.

28. Quoted from Tocqueville's diary by Pierson, *Tocqueville and Beaumont*, p. 381.

29. *Ibid.*, pp. 397–98.

30. *Ibid.*, pp. 398–99.

31. John Fiske, "Manifest Destiny," *Harper's Magazine*, 70:578–90 (1885); *American Political Ideas Viewed from the Standpoint of Universal History* (New York, 1885); and *New France and New England* (Boston, 1902), p. 233. Josiah Strong, *Our Country* (New York [1885]); Lyman Abbott, *The Evolution of Christianity* (Boston, 1892); see also Ira V. Brown, *Lyman Abbott, Christian Evolutionist* (Cambridge, 1953); Merle E. Curti, "Young America," *American Historical Review*, 32:34ff (1926–27); also Oscar Handlin, *Race and Nationality in American Life* (New York, 1957), chap. iv.

32. See Clinton L. Rossiter, *Seedtime of the Republic* (New York, 1953), Introduction, pp. 12ff, and *Conservatism in America* (New York, 1955); Daniel J. Boorstin, *The Genius of American Politics* (Chicago, 1953); also Russell Kirk, *The Conservative Mind: From Burke to Santayana* (Chicago, 1953).

33. Tocqueville, *Democracy in America*, I, 13, 27–43; II, 13ff.

34. *Ibid.*, I, 13.

35. *Ibid.*, I, 47.

36. This is the whole tenor of Rossiter's *Seedtime of the Republic;* see especially p. 301.

37. Tocqueville, *Democracy in America*, I, 47.

CHAPTER III: NATIONAL UNITY: THE AMERICAN INTERPRETATION

1. See Albert F. Pollard, *Factors in American History* (Cambridge, Eng., 1925); Claude H. Van Tyne, *The Causes of the War of Independence* (Boston, 1922).

2. "Report on Letters from the Ministers in Paris," December 20, 1783, Thomas Jefferson, *Writings*, ed. P. L. Ford (New York, 1892–99), III, 357.

3. "Instructions to the Ministers Plenipotentiary Appointed to Negotiate Treaties of Commerce with the European Nations," May 7, 1784, *ibid.*, p. 490.

4. "To James Madison," December 16, 1786, Thomas Jefferson, *Writings*, ed. A. A. Lipscomb *et al.* (Washington, 1903), VI, 9ff; see also letter to Edward Carrington, August 4, 1787, *ibid.*, VI, 227ff; to James Madison, June 20, 1787, *ibid.*, VI, 131ff.

5. "The Anas," Jefferson, *Writings*, ed. Lipscomb, I, 266–67.

6. *The Debates in the Federal Convention of 1787 which framed the Constitution of the United States of America, Reported by James Madison*, eds. Gaillard Hunt and J. B. Scott (New York, 1920), pp. xxvii–xxviii.

7. See Articles II and III of the Articles of Confederation, *Journals of the Continental Congress 1774–1789* (Washington, 1904–34), XIX, 214.

8. See also *Debates in the Federal Convention*, pp. xxviii–xxix.

9. *Ibid.*, p. 308.

10. *Ibid.*, p. 28.

11. *Ibid.*, pp. 81–82; see also Luther Martin, *ibid.*, pp. 130, 136; John Lansing, *ibid.*, pp. 132–34.

12. See Gouverneur Morris in *Debates in the Federal Convention*, pp. 27, 28, and Mason, *ibid.*, p. 28; also Edmund Randolph, *ibid.*, p. 110.

13. See Charles Pinkney, *ibid.*, p. 75.

14. Mason, *Debates in the Federal Convention*, p. 134; see also James Wilson and James Madison on the same question, *ibid.*, pp. 140–43.

15. Alexander Hamilton, in spite of his misgivings and distrust of the masses, suggested, unlike Morris, King, and others, that there should not be any property qualifications for the election of the president. Conscious of the unique importance of the executive in the framework of a national state, he wished to establish the popularity of the president on the broadest basis. See "Hamilton's Draft of a Constitution for the United States," Article IV, pp. 1–4, *Debates in the Federal Convention*, Appendix V, pp. 610–11.

16. See Madison, *ibid.*, pp. 59, 497.

17. Mason, *ibid.*, p. 305; Madison, *ibid.*, p. 309.

18. *The Federalist*, ed. Max Beloff (Oxford, 1948), No. XXXIX, pp. 195–96.

19. See the session of the Convention on June 19 and Rufus King's discussion of the terms which brought about the proposal of Oliver Ellsworth on June 20 to omit the word "national" and retain the proper title "the United States," *Debates in the Federal Convention*, pp. 130–32.

20. *Documentary History of the Constitution of the United States of America, 1786–1870* (Washington, 1894–1905), II, 1.

21. Letter to M. Grand, Oct. 22, 1787, Benjamin Franklin, *Complete Works*, ed. John Bigelow (New York, 1904), XI, 389ff.

22. *Debates in the Federal Convention*, p. 121.

23. *Documentary History of the Constitution*, II, 93. See also the ratification of New Hampshire, *ibid.*, II, 141. Yet a Bill of Rights is added as further safeguard of the Constitutional Compact.

24. *Ibid.*, II, 266, 145–46, 190–203, 267–75, 310–20.

25. *Debates in the Federal Convention*, p. 136.

26. *Federalist*, ed. Max Beloff, No. XXXIII, p. 157.

27. *Ibid.*, No. II, p. 5. "It is well worthy of consideration therefore, whether it would conduce more to the interest of the people of America that they should, to all general purposes, be one nation, under one federal government. . ."

28. *Ibid.*, Nos. III, IV, V.

29. *Ibid.*, No. VII, p. 30.

30. *Debates in the Federal Convention*, pp. 120–27.

31. *Federalist*, No. IX, p. 37.

32. *Ibid.*, p. 39; see also Madison, *ibid.*, No. X, p. 47.

33. *Ibid.*, No. XI, pp. 53–54.

34. See Chapter V below.

35. Kate Mason Rowland, *The Life of George Mason, 1725–1792* (New York, 1892), I, App. IX, p. 430.

36. Quoted by Gilbert Chinard, *Thomas Jefferson; the Apostle of Americanism* (Boston, 1929), p. 81. See letter to Colonel Humphreys, March 18, 1789, Jefferson, *Writings,* ed. Lipscomb, VII, 324.

37. Samuel Adams, *Writings,* ed. H. A. Cushing (New York, 1904–08), I, 271; see also S. Adams and James Otis, "The Rights of the Colonists," November 29, 1770, in *ibid.,* I, 355ff. For a summary of the dominance of the natural-rights theory in the Revolutionary period see, among others: Clinton L. Rossiter, *Seedtime of the Republic* (New York, 1953), pp. 330–430; Charles H. McIlwain, *The American Revolution* (New York, 1924), chap. iii; Carl L. Becker, *The Declaration of Independence* (New York, 1948), chap. ii; and B. F. Wright, Jr., "Natural Law in American Political Theory," unpubl. diss., Harvard University, 1925.

38. Francis N. Thorpe, ed., *Federal and State Constitutions* (Washington, 1909), III, 1889.

39. Gustav H. Blanke, *Amerikanischer Geist; Begriffs und wortgeschichtliche Untersuchungen* (Meisenheim am Glan, Hain, 1956), pp. 47–49, 52–56.

40. For a comprehensive survey of the motivations of the early immigrants and the meaning which America held for them see among others: Perry Miller, *Errand into the Wilderness* (Cambridge, Mass., 1956), chaps. i, ii, and iv; Rossiter, *Seedtime of the Republic;* Max Savelle, *Seeds of Liberty* (New York, 1948), chap. x; M. E. Curti, *The Roots of American Loyalty* (New York, 1946), chap. i; V. L. Parrington, *Main Currents in American Thought* (New York, [1927]), vol. I, pt. 1, chaps. ii–v; Moses Coit Tyler, *A History of American Literature* (New York, 1879), vol. I; Samuel E. Morison, *Builders of the Bay Colony* (Boston, 1930); Oscar Handlin, *Adventure in Freedom; Three Hundred Years of Jewish Life in America* (New York, 1954); Oscar Handlin, *Immigration as a Factor in American History* (New Jersey, 1959); Marcus L. Hansen, *The Atlantic Migration, 1607–1860,* ed. Arthur M. Schlesinger (Cambridge, 1940); M. L. Hansen, *The Immigrant in American History,* ed. Arthur M. Schlesinger (Cambridge, 1940).

41. Blanke, *Amerikanischer Geist,* pp. 15–22.

42. *Ibid.,* p. 46.

43. Francis Bacon, *New Atlantis,* ed. G. C. Moore Smith (Cambridge, Eng., 1900).

44. Blanke, *Amerikanischer Geist,* pp. 46–48.

45. Quoted by V. L. Parrington, *Main Currents in American Thought* (New York, 1930), I, 83, from John Eliot's *Christian Commonwealth.* See also Cotton Mather, *Magnalia Christi Americana* (Hartford, 1820), Introduction and pp. 104–11. See also John Cotton, "God's Promise to his Plantations," in Harry R. Warfel, Ralph H. Gabriel, Stanley T. Williams, eds., *The American Mind* (New York, 1937), I, 26, 27; John Davenport, "Theocracy," *ibid.,* I, 43–45; Cotton Mather, "Wonders of the Invisible World," *ibid.,* I, 51. For the identification of the people and the country with Israel and its

Promised Land see especially "The Fundamental Agreement or Original Constitution of the Colony of New Haven" in Thorpe, *Federal and State Constitutions*, I, 526; and Hans Kohn, *The Idea of Nationalism* (New York, 1951), 664, n. 13, 665, n. 6. For the Puritan concept of history see Perry Miller, *The New England Mind: the Seventeenth Century* (New York, 1939), chap. xiv, pp. 398ff and chap. xvi, pp. 463ff. For similar transmutation of millenary and of eschatological expectations into a philosophy in Puritan England see G. P. Gooch, *English Democratic Ideas in the Seventeenth Century* (Cambridge, Eng., 1927).

46. Jonathan Edwards, "Thoughts on the Revival of Religion in New England," in *Works* (New York, 1844), pt. 2, pp. 313ff.

47. François M. A. de Voltaire: *Lettres sur les Anglais*, ed. Arthur Wilson-Green (Cambridge, Eng., 1931); *Toleration and Other Essays*, trans. Joseph McCabe (New York, 1912); and *Essai sur les moeurs et l'ésprit des nations et sur les principaux faits de l'histoire* (Geneva, 1769).

48. Abbé Guillaume Thomas Raynal, *Histoire philosophique et politique* (Amsterdam, 1770), VI, 425. For the image of America in France see Bernard Faÿ, *The Revolutionary Spirit in France and America* (New York, 1927), pp. 8–20; also Durand Echeverria, *Mirage in the West: A History of the French Image of American Society to 1815* (Princeton, 1957).

49. Faÿ, *The Revolutionary Spirit*, p. 19.

50. George Berkeley, "Verses on the Prospect of Planting Arts and Learning in America," *Works* (London, 1853), II, 294.

51. Georg Simmel, *Grundfragen der Soziologie* (Berlin, 1917), p. 80.

52. See Peter Kalm's account of his travels in North America in Oscar Handlin, *This Was America* (Cambridge, Mass., 1949), pp. 19–20, 35–36. On the prophecies of the coming independence of the American colonies by such Europeans as Thomas Browne, Horace Walpole, Choiseul, Turgot, and the Count de Vergennes, and by the Board of Trade in 1701, see C. H. Van Tyne, *The War of Independence; American Phase* (Boston, 1929), pp. 358–60.

53. "Importance of Gaining and Preserving the Friendship of the Indians," Philadelphia, March 20, 1751, Franklin, *Complete Works*, ed. John Bigelow (New York, 1904), II, 332–38. "Plan of Union Adopted by the Convention at Albany," *ibid.*, III, 25–29.

54. "Observations Concerning the Increase of Mankind and the Peopling of Countries," *ibid.*, II, 338–50.

55. "The Interest of Great Britain Considered, with Regard to Her Colonies and the Acquisitions of Canada and Guadaloupe," *ibid.*, III, 295–96.

56. "Observations Concerning the Increase of Mankind," *ibid.*, II, 341.

57. *Ibid.*, p. 347; also, "Plan for Settling Two Western Colonies in North America," III, 148–57.

58. "The Interest of Great Britain, etc.," *ibid.*, III, 302.

59. *Ibid.*, II, 335.

60. "Observations Concerning the Increase . . . ," *ibid.*, II, 349.

61. "The American Colonies not Dangerous in their Nature to Great

Britain," *ibid.*, III, 322; "Letter Concerning Gratitude of America . . . ," *ibid.*, IV, 166; see also "The Interest of Great Britain, etc.," *ibid.*, III, 322; "Examination of Dr. Benjamin Franklin in the British House of Commons, February 1776," *ibid.*, IV, 202, 208; "Letter to Lord Kames," London, April 11, 1767, *ibid.*, IV, 280. In a letter to Thomas Cushing, July 7, 1773, Franklin writes, "No one doubts the advantage of a strict union between the mother country and the colonies, if it may be obtained and preserved on equitable terms," *ibid.*, VI, 158.

62. See Chapters I and IV of this book. See also Becker, *Declaration of Independence,* chap. iii; John C. Miller, *Origins of the American Revolution* (Stanford, Calif., 1959), pp. 184–85, 225.

63. See "Causes of American Discontent before 1768," Franklin, *Complete Works,* IV, 389; and "Letter Concerning the Gratitude of America," Franklin, *ibid.*, IV, 166–70.

64. "Observations on Passages in 'An Inquiry into the Nature and Causes of the Dispute. . . ,'" Franklin, *Complete Works,* V, 156; "Answer by Franklin to the queries of Mr. Strahan. . . ," *ibid.*, p. 138.

65. See "Some Good Whig Principles," Franklin, *Complete Works,* IV, 435–37; "Positions to Be Examined, Concerning National Wealth," April 1769, *ibid.*, V, 68–71.

66. Letter to Lord Kames, *ibid.*, IV, 286; see also "Letter to Thomas Pownal," *ibid.*, pp. 342–43.

67. "To Joseph Galloway," London, February 25, 1775, *ibid.*, VI, 431–32.

CHAPTER IV: THE FIRST NATIONAL CREED: AMERICAN WHIGGISM

1. See J. T. Adams, *Provincial Society 1690–1763* (New York, 1928), chap. xi; Edward Channing, *History of the United States* (New York, 1905–25), II, chap. xvii; Samuel E. Morison and Henry S. Commager, *The Growth of the American Republic* (New York, 1942), I, chap. v.

2. J. C. Miller, *Origins of the American Revolution* (Stanford, 1959), pp. 48, 60–61; see also Franklin's testimony on the ineradicable jealousy between the colonies, in "The Interest of Great Britain Considered. . ." *Complete Works,* ed. John Bigelow (New York, 1904), III, 320.

3. Jonathan Mayhew, *Two Discourses Delivered October 9th, 1760* (Boston, 1760), p. 47, as quoted by Miller in *Origins of the American Revolution,* p. 71. See also the Reverend Samuel Cooper, *A Sermon Preached before His Excellency Thomas Pownall* (Boston, 1759), p. 46, quoted in Miller, *ibid.*, p. 79.

4. Clinton L. Rossiter, *Seedtime of the Republic* (New York, 1953), p. 141.

5. "Notes on Virginia," Thomas Jefferson, *Writings,* ed. P. L. Ford (New York, 1892–99), III, 189.

6. Rossiter, *Seedtime of the Republic,* p. 266.

7. "Answer of the House of Representatives of Massachusetts to the Governor's Speech, October 23, 1765," Samuel Adams, *Writings,* ed. H. A. Cushing (1904–8), I, 18–19.

8. "Instruction of the Town of Boston to its Representatives, September, 1765," Samuel Adams, *Writings*, I, 8–9. See also "Resolutions of the House of Representatives of Massachusetts, October 29, 1765," *ibid.*, I, 23–25; "Letter to John Smith, December 19, 1765," *ibid.*, I, 45; and "to Dennis de Berdt, December 20, 1765," *ibid.*, I, 64.

9. "The House of Representatives of Massachusetts to the Earl of Shelburne, January 15, 1768," *ibid.*, I, 154.

10. See the protest of the Lords against the repeal of the Stamp Act in which they rejected as a dangerous doctrine, "destructive to all government," the American concept of a free constitution, quoted by C. H. Van Tyne in *The Causes of the War of Independence* (Boston, 1922), pp. 224–26. See also the totally different concept of the Constitution in William Blackstone, *Commentaries on the Laws of England* (London, 1787), I, 63–92.

11. See, e.g., "The Virginia Stamp Act Resolutions," H. S. Commager, ed., *Documents of American History* (New York, 1940), I, 56; "Instructions of the Town of Braintree, Massachusetts," *ibid.*, p. 57; also, "Resolutions of the Stamp Act Congress, No. VI," *ibid.*, p. 58.

12. John Adams, *Works*, ed. C. F. Adams (Boston, 1850–56), II, 523–25.

13. See Andrew C. McLaughlin, *A Constitutional History of the United States* (New York, 1936), pp. 25–28.

14. *The Oxford English Dictionary on Historical Principles* (Oxford, 1888–[1928]), vol. II, confirms the view that the concept was rarely used in English literature before the American Revolution as it has no recognized legal validity or definite institutional meaning.

15. See Perry Miller, *Errand into the Wilderness* (Cambridge, Mass., 1956), chaps. iii, v. Andrew C. McLaughlin, *The Foundations of American Constitutionalism* (New York, 1932), vols. I and III; and *Constitutional History*, pp. 91–96; V. L. Parrington, *Main Currents in American Thought* (New York [1927]), vol. I, pt. 1, chaps. ii–iv; pt. 2, chap. iii, on John Wise; H. L. Osgood, "The Political Ideas of the Puritans," *Political Science Quarterly*, 6:201ff (1891).

16. See Charles H. McIlwain, *Constitutionalism, Ancient and Modern* (Ithaca, 1940).

17. Carl Stephenson and F. G. Marcham, eds., *Sources of English Constitutional History* (New York, 1937), pp. 504, 507, 511, 525, 529.

18. See Ernst Tröeltsch, *Die Soziallehren der Christlichen Kirchen und Gruppen* (Tübingen, 1912), pp. 683–703; A. S. P. Woodhouse, *Puritanism and Liberty* (London, 1938).

19. See Perry Miller, *Errand into the Wilderness*, chaps. ii, iii, v; Georg Jellinek, *Die Erklärung der Menschen und Bürgerrechte* (Leipzig, 1904); Samuel R. Gardiner, *Constitutional Documents of the Puritan Revolution 1625–1660* (Oxford, 1906), Introduction; A. S. P. Woodhouse, *Puritanism and Liberty* (London, 1938); Godfrey Davies, *The Early Stuarts 1603–1660* (Oxford, 1945). See also Walter Rothschild, *Der Gedanke der geschriebenen Verfassung in der englishen Revolution* (Tübingen, 1903); also Joseph R.

Tanner, *English Constitutional Conflicts of the Seventeenth Century 1603–1689* (Cambridge, Eng., 1928).

20. Francis N. Thorpe, ed., *Federal and State Constitutions* (Washington, 1909), I, 519.

21. *Ibid.*, p. 526.

22. *Ibid.*, VI, 3207ff.

23. See G. P. Gooch, *English Democratic Ideas in the Seventeenth Century* (Cambridge, Eng., 1927), pp. 150–51. On Milton, see especially William Haller, *Liberty and Reformation in the Puritan Revolution* (New York, 1955), pp. 178–88, 237–45.

24. See John Milton, *Prose Works* (Philadelphia, 1847), II, 173–90; Gooch, *English Democratic Ideas,* pp. 265–70.

25. John Milton, "The Second Defence of the People of England Against An Anonymous Liberal," *Prose Works,* II, 479–80.

26. H. F. Russell Smith, *Harrington and His Oceana* (Cambridge, Eng., 1914), pp. 133–69; R. H. Tawney, *Harrington's Interpretation of His Age* (London, 1941); Richard Koebner, "Die Geschichtslehre James Harrington's," *Geist und Gessellschaft Festgrift, Kurt Breysig zu seinem sechzigsten Geburtstage* (Breslau, 1927–28), III, 4ff.

27. John Toland, *The Oceana and other Works of James Harrington with an Account of his Life* (London, 1771), p. 35.

28. *Ibid.*, pp. 43–44.

29. *Ibid.*, pp. 41–42.

30. *Ibid.*

31. *Ibid.*, p. 94.

32. See Russell Smith, *Harrington,* pp. 137–43, 162–79; also Gooch, *English Democratic Ideas,* App. A, pp. 305–7.

33. Thorpe, *Federal and State Constitutions,* VI, 2548.

34. *Ibid.;* see also "The Fundamental Constitutions for the Province of East New Jersey in America, Anno Domini 1683," *ibid.*, p. 2547.

35. Thorpe, *Federal and State Constitutions,* V, 3052.

36. *Ibid.*, V, 3054.

37. Charles H. McIlwain, *Constitutionalism, Ancient and Modern,* pp. 4–10.

38. See Chapter I above on the types of modern nationalism.

39. Anthony, Earl of Shaftesbury, *Characteristicks of Men, Manners, Opinions, Times* (London, 1737–38), III, 143.

40. *Ibid.*, III, 143, 146–49.

41. *Ibid.*, III, 145, for Shaftesbury's reflections on the nature of the love of country, and his use of a new term, "patriotism," to describe his concept of "nation" and *patria.* Shaftesbury regrets that there exists no suitable English word for the term *patria* which means "native community," not country-land. It is the idea of a *civil state* or a *nation* not that of the native soil. See *ibid.*, III, 149–50. It is probable that the term "patriotism" took its rise from these ideas. *The Oxford English Dictionary* (Oxford [1909]),

vol. VII, names as the first reference Nathan Bailey's *Universal Etymological English Dictionary*, 3rd ed. (London, 1726), and Bolingbroke's *Letters on the Spirit of Patriotism* (Oxford [1917]).

42. Shaftesbury, *Characteristicks*, III, 146.

43. The word does not occur in the writings of Shaftesbury but it is prominently employed for the first time by Bolingbroke in his *Letters on the Spirit of Patriotism* which were written in the years 1735–48 and published by Pope first in 1741 and then by Bolingbroke himself in 1749. See A. Hassall in "Introduction" to Henry Saint-John Bolingbroke, *Letters* (Oxford [1917]).

44. "An Essay on the Freedom of Wit and Humour," Shaftesbury, *Characteristicks*, I, 104ff; also, "Soliloquy; or Advice to an Author," I, 153ff.

45. Shaftesbury, *Characteristicks*, III, 143n.

46. "Soliloquy," Shaftesbury, *Characteristicks*, I, 216.

47. *Ibid.*, I, 108.

48. "Soliloquy," Shaftesbury, *Characteristicks*, I, 222, 239.

49. "Miscellaneous Reflections," Shaftesbury, *Characteristicks*, III, 150, 312–13.

50. See Rossiter, *Seedtime of the Republic*.

51. [John Trenchard], *Cato's Letters; or Essays on Liberty, Civil and Religious, and Other Important Subjects*, 4 vols. (London, 1748), I, *Dedication*, p. xxiii.

52. *Ibid.*, Letter 26, p. 195.

53. *Ibid.*, p. 191.

54. See *ibid.*, Letter 25, "Considerations on the destructive Spirit of arbitrary Power. With the Blessings of liberty, and our own Constitution," I, 184.

55. *Ibid.*, pp. 185–91.

56. *Ibid.*, p. 185. See also John Trenchard and Thomas Gordon, *A Collection of Tracts* (London, 1751), "An argument showing that a standing Army is inconsistent with Free Government, and absolutely destructive to the Constitution of the English Monarchy."

57. [Trenchard], *Cato's Letters*, II, 192.

58. Trenchard and Gordon, *A Collection of Tracts*, p. 6; [Trenchard], *Cato's Letters*, I, 182.

59. Bolingbroke, *Letters*, pp. 74–75.

60. Charles L. de S., Baron de Montesquieu, *The Spirit of Laws*, trans. Thomas Nugent (New York [1899]), I, 150ff. Though Locke's theory of the civil covenant is compatible with the theory of the British Constitution, he cannot be considered as the source of the American concept. The Americans rather grafted the concept of the Constitution on the contractual theory of society as it had already been done by Bolingbroke and before him by Algernon Sidney in his *Discourses Concerning Government*.

As the main subject of Sidney's *Discourses* is the relation of freedom to the historical forms of government and the question of the legitimate source of authority, the concept of constitution becomes of central importance. See Algernon Sidney, *Discourses Concerning Government* (Philadelphia, 1805),

I, 62, 206, 239, 250, 269, 285, 290, 296; II, 62, 165, 179, 211, 252. See especially II, Sect. 25: "Laws and Constitutions ought to be weighted, and whilst all due reverence is paid to such as are good, every nation . . . ought to exercise that power according to the best of their understanding, and in place of what was either at first mistaken or afterward corrupted, to constitute that which is most conclusive to the establishment of justice and liberty." *Ibid.*, II, 212.

61. Henry St. John, 1st Viscount Bolingbroke, *A Dissertation upon Parties: in Several Letters to Caleb D'Anvers, Esq.* (London, 1771), p. 141.

62. *Ibid.*, p. 144; see also, *ibid.*, Letter XIII, pp. 199–203.

63. *Ibid.*, pp. 183–87, 191–94, 248–55.

64. *Ibid.*, p. 191.

65. *Ibid.*, pp. 204–9.

66. *Ibid.*, pp. 297–98.

67. *Ibid.*, p. 191.

68. *Ibid.*, p. 197.

69. See William Vincent Wells, *The Life and Public Services of Samuel Adams* (Boston, 1888), I, 16–23.

70. James Otis, *The Rights of the British Colonies asserted and Proved* (London [1765]), p. 16.

71. John Locke, *Two Treatises on Government* (London, 1821), Treatise 2, chap. ii–vii.

72. John Locke, *ibid.*, chap. xix, "Of the Dissolution of Government," p. 222.

73. S. Adams, *Writings*, I, 23–24. See also *ibid.*, I, 27–28.

74. *Ibid.*, II, 350–79. See also Charles H. McIlwain, *The American Revolution* (New York, 1924), vol. III.

75. See McIlwain, *ibid.*, chap. ii; Edward Channing, *A History of the United States* (New York, 1912), III, chap. v.

76. Benjamin Franklin, "The Interest of Great Britain Considered," *Complete Works*, III, 293; "Letter Concerning the gratitude of America," *ibid.*, IV, 166ff; "The Examination of Dr. Benjamin Franklin in the British House of Commons," *ibid.*, IV, 191–92.

77. "Observation on Passages in a Pamphlet," Franklin, *Complete Works*, IV, 257–59.

78. "To Lord Kames," April 11, 1767, Franklin, *Complete Works*, IV, 284.

79. S. Adams, *Writings*, I, 19, 24–25.

80. *Ibid.*, p. 73.

81. John Adams, *Works*, I, 66.

82. Richard Henry Lee, *Letters*, ed. J. C. Ballagh (New York, 1911–14), I, 5–6.

83. *Ibid.*, I, 6. Also "To Arthur Lee, July 4, 1765," *ibid.*, pp. 10–11.

84. *Ibid.*, "To Landon Carter, Aug. 15, 1765," p. 11.

85. "Letters from a Farmer in Pennsylvania to the Inhabitants of the British Colonies," in S. E. Morison, ed., *Sources and Documents Illustrating the American Revolution, 1764–1788* (Oxford, 1951), p. 44.

86. *Ibid.*, pp. 34–35.

87. *Ibid.*, p. 43.

88. *Ibid.*, pp. 47, 51–53.

89. *Ibid.*, pp. 42, 45, 47–48.

90. *Ibid.*, p. 53.

91. Samuel White Patterson, *The Spirit of the American Revolution as Revealed in the Poetry of the Period* (Boston [1915]), p. 42, n. 1; also Moses Coit Tyler, *The Literary History of the American Revolution, 1763–1783* (New York, 1897), II, 26–27.

92. Wm. McCarty, comp., *Songs, Odes, and other Poems, on National Subjects* (Philadelphia, 1842), p. 9.

93. Patterson, *Spirit of the American Revolution*, p. 46.

94. *Ibid.*, pp. 48–52; and John Trumbull's Commencement Poem at Yale College, Sept. 12, 1770, "The Prospect of the Future Glory of America," *ibid.*, p. 52. See also, "Free America" by General Warren in McCarty, *Songs, Odes, and other Poems*, p. 14.

95. See Miller, *Origins of the American Revolution*, pp. 268ff.

96. *Ibid.*, pp. 270–74. See also Carl L. Becker, *The Eve of the Revolution* (New Haven, 1918), pp. 50–58, esp. Thomas Hutchinson's Letter, pp. 56–58.

97. Quoted by Miller, *Origins of the American Revolution*, p. 435. See also *ibid.*, pp. 433–37 and John Adams, "Novanglus," in Morison, *Sources and Documents*, pp. 125ff.

98. Lee, *Letters*, I, 29.

99. R. H. Lee to Samuel Adams, February 4, 1773, Lee, *Letters*, I, 82; to Arthur Lee, May 19, 1769, *ibid.*, I, 34.

100. Morison, *Sources and Documents*, pp. 112, 120.

101. *Ibid.*, pp. 126–29, 133–35.

102. Thomas Jefferson, *Writings*, ed. P. L. Ford (New York, 1892–99), "A Summary View of the Rights of British America," I, 429–30.

103. *Ibid.*, pp. 444–45.

104. Morison, *Sources and Documents*, p. 145. See also Jefferson's draft of the same Declaration in *Writings*, ed. Ford, I, 462–76.

105. Thomas Paine, *Life and Works*, ed. W. M. Van der Weyde (New Rochelle, 1925), III, 71. See also *ibid.*, II, 335.

106. See Wilson, "Considerations," in Morison, *Sources and Documents*, 104ff; Jefferson's letter to John Randolph, August 25, 1775, in Jefferson, *Writings*, ed. Ford, I, 482–85; and especially his letter to the same, Nov. 29, 1775, *ibid.*, pp. 491–93. "Believe me, dear Sir, there is not in the British empire a man who more cordially loves a union with Great Britain, than I do. But by the God that made me, I will cease to exist before I yield to a connection on such terms as the British Parliament propose; and in this, I think I speak the sentiments of America." See also R. H. Lee, "Letter of Congress to the Lord Mayor of London," July 8, 1775, *Letters*, I, 141–43.

107. See the argument of Lee, Jay, Rutlege, Livingstone, Sherman, members of the Committee on Stating the Rights and Grievances of the Colonies,

Sept. 8, 1774, whether the colonial rights should be based on the rights of men or not (John Adams, *Works*, II, 370–73).

108. "Warren-Adams Letters," Massachusetts Historical Society, *Collections* (1917), LXXII, 233. On the spirit of hesitancy and fear of independence, see Miller, *Origins of the American Revolution*, pp. 460–62, 482–84.

109. Van Tyne, *War of Independence*, chaps. xv, xvi and pp. 346–50.

110. Letter to Patrick Henry, April 20, 1776, Lee, *Letters*, I, 177.

111. Edmund C. Burnett, ed., *Letters of Members of the Continental Congress* (Washington, 1921–36), I, 118.

112. See Van Tyne, *War of Independence*, pp. 127–39, and Burnett, ed., *Letters of Members of the Continental Congress*, I, 458, 468, 470, 473.

CHAPTER V: THE AMERICAN, THE NEW MAN:
THE IMAGE OF A NEW NATION

1. On the influence of Thomas Paine: C. H. Van Tyne, *The War of Independence* (Boston, 1929), pp. 324, 330–34; J. C. Miller, *Origins of the American Revolution* (Stanford, 1959); George O. Trevelyan, *The American Revolution* (New York, 1909–12), II, 147–54. John Adams conceded, in spite of his early distrust and later hatred of Thomas Paine, that "Paine's pamphlet . . . crystallized public opinion, and was the *first factor* in bringing about the Revolution"; quoted in Mary Agnes Best, *Thomas Paine, Prophet and Martyr of Democracy* (New York, 1927), p. 74. See also, on the same, George Washington, *Writings*, ed. W. C. Ford (New York, 1889–93), III, 396. For a general survey and estimate, see Moncure D. Conway, *The Life of Thomas Paine* (New York, 1893), I, 56–63. See also Edmund C. Burnett, *The Continental Congress* (New York, 1941), pp. 131–37; Carl L. Becker, *The Eve of the Revolution* (New Haven, 1918), pp. 247–51.

2. See M. D. Conway, *Life of Paine*, I, xvi–xix; on John Fiske, *ibid.*, I, 82; V. L. Parrington, *Main Currents in American Thought* (New York, 1927), I, 327–32. On the remarkable vengeance of Morris on Paine, see Conway, *Life of Paine*, II, chaps. v, viii. On the clergy and Thomas Paine, *ibid.*, II, 181–82. An analysis of the attitude toward Thomas Paine would disclose the permanent tension between the universalistic concept of American nationality and the religious-ethnic nationalism of the conservatives in the nineteenth century, especially in its newer version of integral organic nationalism as preached by Theodore Roosevelt.

3. Thomas Paine, "Common Sense," *Life and Works*, ed. W. M. Van der Weyde (New Rochelle, 1925), II, 123–24.

4. *Ibid.*, II, 136–37; also *ibid.*, II, 125, 130–31.

5. *Ibid.*, II, 127.

6. *Ibid.*, II, 144–48.

7. "The Rights of Man, Part II," Thomas Paine, *Writings*, ed. Conway, II, 402.

8. "Common Sense," *Life and Works*, ed. Van der Weyde, II, 179–80.

9. *Ibid.*, II, 101–7.

10. *Ibid.*, II, 150.

11. "Letter to the Abbé Raynal, on the Affairs of North America," Paine, *Writings*, ed. Conway, II, 76.

12. "Letter to Abbé Raynal," *ibid.*, pp. 77, 121.

13. Ludwig Lewisohn, "Introduction," M. G. St. J. de Crèvecœur, *Letters from an American Farmer* (New York, 1908), p. xx.

14. Michel-Guillaume St. John de Crèvecœur, *Letters from an American Farmer* (New York, 1957), Letter III, pp. 42–51 and *ibid.*, Letter XII, p. 198.

15. Robert de Crèvecœur, *Saint John de Crèvecœur, sa vie et ses ouvrages (1735–1813)*, Paris, 1883, pp. 17–62; also Julia Post Mitchell, *St. Jean de Crèvecœur* (New York, 1916), pp. 21–58.

16. Friedrich M. Grimm, *Correspondence litteraire, philosophique, et critique* (Paris, 1877–82), XIV, 88.

17. Crèvecœur, *Letters* (1957), p. 7.

18. *Ibid.*, pp. 51–53.

19. *Ibid.*, p. 54.

20. *Ibid.*, pp. 47–51, 207, 219.

21. The term was used by Crèvecœur.

22. Paine, *Writings*, ed. Conway, II, 402.

23. Crèvecœur, *Letters* (1957 ed.), pp. 37–38.

24. *Ibid.*, p. 40.

25. *Ibid.*, p. 39.

26. Hans Kohn, *The Idea of Nationalism* (New York, 1951), pp. 292–301.

27. See Chapter III above, sec. 4.

28. "To Joshua Babcock," January 13, 1772, Benjamin Franklin, *Complete Works*, ed. John Bigelow (New York, 1904), V, 287–88.

29. Crèvecœur, *Letters* (1957), pp. 41, 51, 52.

30. "To Mr. Bellini, Paris, Sept. 30, 1785," Thomas Jefferson, *Writings*, ed. A. A. Lipscomb (Washington, 1903), V, 152–53; "Letter to George Wythe, Paris, Aug. 13, 1786," Thomas Jefferson, *Writings*, ed. P. L. Ford (New York, 1892–99), IV, 266–70.

31. "Letter to Mrs. Trist, Aug. 18, 1785," Jefferson, *Writings*, ed. Lipscomb, V, 81.

32. "To George Wythe, Aug. 13, 1776," Jefferson, *Writings*, ed. Ford, IV, 269.

33. *Ibid.*, IV, 268.

34. "To Edward Carrington, Jan. 16, 1787," Jefferson, *Writings*, ed. Ford, IV, 360.

35. "To James Monroe, Paris, June 17, 1785," Jefferson, *Writings*, ed. Ford, IV, 59.

36. "To J. Bannister, Junior, Paris, Oct. 15, 1785," Jefferson, *Writings*, ed. Lipscomb, V, 186–87.

37. Van Tyne, *War of Independence*, pp. 349–50.

38. Moses C. Tyler, *The Literary History of the American Revolution* (New York, 1897), I, 505, 509; Carl L. Becker, *The Declaration of Independence* (New York, 1953), pp. 24–29.

39. See Becker, *Declaration of Independence*, pp. 105–13.

40. *Journals of the Continental Congress, 1774–1789* (Washington, 1904–34), V, 425.

41. Jefferson, *Writings*, ed. Ford, I, 22.

42. Tyler, *Literary History*, I, 500.

43. "Thomas Jefferson to Henry Lee, May 8, 1825," Jefferson, *Writings*, ed. Ford, X, 343.

44. See Chapter IV above, pp. 50ff, on "the freest principles of the English Constitution."

45. "John Adams to Timothy Pickering, Aug. 6, 1822," John Adams, *Works*, II, 513–14. See also the excellent anthology, *The Spirit of 'Seventy-Six*, ed. H. S. Commager and R. B. Morris (Indianapolis, 1958), I, 271–324, 367–401.

46. Burnett, *Continental Congress*, pp. 122, 154–55; John Adams, *Works*, III, 13–16; Francis N. Thorpe, *A Constitutional History of the American People* (New York, 1898), I, 111–32.

47. J. Adams, *Works*, III, 45; Burnett, *Continental Congress*, pp. 156–58.

48. "J. Adams to Patrick Henry," *Works*, IX, 387–88; "To William Cushing, June 9, 1776," *ibid.*, IX, 391.

49. "Carter Braxton to Landon Carter, April 14, 1776," in Edmund C. Burnett, ed., *Letters of Members of the Continental Congress* (Washington, 1921–36), I, 421.

50. "To John Jay, June 29, 1776," ed. Burnett, *Letters of Members of the Continental Congress*, I, 518.

51. *The Rights of Man*, Part II, in Paine, *Writings*, ed. Conway, II, 401.

52. See Thorpe, *Constitutional History*, I, 44: "The Declaration of Independence was almost immediately accepted as a national bill of rights."

53. See Tyler, *Literary History*, I, 515–19, for the significance of the Declaration. It is hard to understand how Carl Becker in his very scholarly *The Declaration of Independence* could overlook the twofold significance of the Declaration. Nor is it easy to understand that a historian should ignore or belittle the immense influence of the natural-rights philosophy on the crystallization of the forms of society, state, and nationhood in America. It is surely not the historian's task to show the obsolescence of a philosophy which still remains the backbone of the "American way of life." Ideas and concepts may historically have the utmost creative power and may dominate completely the actions of men, without gaining the approval of the philosopher or making sense in the contemporary climate of opinion.

54. Francis N. Thorpe, *Federal and State Constitutions* (Washington, 1909), IV, 2452.

55. *Ibid.*, V, 2594ff.

56. See *ibid.*, V, secs. XVI–XIX, pp. 2597–98.

57. *Ibid.*, I, 96.

58. The term "freeman" is of course used in all southern slaveholding states, apart from Virginia, to adjust the Declaration of Rights to slavery. See Constitution of Arkansas, in Thorpe, *Federal and State Constitutions*,

I, 269; of Florida, *ibid.*, II, 664; of Mississippi, *ibid.*, IV, 2033; of Texas, *ibid.*, VI, 3547. The Constitution of Kentucky circumvents the same difficulty by introducing the phrase ". . . to secure to all citizens," *ibid.*, III, 1277.

59. *Ibid.*, I, 96–97.

60. *Ibid.*, IV, 1930.

61. *Ibid.*, VI, 3739.

62. See Chapters III and IV above.

63. For an example of the interpretive function of the natural-rights theory, see William Blackstone's exposition of the relation of municipal or civil law and the law of nature in *Commentaries on the Laws of England* (London, 1787), "of the nature of laws in general" and "of the absolute rights of individuals," I, 38–48, 121–45. This is not to deny the impact of the "Natural-Law Philosophy" on the emergence of "enlightened absolutism" in Europe in the second half of the eighteenth century, especially in Spain, Portugal, and Central and Eastern Europe.

64. Paine, *The Rights of Man*, pt. II, in *Writings*, ed. Conway, II, 411.

65. See, for instance, the Constitution of Indiana, in Thorpe, *Federal and State Constitutions*, II, 1057–58.

66. *Ibid.*, VII, 3812.

67. Becker, *Declaration of Independence*, p. 161.

68. *Federal and State Constitutions*, VII, 3813; see, for example, the Constitution of Oregon, *ibid.*, V, 2998.

69. *Ibid.*, IV, 2453–54.

70. John Locke, *Two Treatises on Civil Government* (London, 1821), Treatise II, p. 191.

71. *Ibid.*, p. 234.

72. *Ibid.*

73. *Ibid.*, p. 239.

74. Gilbert Chinard, *Thomas Jefferson, the Apostle of Americanism* (Boston, 1929), p. 81.

75. Blackstone, *Commentaries*, I, 124–25.

76. The Constitution of Massachusetts, 1780, Thorpe, *Federal and State Constitutions*, III, 1888–89.

77. *The Federalist*, ed. Max Beloff (Oxford, 1948), XIV, 65–66.

78. *Ibid.*, p. 66.

79. *Ibid.*

80. See Chapter V, sec. 1, above.

81. *Federalist*, p. 66.

82. Washington, *Writings*, ed. Ford, IV, 292–93.

83. To Abigail Adams, July 3, 1776, John Adams, *Works*, IX, 418, 420.

84. See: Jefferson to Benjamin Galloway, February 2, 1812, *Writings*, ed. Lipscomb, XIII, 130; Jefferson to William Hunter, March 11, 1790, *ibid.*, VIII, 6ff; to Richard Rush, October 20, 1820, *ibid.*, XV, 281–84; Inauguration Address, March 4, 1801, *ibid.*, III, 321–23; The Third Annual Message, *ibid.*, 351–60.

85. *The Rights of Man*, pt. II, in Paine, *Writings*, ed. Conway, II, 402.

86. "The Fortune of the Republic," Ralph W. Emerson, *Complete Writings* (New York, 1929), II, 119; "American Civilization," *ibid.*, II, 1209.

87. Merle E. Curti, *The Roots of American Loyalty* (New York, 1946), p. 63.

88. "America in 1846," *United States Magazine and Democratic Review,* 18:61 (1846).

CHAPTER VI: "NATURAL SOCIETY"—THE EVOLUTION OF A SOCIAL IDEAL

1. Thomas Jefferson, *Writings,* ed. P. L. Ford, X, 227.

2. See Chapter V above.

3. *Common Sense,* Thomas Paine, *Life and Works,* ed. W. M. Van der Weyde (New Rochelle, 1925), II, 97–98.

4. *Ibid.,* p. 99.

5. *Ibid.,* pp. 100–102.

6. "Letter to the Abbé Raynal" (1782), Thomas Paine, *Writings,* ed. M. D. Conway (New York, 1894–96), II, 102–3.

7. See M. D. Conway, *The Life of Thomas Paine* (New York, 1892), I, 315–49.

8. See "Introduction" to *Rights of Man,* in Paine, *Writings,* ed. Conway, II, 292–99; and Gilbert Chinard, *Thomas Jefferson, the Apostle of Americanism* (Boston, 1929), pp. 258–63; also Jefferson to the President, Philadelphia, May 8, 1791, Thomas Jefferson, *Writings,* ed. A. A. Lipscomb (Washington, 1903), VIII, 192–95; and Letter to John Adams, July 17, 1791, *ibid.,* pp. 212–14. See also Chapter VII below on Jefferson and the French Revolution.

9. To Colonel Monroe, July 10, 1791, Jefferson, *Writings,* ed. Lipscomb, VIII, 208; to Thomas Paine, July 29, 1791, *ibid.,* p. 224; for a general and very exalted estimate of Paine's *Writings* see Jefferson's *Writings,* XV, 305.

10. See Conway, *Life of Thomas Paine,* I, 292.

11. *Rights of Man,* Paine, *Writings,* ed. Conway, II, 406.

12. *Ibid.,* p. 407.

13. *Ibid.,* p. 408.

14. *Ibid.,* pp. 408–9.

15. *Ibid.,* pp. 410–11.

16. *Ibid.,* p. 418.

17. *Ibid.,* pp. 419–24.

18. Jean J. Rousseau, *Du Contrat Social,* ed. Maurice Halbwachs (Paris, 1943), p. 153. This edition is hereafter cited, except where otherwise indicated.

19. *Ibid.,* pp. 90, 118, 120.

20. "De plus, l'aliénation se faisant sans réserve, l'union est aussi parfaite qu'elle peut l'être et nul associé n'a plus rien à réclamer" (*ibid.,* p. 91).

21. *Rights of Man,* Paine, *Writings,* ed. Conway, II, 408.

22. "Ainsi, par la nature du pacte, tout acte de souveraineté, c'est-à-dire tout acte authentique de la volonté générale, oblige ou favorise également tous les citoyens." Rousseau, *Contrat Social,* p. 155.

23. J. J. Rousseau, "A Dissertation on Political Economy," in J. J. Rousseau, *Miscellaneous Works* (London, 1767), II, 7.

24. See *ibid.*, II, 21–27 on the virtue of patriotism as the highest expression of good citizenship.

25. See Georg Jellinek, *Allgemeine Staatslehre* (Berlin, 1914), pp. 412–16, 419.

26. See "Considérations sur le gouvernement de Pologne et sur sa réformation projetée en Avril 1772," in *The Political Writings of Jean-Jacques Rousseau*, ed. C. E. Vaughan (Cambridge, Eng., 1915), II, 427ff, 486ff. See also Boyd C. Shafer, *Nationalism, Myth and Reality* (New York, 1955), chaps. vii, viii.

27. Georg Jellinek, *Die Erklärung der Menschen und Bürgerrechte* (Leipzig, 1904), pp. 15ff.

28. *Ibid.*, p. 20. Compare the analysis of the American federal and state constitutions in Chapter V above.

29. Jellinek, *Die Erklärung*, p. 16.

30. *Ibid.*, p. 23.

31. See the Constitution of 1791, Titre II, Article V, "*je jure d'être fidèle à la nation . . .*" in James M. Thompson, ed., *French Revolution; Documents, 1789–94* (Oxford, 1933), p. 114.

32. Titre III, Article I of the Constitution states: "La souveraineté est une, indivisible, inaliénable et imprescriptible; elle appartient à la nation"; *ibid.*, p. 115.

33. "Constitution de 1793," *ibid.*, pp. 239, 241, 243.

34. Thompson, *French Revolution*, "Loi Chapelier," p. 83.

35. Jacob L. Talmon, *The Rise of Totalitarian Democracy* (Boston, 1952), pp. 1–2. See also the analysis of the ambivalence of the Rousseauan tradition toward individual freedom, *ibid.*, pp. 38–49, and the chapters on the Jacobin concept of the general will, *ibid.*, pp. 90–97, 98ff.

36. Roger H. Soltau, *French Political Thought in the Nineteenth Century* (New York, 1959), Introduction, pp. xix, xx. On the influence of the French Revolution on the rise of the concept of nationality see Lord Acton's "Nationality," in John N. Figgis and Reginald V. Laurence, eds., *The History of Freedom and Other Essays* (London, 1907), pp. 277ff. See also the tracing of the Jacobin influence in Hans Kohn, *Prophets and Peoples; Studies in Nineteenth Century Nationalism* (New York, 1946), especially his chapter on Michelet.

37. To my knowledge, the first historian who has paid attention to the importance of Paine's concept of society is Elie Halévy in *La Formation du radicalisme philosophique*, II: "L'Evolution de la doctrine utilitaire" (Paris, 1901–04), pp. 66–73: "The idea of the new economic doctrine is that the two notions of *society* and *government* are separable. . . It remained for Thomas Paine to push this idea to its revolutionary conclusions." (Quoted from Elie Halévy, *The Growth of Philosophic Radicalism*, trans. Mary Morris, New York, 1928, p. 129.) See also Norman Sykes, "Thomas Paine," in F. J. C. Hearnshaw, ed., *The Social and Political Ideas of Some Represen-*

Sept. 8, 1774, whether the colonial rights should be based on the rights of men or not (John Adams, *Works*, II, 370–73).

108. "Warren-Adams Letters," Massachusetts Historical Society, *Collections* (1917), LXXII, 233. On the spirit of hesitancy and fear of independence, see Miller, *Origins of the American Revolution*, pp. 460–62, 482–84.

109. Van Tyne, *War of Independence*, chaps. xv, xvi and pp. 346–50.

110. Letter to Patrick Henry, April 20, 1776, Lee, *Letters*, I, 177.

111. Edmund C. Burnett, ed., *Letters of Members of the Continental Congress* (Washington, 1921–36), I, 118.

112. See Van Tyne, *War of Independence*, pp. 127–39, and Burnett, ed., *Letters of Members of the Continental Congress*, I, 458, 468, 470, 473.

CHAPTER V: THE AMERICAN, THE NEW MAN:
THE IMAGE OF A NEW NATION

1. On the influence of Thomas Paine: C. H. Van Tyne, *The War of Independence* (Boston, 1929), pp. 324, 330–34; J. C. Miller, *Origins of the American Revolution* (Stanford, 1959); George O. Trevelyan, *The American Revolution* (New York, 1909–12), II, 147–54. John Adams conceded, in spite of his early distrust and later hatred of Thomas Paine, that "Paine's pamphlet . . . crystallized public opinion, and was the *first factor* in bringing about the Revolution"; quoted in Mary Agnes Best, *Thomas Paine, Prophet and Martyr of Democracy* (New York, 1927), p. 74. See also, on the same, George Washington, *Writings*, ed. W. C. Ford (New York, 1889–93), III, 396. For a general survey and estimate, see Moncure D. Conway, *The Life of Thomas Paine* (New York, 1893), I, 56–63. See also Edmund C. Burnett, *The Continental Congress* (New York, 1941), pp. 131–37; Carl L. Becker, *The Eve of the Revolution* (New Haven, 1918), pp. 247–51.

2. See M. D. Conway, *Life of Paine*, I, xvi–xix; on John Fiske, *ibid.*, I, 82; V. L. Parrington, *Main Currents in American Thought* (New York, 1927), I, 327–32. On the remarkable vengeance of Morris on Paine, see Conway, *Life of Paine*, II, chaps. v, viii. On the clergy and Thomas Paine, *ibid.*, II, 181–82. An analysis of the attitude toward Thomas Paine would disclose the permanent tension between the universalistic concept of American nationality and the religious-ethnic nationalism of the conservatives in the nineteenth century, especially in its newer version of integral organic nationalism as preached by Theodore Roosevelt.

3. Thomas Paine, "Common Sense," *Life and Works*, ed. W. M. Van der Weyde (New Rochelle, 1925), II, 123–24.

4. *Ibid.*, II, 136–37; also *ibid.*, II, 125, 130–31.

5. *Ibid.*, II, 127.

6. *Ibid.*, II, 144–48.

7. "The Rights of Man, Part II," Thomas Paine, *Writings*, ed. Conway, II, 402.

8. "Common Sense," *Life and Works*, ed. Van der Weyde, II, 179–80.

9. *Ibid.*, II, 101–7.

10. *Ibid.*, II, 150.

11. "Letter to the Abbé Raynal, on the Affairs of North America," Paine, *Writings*, ed. Conway, II, 76.

12. "Letter to Abbé Raynal," *ibid.*, pp. 77, 121.

13. Ludwig Lewisohn, "Introduction," M. G. St. J. de Crèvecœur, *Letters from an American Farmer* (New York, 1908), p. xx.

14. Michel-Guillaume St. John de Crèvecœur, *Letters from an American Farmer* (New York, 1957), Letter III, pp. 42–51 and *ibid.*, Letter XII, p. 198.

15. Robert de Crèvecœur, *Saint John de Crèvecœur, sa vie et ses ouvrages (1735–1813)*, Paris, 1883, pp. 17–62; also Julia Post Mitchell, *St. Jean de Crèvecœur* (New York, 1916), pp. 21–58.

16. Friedrich M. Grimm, *Correspondence litteraire, philosophique, et critique* (Paris, 1877–82), XIV, 88.

17. Crèvecœur, *Letters* (1957), p. 7.

18. *Ibid.*, pp. 51–53.

19. *Ibid.*, p. 54.

20. *Ibid.*, pp. 47–51, 207, 219.

21. The term was used by Crèvecœur.

22. Paine, *Writings*, ed. Conway, II, 402.

23. Crèvecœur, *Letters* (1957 ed.), pp. 37–38.

24. *Ibid.*, p. 40.

25. *Ibid.*, p. 39.

26. Hans Kohn, *The Idea of Nationalism* (New York, 1951), pp. 292–301.

27. See Chapter III above, sec. 4.

28. "To Joshua Babcock," January 13, 1772, Benjamin Franklin, *Complete Works*, ed. John Bigelow (New York, 1904), V, 287–88.

29. Crèvecœur, *Letters* (1957), pp. 41, 51, 52.

30. "To Mr. Bellini, Paris, Sept. 30, 1785," Thomas Jefferson, *Writings*, ed. A. A. Lipscomb (Washington, 1903), V, 152–53; "Letter to George Wythe, Paris, Aug. 13, 1786," Thomas Jefferson, *Writings*, ed. P. L. Ford (New York, 1892–99), IV, 266–70.

31. "Letter to Mrs. Trist, Aug. 18, 1785," Jefferson, *Writings*, ed. Lipscomb, V, 81.

32. "To George Wythe, Aug. 13, 1776," Jefferson, *Writings*, ed. Ford, IV, 269.

33. *Ibid.*, IV, 268.

34. "To Edward Carrington, Jan. 16, 1787," Jefferson, *Writings*, ed. Ford, IV, 360.

35. "To James Monroe, Paris, June 17, 1785," Jefferson, *Writings*, ed. Ford, IV, 59.

36. "To J. Bannister, Junior, Paris, Oct. 15, 1785," Jefferson, *Writings*, ed. Lipscomb, V, 186–87.

37. Van Tyne, *War of Independence*, pp. 349–50.

38. Moses C. Tyler, *The Literary History of the American Revolution* (New York, 1897), I, 505, 509; Carl L. Becker, *The Declaration of Independence* (New York, 1953), pp. 24–29.

73. See Walter McIntosh Merrill, *From Statesman to Philosopher, A Study in Bolingbroke's Deism* (New York, 1949), pp. 214–15.

74. Bolingbroke, "Fragments," *Works*, IV, 160.

75. *Ibid.*, p. 147.

76. *Ibid.*, p. 164.

77. *Ibid.*, p. 165.

78. *Ibid.*, pp. 165, 181–82.

79. *Ibid.*, p. 185.

80. *Ibid.*, p. 187.

81. *Ibid.*, pp. 189–90.

82. See Ferdinand Tönnies, *Gemeinschaft und Gesellschaft, Grundbegriffe der reinen Soziologie* (Berlin, 1920), pp. 1–6; for Shaftesbury, see "Essay on Freedom, Wit and Humour," *Characteristicks*, I, 111–20.

83. "Fragments," Bolingbroke, *Works*, IV, 181ff.

84. *Ibid.*, p. 181.

85. *Ibid.*, p. 188.

86. Arthur O. Lovejoy, *The Great Chain of Being: A Study of the History of an Idea* (Cambridge, Mass., 1950), pp. 188–89, 191–93, 359, n. 9; Walter Sichel, *Bolingbroke and His Times* (London, 1901–02), II, chap. vi.

87. See Moritz Brosch, *Lord Bolingbroke und die Whigs und Tories Seiner Zeit* (Frankfurt a.M., 1883), on his influence on historiography, *ibid.*, pp. 296–300, and on Voltaire, *ibid.*, pp. 296–97. See also Sichel, *Bolingbroke*, II, 448–50.

88. Arthur Hassall, *Life of Viscount Bolingbroke* (Oxford, 1915), pp. 200–4.

89. See Bryson, *Man and Society;* Werner Sombart, "Anfange der Soziologie," in Melchior Palyi, ed. *Hauptprobleme der Soziologie. Erinnerungs-gabe für Max Weber* (Munich, 1923); Jellinek, *Allgemeine Staatslehre;* Meinecke, *Die Entstehung des Historismus;* Ernst Cassirer, *The Philosophy of Enlightenment* (Boston, 1955), chap. vi; W. C. Lehman, *Adam Ferguson and the Beginnings of Modern Sociology* (New York, 1930); Huth, *Soziale Auffassungen;* Hasbach, *Grundlagen.*

90. Immanuel Kant, *Beantwortung der Frage: Was ist Aufklärung?* (Wiesbaden, 1914). See also Paul Hazard, *La Pensée européenne au XVIIIème siècle de Montesquieu à Lessing* (Paris, 1946), vol. I, chap. iii.

91. Bryson, *Man and Society*, p. 33.

92. Bolingbroke, *Letters on the Study and Use of History*, in *Works*, II, 193.

93. *Ibid.*, II, 191.

94. David Hume, *Essays and Treatises on General Subjects* (London, 1777), I, 88–89; see also Becker, *Heavenly City*, pp. 88–118. Becker's evaluation of the eighteenth-century attitude toward history does not do justice to its achievements nor does it grasp its real motives for historical inquiry, namely, to discover the laws of society and to formulate a philosophical anthropology. See Bryson, "Man's Past," in *Man and Society*, pp. 109–13.

This is confirmed by Meinecke, *Die Entstehung des Historismus,* vol. I, and by Herbert Butterfield, *Man on His Past; the Study of the History of Historical Scholarship* (Cambridge, Mass., 1955).

95. Bryson, *Man and Society,* pp. 63–66.

96. Jefferson, "Notes on Virginia," *Writings,* ed. P. L. Ford, III, query XIV, pp. 245–52.

97. Henry Home, Lord Kames, "Discourse Concerning the Origin of Man and of Language," in *Sketches of the History of Man* (Edinburgh, 1778), I, 23, 30–50. On his influence on Jefferson, see Chinard, *Thomas Jefferson,* pp. 29–30.

98. Jefferson, "Notes on Virginia," *Writings,* ed. Ford, III, 248. See also Daniel F. Boorstin, *The Lost World of Thomas Jefferson* (New York, 1948), and Oscar Handlin, *Race and Nationality in American Life* (New York, 1954), pp. 24–28, 57–63.

99. See Hazard, *La Pensée européenne,* I, chap. iii, III, chap. ii, on Leibnitz's influence; also Hasbach, *Grundlagen,* pp. 46–47, on Wolff.

100. Thomas Paine was probably the first to give currency to the term "religion of humanity"; he did so in connection with his society of theophilanthropy, founded in 1797. See Conway, *Life of Paine,* II, 251–56.

101. "A Vindication of Natural Society; or a View of the Miseries and Evils Arising to Mankind from Every Species of Artificial Society," Edmund Burke, *Writings and Speeches* (Boston, 1901), I, 3–66. Almost all writers have accepted Burke's statement that this work was intended as a parody of the deistic attacks on the evils of the state churches by way of comparing deism with the consequences of a radical philosophy of natural rights which would attempt to base social institutions on its own premises. See Thomas W. Copeland, *Our Eminent Friend Edmund Burke; Six Essays* (New Haven, 1949), p. 133; John Morley, *Burke* (London, 1892), p. 70; Richmond Lennox, *Edmund Burke und sein politisches Arbeitsfeld in den Jahren 1760 bis 1790* (Munich, 1923), pp. 18–19. On the influence of Rousseau's *Discours,* the opinions are divided.

102. Burke, *Vindication,* in *Writings and Speeches,* I, 11.

103. *Ibid.,* pp. 25–33, 46.

104. *Ibid.,* pp. 57–58.

105. *Ibid.,* p. 5.

106. See the repeated references by William Godwin to the *Vindication* in *Political Justice* (Toronto, 1946), I, 13, n.13 and the interesting reprint of the *Vindication* in *The Inherent Evils of all State Governments Demonstrated, Being a Reprint of Edmund Burke's Celebrated Essay Entitled "A Vindication of Natural Society"* (London, 1858).

107. Adam Ferguson, *An Essay on the History of Civil Society* (Edinburgh, 1767), p. 7.

108. *Ibid.,* p. 9.

109. *Ibid.,* p. 12.

110. *Ibid.,* pp. 16–18.

111. *Ibid.,* pp. 23–29.

112. *Ibid.*, pp. 29–36.

113. *Ibid.*, pp. 123–27.

114. *Ibid.*, pp. 130–31.

115. *Ibid.*, p. 131.

116. Lois Whitney, *Primitivism and the Idea of Progress in English Popular Literature of the Eighteenth Century* (Baltimore, 1934). See Samuel Kliger, *The Goths in England* (Cambridge, Mass., 1952), pp. 72–94, 113–144.

117. See Jefferson, "Notes on Virginia," *Writings,* ed. P. L. Ford, III, 151ff and 167n.

118. Ferguson, *An Essay,* p. 133.

119. *Ibid.*, p. 134.

120. *Ibid.*, p. 143.

121. *Ibid.*, p. 155.

122. *Ibid.*, pp. 198–202.

123. *Ibid.*, p. 219.

124. *Ibid.*, pp. 221–44.

125. *Ibid.*, pp. 86–87.

126. *Ibid.*, p. 87.

127. *Ibid.*, p. 95. Compare this with Emerson's "New England Reformers": The world is awaking to the idea of union. . . Men will live And communicate . . . as by added ethereal power, when once they are united . . . leave him alone, to recognize in every hour and place the secret soul; he will go up and down doing the works of a true member, and, to the astonishment of all, the work will be done with concert, though no man spoke. Government will be adamantine without any governor. R. W. Emerson, *Complete Writings* (New York, 1929), pp. 317–18.

128. William Blackstone, *Commentaries on the Laws of England* (London, 1787), I, 40–41. Howard Mumford Jones, in his delightful *The Pursuit of Happiness* (Cambridge, Mass., 1953), pp. 92–97, has interpreted Blackstone in terms of the Lockian concept of the law of nature. Yet the eighteenth-century interpretation of the law of nature and of human happiness is absolutely different from the Lockian outlook. For the same reason the usual interpretation of the Jeffersonian concept of happiness lacks all the essential elements of liberal humanism which mark late eighteenth-century thought.

129. Bentham admitted to having adopted the formula of Priestley for his own system of utilitarianism. For the real origin of the greatest-happiness principle see *Cambridge History of English Literature,* A. W. Ward and A. R. Waller, eds., X, 342ff, and IX, 302,n.1.

130. Joseph Priestley, *An Essay on the First Principles of Government, and on the Nature of Political, Civil, and Religious Liberty* (London, 1771), p. 13.

131. Marie Jean Antoine Nicholas de Caritat Marquis de Condorcet, *Outlines of an Historical View of the Progress of the Human Mind* (Philadelphia, 1796), pp. 188, 189.

132. *Ibid.*, p. 260.

133. Adam Smith, *The Theory of Moral Sentiments* (London, 1792), I, 213–15.

134. P. F. Le Mercier de la Rivière, *L'Ordre naturel et essentiel des sociétés politiques* (London, 1767), pp. 12–13, 14–16. See Edmund Richner, *Le Mercier de la Rivière: Ein Führer der physiokratischen Bewegung in Frankreich* (Zürich, 1931), pp. 146ff.

135. Mercier de la Rivière, *L'Ordre naturel*, pp. 36 and ·33·

136. *Ibid.*, p. 36.

137. Quoted from Eugène Dairé, *Physiocrates* (Paris, 1846), I, 337·

138. Smith, *Theory of Moral Sentiment*, I, 292–93·

139. *Ibid.*, pp. 295ff.

140. Adam Smith, *An Inquiry into the Nature and Causes of the Wealth of Nations* (London, 1929–30), II, 180–81.

141. *Ibid.*, 180–81.

142. Smith, *Theory of Moral Sentiment*, I, 205·

143. Smith, *Wealth of Nations*, I, 48–56, 117–30.

144. *Ibid.*, I, 341–70.

145. *Ibid.*, II, 40.

146. *Ibid.*, pp. 137–56. See also "Of Bounties," *ibid.*, pp. 6–42·

147. *Ibid.*, pp. 137–56.

148. *Ibid.*, pp. 436–40 and 299–306.

149. *Ibid.*, I, 341–52.

150. See Huth, *Soziale Auffassungen*, p. 133; and *Wealth of Nations*, I, 341–51·

151. *Ibid.*, I, 341–51 and II, 63–87, "Causes of the Prosperity of colonies."

152. *Wealth of Nations*, II, 297–98.

CHAPTER VII: FREE SOCIETY—THE FORMULATION OF THE JEFFERSONIAN SOCIAL IDEAL

1. See Chapter V, sec. 2, above. This was the opinion of the leaders of the French Enlightenment, who survived the Revolution, such as Du Pont de Nemours, Destutt de Tracy, La Fayette, and the Ideologists in general. See Bernard Faÿ, *The Revolutionary Spirit in France and America* (New York, 1927), pp. 317–20, 384–91; Durand Echeverria, *Mirage in the West, A History of the French Image of American Society to 1815* (Princeton, 1957), pp. 267–79; Gilbert Chinard, *Jefferson et les idéologues* (Baltimore, 1925), and *The Correspondence of Jefferson and Du Pont de Nemours* (Baltimore, 1931).

2. Elie Halévy says: "Entre la philosophie politique qui se trouve exposée dans la seconde partie des 'Droits de l'Homme' et celle que va développer William Godwin, un an plus tard, dans sa 'Justice politique,' la distance est courte." *La Formation du radicalisme philosphique* (Paris, 1901–04), II, 71–72 *passim*. See also F. E. L. Priestley, in Introduction to *Enquiry Concerning Political Justice and Its Influence on Morals and Happiness* (Toronto, 1946), III, 29, nn. 12 and 48.

3. On the influence of Thomas Paine see Walter P. Hall, *British Radi-*

calism, 1791–1797 (New York, 1912), pp. 85, 95. Also Simon Maccoby, *English Radicalism* (London, 1935–1955), vol. II. On his influence on the Democratic societies in the United States see Eugene P. Link, *Democratic-Republican Societies 1790–1800* (New York, 1942), pp. 34–43, 104.

4. Marie Jean Antoine Nicholas Caritat Condorcet, *Outlines of an Historical View of the Progress of the Human Mind* (Philadelphia, 1796), pp. 205–6.

5. "Agrarian Justice," Thomas Paine, *Writings*, ed. M. D. Conway (New York, 1894–96), III, 340.

6. *Ibid.,* pp. 328–31.

7. *Ibid.,* p. 337; see also *Rights of Man*, in Paine, *Writings*, ed. Conway, II, chap. v, and *Public Good, ibid.,* pp. 34–35 in which he urged a nationalization of western lands.

8. "Agrarian Justice," *ibid.,* III, 341.

9. See Conway's introduction to "Agrarian Justice," *ibid.,* III, 323–25.

10. See Chapter V, "The Promise of American Life." On the great fame and influence of Crèvecœur in France, see Faÿ, *The Revolutionary Spirit,* p. 222.

11. M. G. St. John de Crèvecœur, *Letters from an American Farmer* (New York, 1957), p. 36.

12. *Ibid.,* pp. 36–37.

13. *Ibid.,* pp. 85–86.

14. *Ibid.,* p. 87.

15. *Ibid.,* p. 124.

16. *Ibid.,* pp. 135–36.

17. Jefferson used and probably coined the word "Americanism." See letter to Governor William Plumer, Jan. 31, 1815, Thomas Jefferson, *Writings,* ed. Andrew A. Lipscomb (Washington, 1903), XIV, 238.

18. For a different view see Gilbert Chinard, *Thomas Jefferson, Apostle of Americanism* (Boston, 1939), p. 397.

19. See letter to the Marquis de La Fayette, Feb. 28, 1787, Jefferson, *Writings,* ed. Lipscomb, VI, 101–2; to Comtesse De Tesse, March 20, 1787, *ibid.,* VI, 105; to La Fayette, May 6, 1789, *ibid.,* VII, 333–35; to Monsieur de Crève-Cœur, May 20, 1789, *ibid.,* VII, 367–69; to La Fayette, June 3, 1789, *ibid.,* VII, 370; and especially to Monsieur de St. Etienne, June 3, 1789, *ibid.,* VII, 370–74. See also *Autobiography, ibid.,* I, 127–57; the letters to Thomas Paine, July 11, 1789, *ibid.,* VII, 404–8, and letter to L'Abbé Arnoud, July 19, 1789, *ibid.,* VII, 422–24. See also letter to Count de Moustier, May 17, 1788, *ibid.,* VII, 12–15. Jefferson himself reviews the part taken in his letter to La Fayette, Feb. 14, 1815, *ibid.,* XIV, 245–52. Chinard tries to minimize the participation of Jefferson in the guidance of the Revolution. Yet the letter to James Madison of Aug. 28, 1789, throws a different light on the role of Jefferson (see *ibid.,* VII, 448–50). So does the fact that La Fayette submitted his *Declaration européenne des droits de l'homme et du citoyen* to Jefferson's criticism. See Chinard, *Thomas Jefferson, Apostle of Americanism,* pp. 232–34.

20. See letter to Lafayette, Feb. 14, 1815, Jefferson, *Writings*, ed. Lipscomb, XIV, 245–55.

21. See letter to William Short, Jan. 3, 1793, *ibid.*, IX, 9–12. See also letter to James Madison about the reception and mission of Genêt, May 19, 1793, *ibid.*, IX, 96–98.

22. See Jefferson's attitude to *Rights of Man* by Thomas Paine in Chapter VI, sec. 1, above. As remarked there, American republicanism crystallized only with the debate on the French Revolution. John Adams' *Discourses on Davila*, and John Quincy Adams' *Publicola*, opened the conservative counterattack which was answered by "Brutus" and *The National Gazette*, the mouthpiece of republicanism. See also letter to George Gilmer, Dec. 15, 1792, in Jefferson, *Writings*, ed. Lipscomb, VIII, 444, 445. For the whole question of the influence of the French Revolution on American republicanism see Link, *Democratic-Republican Societies*. Though it is hard to agree with Link's interpretation of American democracy, the book proves the profound upsurging of ideological forces in American society. See also Charles D. Hazen, *Contemporary American Opinion of the French Revolution* (Baltimore, 1897); Fäy, *The Revolutionary Spirit*, and Howard M. Jones, *America and French Culture* (Chapel Hill, 1927).

23. To Colonel Mason, Feb. 4, 1791, Jefferson, *Writings*, ed. Lipscomb, VIII, 123–24; see also the letter to Edward Rutledge, Aug. 25, 1791, *ibid.*, VIII, 234.

24. To E. Rutledge, *ibid.*

25. To William Short, Jan. 3, 1793, *ibid.*, IX, 9. See also letter to Governor William Plumer, Jan. 31, 1815, *ibid.*, XIV, 235–38; "The Anas," *ibid.*, I, esp. 380–83, 385–87, 389–93.

26. See letter to Samuel Adams, Feb. 26, 1800, *ibid.*, X, 153, and to Henry Innis, Esq., Jan. 23, 1800, *ibid.*, p. 143.

27. Letter to Madame La Baronne De Staël-Holstein, May 24, 1813, *ibid.*, XIII, 245; to John Adams, June 15, 1813, *ibid.*, XIII, 254. The view expressed here that the French Revolution created in America for the first time a full-fledged ideological movement of democracy, international in its outlook, and that the collapse of the former was instrumental in shaping an American-centered democratic and nationalistic orientation is confirmed by Link, *Democratic-Republican Societies*, pp. 44–56, 108–10, 125, 133. The writer exaggerates the ideological influence of France and is apparently unaware of the basic differences between the Jacobin and the American democracy.

28. To John Adams, Oct. 28, 1813, Jefferson, *Writings*, ed. Lipscomb, XIII, 402. See also letter to John Adams, Sept. 4, 1823, *ibid.*, XV, 464–67.

29. See letter to Baron Alexander von Humboldt, Dec. 6, 1813, *ibid.*, XIV, 21–22; to John Adams, Sept. 4, 1823, *ibid.*, XV, 464. See also his letter to La Fayette, Feb. 14, 1815, on the causes of the failure of the French Revolution, *ibid.*, XIV, 245, and to Du Pont de Nemours, Feb. 28, 1815, on the same, *ibid.*, XIV, 256.

30. To Roger C. Weightman, June 24, 1826, *ibid.*, XVI, 182. See also Inaugural Address, March 4, 1801, *ibid.*, III, 319.

31. See Jefferson to Monsieur Du Pont de Nemours, Dec. 31, 1815, *ibid.*, XIV, 369.

32. See Chinard, *Jefferson, Apostle of Americanism*, pp. 400–14 and *Correspondence between Thomas Jefferson and Pierre Samuel Du Pont de Nemours, 1798–1817*, ed. Dumas Malone (Boston, New York, 1930), pp. 46–79.

33. See Chapter III, sec. 4, above.

34. To Governor James Monroe, Nov. 24, 1801, Jefferson, *Writings*, ed. Lipscomb, X, 296.

35. Third Annual Message, Oct. 17, 1803, *ibid.*, III, 353.

36. Letter to Du Pont de Nemours, Dec. 31, 1815, *ibid.*, XIV, 371–72.

37. To Dr. John Crawford, Jan. 2, 1812, *ibid.*, XIII, 119.

38. To William Short, Aug. 4, 1820, *ibid.*, XV, 263.

39. To James Monroe, Oct. 24, 1823, *ibid.*, XV, 477, and letter to the same, June 11, 1823, *ibid.*, XV, 435; also to John Adams, Aug. 1, 1816, *ibid.*, XV, 58–59; and letter to the Baron Alexander von Humboldt, Dec. 6, 1813, *ibid.*, XIV, 22; to J. Correa De Serra, Oct. 24, 1820, *ibid.*, XV, 285.

40. See Jefferson's attitude toward the conquest of Canada, the Floridas, and Cuba in letter to Colonel William Duane, Oct. 1, 1812, *ibid.*, XIII, 187, and to Du Pont de Nemours, Nov. 29, 1813, in *Correspondence between Jefferson and Du Pont de Nemours*, ed. Dumas Malone, pp. 147–49; also to James Monroe, Oct. 24, 1823, Jefferson, *Writings*, ed. Lipscomb, XV, 479.

41. See letter to Monsieur Barré de Marbois, June 14, 1817, *ibid.*, XV, 131. See also, *Correspondence between Jefferson and Du Pont de Nemours*, ed. Malone, p. 145; and Chinard, *Correspondence of Jefferson and Du Pont de Nemours*, pp. 179–91, 193–95. Destutt de Tracy dealt with this subject in *A Commentary and Review of Montesquieu's Spirit of Laws* (Philadelphia, 1811), Bk. VIII, pp. 75–81. As Jefferson considered the *Commentary* the best book yet written on the true and real basis of representative democracy, Destutt de Tracy's opinions can be taken as those of Jefferson. See letter to Nathaniel Niles, Esq., March 22, 1801, Jefferson, *Writings*, ed. Lipscomb, X, 232–33, and to Monsieur Destutt de Tracy, Jan. 26, 1811, *ibid.*, XIII, 15–20.

42. Destutt de Tracy, in his *Commentary and Review of Montesquieu's Spirit of Laws*, had equated liberty with happiness. "Liberty, in the most general acceptation of the word, is nothing else than the power of executing the will, and accomplishing our desires; now the nature of every being endowed with will, is such that this faculty of willing causes his happiness or unhappiness; he is happy when his desires are accomplished, and unhappy when they are not; and happiness or misery are proportioned in him according to the degree of his gratification or disappointment. It follows that his liberty and happiness are the same thing. . . The second consequence of the observation which we have made above is, that the government under which the greatest liberty is enjoyed . . . is that which governs the best, for in it the greatest number of people are happiest. . . The only circumstance, therefore, which renders any one social organization preferable to another, is its being

better adapted to render the members of society happy; and if in general it be desired, that the social constitution should leave to the people a great facility to make known their wishes, it is then more probable that under a government which secures this power, they are governed as they desire." *Ibid.*, pp. 97–101.

43. This is not to claim that these theories were determining the formation of the American democratic ideology. Late eighteenth-century thought was as much indebted to the American Revolution as it was instrumental in supplying the theoretical framework for American democracy. Yet undoubtedly it would be hard to eliminate the ideas and opinions of the Enlightenment from the crystallization of American democratic thought.

44. To John Melish, Jan. 13, 1813, Jefferson, *Writings*, ed. Lipscomb, XIII, 212.

45. *The Commonplace Book of Thomas Jefferson*, ed. Gilbert Chinard (Baltimore, 1926), pp. 107–8. Gilbert Chinard strangely connects this quotation with the influence of Locke, ignoring the whole trend of the Scottish moral philosophy. See *ibid.*, p. 19, and compare it with Gladys Bryson, *Man and Society: The Scottish Inquiry of the Eighteenth Century* (Princeton, 1945).

46. Peter Carr, Aug. 10, 1787, Jefferson, *Writings*, ed. Lipscomb, VI, 257–58. See also the letter to John Adams, Oct. 14, 1816, *ibid.*, XV, 76–77; to Thomas Law, Esq., June 13, 1814, *ibid.*, XIV, 138–44; to Francis W. Gilmer, June 7, 1816, *ibid.*, XV, 25; to Monsieur Du Pont de Nemours, April 24, 1816, *ibid.*, XIV, 487, 490–91.

47. To Thomas Law, *ibid.*, XIV, 140–42.

48. To Francis Gilmer, June 7, 1816, *ibid.*, XV, 25.

49. See Chapter VI, sec. 4, above, and Chapter VI, nn. 113–20.

50. To Francis Gilmer, June 7, 1816, Jefferson, *Writings*, ed. Lipscomb, XV, 25–26.

51. *Ibid.*

52. See letter to John Adams, Oct. 28, 1813, *ibid.*, XIII, 400; to Joseph C. Cabell, Feb. 2, 1816, *ibid.*, XIV, 421–22; to John Taylor, May 28, 1816, *ibid.*, XV, 17–20; to Samuel Kercheval, Sept. 5, 1816, *ibid.*, pp. 70–71; to Major John Cartwright, June 5, 1824, *ibid.*, XVI, 46.

53. Jefferson, "Notes on Virginia," Jefferson, *Writings*, ed. Paul L. Ford (New York, 1892–99), III, 155.

54. *Ibid.*, p. 167n.

55. *Ibid.*, p. 195,n.1.

56. *Ibid.*, p. 199n.

57. *Ibid.*, p. 195,n.1.

58. On the relation between conservative thought and historical orientation see Karl Mannheim, "Das konservative Denken. Soziologische Beiträge zum Werden des politisch-historischen Denkens in Deutschland," *Archiv für Sozialwissenschaft und Sozialpolitik*, 57 (1927), 68–142, 470–95.

59. *Discourses on Davila*, in *Works of John Adams*, ed. Charles F. Adams (Boston, 1851), VI, 232.

60. *Ibid.*

61. *Ibid.*, p. 234.

62. *Ibid.*

63. *Ibid.*, pp. 249–57.

64. *Ibid.*, p. 253.

65. *Ibid.*, p. 276.

66. From "Letters to John Taylor of Carolina, Virginia in Reply to his strictures on some Parts of the Defence of the American Constitutions," John Adams, *Works*, VI, Letter XVIII, p. 484.

67. *Discourses on Davila, ibid.*, VI, 279–80, 285–86.

68. "Letters to John Taylor," *ibid.*, Letter XXXI, p. 517. See also John Adams' letters to Jefferson on the "Ideologists," the ignorance of Turgot, Price, Condorcet, Rousseau, Paine, and Franklin, and the vicious effects of their visionary views, in Jefferson, *Writings*, ed. Lipscomb, XIII, 306–10, 313–16; and *ibid.*, XIV, 156–61.

69. *Discourses on Davila*, John Adams, *Works*, VI, 280.

70. See letters of John Adams to Jefferson, June 28, 1813, *ibid.*, XIII, 293–94; July 15, 1813, *ibid.*, p. 314; on Bolingbroke, Dec. 25, 1813, *ibid.*, XIV, 34; and letter of Nov. 13, 1815, *ibid.*, XIV, 359–60.

71. *Discourses on Davila*, in John Adams, *Works*, VI, 280; see John Adams' correspondence with John Taylor, Letters XVIII to XXVII in *ibid.*, VI, 484–510 and his correspondence with Samuel Adams, *ibid.*, 415–19.

72. See "Letters of Publicola," John Quincy Adams, *Writings*, ed. W. Chauncey Ford (New York, 1913), I, 66–147.

73. For other representatives of conservatism see Fisher Ames, "The Dangers of American Liberty," *Works* (Boston, 1809). For Jefferson's evaluation of the nature of federalism see "The Anas," Jefferson, *Writings*, ed. Lipscomb, I, 266–81; Daniel Webster, "The Basis of the Senate," *Writings and Speeches* (Boston, 1903), III; James Kent's speech at the New York Constitutional Convention, 1821, *Reports of the Proceedings and Debates of the Convention of 1821* (Albany, 1821), 219–21; John T. Horton, *James Kent, A Study in Conservatism, 1763–1847* (New York, 1939), chaps. vi–vii. For various facets of early conservatism see Vernon L. Parrington, *Main Currents in American Thought* (New York [1927]), bk. II, chap. ii, and bk. III, chap. iii. A faithful description of the New England mind can be gained from the Notes and Journals of Tocqueville as quoted by G. W. Pierson, *Tocqueville and Beaumont in America* (New York, 1938), pp. 370–420.

74. To Samuel Adams, October 18, 1790, John Adams, *Works*, VI, 415.

75. "Defence of the Constitutions of Government of the United States of America," *ibid.*, IV, 489–90. See also John Adams to Thomas Jefferson, Nov. 15, 1813, Jefferson, *Writings*, ed. Lipscomb, XIV, 8.

76. See Howard M. Jones, *The Pursuit of Happiness* (Cambridge, Mass., 1953). Professor Jones has not analyzed the contemporary European literature of moral philosophy, which surely would be highly significant for Jefferson's notions of happiness, especially the work of Hutcheson, Ferguson, Price, and Priestley. On the sources of the Jeffersonian concept see also

Charles H. Wiltse, *The Jeffersonian Tradition in American Democracy* (Chapel Hill, 1935), chap. iv, "The Pursuit of Happiness." Yet Charles Wiltse identifies the moral sense with the urge or the right of happiness. See *ibid.*, pp. 67–68.

77. See Wiltse, *Jeffersonian Tradition*, pp. 136–39. See Jefferson's criticism of La Fayette's proposed *Declaration européenne des droits*, in Chinard, *Thomas Jefferson, the Apostle of Americanism*, pp. 232–34.

78. Destutt de Tracy, *A Commentary and Review of Montesquieu's Spirit of Laws*, pp. 192–93.

79. *Ibid.*, pp. 185–86.

80. The clearest exposition of Jefferson's views on this subject is to be found in his letter to Monsieur Du Pont de Nemours, April 24, 1816, *ibid.*, XIV, 487–93, which was written in answer to Du Pont de Nemours' proposals for a constitution of a Spanish-American federal republic. In this plan citizenship rights are based exclusively on landed property, and representative democracy is rejected for a highly selective and indirectly chosen government. See Du Pont de Nemours to Jefferson, Dec. 12, 1811, and Jefferson to Du Pont de Nemours, April 24, 1816, in *Correspondence between Jefferson and Du Pont de Nemours*, ed. Dumas Malone, pp. 137–44.

81. To Monsieur A. Corray, Oct. 31, 1823, Jefferson, *Writings*, ed. Lipscomb, XV, 482. See also Jefferson to F. A. Van der Kemp, March 22, 1812, *ibid.*, XIII, 135.

82. "Inaugural Address," March 4, 1801, Jefferson, *Writings*, ed. Lipscomb, III, 320–21.

83. John Adams to Thomas Jefferson, June 30, 1813, *ibid.*, XIII, 297. See also to the same, July 13, 1813, *ibid.*, p. 309.

84. To James Madison, Jan. 30, 1787, *ibid.*, VI, 65.

85. "Inaugural Address," March 4, 1801, *ibid.*, III, 319.

86. To James Madison, Jan. 30, 1787, *ibid.*, VI, 64, 65. See also letter to James Monroe concerning the right size for the western states, July 9, 1786, Jefferson, *Writings*, ed. Ford, IV, 245–51, and on the same point to Madison, Dec. 16, 1786, *ibid.*, 331–37.

87. To Joseph C. Cabell, Feb. 2, 1816, Jefferson, *Writings*, ed. Lipscomb, XIV, 421.

88. *Ibid.*, pp. 421–22.

89. *Ibid.*, p. 421.

90. "Inaugural Address," March 4, 1801, *ibid.*, III, 319–20.

91. To Joseph C. Cabell, *ibid.*, XIV, 422.

92. To Abbé Arnould, July 19, 1789, *ibid.*, VII, 422. See letter to John Adams, Oct. 28, 1813, *ibid.*, XIII, 400; to John Taylor, May 28, 1816, *ibid.*, XV, 19; to Isaac H. Tiffany, Aug. 26, 1816, *ibid.*, p. 66; to Samuel Kercheval, Sept. 5, 1816, *ibid.*, 70–71.

93. See letter to Edward Carrington, Aug. 4, 1787, *ibid.*, VI, 227; to John Adams, Feb. 23, 1787, *ibid.*, p. 97; to James Madison, June 20, 1787, *ibid.*, p. 132; to William Carmichael, Dec. 11, 1787, *ibid.*, 380; to James Madison, Dec. 20, 1787, *ibid.*, p. 393; to John Taylor, May 28, 1816, *ibid.*, XV, 20–22;

to Samuel Kercheval, July 12, 1816, *ibid.*, pp. 32–39; to Judge Spencer Roane, Sept. 6, 1819, *ibid.*, p. 214; to Thomas Ritchie, Dec. 25, 1820, *ibid.*, p. 298; to Judge Spencer Roane, June 27, 1821, *ibid.*, pp. 327–32; to William T. Barry, July 2, 1822, *ibid.*, p. 389; to Edward Livingston, April 4, 1824, *ibid.*, XVI, 23–25.

94. To Archibald Stuart, Dec. 23, 1791, *ibid.*, VIII, 276.

95. Letter of April 24, 1816 in *Correspondence between Jefferson and Du Pont de Nemours*, ed. Dumas Malone, p. 184.

96. *Ibid.*, pp. 181–82.

97. See Jefferson's radical and stringent criticism of the Constitution of Virginia in "Notes on Virginia," Query XIII, Jefferson, *Writings*, ed. Ford, III, 222–34; to Archibald Stuart, Dec. 23, 1791, Jefferson, *Writings*, ed. Lipscomb, VIII, 277–78; to John Hambden Pleasants, *ibid.*, XVI, 27–29; to Major John Cartwright, *ibid.*, pp. 44–46; see also to John Taylor, *ibid.*, XV, 20–23.

98. "The Kentucky Resolution of 1798," Jefferson, *Writings*, ed. Ford, VIII, 474.

99. "Notes on Virginia," *ibid.*, III, 224–25.

100. See Adams' letter to Jefferson, July 13, 1813, in Jefferson, *Writings*, ed. Lipscomb, XIII, 309.

101. John Adams, *Works*, VI, 227.

102. John Adams to Jefferson, July 13, 1813, in Jefferson, *Writings*, ed. Lipscomb, XIII, 309.

103. Condorcet, *Outlines of an Historical View of the Progress of the Human Mind*, pp. 209–10.

104. *Ibid.*, pp. 209–10.

105. *Ibid.*, pp. 212–13.

106. To Major John Cartwright, Jefferson, *Writings*, ed. Lipscomb, XVI, 44.

107. On Anglo-Saxon freedom see *ibid.*, and Chinard, *Thomas Jefferson, Apostle of Americanism*, pp. 31, 32, 86–87. See also "Notes on Virginia," in Jefferson, *Writings*, ed. Ford, III, 189.

108. To La Fayette, Feb. 14, 1815, Jefferson, *Writings*, ed. Lipscomb, XIV, 246; see also Jefferson to Du Pont de Nemours, *ibid.*, p. 256, and to Madame de Staël-Holstein, *ibid.*, XIII, 245.

109. Jefferson to Destutt de Tracy, Jan. 26, 1811, in Gilbert Chinard, *Jefferson et les Idéologues*, pp. 77–78.

110. To John Adams, Oct. 28, 1813, Jefferson, *Writings*, ed. Lipscomb, XIII, 401–2.

111. See Chapter III, secs. 3 and 4, above; also Chapter V, sec. 1, above.

112. "Notes on Virginia," Jefferson, *Writings*, ed. Ford, III, 269.

113. *Ibid.*, III, 269.

114. See nn. 76–86 above.

115. See above, Chapter V, nn. 30–34.

116. To John Watson, May 17, 1814, Jefferson, *Writings*, ed. Lipscomb, XIV, 136.

117. To Dr. Thomas Cooper, Sept. 10, 1814, *ibid.*, XIV, 182.

118. To Governor William Plumer, Jan. 31, 1815, *ibid.*, p. 237.

119. To Judge William Johnson, June 12, 1823, *ibid.*, XV, 440.

120. *Ibid.*, pp. 441–42.

121. See letter to James Madison, Sept. 6, 1789, *ibid.*, VII, 454–61; also *ibid.*, pp. 462–63; to Isaac McPherson, Aug. 13, 1813, *ibid.*, XIII, 333–35; to John W. Eppes, June 24, 1813, *ibid.*, pp. 270–72; to Samuel Kercheval, July 12, 1816, *ibid.*, XV, 41–44; to Governor Plumer, July 21, 1816, *ibid.*, pp. 46–47; to Thomas Earle, Sept. 24, 1823, *ibid.*, pp. 47–71.

122. To James Madison, Sept. 6, 1789, *ibid.*, VII, 459.

123. To S. Kercheval, July 12, 1816, *ibid*, XV, 41.

124. To Francis Gilmer, June 7, 1816, *ibid.*, p. 24.

125. To Du Pont de Nemours, April 24, 1816, *ibid.*, XIV, 490; and to Mr. Joseph Milligan, April 6, 1816, *ibid.*, 466.

126. To Thomas Earle, Sept. 24, 1823, *ibid.*, XV, 470–71.

127. To James Madison, Sept. 6, 1789, *ibid.*, VII, 460.

128. "Agrarian Justice," Paine, *Writings*, ed. Conway, III, 342.

129. Paine, *Writings*, ed. Conway, III, 337.

130. See Chinard, *Thomas Jefferson, the Apostle of Americanism*, pp. 29–32, on Jefferson's studies of the history of property. See also Chinard, *The Commonplace Book of Thomas Jefferson*.

131. See Jefferson, *Writings*, ed. Lipscomb, I, Appendix [Note C], 207.

132. To Rev. James Madison, Oct. 28, 1795, Jefferson, *Writings*, ed. Lipscomb, XIX, 17–18.

133. To Isaac McPherson, Aug. 13, 1813, Jefferson, *Writings*, ed. Lipscomb, XIII, 333.

134. To Rev. James Madison, Oct. 28, 1785, Jefferson, *Writings*, ed. Lipscomb, XIX, 17–18.

135. See, for the same view, Henry George, *Progress and Poverty* (New York, 1880), pp. 506–20, which was avowedly based on Jefferson, the physiocrats, and the Ideologists.

136. Antoine Louis Claude Destutt de Tracy, *A Treatise on Political Economy; to which is prefixed a supplement to a preceding work on the Understanding or Elements of ideology; with an analytical table, and an introduction on the faculty of the will*, translated from the unpublished French original (Georgetown, D. C., 1817), pp. 156–58. The treatise was sent to Jefferson, who superintended its translation. For the identity of the views between Jefferson and Destutt de Tracy see Gilbert Chinard, *Jefferson et les Idéologues*, pp. 45–55.

137. *Ibid.*, pp. 158–59; also Adam Smith, *Wealth of Nations*, ed. Edwin Cannon (London, 1961), I, 409ff.

138. To Judge William Johnson, June 12, 1823, Jefferson, *Writings*, ed. Lipscomb, XV, 442.

139. To John Adams, Oct. 28, 1813, *ibid.*, XIII, 402.

140. See Chinard, Introduction to *Correspondence of Jefferson and Du Pont de Nemours*, pp. ix–xiv, xlv–lxxvi. See also letter to Colonel William

Duane, Jan. 22, 1813, Jefferson, *Writings,* ed. Lipscomb, XIII, 214, and to the same, April 4, 1813, *ibid.,* XIII, 231, where he identifies himself fully with Destutt de Tracy's criticism of the physiocrats.

141. See Du Pont de Nemours to Jefferson, Dec. 12, 1811, *Correspondence between Jefferson and de Nemours,* ed. Dumas Malone, pp. 139–44, and Jefferson's letter to the same, April 24, 1816, *ibid.,* pp. 181–87 and, particularly, to Mr. Joseph Milligan, April 6, 1816, Jefferson, *Writings,* ed. Lipscomb, XIV, 460–61.

142. Charles Gide observes "that the Physiocrats were certainly the first to grasp the conception of a unified science of society." Charles Gide and Charles Rist, *A History of Economic Doctrines from the Time of the Physiocrats to the Present Day* (Boston, New York [1915]), p. 2. This may be doubted, yet certainly they were the first to demonstrate the laws of natural society in those of economic society. See Gide and Rist, *ibid.,* chap. i, sec. 1, "The Natural Order," pp. 5–12.

143. "Notes on Virginia," Jefferson, *Writings,* ed. Ford, III, 268; Jefferson to John Jay, Aug. 23, 1785, Jefferson, *Writings,* ed. Lipscomb, V, 93–96. See also Dr. Edmund Richner, *Le Mercier de la Rivière; ein Führer der physiokratischen Bewegung in Frankreich* (Zurich, 1931), pp. 213–69.

144. See H. M. Jones, *The Pursuit of Happiness,* on the classical inspiration of the identification of the good life with the life in nature, *ibid.,* pp. 79–80; also pp. 85–92.

145. On the religious implications and sources of the physiocrats see Gide and Rist, *A History of Economic Doctrines;* on the cult of nature and its meaning, see Chapter III, secs. 3 and 4, above; also Chapter V, sec. 1.

146. See his "Positions to Be Examined, Concerning National Wealth," Benjamin Franklin, *Works,* ed. John Bigelow (New York, 1904), V, 68–71.

147. See Chapter III, sec. 4, above.

148. "The Interest of Great Britain Considered," in Franklin, *Works,* ed. Bigelow, III, 295–96.

149. "Positions to Be Examined," *ibid.,* V, 71.

150. "Notes on Virginia," Jefferson, *Writings,* ed. Ford, III, 268–69.

151. On Jefferson's absolute acceptance of Destutt de Tracy's views see his letters to Colonel William Duane, Jan. 22, 1813, Jefferson, *Writings,* ed. Lipscomb, XIII, 214; and to the same, April 4, 1813, *ibid.,* p. 231. See also his letter to Joseph C. Cabell, Feb. 2, 1816, *ibid.,* XIV, 419; to John Adams. March 14, 1820, *ibid.,* XV, 240.

152. Destutt de Tracy, *A Treatise on Political Economy,* pp. 6, 17.

153. *Ibid.,* p. 24.

154. To Dr. Thomas Cooper, Sept. 10, 1814, Jefferson, *Writings,* ed. Lipscomb, XIV, 180–85.

155. *Ibid.,* pp. 182–83.

156. *Ibid.,* pp. 184–85.

157. To William H. Crawford, June 20, 1816, *ibid.,* XV, 28.

158. *Ibid.,* p. 29. See also to Dr. Josephus B. Stuart, May 10, 1817, *ibid.,* pp. 112–13; to Nathaniel Macon, Esq., Jan. 12, 1819, *ibid.,* p. 180.

CHAPTER VIII: THE JEFFERSONIAN IDEAL—SOCIAL AND
POLITICAL DEMOCRACY

1. See Chapter VII, sec. 2, above.

2. See "Third Annual Message," Oct. 17, 1803, in Thomas Jefferson, *Writings*, ed. A. A. Lipscomb (Washington, 1903), III, 353. See Albert K. Weinberg, *Manifest Destiny, A Study of Nationalist Expansionism in American History* (Baltimore, 1955), chap. vi.

3. To Monsieur Barré de Marbois, June 13, 1817, Jefferson, *Writings*, ed. Lipscomb, XV, 131.

4. Thomas Jefferson, *Works*, ed. P. L. Ford (New York, 1904), II, 178.

5. To Rev. James Madison, Oct. 28, 1785, Jefferson, *Writings*, ed. Lipscomb, XIX, 18. On the Jeffersonian-Republican land policy see: Thomas Donaldson, *The Public Domain* (Washington, 1884), pp. 196–208, 214, 216; Payson Jackson Treat, *The National Land System, 1785–1820* (New York, 1910), chaps. v, vi.

6. See letter to William B. Giles, Dec. 26, 1825, Jefferson, *Writings*, ed. Lipscomb, XVI, 148–49.

7. To Du Pont de Nemours, April 15, 1811, in Dumas Malone, ed., *Correspondence between Thomas Jefferson and Pierre Samuel Du Pont de Nemours* (Boston, 1930), p. 133; for identical view see letter to Thaddeus Kosciusko, April 13, 1811, Jefferson, *Writings*, ed. Lipscomb, XIII, 42; also to John W. Eppes, Sept. 11, 1813, *ibid.*, XIII, 354. "The fondest wish of my heart ever was that the surplus portion of these taxes, destined for the payment of that debt, should . . . be continued by annual or biennial re-enactments, and applied, in time of peace, to the improvement of our country by canals, roads and useful institutions, literary or others."

8. See Jefferson, *Writings*, ed. Lipscomb, III, 377.

9. To Albert Gallatin, June 16, 1817, *ibid.*, XV, 134. See also letter to William B. Giles, *ibid.*, XVI, 148–49. See also Second Inaugural Address, March 4, 1805, *ibid.*, III, 375ff; and Sixth Annual Message, Dec. 2, 1806, *ibid.*, III, 423–24.

10. See Chapter VII, above, on equality.

11. "Autobiography," Jefferson, *Writings*, ed. Lipscomb, I, 54.

12. To John Adams, Oct. 28, 1813, *ibid.*, XIII, 399–400.

13. *Ibid.*, p. 400.

14. See Jefferson to John Eppes, Nov. 6, 1813, *ibid.*, p. 423. See also A. L. C. Destutt de Tracy, *A Commentary and Review of Montesquieu's Spirit of Laws* (Philadelphia, 1811), p. 213: "*All labor is productive which produces property greater in value than the amount of the expences employed in procuring it.*"

15. Destutt de Tracy, *Commentary*, pp. 205–6.

16. A. L. C. Destutt de Tracy, *Treatise on Political Economy* (Georgetown, 1817), p. 6.

17. To Joseph Milligan, April 6, 1816, Jefferson, *Writings*, ed. Lipscomb, XIV, 466.

18. "Inaugural Address," March 4, 1801, *ibid.*, III, 320–21.

19. "Report on the privileges and restrictions on the commerce of the United States in foreign countries." Dec. 16, 1793, *ibid.*, III, 275.

20. See "First Annual Message," Dec. 8, 1801, *ibid.*, III, 337; "Second Annual Message," *ibid.*, p. 348; and "Eighth Annual Message," Nov. 8, 1808, *ibid.*, p. 483. To William Short, Esq., Nov. 28, 1814, *ibid.*, XIV, 214. "Our enemy has indeed the consolation of Satan . . . from a peaceable and agricultural nation, he makes us a military and manufacturing one."

21. To Du Pont de Nemours, June 28, 1809, Malone, ed., *Correspondence,* 124–25; to Jean Batiste Say, March 2, 1815, Jefferson, *Writings,* ed. Lipscomb, XIV, 259–60; to Benjamin Austin, Esq., Jan. 9, 1816, *ibid.*, XIV, 389–93.

22. To Benjamin Austin, Esq., Jan. 9, 1816, *ibid.*, XIV, 392. To Governor John Jay, April 7, 1809, *ibid.*, XII, 271.

23. See on the general philosophy of the Federalist party Chapter VII, sec. 3, above; see also "The Anas," Jefferson, *Writings,* ed. Lipscomb, I, 278–85; also *ibid.*, pp. 317–19, 332–53, 411–13, 420–21. See also letter to Henry Lee, Aug. 10, 1824, *ibid.*, XVI, 74; to William Short, Jan. 8, 1825, *ibid.*, pp. 92–96; to Judge William Johnson, June 12, 1823, *ibid.*, XV, 440–42; to Martin Van Buren, June 29, 1824, *ibid.*, XVI, 60–68.

24. Jefferson, "The Anas," *ibid.*, I, 267–77, 290–91, 311–12.

25. *Ibid.*, p. 290.

26. "The Anas," *ibid.*, I, 271–77; to John W. Eppes, Sept. 11, 1813, *ibid.*, XIII, 358–61; also to Josephus B. Stuart, May 10, 1817, *ibid.*, XV, 112–13; see also to Nathaniel Macon, Esq., Jan. 12, 1819, *ibid.*, XV, 180.

27. To John W. Eppes, Nov. 6, 1813, *ibid.*, XIII, 423.

28. *Ibid.*, p. 430.

29. To Dr. Thomas Cooper, Jan. 16, 1814, *ibid.*, XIV, 61; also to William Short, Esq., Nov. 28, 1814, *ibid.*, p. 215; to Thomas Cooper, Sept. 10, 1814, *ibid.*, XIV, 187–88.

30. To Horatio G. Spafford, March 17, 1814, *ibid.*, XIV, 119–20; to William H. Crawford, June 20, 1816, *ibid.*, XV, 28–29; see also "The Anas," *ibid.*, I, 347–48.

31. To Governor William Plumer, Jan. 31, 1815, *ibid.*, XIV, 235–37.

32. To William Crawford, *ibid.*, XV, 29; to Samuel Kercheval, *ibid.*, 39–40; see also letter to Josephus Stuart, *ibid.*, p. 112.

33. See "The Anas," *ibid.*, I, 291–92; see letter to Albert Gallatin, *ibid.*, XV, 133–34; to Charles Pinkney, Sept. 30, 1820, *ibid.*, XV, 280; to William B. Giles, Dec. 26, 1825, *ibid.*, XVI, 146–47.

34. To Joseph B. Cabell, Feb. 2, 1816, *ibid.*, XIV, 421.

35. To Charles Hammond, Aug. 18, 1821, *ibid.*, XV, 332. See also letter to William T. Barry, July 2, 1822, *ibid.*, XV, 389.

36. See Jefferson to John Dickinson, Dec. 19, 1801, *ibid.*, X, 301; to George Hay, June 2, 1807, *ibid.*, XI, 213–16; to the same, June 20, 1807, *ibid.*, 239–42; see also letter to Judge William Johnson, June 12, 1823, *ibid.*, XV, 444–52.

37. To George Hay, June 2, 1807, *ibid.*, XI, 213, 215; to Judge William Johnson, *ibid.*, XV, 447. Yet as Charles Beard points out, Federalism having shaped the Constitution, John Marshall continued its true intent in his juridical construction. See Charles Beard, *The Supreme Court and the Constitution* (New York, 1926). For the same view see also Homer Carey Hockett, *The Constitutional History of the United States* (New York, 1939), pp. 267, 277–81, 308–09, 357–62; see also Andrew C. McLaughlin, *A Constitutional History of the United States* (New York, [1935]), pp. 387–89.

38. See McLaughlin, *Constitutional History*, p. 386, and nn. 9–11. For the defense of the still more fraudulent claims of the Holland Company *versus* Pennsylvania see Gustavus Myers, *History of the Supreme Court of the United States* (Chicago, 1918), pp. 247–52. See the same author on the Fairfax Case and that of *Fletcher vs. Peck*, *ibid.*, pp. 258–67. See also the connections between the Supreme Court and Banking, *ibid.*, pp. 267–69.

39. Quoted from McLaughlin, *Constitutional History*, p. 397.

40. Quoted by Beard, *Supreme Court*, p. 114.

41. See letter to Horatio G. Spafford, March 17, 1814, Jefferson, *Writings*, ed. Lipscomb, XIV, 119–20. See also letter to Samuel Kercheval, July 12, 1816, *ibid.*, XV, 35–42, and to Judge Spencer Roane, Sept. 6, 1819, *ibid.*, XV, 213–14.

42. To Thomas Ritchie, Dec. 25, 1820, *ibid.*, pp. 296–98; to Spencer Roane, *ibid.*, p. 326.

43. To Charles Hammond, Aug. 18, 1821, *ibid.*, p. 332.

44. See letter to Judge Spencer Roane, *ibid.*, XV, 326–29; and to Judge William Johnson, *ibid.*, pp. 440–48; to William Short, Jan. 8, 1825, *ibid.*, XVI, 96.

45. To William T. Barry, July 2, 1822, *ibid.*, XV, 389; also to Robert J. Garnett, Feb. 14, 1824, *ibid.*, XVI, 15.

46. To Samuel Kercheval, July 12, 1816, *ibid.*, XV, 35–39. The letter was addressed primarily to a reform of the Constitution of Virginia but the general validity of its views is obvious.

47. The word "Americanism" in this sense is used by Jefferson in a letter to Governor William Plumer, Jan. 31, 1815, *ibid.*, XIV, 238.

48. John Adams to Thomas Jefferson, Nov. 13, 1815, *ibid.*, XIV, 359.

49. See Eugene Tenbroeck Mudge, *The Social Philosophy of John Taylor of Caroline: A Study in Jeffersonian Democracy* (New York, 1939); also Henry H. Sims, *Life of John Taylor* (Richmond, 1932), chap. vi; and Benjamin F. Wright, Jr., "The Philosopher of Jacksonian Democracy," in *American Political Science Review*, 22:870 (1928).

50. See Charles M. Wiltse, *The Jeffersonian Tradition in American Democracy* (Chapel Hill, 1935), pp. 216–22.

51. John Taylor, *Construction Construed and Constitutions Vindicated* (Richmond, 1820), p. 13.

52. John Taylor, *An Inquiry into the Principles and Policy of the Government of the United States* (Fredericksburg, 1814), "To the Publick," and *ibid.*, pp. 4, 142–44, 408–15, 422.

53. Taylor, *Construction Construed*, p. 37.

54. *Ibid.*, pp. 25–28; this is the basic proposition of the whole argument of the *Inquiry into the Principles and Policy of the Government of the United States*, especially secs. I and VI.

55. Taylor, *Inquiry*, p. 424.

56. *Ibid.*, pp. 6–7.

57. *Ibid.*, p. 1.

58. *Ibid.*, pp. 83, 84, 85.

59. *Ibid.*, p. 35.

60. *Ibid.*, p. 76.

61. *Ibid.*, p. 159.

62. *Ibid.*, p. 143.

63. *Ibid.*

64. *Ibid.*, p. 159.

65. *Ibid.*, sec. 1, "Aristocracy."

66. See Chapter VII, above.

67. See Taylor, *Construction Construed*, pp. 2–5, 9–11, 14–19.

68. Taylor, *Inquiry*, pp. 76, 78.

69. Taylor, *Construction Construed*, pp. 25, 26.

70. *Ibid.*, pp. 27–28.

71. *Ibid.*, p. 37.

72. *Ibid.*, pp. 25ff.

73. *Ibid.*, pp. 32–33.

74. Taylor, *Inquiry*, p. 424; see also p. 412.

75. *Ibid.*, pp. 408–9.

76. Taylor, *Construction Construed*, pp. 40–64, and Taylor, *Inquiry*, p. 409.

77. Taylor, *Inquiry*, pp. 412–20.

78. *Ibid.*, pp. 444–46.

79. *Ibid.*, pp. 414–15.

80. *Ibid.*, p. 412.

81. *Ibid.*, p. 414.

82. See Chapter III, sec. 2, and Chapter V, sec. 2, above.

83. Taylor, *Inquiry*, p. 422.

84. *Ibid.*, p. 113. See Taylor, *Construction Construed*, pp. 67ff.

85. Taylor, *Construction Construed*, pp. 14–15.

86. *Ibid.*, pp. 167–68.

87. Taylor, *Inquiry*, pp. 37–38, 445–46; *Construction Construed*, pp. 16–19.

88. Taylor, *Inquiry*, pp. 41–63; *Construction Construed*, pp. 213–33, 246–53.

89. Taylor, *Inquiry*, p. 66; *Construction Construed*, pp. 203ff.

90. Taylor, *Inquiry*, pp. 63–64.

91. Taylor, *Construction Construed*, p. 77.

92. *Ibid.*, pp. 77–78.

93. *Ibid.*, pp. 203–7.

94. *Ibid.*, p. 208.

95. Taylor, *Inquiry*, pp. 41–42; *Construction Construed*, pp. 4–5, 77–78.

96. Taylor, *Construction Construed*, p. 207.

97. Ralph Barton Perry, *Characteristically American* (New York, 1949), pp. 37ff.

98. See Chapter XII below, on Josiah Warren and American anarchism.

99. See Arthur M. Schlesinger, Jr., *The Age of Jackson* (Boston, 1946); and Marvin Meyers, *The Jacksonian Persuasion, Politics and Belief* (New York, 1960), chap. ix.

100. As quoted by A. M. Schlesinger, Jr., *Jackson*, p. 316; see also Meyers, *Jacksonian Persuasion*, "Appendix B," pp. 280–82.

101. Julius W. Pratt, "John L. O'Sullivan and Manifest Destiny," *New York History*, 14:224 (1933); on O'Sullivan see also M. E. Curti, "Young America," *The American Historical Review*, 32:34–55 (1926); and Frank L. Mott, *A History of American Magazines, 1741–1850* (Cambridge, Mass., 1957), pp. 678–80.

102. "The Democratic Principle," Introduction, *The United States Magazine and Democratic Review*, 1:1 (January 1938).

103. See "Radicalism," *ibid.*, 3:99–111 (October 1838); "How Stands the Case," *ibid.*, 9:4–7 (September 1838); and Tocqueville, "European Views of American Democracy. II," *ibid.*, 2:338–55 (July 1838).

104. "The Democratic Principle," *ibid.*, pp. 2–4 and 6–11; see also "The Course of Civilization," *ibid.*, 6:208–17 (September 1839).

105. "The Democratic Principle," *ibid.*, 1:6–7 (October 1839).

106. See J. W. Pratt, "John L. O'Sullivan and Manifest Destiny," pp. 222–31; M. E. Curti, "Young America"; also Lawrence Sargent Hall, *Hawthorne, Critic of Society* (New Haven, 1944), pp. 102–10; also Weinberg, *Manifest Destiny*, chaps. iv and v; pp. 100–54.

CHAPTER IX: A EUROPEAN CONCEPT CROSSES THE ATLANTIC

1. See Marvin Meyers, *The Jacksonian Persuasion* (New York, 1960), chap. xi. See also Louis Hartz, *The Liberal Tradition: An Interpretation of American Political Thought Since the Revolution* (New York, 1955). The change in the orientation of the Federalist Whig in the 1830's can be observed in a comparison of the Inaugural Speech of Charles Quincy Adams in 1825 with that of Benjamin Harrison in 1841—the one exhibits the National Republican principle with dignity and clarity, the other flounders between its protestation of democratic principles and its eager attempt to circumscribe as narrowly as possible the powers of the sovereign people.

2. George W. Pierson, *Tocqueville and Beaumont in America* (New York, 1938), p. 118.

3. *Ibid.*, p. 152.

4. Alexis de Tocqueville, *Democracy in America*, ed. Phillips Bradley (New York, 1945), I, chaps. iv, ix, xiii, xv.

5. Tocqueville to M. Stoffels, Paris, Feb. 21, 1835, quoted by Phillips Bradley in Tocqueville, *Democracy in America*, I, pp. xx–xxi. See also

Tocqueville's introduction to the second part of *Democracy in America*, pp. iv–v.

6. Tocqueville, *Democracy in America*, I, 404.

7. *Ibid.*, I, 383.

8. *Ibid.*, I, 416, 383.

9. Tocqueville, *Democracy in America*, I, 26–28, 243–44, 271–87.

10. *Ibid.*, I, 393–94.

11. Pierson, *Tocqueville and Beaumont*, p. 70.

12. *Ibid.*, p. 76.

13. *Ibid.*, pp. 113–19. See also Tocqueville, *Democracy in America*, I, 243.

14. Tocqueville, *Democracy in America*, I, 392ff. See also chap. ii.

15. Pierson, *Tocqueville and Beaumont*, p. 693.

16. Tocqueville, *Democracy in America*, I, 13.

17. Pierson, *Tocqueville and Beaumont*, pp. 370–424.

18. Tocqueville, *Democracy in America*, I, 416.

19. Pierson, *Tocqueville and Beaumont*, p. 381.

20. *Ibid.*, p. 381.

21. *Ibid.*, p. 413.

22. See Pierson, *Tocqueville and Beaumont*, p. 414; Tocqueville, *Democracy in America*, I, 429–34. See also II, bk. 2, chaps. iv–ix.

23. Tocqueville, *Democracy in America*, I, 70ff.

24. Pierson, *Tocqueville and Beaumont*, p. 661.

25. Tocqueville, *Democracy in America*, I, 416.

26. *Ibid.*

27. *Ibid.*, p. 417.

28. *Ibid.*, p. 418.

29. Pierson, *Tocqueville and Beaumont*, pp. 152–53.

30. Tocqueville, *Democracy in America*, I, 393.

31. See the discussion of the influence of the New England leaders on Tocqueville in Pierson's *Tocqueville and Beaumont*, pp. 364–422. See also Charles M. Andrews on Jared Sparks as quoted by Pierson, *ibid.*, p. 410; and Meyers, *Jacksonian Persuasion*, chap. iii.

32. Pierson, *Tocqueville and Beaumont*, p. 32. On Tocqueville's influence on Francis Lieber see Merle Curti, *The Growth of American Thought* (New York, 1943), p. 395.

33. On the reception of Tocqueville, see "Introduction" of Phillips Bradley to Tocqueville, *Democracy in America*, I, xxi–xxxviii. On the sociological aspect of Tocqueville's work see J. P. Mayer, *Prophet of the Mass Age, A Study of Alexis De Tocqueville*, trans. M. M. Bozman and C. Hahn (London, 1939); also Albert Salomon, "Tocqueville, Moralist and Sociologist," *Social Research*, 2:420–22 (1935). On the origins of some of the guiding principles and concepts in Tocqueville's work see Bernhard Fabian, *Alexis de Tocqueville's Amerikabild* (Heidelberg, 1957).

34. Tocqueville, *Democracy in America*, II, bk. 4, esp. chap. vi.

35. *Ibid.*, II, 328–29.

36. See Chapter VIII above.

37. "The Course of Civilization," *The United States Magazine and Democratic Review*, 6:213–14 (1839).

38. *Ibid.*, p. 214. See also "Radicalism," *The United States Magazine and Democratic Review*, 3:109–11 (1838).

39. "The Course of Civilization," *U.S. Magazine and Democratic Review*, 6:209 (1839).

40. *Ibid.*, pp. 208ff, 211.

41. See Chapter II, Sect. 3, above.

42. See, for instance, Charles A. and Mary R. Beard, *A Basic History of the United States* (New York, 1944), p. 361, in which the authors mistakenly date the publication of the book in 1835 instead of 1840; also A. D. Lindsay, "Individualism," *Encyclopaedia of Social Sciences*, ed. E. R. A. Seligman (New York, 1932), VII, 674ff, and the *Oxford English Dictionary*, V, 224.

43. Tocqueville, *Democracy in America*, ed. P. Bradley (New York, 1945), I, vi, note.

44. See "Michel Chevalier," *Grand Dictionnaire Universel Du XIXᵉ siècle* (1869), vol. IV; Chevalier's work was published under the name Michael Chevalier, *Society, Manners and Politics in the United States* (Boston, 1839).

45. Albert Brisbane's book, *Social Destiny of Man*, was published in Philadelphia in 1840.

46. List's book was translated and published through the exertions of Stephen Colwell as *The National System of Political Economy*, translated from the German, which was published in 1841, by G. A. Matile, including the notes of the French translation by Henri Richelot with a preliminary essay and notes by Stephen Colwell (Philadelphia, 1856).

47. See Tocqueville, *Democracy in America*, II, bk. 2, chaps. ii–iv, viii, and bk. 4. See also *ibid.*, II, bk. 1, chap. iii, and App. BB, p. 368. For further discussion of the term in Tocqueville's work see Fabian, *Amerikabild*, pp. 33, 36–37. The last-named author has not grasped the negative meaning of Tocqueville's concept of individualism and he is also unaware of the origin and development of the concept in France.

48. See Chapter II above on Tocqueville's sociology of knowledge. For his treatment of general concepts and the interrelation between social structure and intellectual perspectives see Tocqueville, *Democracy in America*, II, bk. 1, chaps. i, ii–iv, vii, vii, x, xiii, xvi, xvii, and esp. xx.

49. Tocqueville, *Democracy in America*, II, 99.

50. *Ibid.*, p. 98.

51. *Ibid.*

52. *Ibid.*, p. 319.

53. *Ibid.*, pp. 318–19.

54. See Richard Koebner, "Semantics and Historiography," *The Cambridge Journal*, 7:133–34 (1953), on the significance of the Greek suffixes *ismos, izein*, in the evolution of the political "isms" of the nineteenth century.

55. See Richard Koebner, "Zur Begriffsbildung der Kultur-Geschichte," *Historische Zeitschrift*, 149:26off (1934). I have been guided in my research

on the origins of the concept of individualism by Richard Koebner's pioneering research on the European origins of the idea of individualism. On Tocqueville see *ibid.*, pp. 260–65.

56. Tocqueville, *Democracy in America*, II, 329ff.

57. Tocqueville to Reeve, February 3, 1840, Alexis de Tocqueville, *Correspondence Anglaise* (in *Oeuvres complètes*, ed. J. P. Mayer [Paris, 1954]), VI, 52–53.

58. See Fabian, *Amerikabild*, pp. 36–37.

59. See Alexandre Vinet, *Philosophie morale et sociale* (Lausanne, 1913), I, 322–35. The resemblance between the ideas of Alexandre Vinet and Tocqueville not only concerning individualism and the age of the masses but also concerning the process of leveling and generalization in the field of intellectual orientations is so remarkable that one suspects more than a coincidence. Yet though Tocqueville must have been aware of the literary and political activity of Alexandre Vinet, being particularly interested in the destiny of Switzerland and its democracy, I have been unable to prove his acquaintance with Vinet's work.

60. Alexis de Tocqueville, *De la démocratie en Amérique* (in *Oeuvres Complètes*, J. P. Mayer ed. [Paris, 1951]), II, 110.

61. *Ibid.*, pp. 109–12.

62. See Tocqueville, *Democracy in America*, ed. Bradley, I, "Author's Introduction," p. 13.

63. See Pierson, *Tocqueville and Beaumont*, pp. 113–14; Tocqueville, *Democracy in America*, II, 121ff.

64. Tocqueville, *Democracy in America*, II, 102ff.

65. Quoted from Pierson, *Tocqueville and Beaumont*, pp. 113–14.

66. Tocqueville, *Democracy in America*, II, bk. 2, chap. viii, pp. 121–22.

67. See Tocqueville to Henry Reeve, March 22, 1837, as quoted by Pierson in *Tocqueville and Beaumont*, p. 695.

68. See Phillips Bradley's survey of the reception of both volumes in Tocqueville, *Democracy in America*, I, xl–xlviii.

69. See Noah Webster, *American Dictionary of the English Language*, rev. ed. (New York, 1847); and the edition of 1864, ed. Noah Porter.

70. John Ogilvie, *The Imperial Dictionary of the English Language* (London, 1882–83), II, 596; see also Robert Hunter, ed., *The Encyclopaedic Dictionary*, II (1896), in which the following definition is given: "The selfishness of the small proprietor has been described by the best writers as individualism."

71. "Catholicism," *Boston Quarterly Review*, 4:320ff (1841).

72. *Ibid.*, p. 323.

73. *Ibid.*, p. 326.

74. *Ibid.*, pp. 331ff.

75. *Ibid.*, p. 332.

76. E. L. Godkin, "Aristocratic Opinions of Democracy," *Problems of Modern Democracy* (New York, 1896).

77. *Ibid.*, pp. 20–25.

78. *Ibid.*, p. 26. The essay was first published in *The North American Review*, January 1865.

79. *Ibid.*, p. 28.

80. *Ibid.*, p. 39.

81. *Ibid.*, pp. 40, 42, 55–56, 58, 61.

82. John W. Nevin, "Human Freedom," *The American Review*, 7:406–18 (1848). *The American Review* was a Whig journal devoted to politics and literature.

83. *Ibid.*, pp. 416–17.

84. *Ibid.*, pp. 415–16.

85. *Ibid.*, p. 416.

86. See the declaration of Whig principles in "Prospectus of the New Series," *The American Review*, 1:2 (1848).

87. "The Future Policy of the Whigs," *The American Review*, 1:330–31 (1848).

88. *Ibid.*, p. 330.

89. See Marlis Steinert, *Michel Chevalier: l'evolution de sa pensée economique, sociale et politique, 1830–1852* ([Saarbrucken], 1956). See also Sébastien Charléty, *Histoire du Saint Simonisme (1815–1864)*, Paris, 1931, p. 95.

90. A. Legoyt, "Michel Chevalier," in *Nouvelle Biographie Générale depuis les temps les plus reculés jusqu'a nos jours* (Paris, 1852–66), X, 261.

91. *Ibid.*, p. 262.

92. See Lewis Freeman Mott, *Sainte Beuve* (New York, 1925), p. 76.

93. Chevalier became acquainted with the first part of Tocqueville's work after his "Letters" had already been published in the *Journal des débats*. See note to Letter XXXIV, "La Democratie," in *Lettres sur L'Amérique du Nord*, 3rd ed. (Paris, 1838), III, 396. It is impossible to determine to what degree Tocqueville was acquainted with Chevalier's "Letters," which were printed in book form a year after the appearance of Part One of *De la démocratie*. Pierson quotes a letter of Tocqueville of Nov. 4, 1836, which refers to Chevalier's book: "Blosseville informed me the other day that Chevalier's book had appeared. You realize that I am always on the *qui vive* where America is concerned. Yet I will not read Chevalier's work; you know that it's a principle with me. Have you glanced at it and, in that case, what do you think of it? What is its tone? What is its object. . . And in what way might it be prejudicial to the philosophico-political work that I am preparing? If, without *distracting yourself*, you can reply to these questions, you will do me pleasure." Pierson, *Tocqueville and Beaumont*, p. 726n.

94. Michel Chevalier, *Lettres sur L'Amérique du Nord* (Paris, 1836), "Introduction," I, iv–viii. Except where otherwise noted, this edition is cited.

95. *Ibid.*, Lettre XXXIII, "L'Aristocratie," II, 376–88.

96. "Introduction," I, x–xv; see also "Lettre XVI" (3rd ed., Paris, 1838), I, 252ff.

97. The concept of Western civilization prominent in Chevalier gains momentum in the historical speculations of the Saint-Simonians.

98. Chevalier, *Lettres,* "La Démocratie," II, 405.

99. *Ibid.,* p. 406.

100. *Ibid.,* 406–7.

101. See Chapter IX above.

102. Letter XXIX, "Amelioration sociale," *Lettres,* II, 306–7.

103. *Ibid.*

104. *Ibid.,* p. 307; see also "De l'association," ibid., pp. 502–7.

105. *Ibid.,* p. 372.

106. "L'Yankée et le Virginien," *ibid.,* I, 161–75.

107. See Charles Gide and Charles Rist, *History of Economic Doctrines* (London, 1915), pp. 264ff.

108. Friedrich List, *Das Nationale System der Politischen Ökonomie,* in *Werke* [Berlin, 1927], IV, 209.

109. See Koebner, "Zur Begriffsbildung," *Hist. Z.,* 149:260ff (1934), and List, *Das Nationale System,* pp. 355–56.

110. Charles Jared Ingersoll, Vice-President of the "Pennsylvania Society for the Promotion of Manufactures and the Mechanic Arts," impressed by List's abilities, had invited him to prepare a popular pamphlet in support of the protectionist cause against the free-trader arguments, especially those of Cooper. See Margaret E. Hirst, *Life of Friedrich List and Selections from His Writings* (London, 1909), p. 42.

111. Friedrich List, Letter I, in *Outlines of American Political Economy* (in *Werke* [Berlin, 1931]), II, 99–103. See also Joseph Dorfman, *The Economic Mind in American Civilization* (New York, 1946), II, 577.

112. List, *Outlines,* Letter II, July 12, 1827, p. 107, and Letter VI, "Individual Economy is not Political Economy," pp. 127ff; Letters VII–XII, "Political Economy is not Cosmopolitical Economy," *ibid.,* pp. 130–56.

113. Hirst, *Life of List,* pp. 43–47.

114. See William Notz, "Friedrich List in America," *American Economic Review,* 16:249ff (June, 1926); also Hirst, *Life of List,* p. 112, on Daniel Raymond.

115. See Stephen Colwell's "Preliminary Essay" on the history of political economy in *National System of Political Economy* (Philadelphia, 1856), pp. xvii–lxxvii.

116. As quoted in Henry C. Carey, *Memoir of Stephen Colwell* (Philadelphia, 1871), pp. 17–24.

117. Carey, *Colwell,* p. 24.

118. The difference between Colwell's social Christianity and the Christian Socialism of Maurice and Kingsley lies exactly in their respective different attitudes toward the state. Colwell himself refers to Sismondi and Adolphe Blanqui as having laid bare the pernicious effects of a laissez-faire and free-trade policy; see "Preliminary Essay" in *National System of Political Economy,* pp. xxxiii, xxxviii.

119. F. A. von Hayek, in "The Counter Revolution in Science," *Economica*, 8:281–330 (August 1941), attempts to demonstrate Saint-Simonian influence on the thought of Friedrich List. He cites, in support of his thesis, List's contact with the first editors of the *Revue Encyclopaedique* in the years of 1823–1824, which during his second visit had fallen into the hands of Saint-Simonians. As further support, he mentions List's acquaintance with Chevalier and his attempt to meet D'Eichthal, *ibid.*, 290–91. See Hirst, *Life of List*, p. 124. Gide and Rist, *Economic Doctrines*, p. 277, no. 2, on the influence of Adam Müller and the French Protectionists. It could be also shown that the dialectic of the idea of nationalism had brought the German philosopher G. E. Fichte to similar even though far more radical conclusions in the idea of *Der Geschlossene Handelsstaat*.

CHAPTER X: INDIVIDUALISM AND SOCIALISM:
THE BIRTH OF TWO NEW CONCEPTS

1. Among the ever-increasing studies on Saint-Simonism and its influence see in particular: Friedrich A. von Hayek, *The Counter-Revolution of Science: Studies on the Abuse of Reason* (Illinois, 1952); Eliza M. Butler, *The Saint-Simonian Religion in Germany, A Study of the Young German Movement* (Cambridge, Eng., 1926); Sébastian Charléty, *Histoire du Saint-Simonisme* (Paris, 1931); Frank E. Manuel, *The New World of Henri Saint-Simon* (Cambridge, 1956); Richard K. P. Pankhurst, *The Saint-Simonians Mill and Carlyle* (London, 1957); Jacob L. Talmon, *Political Messianism, the Romantic Phase* (London, 1960), chap. i. See also Georg G. Iggers' "Introduction" to *The Doctrine of Saint-Simon: An Exposition; First Year, 1828–1829* (Boston [1958]); and also the Introduction of Célestin C. Bouglé and Elie Halévy in *Doctrine de Saint-Simon, exposition, première Année, 1829* (Paris, 1924).

2. See Talmon, *Political Messianism*, Part II, "Messianic Nationalism"; Butler, *Saint-Simonian Religion in Germany;* Hans Kohn, *Prophets and Peoples* (New York, 1952), chaps. ii, iii. See also Roger H. Soltau, *French Political Thought in the Nineteenth Century* (New York, 1959).

3. See Hayek, *Counter-Revolution of Science*, p. 164; Charles Gide and Charles Rist, *A History of Economic Doctrines from the Time of the Physiocrats to the Present Day* (London [1915]), pp. 225–31.

4. On the influence of the "Socialists of the Chair" (Katherdersozialismus) on the social program of the German Reich, see Moritz Wirth, *Bismarck, Wagner und Rodbertus* (Leipzig, 1885). On Louis Napoleon see Hayek, *Counter-Revolution of Science*, pp. 166–67; Gide and Rist, *History of Economic Doctrines*, pp. 407ff; see also Soltau, *French Political Thought*, pp. 146–50. On Carlyle and hero worship see David B. Cofer, *Saint-Simonism in the Radicalism of Thomas Carlyle* (Austin, 1931) and Eugene d'Eichthal, "Carlyle et le Saint-Simonisme; Lettres à Gustave d'Eichthal, *Revue historique*, 82:292ff (1903).

5. Iggers' "Introduction," *Doctrine of Saint-Simon*, pp. xxxv–xlvii.

6. *Ibid.*, First Session, p. 1.

7. *Ibid.*, Third Session, "Conception, Method and Historical Classification."

8. See *ibid.*, First and Second Sessions and "Introduction" to *Doctrine de Saint-Simon*, Bouglé and Halévy eds., pp. 73–74.

9. See "Introduction" to Claude H. Saint-Simon, *Opinions littéraires, philosophiques et industrielles* (Paris, 1825), pp. 15–19.

10. Iggers, *Doctrine of Saint-Simon*, Fourth Session, p. 58. On the meaning and significance of the term "association" see the explanation of Bouglé and Halévy in their edition of *Doctrine de Saint-Simon*, pp. 203–5, n.91.

11. Iggers, *Doctrine of Saint-Simon*, Fourth Session, pp. 69–70.

12. Eugène Rodrigues, *Lettres sur la religion et la politique, 1829* (Paris, 1832), pp. 174–75. On the significance of the Jewish ingredient in Saint-Simonism see Talmon, *Political Messianism*, pp. 77–81. Among the first to notice the impact of Jewish messianism and the preponderance of Jews in the Saint-Simonian movement was Sainte-Beuve. See Charles A. Sainte-Beuve, *Premiers Lundis* (Paris, 1874–75), pp. 55–57. The answer which Sainte-Beuve gives is that the parallels between Mosaism and Saint-Simonism are marked. Like the former, Saint-Simon negates the dualism of Christianity. To him it is essentially a social religion, unitary and theocratic, and seeks the realization of the absolute on earth.

13. See Marie Jean Antoine-Nicolas Caritat de Condorcet, *Outlines of an Historical View of the Progress of the Human Mind* (Philadelphia, 1796), p. 289. See Claude H. Saint-Simon, "Introduction aux travaux scientifiques du XIX siècle," *Oeuvres choisies* (Brussels, 1859), I, 98–110. Also Hayek, *Counter-Revolution of Science*, 106–8 and Manuel, *New World of Henri Saint-Simon*, pp. 158–67, 75–76.

14. See Manuel, *ibid.*, pp. 148–57, 140; Iggers, *Doctrine of Saint-Simon*, Third Session, *passim*.

15. This is the aspect which Hayek has treated exclusively in his *Counter-Revolution of Science*. See also Saint-Simon, "Introduction aux travaux scientifiques," *Oeuvres choisies*, I, 164–65, n.1.

16. Hayek, *Counter-Revolution of Science*; Lorenz von Stein, *Geschichte der sozialen Bewegung in Frankreich* (Munich, 1921), II, 192ff, 208, 256. See also François de Corcelle, *Documents pour servir à l'histoire des conspirations, des partis et des sectes* (Paris, 1831), chaps. iii–iv, on the dominant influence of *l'école polytechnique*.

17. All the *idéologues* were persuaded that a science of politics and society could be found through which rationality could be introduced into politics and the statesmen would be able to calculate scientifically the correct policy and legislation for their country. This is true for the work of Destutt de Tracy and even that of Du Pont de Nemours. See Madame de Staël's defense of such comprehensive sciences of society in *The Influence of Literature upon Society* (Boston, 1813), II, 208–24. See also Raymond G. Carey's *The Liberals of France and Their Relation to the Development of Bonaparte's Dictatorship, 1799–1804* (Chicago, 1947).

18. See Chapter VI above, esp. secs. 4 and 5.

19. *Ibid.*, pp. 108–11.

20. On the profound influence of the "Ultras" and their ideology, especially that of Joseph de Maistre, Louis G. A. de Bonald, and Pierre Ballanche on Saint-Simon, see Saint-Simon, "Introduction aux travaux scientifiques," in *Oeuvres choisies*, I, 211–12. See also *Doctrine de Saint-Simon*, Bouglé and Halévy eds., p. 122f, n. 4, and Iggers, *Doctrine of Saint-Simon*, Ninth Session, pp. 145–46, and *ibid.*, Thirteenth Session, p. 213, Sixteenth Session, pp. 251–52. On the influence of the German historical world view as evolved by the conservative-romantic reaction toward the French revolutionary rationalism see Saint-Amand Bazard, "Consideration sur l'histoire," in *Le Producteur: journal philosophique de l'industrie, des sciences et des beaux-arts*, 4:390–415 (1826). Also, the very enlightening remarks of François de Corcelle in *Documents pour servir a l'histoire des conspirations*, chaps. iii, iv; "De la tendance nouvelle des idées," *Revue encyclopedique*, 53:2ff (1832); and Jean Reynaud, "De la société Saint-Simonienne," *ibid.*, pp. 17–18. See also Robert Spaemann, *Der Ursprung der Soziologie aus dem Geist der Restauration* (Munich, 1959), pp. 18–184, and Manuel, *New World of Henri Saint-Simon*, pp. 262–63, 271–72.

21. See Karl Mannheim's masterly analysis of the emergence of the historical world view as the conservative answer to revolutionary rationalism in "Das konservative Denken, soziologische Beiträge zum Werden des politisch-historischen Denkens in Deutschland," *Archiv fur Sozialwissenschaft und Sozialpolitik*, 57:68–142, 470–95 (1927).

22. See Joseph de Maistre, *Consideration sur la France* (Paris, 1936), chap. vi, pp. 75–82; Louis G. A. de Bonald, *Theorie du pouvoir politique et religieux dans la société* (Paris, 1834), pt. II, Introduction; Paul Bourget and Michel Salomon, *Bonald* (Paris, 1904), pp. 78–79, 131–36.

23. Mannheim, "Das Konservative Denken," p. 75.

24. Joseph de Maistre, "Etude sur la souveraineté," *Oeuvres complètes* (Lyons, 1884–86), I, 375–76; Louis G. A. de Bonald, *Oeuvres complètes* (Paris, 1859), III, 13–22, 536.

25. See E. Rothacker, "Savigny, Grimm, Ranke," *Historische Zeitschrift*, 128:433–40 (1923).

26. Bonald, "De la philosophie morale et politique du XVIIIième siècle," *Oeuvres complètes*, III, 470–85; Spaemann, *Ursprung der Soziologie*, pp. 25–31, 41. See also Karl Mannheim, "Das Konservative Denken," pp. 142, 471–77.

27. See Louis G. A. de Bonald, *Récherches philosophiques sur les premiers objets des connaissances morales* (Paris, 1818), III, 62–122. See also Talmon, *Political Messianism*, p. 300.

28. The profound significance of the phenomenon of language for the rejection of the Lockian tradition of rationalism in England and France and for the emergence of historicism and the romantic world view can be seen in Vico, Herder, Wilhelm von Humboldt and the Romantics, the Schlegel brothers, Novalis, and Grimm, no less than in Bonald's theories.

29. For the meaning of the word "historicism" see Friedrich Meinecke,

Die Entstehung des Historismus (Munich, 1936), vol. I, "Vorbemerkung," pp. 1–5.

30. See Meinecke, *ibid.*, I, 67.

31. See Otto Freiherrn von Gemmingen, *Vico, Hamann und Herder, Eine Studie zur Geschichte der Erneuerung des Deutschen Geisteslebens im 18. Jahrhundert* (Borna-Leipzig, 1918).

32. Elio Gianturco, *Joseph de Maistre and Giambattista Vico (Italian Roots of De Maistre's Political Culture)*, Washington, D.C., 1937. On the influence of Vico on Pierre-Simon Ballanche, see Robert Flint, *History of the Philosophy of History* (Edinburgh, 1893), pp. 382–83.

33. See the interesting list of authors who dealt with the philosophy of history in Jules M. Michelet's "Discourse sur le système et la vie de Vico," *Oeuvres choisies de Vico* (Paris, 1835), pp. 128–30, in which the German authors Herder, Lessing, Kant, and others are listed. For Vico's general influence see also Robert Flint, *Vico* (London, 1884), pp. 230–32, note, and Marcel Cochery, *Les grand lignes de la philosophie historique et juridique de Vico* (Paris, 1923), chap. iv; also Meinecke, *Die Entstehung des Historismus*, vol. I, on Vico.

34. See Meinecke, *ibid.*, II, 644.

35. Yet for important exceptions see the attitudes of Pierre Ballanche and, of course, Lamennais, Montalembert, Lacordaire, and other liberal Catholics.

36. See Leibnitz, "De Principio Individui," and his proposition "omne individuum sua tota entitate individuatur" in Meinecke, *Die Entstehung des Historismus*, I, 32; see *ibid.* on Justus Möser, Herder, and Ranke; also Karl Mannheim, "Das Konservative Denken," pp. 112–42.

37. "The Progressive Development of Religious Ideas," in George Ripley, ed., *Specimens of Foreign Standard Literature* (Boston, 1838–42), II, 293.

38. For the Catholic side, see Louis G. A. de Bonald, "Démonstration philosophique du principe constitutif de la société," *Oeuvres* ([Paris, 1817–30]), XII, chaps. xx–xxi, and Friedrich von Schlegel, *The Philosophy of History* (New York, 1841), II, Lectures XI–XVI. See also de Maistre, "Examen de la philosophie de Bacon," *Oeuvres complètes*, VI, 472, and "Réflexions sur le protestantisme," *ibid.*, VIII, 66–68, 79–82. The liberal counterposition is represented by the friend of Benjamin Constant and Madame de Staël, Charles Villers, in his *Essai sur l'ésprit et l'influence de la Réformation de Luther* (Paris, 1804). See also François Pierre Guillaume Guizot, *General History of Civilization in Europe from the Fall of the Roman Empire to the French Revolution* (New York, 1840), Lecture XIII, "The Reformation." For the German Protestant position, Hegel's evaluation of Protestantism may stand as representative. See his "Vorlesungen über die Philosophie der Geschichte," *Sämtliche Werke* (Stuttgart, 1927–40), XI, 441, 519–48.

39. H. Richard Niebuhr, "The Protestant Movement and Democracy in the United States," in James W. Smith and A. Leland Jamison, eds., *Religion in American Life* (Princeton, 1961), I, 22. On the influence of sectarian Protestantism on the German historical world view see Meinecke, *Die*

Entstehung des Historismus, I, 47–55, 389–91, 628. See also Ernst Troëltsch, *Die Bedeutung des Protestantismus für die Entstehung der modernen Welt* (Munich, 1924).

40. Quoted from Dietrich H. Iyer, *Edmund Burke und Seine Kritik der Franzosischen Revolution* (Stuttgart, 1960), p. 5. The views of Burke on the French Revolution changed considerably from the "Reflection" to the "Regicide Peace." In the former, the fear of anarchism, of the leveling spirit of a rationalistic equalitarian approach, predominates. In the latter, the fear of the immense leviathan state, the Republic "une et indivisible" predominates. "To them, the will, the wish, the want, the liberty, the toil, the blood of individuals, is nothing. Individuality is left out of their scheme of government. The State is all in all" ("Three Letters on a Regicide Peace," Edmund Burke, *Works,* London, 1803, VIII, 253).

41. Edmund Burke, "Thoughts on French Affairs," *Works,* VII, 13–14, 18; and "Reflections on the Revolution in France," *ibid.,* V, 39–40. See also "Regicide Peace," *ibid.,* VIII, 98, 214, 235.

42. See "Reflections," *ibid.,* V, 109–11, 113–14, 149–51.

43. *Ibid.,* pp. 122–23.

44. *Ibid.,* p. 149.

45. *Ibid.*

46. *Ibid.,* p. 151.

47. *Ibid.,* pp. 151–52.

48. *Ibid.,* p. 184.

49. *Ibid.,* p. 168.

50. *Ibid.,* p. 183.

51. On the influence of Burke's "Reflections" on European conservatism see Soltau, *French Political Thought,* p. 19, n. 1.

52. See Bonald, *Oeuvres complètes,* III, 13–31, 536; de Maistre, "Etude sur la souveraineté," *Oeuvres,* I, 524, and "Essai sur le principle générateur," *ibid.,* I, 244. See Andreas Müller, *Die Auseinandersetzung der Romantik mit den Ideen der Revolution* (Halle, 1929); see also Gunmar Rexius, "Studie zur Staats lehre der Historischen Schule," *Historische Zeitschrift,* 107:496ff (1911). For Hegel see *Grundlinien der Philosophie des Rechtes,* ed. Georg Lasson (Leipzig, 1921), VI, esp. p. 258. See also Friedrich von Schlegel's rejection of modern history as a rebellion of individual reason, will, and morality against the unity of mankind in his *Philosophie der Geschichte* (Vienna, 1829); see also Adam H. Müller, *Die Elemente der Staatskunst* (Berlin, 1809), vol. I, Lecture II, pp. 35–69; vol. II, Lecture XIX; vol. III, Lecture XXXVI. On Adam Müller see Reinhold Aris, *Die Staatslehre Adam Müllers in ihrem Verhältnis zur Deutschen Romantik* (Tübingen, 1929), pp. 43–51.

53. See his "Regicide Peace," Burke, *Works,* VIII, 253.

54. Characteristic of this rejection of eighteenth-century French rationalism is Benjamin Constant's "De Godwin, et de son Ouvrage sur la Justice Politique," in *Mélanges de litterature et de politique* (Paris, 1829), I, 188–92. While Benjamin Constant rejects Godwin's metaphysics, psychology and

morality, he agrees completely with his ideal of laissez-faire. See *ibid.*, pp. 188, 190–91.

55. See Benjamin Constant, "De Madame de Staël, et de ses ouvrages," *ibid.*, pp. 166–77, on the French Revolution. See also Soltau, *French Political Thought*, pp. 38–42.

56. On the American influence see Chapter VII above. On the German influence no better survey can be given than that of Victor Cousin in "Exposition of Eclecticism," the preface to *Philosophical Fragments* in George Ripley, comp., *Philosophical Miscellanies* (Boston, 1838), I, 55, 79–100, 120–31; Madame de Staël's *Influence of Literature upon Society* and her *De L'Allemagne* (London, 1813), no less than Benjamin Constant's profound knowledge of German thought mediated by the Schlegels, represented the beginnings.

57. On the Anglophile orientation of the doctrinaire liberals see also Armand Marrast, "La Presse révolutionnaire," *Paris révolutionnaire* (Paris, 1833–34), II, 106–8.

58. Preface to Benjamin Constant's *Mélanges*, translated in George Ripley, *Specimens of Foreign Standard Literature*, II, 265–66.

59. See Lecture I in Guizot, *General History*, pp. 17–22.

60. *Ibid.*, pp. 22–23.

61. *Ibid.*, p. 25.

62. *Ibid.*, pp. 31–32. See Victor Cousin's "Exposition of Eclecticism," in Ripley, *Specimens of Foreign Standard Literature*, I: Introduction to the *History of Modern Philosophy* (Boston, 1832) to which Guizot refers in the conclusion of his *General History*, p. 341.

63. Guizot, *General History*, p. 31.

64. See Victor Cousin's "Moral Law and Liberty," which, elaborating the Kantian philosophy of morality, anticipates clearly the American transcendentalist philosophy; in Ripley, *Specimens of Foreign Standard Literature*, I, 158–62. The relation between the doctrinaire liberalism of Royer-Collard and Guizot and the philosophical eclecticism of Cousin and Jouffroy has been stated clearly by Cousin in his "Exposition of Eclecticism," *ibid.*, pp. 105–7. See also Flint, *History of the Philosophy of History*, chap. viii, on the relation between eclectic and doctrinaire historical philosophy.

65. See Soltau, *French Political Thought*, pp. 6–14, 26–31.

66. *Ibid.*, pp. 32–37.

67. It is of course impossible to ascertain positively the first use of a term as ambiguous and varied in connotation as that of "individualism." Our endeavor has been only to trace the emergence of the concept in its relation to the great ideological and historical tensions of the times. It is interesting to note that Thomas Jefferson used this term as early as February 1814 in order to characterize the nominalistic and anti-Linnaean concept of nature of Buffon. See Jefferson to Dr. John Manners, Feb. 22, 1814, in Jefferson, *Writings*, ed. A. A. Lipscomb, *et al.* (Washington, D.C., 1903), XIV, 101. Jefferson's own inclination to neologisms and his free use of "isms" is in harmony with the growing inclination of the early nineteenth century,

especially of the *idéologues,* to introduce generalized words in order to connote general tendencies and principles of action to the various fields of knowledge. See Jefferson's defense of neologisms in his letter to Joseph Milligan, April 6, 1816, *ibid.,* pp. 463–64.

68. François de Corcelle, *Documents pour servir à l'histoire des conspirations, des partis et des sectes,* p. 19.

69. *Ibid.,* pp. 18–19. See also Lorenz von Stein, *Geschichte der Sozialen Bewegung in Frankreich,* II, 353–55.

70. Corcelle, *Documents,* p. 20.

71. *Ibid.*

72. Armand Marrast, "La Presse révolutionnaire," *Paris révolutionnaire,* II, 106–8.

73. *Ibid.,* II, 109.

74. See *ibid.,* I, 120–26.

75. See J. T. Flottard, "Une Nuit d'etudiant sous la Restauration," *Paris révolutionnaire,* II, on the credo of the *Loge des amis de la vérité,* 454–57.

76. Chapter VII, above; and Chapter VIII.

77. See Claude H. Saint-Simon, *Oeuvres de Saint-Simon, et d'Enfantin* (Paris, 1865–78), XX, 118–19.

78. *Ibid.,* XX, 17–26, 50–59, 199–200, and XXI, 14–16.

79. Saint-Amand Bazard, "Considération sur l'histoire," *Le Producteur,* 4:405 (1826).

80. See Prosper Enfantin, "Considérations sur les progrès de l'économie politique, dans ses rapports avec l'organisation sociale," *ibid.,* pp. 373ff.

81. Iggers, *Doctrine of Saint-Simon,* Second Session, p. 28.

82. Saint-Amand Bazard, "De l'esprit critique," *Le Producteur,* 3:117–19 (1826). Iggers, *Doctrine of Saint-Simon,* Second Session; Third Session, pp. 51–56; Fourth Session, pp. 58–70; Fifth Session; Seventh Session, pp. 95–98.

83. Iggers, *Doctrine of Saint-Simon,* First Session, p. 5; see also Saint-Simon, *Opinions littéraires, philosophiques et industrielles* (Paris, 1825).

84. See also Arthur E. Bestor, Jr., "The Evolution of the Socialist Vocabulary," *Journal of the History of Ideas,* 9:259–302 (1948). The term individualism was used first in *Le Producteur,* 4:241 (1826). It appears again in *Doctrine de Saint-Simon,* ed. Bouglé et Halévy, Twelfth Session, pp. 274 and 381, and in "Lettre" of the Sixteenth Session, Iggers, *Doctrine of Saint-Simon,* p. 464; see also *ibid.,* Seventh Session, "Constitution de la Propriété," pp. 262–63. See also Gabriel Deville, "Origine des mots 'socialisme' et 'Socialist' et de certains autres," *La Révolution Française; revue d'histoire moderne et contemporaine,* 54:385–401 (1908); also Richard Koebner, "Zur Begriffbildung der Kulturgeschichte," *Historische Zeitschrift,* 149:261–62 (1934). Heinrich Dietzel, "Individualism," *Handwörterbuch der Staatswissenschaften* (Jena, 1923–28), V, 408–23.

85. See Iggers, *Doctrine of Saint-Simon,* First Session, for a summary of the contemporary state of anarchy. See also Sixth Session, "The Successive Transformation of Man's Exploitation by Man and of the Rights of Property," *ibid.,* pp. 8off.

86. *Ibid.*, Twelfth Session, p. 178.

87. *Ibid.*, p. 179; also "Sad deities of the doctrine of individualism, two creatures of reason—conscience and public opinion. . . ," *ibid.*, p. 182.

88. *Ibid.*, Eighth Session, "Modern Theories of Property," pp. 113ff, and Twelfth Session, "Legislation," pp. 178–82.

89. This is already clearly expressed by Saint-Simon. See his *Oeuvres de Saint-Simon et d'Enfantin*, XXI, 16, 83. See also Saint-Amand Bazard, "De l'esprit critique," *Le Producteur*, 3:111 (May 1826).

90. *Ibid.*, pp. 117–18.

91. Bazard, "De l'esprit critique," *ibid.*, p. 113.

92. *Ibid.*, pp. 118–19.

93. *Organisateur*, Sept. 5, 1829, as quoted in Iggers, *Doctrine of Saint-Simon*, pp. xxxiiiff.

94. On the origin of the term "socialism" see Carl Grünberg, "Der Ursprung der Worte 'Sozialismus' und 'Sozialist,' " *Archiv für die Geschichte des Sozialismus und der Arbeiterbewegung*, II (1912), 372ff. See also Deville, "Origine des Mots"; also Charles Gide and Charles Rist, *Histoire des doctrines economiques depuis les physiocrats jusqu'à nos jours* (Paris, 1922), p. 308, n. 1, and Robert Flint, *Socialism* (London, 1895), pp. 12ff, n. 1.

95. See P. M. Laurent, "Les Monarchiens et les doctrinaires," *Revue encyclopédique*, 52:586 (October 1831). See also P. Leroux, "De la philosophie et du Christianisme," *ibid.*, 55:281–340 (1832).

96. Sainte-Beuve started to discuss and propagate the Saint-Simonian teaching for the first time in August 1830. See his "J. Fievée," in *Premiers Lundis*, I, 358, and "Deux Révolutions," *ibid.*, pp. 365–67. In February 1831 appeared his "Doctrine de Saint-Simon," *ibid.*, II, 50–57, in which he discussed the concept of individualism.

97. See C. A. Sainte-Beuve on the influence of Saint-Simon on Théodore Jouffroy in "Jouffroy, cours de philosophie moderne," *ibid.*, II, 9–13. The Protestant *Le Semeur* discussed first the theory of Saint-Simonians in "La Doctrine de Saint-Simon," September 1831. Other Protestant periodicals such as the Swiss *Le Nouvelliste vaudois* discussed the doctrine at the same time. La Société de la Morale Chrétienne offered a prize "for the best refutation of the doctrine of Saint-Simon." See Preface of Alexandre Vinet's *Philosophie morale et sociale* in *Oeuvres* (Lausanne [1913]), I, xxviii.

98. It seems that Alexandre Vinet first introduced the term "socialism" in *Le Semeur* in November 1831. See his "Catholicisme et socialisme" as quoted by Carl Grünberg, "Der Ursprung der Worte 'Sozialismus,' " pp. 374–75.

99. See Pierre Leroux, "Cours d'economie politique," *Revue Encyclopédique*, 60:104–14 (December 1833). The motto of the *Revue Encyclopédique*, newly taken over by H. Carnot and P. Leroux, was "Liberté, Egalité, Association." See "De la tendance nouvelle des idées," *Revue encyclopédique*, vol. 53 (January–March 1832), *Prospectus*.

100. On the fate of the Saint-Simonian church, see Talmon, *Political Messianism*, pp. 100–24. For the dispersal of the Saint-Simonians and the

development of socialistic theories based on Saint-Simonism see Lorenz von Stein, *Geschichte der Sozialen Bewegung in Frankreich*, II, 213–31.

101. See Louis Blanc, *Histoire de dix ans, 1830–1840* (Brussels, 1846), II, 289.

102. Lamennais' *Le Livre du peuple* expressed this attitude in the words, *"Des saintes maximes d'égalité, de liberté, de fraternité immuablement établies, émanera l'organisation sociale."* Quoted by Lorenz von Stein, *Geschichte Sozialen Bewegung in Frankreich*, II, 430. These are the principles of most of the Fourierists as well as of Louis Blanc, Proudhon, Lamennais, Leroux, and, in spite of his communism, of the disciples of Étienne Cabet. See Lorenz von Stein, *ibid.*, pp. 439–53.

103. "De la société Saint Simonienne," *Revue encyclopédique*, 53:29 (January–March 1832).

104. Alexandre de Saint-Cheron, "Philosophie du droit," *Revue encyclopédique*, 52:600 (October 1831).

105. See H. Joncières, "Feuilles d'automme," *Globe* (Feb. 13, 1832), as quoted by Carl Grünberg, "Der Ursprung der Worte 'Sozialismus,' " p. 375.

106. See Pierre Leroux, "De la philosophie et du Christianisme," *Revue encyclopédique*, 55:299–301 (1832).

107. *Ibid.*, p. 303.

108. *Ibid.*, p. 304.

109. *Ibid.*, pp. 308–19.

110. "Cours d'economie politique," *Revue encyclopédique*, 60:104 (1833).

111. *Ibid.*, p. 106.

112. *Ibid.*, pp. 106–8.

113. *Ibid.*, pp. 110–11.

114. On the significance of Fourier and his influence on Saint-Simonism see Lorenz von Stein, *Geschichte der Sozialen Bewegung in Frankreich*, II, 209–10, 228. On the influence of Victor Considérant on Louis Blanc, see *ibid.*, II, 352; also "Social Destiny of Man" in *United States Magazine and Democratic Review*, 8:431ff (November 1840).

115. Robert Owen adopted the term individualism in contrast to socialism in his *Development of the Principles and Plans on which to Establish Self-supporting Home Colonies* (London, 1841), p. 31. See also his *Moral World* (1845) where he says: "To effect these changes there must be not only a new organization of society, on the principle of *attractive* union, instead of *repulsive individualism*. . . ," quoted in "Review, Historical and Critical," *Hunt's Merchants' Magazine*, 44:292ff (1861).

Chapter XI: Social Criticism in America

1. Pierre Leroux's statement in this connection has generally been misunderstood. See Charles Gide and Charles Rist, *A History of Economic Doctrines from the Time of the Physiocrats to the Present Day* (Boston, New York, 1915), p. 263, n. 3; also Robert Flint, *Socialism* (London, 1895), pp. 12ff.

2. See Chapter IX, secs. 1–4, above. See also Carl Brinkmann, *Versuch*

einer Gesellschaftswissenschaft (Munich, 1919). The revolution produced
by the sociological mode of Saint-Simonian thought is strikingly confirmed in
the work of Lorenz von Stein, whose *Geschichte der Sozialen Bewegung in
Frankreich* (Munich, 1921), apart from Comte's work, is among the most
impressive sociological works of the first half of the nineteenth century. Lorenz
von Stein wrote in the preface to the above-named work, whose first part
carries the title "The Concept of Society and the Social History of the French
Revolution to the Year 1830," the following words: "The introduction of the
work, the theory of society, will prove that the constitutions as well as the
administration of the states are subject to the elements and movements of
the social order . . . this is the real character, the spiritual (*geistige*) phase
of our time that it arrived at the conscious realization of the existence of the
social order and that it begins to recognize the dominion of this order over
the state and the law." *Ibid.*, I, 3, and the "Introduction" on the concept of
society, *ibid.*, pp. 11–104.

3. See Albert Brisbane, *Social Destiny of Man; or, Association and Reorganization of Industry* (Philadelphia, 1840), p. 201. The first Fourierist
publication in the United States appeared in New York in 1838. See *Socialism
and American Life,* ed. Donald D. Egbert and Stow Persons (Princeton,
1952), II, 134. On the role of Albert Brisbane in the propagation of
Fourierism see Arthur E. Bestor, Jr., "Albert Brisbane—Propagandist for
Socialism in the 1840's," *New York History,* 45:128ff (1947).

4. This analysis was based on Prosper Considérant, *Destinée sociale*
(Paris, 1834–44). On the importance of Victor Considérant see Lorenz von
Stein, *Geschichte der Sozialen Bewegung in Frankreich,* II, 256–72.

5. Brisbane, *Social Destiny of Man,* p. 280.

6. *Ibid.,* p. 281.

7. See "Table of the Movement of Civilization," *ibid.*, pp. 284, 315–30.
The analysis and prognosis of the economic development of competitive
capitalism anticipates the whole Marxist theory. Its relevance to the depression of 1837 was obvious.

8. "Social Destiny of Man," U.S. *Magazine and Democratic Review,*
8:431ff (November 1840).

9. *Ibid.,* p. 431; see editor's note.

10. *Ibid.,* p. 449.

11. *Ibid.,* p. 448.

12. Albert Brisbane, "The American Associationists," U.S. *Magazine and
Democratic Review,* 18:145–46 (February 1846).

13. The doctrines of the English school of political economy were criticized as a theory of economic individualism. See "Social Destiny of Man,"
U.S. *Magazine and Democratic Review,* 8:448–49 (November 1840). See
also William H. Channing, "Call of the Present," in *The Present,* 1:37ff
(Oct. 15, 1843). Also, William Elder, *The Enchanted Beauty, and other
Tales, Essays, and Sketches* (New York, 1855): "Free industrial competition
is, in principle, a system of masked fratricide. . . That liberty which dissolves
society into separate individualism, and turns everybody into the mêlée of

a deadly antagonism is, in effect, the political system of the savage state mixed with the social and industrial economy of civilization" (*ibid.*, p. 305). The essay was written in the 1840's under the influence of Fourierism. See Luther L. Bernard and Jessie Bernard, *Origins of American Sociology* (New York [1943]), pp. 443–44.

14. Quoted from John T. Codman, *Brook Farm; Historic and Personal Memoirs* (Boston, 1894), pp. 11–12. The statement of Codman that Ripley was not acquainted with Fourierist thought is doubtful.

15. On the immediate success of Brisbane's book see Frederick E. Haynes, *Social Politics in the United States* (Boston, 1924), pp. 31–32; Bestor, "Albert Brisbane," *New York History*, 45:130, 145–150 (1947). On the spread of Fourierism in America see John R. Commons *et al.*, *History of Labor in the United States* (New York, 1918), I, 498–506, 547ff. For a general survey, see *Socialism and American Life*, ed. Egbert and Persons, II, 132–37; see also John H. Noyes, *History of American Socialism* (Philadelphia, 1870), pp. 233–50. See Codman, *Brook Farm*, chaps. i, ii, iv, vi, on the connection between Fourierists and the New England intellectuals. See also Lindsay Swift, *Brook Farm; Its Members, Scholars, and Visitors* (New York, 1900). See also Arthur M. Schlesinger, Jr., *The Age of Jackson* (Boston, 1946), pp. 361–68.

16. Brisbane, *Social Destiny of Man*, chaps. viii–x.

17. Albert Brisbane had traveled extensively in Europe and the Near East, studied in Germany and France, disseminated Saint-Simonian thought in Germany, and then studied for two years (1832–1834) with Fourier. See Redelia Brisbane, *Albert Brisbane* (Boston, 1893), and Eliza M. Butler, *The Saint-Simonian Religion in Germany: A Study of the Young German Movement* (Cambridge, 1926), on Brisbane in Germany; also Bestor, "Brisbane," *New York History*, 45:132 (1947).

18. "Address to the Workingmen of Charlestown, Mass.," *Boston Quarterly Review*, 4:117 (Boston, 1841). See also "The Laboring Classes," *ibid.*, 3:358–95, 420–510 (1840), in which he proposed to abolish the right to transfer property by inheritance. In this article he states: "Universal suffrage is little better than a mockery, where the voters are not socially equal" (*ibid.*, 474). The proposal to abolish hereditary property was initiated by the Saint-Simonians. The proposals, taken to be those of radical democracy, and coming in the election year of 1840, caused a tremendous sensation and were said to have contributed to the victory of the Whigs. See Arthur M. Schlesinger, Jr., *Orestes A. Brownson: A Pilgrim's Progress* (Boston, 1939), pp. 89–111, and Theodore Maynard, *Orestes Brownson, Yankee, Radical, Catholic* (New York, 1943), p. 92.

19. "The Times—Past, Present, and Future," *Boston Quarterly Review*, 6:64 (January 1841).

20. Founded in 1838, the *Boston Quarterly Review* counted among its contributors George Bancroft, George Ripley, Bronson Alcott, Margaret Fuller, Theodore Parker, Alexander H. Everett, William H. Channing, John S. Dwight, and Albert Brisbane; see Schlesinger, *Orestes A. Brownson*, p. 45.

21. *Ibid.*, p. 48; Clarence L. F. Gohdes, *The Periodicals of American Transcendentalism* (Durham, 1931), chap. iii, "Orestes A. Brownson and the *Boston Quarterly Review*."

22. It is interesting in this context to note that Brownson had already asserted in his *New Views of Christianity, Society and Church* (Boston, 1836) that Protestantism represented the "rebellion . . . of the material order against the spiritual. . ." (*ibid.*, p. 27), that it was the antithesis of the pure spirituality of early Christianity and the corrupted materialism of the Renaissance Church, and that it had fulfilled its historic function with the French Revolution. "A new Church" embracing all humanity therefore had to be built up embodying both spiritual and material values (*ibid.*, pp. 31, 47ff, 57). See also "Democracy and Reform," *Boston Quarterly Review*, 2:478–577 (October 1839); "Address to the Workingmen. . . ," *ibid.*, 4:112ff (January 1841); also, "The Times—Past, Present, and Future," *ibid.*, pp. 41ff.

23. "In forming my own system of philosophy, I have also been greatly assisted by the Saint-Simonian school, in which I reckon . . . Bazard and Enfantin, Leroux, Lerminier, De La Mennais." *Brownson's Quarterly Review*, 1:7 (1844).

24. See *ibid.*: "Leroux is, indisputably, a great man; his, so far as I am able to judge, is the greatest name in contemporary French literature." See also "Liberalism and Socialism," *ibid.*, 3[3rd ser.]:184 (April 1855): "They [Leroux's writings] revolutionized our own mind . . . and by the grace of God became the occasion of our conversion to Catholicity."

25. *Le Livre du peuple*, by Lamennais, had been translated by his friend Nathaniel Greene in 1839 as *The People's Own Book* (Boston, 1839). Lamennais' *Modern Slavery* was printed in London in 1840.

26. "The Laboring Classes," *Boston Quarterly Review*, 3:370 (July 1840).

27. See "White Slavery," *U.S. Magazine and Democratic Review*, 11:260–72 (September 1842), and "The Present State of Society," *ibid.*, 13:27 (July 1843).

28. See Calhoun's speech in the Senate in 1837 in the debate on the "Independent Treasury Plan" of Van Buren as quoted by Schlesinger in *The Age of Jackson*.

29. See Chapter XIV, pp. 300ff, above.

30. "Democracy and Reform," *Boston Quarterly Review*, 2:505–6 (October 1839).

31. See Brownson's quotations from Pierre Leroux's *L'Humanité* in "Community System," *U.S. Magazine and Democratic Review*, 12:137 (February 1842).

32. *Ibid.*, p. 134.

33. *Ibid.*, pp. 135–38. See also "Social Evils and Their Remedy," *Boston Quarterly Review*, 4:271 (July 1841).

34. "Social Evils and Their Remedy," p. 271.

35. "Brook Farm," *U.S. Magazine and Democratic Review*, 11:482 (November 1842).

36. *Ibid.*, pp. 482–84.

37. *Ibid.*, pp. 484–86.

38. *Ibid.*, p. 486.

39. *Ibid.*

40. *Ibid.*, p. 487. For another analysis of communism and individualism see "The Community System," *U.S. Magazine and Democratic Review,* 12:129–44 (February 1843).

41. See "Origins and Ground of Government," *U.S. Magazine and Democratic Review,* 13:133, 136–42 (August 1843). See also Part II, *ibid.* (September 1843), p. 254.

42. In "The Present State of Society," *U. S. Magazine and Democratic Review,* 13:17ff (July 1843), O. A. Brownson reviews Carlyle's *Past and Present.*

43. O. A. Brownson, "Origin and Ground of Government," *ibid.* (October 1843), p. 359.

44. See "Present State of Society," *ibid.*, p. 34, where Brownson mentions with approval Friedrich von Schlegel's discourses on history. See also "Remarks on Universal History," in which he deals with the French philosophers of history, Michelet, Jouffroy, Cousin, *ibid.*, 12:473–74 (May 1843).

45. On the influence of Brownson on his American contemporaries, see also Sister Mary R. G. Whalen, *Some Aspects of the Influence of Orestes A. Brownson on His Contemporaries* (Indiana, 1933), pp. 22ff, 38ff.

46. Isaac Hecker, editor of the *Catholic World,* and Sophie Ripley became Catholics through his influence. Outside the United States *Brownson's Quarterly Review* was highly appreciated. Cardinal Newman offered him a lectureship at the newly established Catholic University of Ireland. See Schlesinger, *O. A. Brownson,* pp. 154, 216.

47. See also Lord Acton's letter to Brownson acknowledging the influence the latter exercised on him. Quoted in Schlesinger's *O. A. Brownson,* p. 217. See also the excellent short description of Brownson in Van Wyck Brooks, *The Flowering of New England 1815–1865* (Cleveland, 1946), pp. 246–49.

48. On William H. Channing see Gohdes, *The Periodicals of American Transcendentalism,* chaps. iv, vi.

49. George W. Cooke, *Ralph Waldo Emerson* (Boston, 1881), pp. 77, 204–5.

50. See Octavius B. Frothingham, *Memoir of William Ellery Channing* (Boston, 1886), p. 203.

51. He printed lengthy extracts from Pierre Leroux's *L'Humanité* and from Victor Considérant's writings, a series of articles by Parke Godwin, "Constructive and Pacific Democracy," which was a précis of Considérant's writings on the socio-economic development of mankind. See *The Present,* 1:181–96 (Dec. 15, 1843).

52. *Ibid.* (Oct. 15, 1843), p. 43.

53. *The Spirit of the Age,* ed. William H. Channing, 1:8–10 (July 7, 1849).

54. "Cheering Signs," *The Present,* 1:212–15 (December 1843).

55. "The Judgment of Christendom," *The Spirit of the Age*, 1:265 (Oct. 27, 1849).

56. See Chapter X, sec. 4, above.

57. The term *"souverainété individuelle"* appeared in the Introduction to the *Doctrine de Saint-Simon, exposition, premier année, 1828–1829* (Paris, 1831), p. 12.

58. "The Judgment of Christendom," *The Spirit of the Age*, p. 264.

59. Octavius B. Frothingham, *Transcendentalism in New England: A History* (New York, 1876), p. 157.

60. "Catholicism," *Boston Quarterly Review*, 4:332 (July 1841).

CHAPTER XII: FOUNDATIONS OF THE AMERICAN IDEAL OF INDIVIDUALISM

1. See Chapter VII above.

2. On John Adams and the French Revolution see Chapter VII, sec. 4, above. A typical version of this view may be found in Robert Baird's *Religion in America* (New York, 1844), chap. ix: "How a correct knowledge of the American People, the Nature of their Government and of their national character may be best attained," pp. 29–31. Neither the word "democracy" nor the phenomenon of democracy is mentioned in the entire book.

3. See Gustav A. Koch, *Republican Religion; the American Revolution and the Cult of Reason* (New York, [1933]), chap. viii.

4. See John W. Thornton, ed., *The Pulpit and the American Revolution, or the Political Sermons of the Period of 1776* (Boston [1876]).

5. See Edward F. Humphrey, *Nationalism and Religion in America, 1774–1789* (Boston, 1924); and Alice M. Baldwin, *The New England Clergy and the American Revolution* (Durham, N.C., 1928). On the situation of the Anglican Church, William W. Sweet, *Religion in the Development of American Culture* (New York, 1952), pp. 14–24.

6. Yet for the various religious limitations of the rights of citizenship see Humphrey, *Nationalism and Religion in America*, pp. 483–501.

7. See *Federal and State Constitutions*, ed. Francis N. Thorpe (Washington, 1909), III, 1889–90.

8. Baird, *Religion in America*, p. 225.

9. On the prevalence of deism and its alliance with political radicalism, see Koch, *Republican Religion*, "The Triumph of Fidelity." See also Leonard W. Bacon, *A History of American Christianity* (New York, 1897), pp. 219–30. See also Howard M. Jones, *America and French Culture, 1750–1848* (Chapel Hill, 1927), pp. 389–99.

10. See Ezra Stiles, "The United States Elevated to Glory and Honor," in Thornton, *The Pulpit and the American Revolution*, pp. 470–98.

11. Timothy Dwight, "A Discourse of Some Events of the Last Century," quoted in Koch, *Republican Religion*, pp. 246–47.

12. Uzal Ogden, "Antidote to Deism," as quoted in *ibid.*, p. 249.

13. *Ibid.*, pp. 251–59.

14. *Ibid.*, p. 225.

15. See Sidney E. Ahlstrom, "Theology in America: A Historical Survey," in James W. Smith and A. Leland Jamison, eds., *Religion in American Life* (Princeton, 1961), I, 243–45.

16. *Ibid.*, pp. 245–51. See also Arthur A. Ekirch, *The Idea of Progress in America, 1815–1860* (New York, 1944), chap. iv.

17. Yet even Francis Hutcheson, the disciple of Shaftesbury, was suspected of heterodoxy. See Sidney E. Ahlstrom, "The Scottish Philosophy and American Theology," *Church History*, 29:260 (September 1955).

18. *Ibid.*, pp. 267–68.

19. For the Scottish concept of man and society in the second half of the eighteenth century, see Chapter VI, sec. 4, above.

20. On the question of the evolution of the economic and social morality of Calvinism, see Richard H. Tawney, *Religion and the Rise of Capitalism; A Historical Study* (New York, 1952); his discussion of the thesis of Max Weber; and also his *Acquisitive Society* (New York [1947]), pp. 15–16.

21. Cliffe Leslie, "Political Economy in the United States," *Fortnightly Review*, 34:496–698 (October 1880).

22. Henry F. May, *Protestant Church and Industrial America* (New York [1949]), p. 12, n. 32; Joseph Dorfman, *The Economic Mind in American Civilization* (New York, 1946–59), II, 512; and *Thorstein Veblen and His America* (New York, 1934), chap. ii.

23. Dorfman, *Veblen*, pp. 22–23.

24. *Ibid.*, p. 21.

25. *Ibid.*, p. 21ff.

26. Francis Walker, "Recent Progress of Political Economy in the United States," *American Economic Association Publications*, 4:254 (1889).

27. Sidney Fine, "Laissez Faire and the General-Welfare State," unpub. diss. University of Michigan, 1948, pp. 72, 75–100.

28. Timothy Dwight, *Travels in New-England and New-York* (New Haven, 1821–1822), II, 462–63.

29. Sidney Fine, *Laissez Faire and the General-Welfare State*, pp. 16–17.

30. Quoted by Perry Miller in Preface to Philip Schaff, *America, A Sketch of Its Political, Social, and Religious Character*, ed. Perry Miller (Cambridge, Mass., 1961), p. 26.

31. See Michael Kraus, *The Writing of American History* (University of Oklahoma Press, 1953), pp. 81, 89.

32. Lyman Beecher, *A Plea for the West* (Cincinnati, 1835), pp. 8–10.

33. See *The Puritans*, ed. Perry Miller and Thomas H. Johnson (New York, [1938]), p. 4.

34. Beecher, *A Plea for the West*, pp. 11, 12.

35. *Ibid.*, pp. 12–13.

36. *Ibid.*, pp. 30–31, 39–40.

37. *Ibid.*, pp. 36–37.

38. Quoted by Josiah Strong, *Our Country* (New York [1885]), pp. 175–76.

39. Philip Schaff, *America*, pp. xii and 47.

40. *Ibid.*, pp. 47–48.

41. *Ibid.*, p. 51. For similar views see George P. Marsh, *The Goths in New England* (Middlebury, Vermont, 1843).

42. See "Epilogue," Chapter XV, below.

43. See Chapter IX, sec. 4, above.

44. See Ahlstrom, "Theology in America," pp. 267–71, and Perry Miller's Preface to Schaff's *America*, pp. xviii–xxv.

45. Schaff, *America*, pp. 94, 213–14.

46. *Ibid.*, p. 101.

47. *Ibid.*, p. 212.

48. *Ibid.*, p. 214.

49. *Ibid.*, pp. 37–38.

50. *Ibid.*, p. 102.

51. See Koch, *Republican Religion*, chap. vii. See also Joseph H. Allen and Richard Eddy, eds., *A History of the Unitarians and the Universalists in the United States* (New York, 1894), chap. viii.

52. Koch, *Republican Religion*, pp. 203–7.

53. Luther on Erasmus, as quoted by Philip Schaff, *History of the Christian Church* (New York, 1901), VI, 429, n. 1.

54. James Freeman, *Sermons and Charges*, quoted in Koch, *Republican Religion*, pp. 207–8.

55. See Ernst Troeltsch, "Renaissance and Reformation," *Aufsätze zur Geistesgeschichte und Religionssoziologie* (Tübingen, 1925), pp. 267ff.

56. See the definition of humanism given by F. L. S. Schiller in Hasting's *Encyclopedia of Religion and Ethics* (Edinburgh, 1908–15), VI, 830.

57. William Bentley, *A Sermon Preached at the Stone Chapel*, quoted by Koch, *Republican Religion*, p. 215.

58. See George W. Cooke, *Unitarianism in America; A History of Its Origin and Development* (Boston, 1902), pp. 156–59; Octavius B. Frothingham, *Boston Unitarianism, 1820–1850* (New York, 1890).

59. See Kraus, *The Writing of American History*, pp. 58–103, on the late eighteenth-century historical literature.

60. *Ibid.*, pp. 60–61.

61. John Adams, "Discourses on Davila," *Works* (Boston, 1850–56), pp. 494–95.

62. See Van Wyck Brooks, *The Flowering of New England, 1815–1865* (Cleveland, 1946), chap. vi; see also Kraus, *The Writing of American History*, pp. 93–100.

63. Quoted by Kraus, *ibid.*, p. 102.

64. *Ibid.*, p. 123.

65. G. W. Pierson, *Tocqueville and Beaumont in America* (New York, 1938), pp. 398–99.

66. *Ibid.*, p. 381.

67. *Ibid.*, pp. 377–78.

68. See Merle E. Curti, "Francis Lieber and Nationalism," *Huntington Library Quarterly*, 4:263–92 (April 1941); and Bernard E. Brown, *Ameri-*

can Conservatives: The Political Thoughts of Francis Lieber and John W. Burgess (New York, 1951).

69. See Chapter X, secs. 2 and 3, above.

70. See Russell Kirk in Preface to Friedrich von Gentz, *The French and American Revolutions Compared,* trans. John Quincy Adams (Chicago [1955]). On the quest for nationality in letters, see Howard M. Jones, *The Theory of American Literature* (Ithaca, 1948), chap. iii; Benjamin T. Spencer, *The Quest for Nationality; An American Literary Campaign* (Syracuse, 1957), pp. 90–101; Henry A. Pochmann, *German Culture in America, Philosophical and Literary Influences, 1600–1900* (Madison, 1957), pp. 50–57. See also Koch, *Republican Religion.*

71. The publication by Wells and Watt in 1813 seems to have escaped Pochmann's comprehensive survey.

72. See also Brooks, *The Flowering of New England* (1946), pp. 111ff. See also Frank L. Mott, *A History of American Magazines, 1791–1850* (New York, London, 1930), pp. 190–92.

73. Pochmann, *German Culture in America,* pp. 114–24.

74. *Ibid.,* pp. 131–32.

75. *Ibid.,* p. 132.

76. *Ibid.,* pp. 85–119.

77. Yet on the dominant influence of non-German historians see Harry H. Clark, "The Vogue of Macaulay in America," *Wisconsin Academy of Sciences, Arts and Letters,* 1941, and on Guizot, Kraus, *The Writing of American History,* p. 122.

78. Octavius B. Frothingham, *Transcendentalism in New England; A History* (Boston, 1903), pp. 109–110.

79. See David P. Edgell, *William Ellery Channing; An Intellectual Portrait* (Boston [1955]), pp. 63–69; William H. Channing, *The Life of William Ellery Channing* (Boston, 1890), p. 34. See also Merrell R. Davis, "Emerson's 'Reason' and the Scottish Philosophers," *New England Quarterly,* 17:209–228 (1944); and Pochmann, *German Culture in America,* p. 159.

80. See Richard Koebner, "Zur Begriffsbildung der Kulturgeschichte," *Historische Zeitschrift,* 149:274–78. See also Friedrich Meinecke, *Weltbürgertum und Nationalstaat* (Munich, 1917), chaps. iii, iv; Jacob L. Talmon, *Political Messianism, The Romantic Phase* (London, 1960), pp. 177–86; also Friedrich Meinecke, *Zur Theorie und Philosophie der Geschichte* (Stuttgart, 1959), "Möser, Herder, Goethe," pp. 244ff, and "Schiller," pp. 285ff.

81. See Wilhelm von Humboldt, *The Sphere and Duties of Government,* trans. Joseph Coulthard (London, 1854), pp. 17–18.

82. Nathan Rotenstreich, "Marx' Thesen über Feuerbach," *Archiv für Rechts-und Sozialphilosophie,* 39:338ff (1951); Theodor Zlocisti, *Moses Hess, der Vorkämpfer des Sozialismus und Zionismus* (Berlin, 1921); Auguste Cornu, *Moses Hess et la gauche hégélienne* (Berlin, 1934).

83. See Talmon, *Political Messianism,* pp. 183–84.

84. Heinrich Heine, *Prose Miscellanies from Heinrich Heine*, trans. S. L. Fleishman (Philadelphia, 1876), pp. 143–44, 152–53.

85. Pierson, *Tocqueville and Beaumont*, p. 422.

86. *Ibid.*, pp. 156–57.

87. Bernhard Fabian, *Alexis de Tocqueville's Amerikabild* (Heidelberg, 1957), pp. 42–61.

88. See Jefferson to Jared Sparks, Nov. 4, 1820, in Jefferson, *Writings*, ed. Andrew A. Lipscomb *et al.* (Washington, 1903), XV, 288; to Dr. Thomas Cooper, Nov. 2, 1822, *ibid.*, pp. 403–7; and to James Smith, Dec. 8, 1822, *ibid.*, pp. 408–410.

89. See Fabian, *Alexis de Tocqueville's Americabild*, p. 61, n. 16.

90. See the opposition of the conservatives to creation of a broad movement through the establishment of a Unitarian Association in January 1825 in Cooke, *Unitarianism in America*, pp. 130–33.

91. Frothingham, *Transcendentalism in New England*, p. 110. On the later relationship between Channing and the upper classes of Boston see Van Wyck Brooks, *The Flowering of New England*, pp. 106ff.

92. W. H. Channing, *Life of William Ellery Channing*, p. 427; William E. Channing, "Self-Denial," *Complete Works* (London, 1884), p. 260.

93. "The Essence of the Christian Religion," W. E. Channing, *Complete Works*, pp. 44–45.

94. Compare the Twenty-Eighth Report of the American Unitarian Association as quoted by Cooke, *Unitarianism in America*, p. 157, with Channing's "God Revealed in the Universe and in Humanity," W. E. Channing, *Complete Works*, p. 8.

95. Andrew Norton, "The Latest Form of Infidelity," quoted by Frothingham, *Transcendentalism in New England*, p. 124.

96. Cooke, *Unitarianism in America*, p. 157.

97. *Ibid.*, pp. 227–28.

98. See Pochmann, *German Culture in America*, pp. 85, 117, 219–21, and, on Coleridge, pp. 88ff.

99. "On the Elevation of the Laboring Classes," W. E. Channing, *Complete Works*, p. 90.

100. "Remarks on Association," *ibid.*, p. 144; see also "The Duty of the Free States," p. 607.

101. W. H. Channing, *The Life of William Ellery Channing*, p. 432. On the concept of individuality developed by Humboldt, Schleiermacher, Schelling and the Romantic circles, see Meinecke, *Zur Theorie und Philosophie der Geschichte*, pt. III.

102. "Remarks on National Literature," W. E. Channing, *Complete Works*, p. 140.

103. *Ibid.*, p. 135.

104. W. H. Channing, *The Life of William Ellery Channing*, pp. 346–48.

105. See Koch, *Republican Religion*, pp. 247ff. See Reinhold Niebuhr, *The Irony of American History* (New York, 1952), p. 69. Also Helmut R.

Niebuhr, *The Kingdom of God in America* (Chicago, 1937); *The Pulpit and the American Revolution*, ed. Thornton, pp. 311, 481; and Perry Miller, "From the Covenant to the Revival," in Smith and Jamison, *Religion in American Life*, I, 322–66. See also Edward M. Burns, *The American Idea of Mission; Concepts of National Purpose and Destiny* (New Brunswick, 1957).

106. Beecher, *A Plea for the West*, pp. 9–10.

107. James W. Smith, "Religion and Science in American Philosophy," in Smith and Jamison, *Religion in American Life*, I, 402–3.

108. Perry Miller, "From the Covenant to the Revival," in Smith and Jamison, *Religion in American Life*, I, 353, 350.

109. See Samuel Adams' letter to Thomas Paine, Nov. 30, 1802: "When I heard you had turned your mind to a defence of infidelity, I felt myself much astonished and more grieved, that you had attempted a measure so injurious to the feelings and so repugnant to the true interest . . . of the citizens of the United States." Samuel Adams, *Writings* (New York, 1904–08), IV, 412. On the fate of Paine after his return to America see Koch, *Republican Religion*, pp. 130–46. For the decline of deism and the "Triumph of Fidelity" see *ibid.*, chap. viii.

110. See John M. Mecklin, *The Story of American Dissent* (New York [1934]), pp. 312–17, 320–35; for a survey of the political aspect of revival movements, see Russel B. Nye, *The Cultural Life of the New Nation, 1776–1830* (New York [1960]), pp. 216–21.

111. Quoted by Helmut R. Niebuhr, *The Social Sources of Denominationalism* (Hamden [1954]). For the class character of the revivalist movement see also William W. Sweet, *Revivalism in America; Its Origin, Growth and Decline* (New York, 1944), pp. 38–43, 45.

112. Sweet, *Religion in the Development of American Culture*, p. 97.

113. See A. Leland Jamison, "Religions on the Christian Perimeter," in Smith and Jamison, *Religion in American Life*, I, 194.

114. Sweet, *Revivalism in America*, p. 43. See Wesley M. Gewehr, *The Great Awakening in Virginia, 1740–1790* (Durham, 1930), chap. viii.

115. See A. L. Jamison, "Religions on the Christian Perimeter," in *Religion in American Life*, p. 195; Sidney E. Ahlstrom, "Theology in America," pp. 256–60; William W. Sweet, *The American Churches, An Interpretation* (New York [1948]), chap. vii, and *Revivalism in America*, chap. vi.

116. See Miller, "From the Covenant to the Revival," Smith and Jamison, *Religion in American Life*, I, 350.

117. Helmut R. Niebuhr, "The Protestant Movement and Democracy in the United States," Smith and Jamison, *Religion in American Life*, I, 50.

118. Donald D. Egbert and Stow Persons, eds., *Socialism and American Life* (Princeton, 1951), I, 128ff; Jamison, "Religions on the Christian Perimeter," in Smith and Jamison, *Religion in American Life*, I, 162ff; Timothy L. Smith, *Revivalism and Social Reform in Mid-Nineteenth Century America* (New York [1957]). See also Carl R. Fish, *The Rise of the Common Man* (New York, 1927), chap. xii.

119. See Alfred W. Griswold, *Farming and Democracy* (New York,

1948), and Chester E. Eisinger, "The Influence of Natural Rights and Physiocratic Doctrines on American Agrarian Thought during the Revolutionary Period," *Agricultural History*, 21:13–23 (1947).

120. See Richard Hofstadter, *The Age of Reform—From Bryan to F.D.R.* (New York, 1955), esp. Introduction; H. R. Niebuhr, *The Social Sources of Denominationalism*, pp. 142–45; Sweet, *American Churches*, pp. 68ff, and *Revivalism in America*, p. xii. Most of these interpretations can be traced back to the publication of Frederick Jackson Turner's "The Significance of the Frontier in American History," in 1893. The explanation of the frontier in terms of "individualism" can be traced back to Edwin L. Godkin's "Aristocratic Opinions of Democracy," in *Problems of Modern Democracy* (New York, 1896) which was written in 1865.

121. Perry Miller, *Errand into the Wilderness* (Cambridge, Mass., 1956), pp. 98–99.

122. John W. Chadwick, *William Ellery Channing, Minister of Religion* (Boston, 1903), p. 246.

123. Summary of Channing's "Remarks on National Literature," in Merle E. Curti, *The Growth of American Thought* (New York and London [1943]), pp. 249–5. See the somewhat one-sided but brilliant analysis of Channing by Vernon L. Parrington, *Main Currents in American Thought* (New York [1927]), vol. II; also Van Wyck Brooks, *The Flowering of New England*, pp. 104–10.

124. Merle E. Curti, *The Root of American Loyalty* (New York, 1946), p. 63.

125. "Imitableness of Christ's Character," W. E. Channing, *Complete Works*, p. 245.

126. "The Present Age," *ibid.*, pp. 157ff.

127. "On National Literature," *ibid.*, p. 140.

128. George Bancroft, *Memorial Address on the Life and Character of Abraham Lincoln* (Washington, 1866), pp. 4–61. See also his oration delivered before the Adelphi Society of Williamstown College, 1875, "The Office of the People in Art, Government, and Religion," in George Bancroft, *Literary and Historical Miscellanies* (New York, 1855), pp. 408–35.

129. "America in 1846. The Past—The Future." *U. S. Magazine and Democratic Review*, 18:61 (January 1846); "Bancroft's History," *Boston Quarterly Review*, 4:512–18 (October 1841).

130. See George Bancroft, *History of the United States* (Boston, 1874), II, 326–30.

131. Henry James, *Lectures and Miscellanies* (New York, 1852). Lecture I, "Democracy and Its Issues," pp. 4, 8, 10–11.

132. "Progress of Society," *U. S. Magazine and Democratic Review*, 7:87 (July 1840).

133. See "Social Tendencies," *The Dial*, 4:76 (July 1843).

134. See Cooke, *Unitarianism in America*, chap. xvi, "Unitarians and Reforms"; Frothingham, *Transcendentalism in New England*, chap. vii, "Practical Tendencies"; Brooks, *The Flowering of New England*, chaps. xiv,

xv, xix, and xxi. See also Parrington, *Main Currents*, II, pp. 328–38, 386–425.

135. *Socialism and American Life*, ed. Stow and Persons, I, 125ff.

136. From John H. Noyes to W. L. Garrison, March 22, 1837, in Wendell P. Garrison, *William Lloyd Garrison, 1805–1879: The Story of His Life* (New York, 1885–1889), II, 145, 147, 148.

137. *Ibid.*, III, 412.

138. *Ibid.*, II, 151.

139. Quoted by Parrington, *Main Currents*, II, 410.

140. "On the Annexation of Texas to the United States," W. E. Channing, *Complete Works*, p. 542.

141. See C. N. Curtis, "American Opinion of the French Nineteenth-Century Revolutions," *American Historical Review*, 29:249–70 (January 1924). The author describes the apprehensions of the commercial classes as expressed in the Whig papers of the North (*ibid.*, pp. 255–62), and their coalition with the southern Democrats who were infuriated by the emancipation decrees of the French Republic.

142. See "Socialists, Communists and Red Republicans," *The American Review*, 10:401–18 (October 1849); J. M. Mackie, "Three Stages of the French Revolution," *ibid.*, 9:358–66 (April 1849); J. A. McMaster, "Societary Theories," *ibid.*, 7:632–46 (June 1848); Francis Bowen, "Population and Property," *North American Review*, 67:370–419 (October 1848); "The True Progress of Society," *Biblical Repertory and Princeton Review*, 24:16–38 (January 1852); Francis Bowen, "French Ideas of Democracy and Community of Goods," *North American Review*, 69:277–325 (October 1849); "Socialism," *The American Church Review*, 2:491–564 (January 1850); "Social Inequalities," *The Christian Examiner and Religious Miscellany*, 39:63–81 (July 1845).

143. "True Progress of Society," *Biblical Repertory and Princeton Review*, 24:19 (January 1852).

144. *Ibid.*, p. 24.

145. "Three Stages in the French Revolution," *The American Review*, 10:361 (1849).

146. See, for a similar argument, Chapter IX, sec. 4, above.

147. See letter to J. C. L. Simonde de Sismondi, June 16, 1831, in Channing, *William Ellery Channing*, p. 430; to Joseph Tuckerman, April 6, 1831, *ibid.*, pp. 510–11; and to Reverend Adin Ballou, Feb. 27, 1841, *ibid.*, pp. 511–13; see also *ibid.*, pp. 514–15.

148. "On the Elevation of the Laboring Classes," *U. S. Magazine and Democratic Review*, 18:60 (January 1846).

149. Channing, *William Ellery Channing*, p. 511.

150. To Joseph Tuckerman, April 1831, *ibid.*, pp. 510–11. It is interesting to note that Channing himself, as a young man, advocated Christian communism in order to destroy selfishness. See Frothingham, *Transcendentalism in New England*, pp. 63–66.

151. For a characteristic expression of these views, see Henry James, *The*

Social Significance of Our Institutions: An Oration Delivered by Request of the Citizens of Newport, R. I., July 4th, 1861 (Boston, 1861).

CHAPTER XIII. UTOPIAN INDIVIDUALISM: THEORY AND PRACTICE

1. Ralph W. Emerson, *Journals* (Boston, 1912), VII, 322–23.

2. *Ibid.*, V, 473–74.

3. *Ibid.*, VII, 134–35.

4. See the analysis of influences by Henry A. Pochmann, *German Culture in America* (Madison, 1957), pp. 193–203; also John S. Harrison, *The Teachers of Emerson* (New York, 1910), chap. i, and George W. Cooke, *Ralph Waldo Emerson: His Life, Writings and Philosophy* (Boston, 1881).

5. Emerson, *Journals*, II, 166, 209–11, 278–79; Pochmann, *German Culture in America*, p. 169.

6. Emerson, *Journals*, III, 200–1.

7. *Ibid.*, p. 201.

8. Cooke, *Ralph Waldo Emerson*, p. 269.

9. "Nature," Ralph Waldo Emerson, *The Complete Writings* (New York, 1929), I, 13. See also "The Nominalist and Realist," *ibid.*, I, 311ff. See also Cooke, *Ralph Waldo Emerson*, chap. xix.

10. "Nature," Emerson, *Complete Writings*, I, 20.

11. See Emerson, *Journals*, IV, 78, 247–49.

12. See his critique of Swedenborg in "Swedenborg, or the Mystic," in Emerson, *Complete Writings*, I, 366–67; also "Culture," *ibid.*, pp. 559ff.

13. "The Fortune of the Republic," *ibid.*, II, 1192.

14. "The Times," *ibid.*, I, 86.

15. "Self-Reliance," *ibid.*, p. 146.

16. "An Address," *ibid.*, p. 45.

17. "Self-Reliance," *ibid.*, p. 139.

18. "Character," *ibid.*, p. 268.

19. See "Self-Reliance," *ibid.*, p. 143. "Every true man is a cause, a country and an age. . . An institution is the lengthened shadow of one man. . ." See also George E. Woodbury, *Ralph Waldo Emerson* (New York, 1907), pp. 123ff.

20. "Character," Emerson, *Complete Writings*, I, 272–73.

21. "Self-Reliance," *ibid.*, p. 148.

22. Emerson, *Journals*, III, 369–70.

23. *Ibid.*, p. 390.

24. "Man the Reformer," Emerson, *Complete Writings*, I, 76–77.

25. *Ibid.*, p. 77; "The Times," *ibid.*, pp. 86–87. See also "The Times," p. 86, where he states: "I think that the soul of reform; the conviction that . . . not even government, are needed,—but in lieu of them all, reliance on the sentiment of man, which will work best the more it is trusted"; also, "New England Reformers," *ibid.*, I, 316.

26. "The Times," *ibid.*, pp. 86–87; "New England Reformers," *ibid.*, p. 316.

see 281   — link to Garrison?

27. "New England Reformers," *ibid.*, pp. 317–18.

28. See sec. 2 of this chapter.

29. "The Young American," Emerson, *Complete Writings*, I, 113.

30. "The Fortune of the Republic," *ibid.*, II, 1191; "The Young American," *ibid.*, I, 120; "American Civilization," *ibid.*, II, 1209.

31. "The Fortune of the Republic," *ibid.*, II, 1186.

32. "The Young American," *ibid.*, I, 120.

33. "Politics," *ibid.*, pp. 301ff.

34. *Ibid.*

35. *Ibid.*, p. 302.

36. *Ibid.*

37. *Ibid.*

38. See Wendell P. Garrison, *William Lloyd Garrison, 1805–1879; The Story of His Life* (New York, 1885–89), II, 150, 152.

39. "Politics," Emerson, *Complete Writings*, I, 302.

40. "War," *ibid.*, II, 1146.

41. *Ibid.*, p. 1140.

42. See the whole essay on "War," "Nature," *ibid.*, I, 20ff; "The Young American," I, 113ff; "Politics," I, 299ff; also "Wealth," I, 551ff.

43. "Politics," *ibid.*, I, 299.

44. "Wealth," *ibid.*, p. 551; on the merits of laissez-faire, see also "Politics," I, 300, "New England Reformers," I, 314, and "Speech at Manchester," I, 51ff, in "English Traits" and also "The Fortune of the Republic," I, 1194.

45. "The Young American," *ibid.*, I, 114–15.

46. *Ibid.*, p. 116.

47. *Ibid.*

48. *Ibid.*, p. 118. See also "Politics," I, 304, "Character," II, 982–83, and "Worship," I, 585.

49. "Catholicism," *Boston Quarterly Review*, 4:332 (1841).

50. See for instance: "Politics," Emerson, *Complete Writings*, I, 304: "The tendencies of the times favor the idea of self-government, and leave the individual . . . to the rewards and penalties of his own constitution; which work with more energy than we believe whilst we depend on artificial restraints. . . It separates the individual from all party, and unites him at the same time to the race. It promises a recognition of higher rights than those of personal freedom, or the security of property. . . The power of love, as the basis of a State, has never been tried." See also "Character," *ibid.*, II, 982: "In the present tendency of our society, in the new importance of the individual . . . society is threatened with actual granulation, religious as well as political . . . but this rude stripping him of all support drives him inward, and he finds himself . . . face to face with the majestic Presence, reads the original of the Ten Commandments; the original of Gospels and Epistles. . ." See also "Worship," *ibid.*, I, 585: "The energetic action of the times develops individualism, . . . I esteem this a step in the right direction."

51. See "The Young American," *ibid.*, I, 119ff.

52. "The Fortune of the Republic," *ibid.*, II, 1186. While "The Fortune"

was not written until 1878 and the essays "The F
and "American Civilization" in 1863, they only r
"The Young American" and *The Dial.*

53. "The Fortune of the Republic," *ibid.*, II, 1

54. *Ibid.*, p. 1194.

55. John Stuart Mill, *Autobiography* (Oxford

56: William Bailie, *Josiah Warren, The Fi
Sociological Study* (Boston, 1906), p. xxii.

57. Peter A. Kropotkin, "Anarchism," *Encyclo
1929), ·I, 876ff.

58. See, apart from William Bailie's work, James J. Martin, *Men Against
the State; the Expositors of Individualist Anarchism in America, 1827–1908*
(De Kalb, Ill., 1953), pp. 15ff.

59. Bailie, *Josiah Warren*, p. 6.

60. *Periodical Letter,* II (July 1856), pp. 55–56, quoted by Martin, *Men
Against the State*, p. 15.

61. Josiah Warren, *Equitable Commerce; a New Development of Principles for the Harmonious Adjustment and Regulation of the Pecuniary,
Intellectual ˙and Moral Intercourse of Mankind, Proposed as Elements of
New Society* (Utopia, Ohio, 1849), p. 4. The first edition was published in
1846.

62. Quoted from Warren by Bailie, *Josiah Warren*, p. 102.

63. See Josiah Warren, *True Civilization, an Immediate Necessity and
the Last Ground of Hope for Mankind. Being the Results and Conclusions of
Thirty-Nine Years Laborious Study and Experiments in Civilization as it is,
and in Different Enterprises for Reconstruction* (Boston, 1863), pp. 10–11.

64. *Ibid.*, pp. 11–14, 181; Warren, *Equitable Commerce*, p. 21.

65. Stephen P. Andrews, *The Science of Society*, No. 1, "The True Constitution of Government in the Sovereignty of the Individual as the Final
Development of Protestantism, Democracy and Socialism" (New York,
1851–52), p. 63.

66. Warren, *True Civilization*, p. 168.

67. See Bailie, *Josiah Warren;* John H. Noyes, *History of American
Socialisms* (Philadelphia, 1870), pp. 84–94, and the interesting letters of
Henry Edgar to Auguste Comte published by Richmond L. Hawkins in
Positivism in the United States (1853–1861) (Cambridge, 1938), pp. 133–
38.

68. Printed on the labor note which is reproduced in Warren, *Equitable
Commerce.*

69. *Ibid.*, pp. 10, 32–33.

70. Bailie, *Josiah Warren*, pp. 48–49.

71. Warren, *Equitable Commerce*, p. 57.

72. Quoted by Bailie, *Josiah Warren*, pp. 54–55.

73. Warren, *Equitable Commerce*, p. 6.

74. *Ibid.*, p. 22.

75. *Ibid.*, p. 8; Warren, *True Civilization*, p. 162.

76. The title of the last edition of *True Civilization*, which Warren published one year before his death, reads as follows: *Practical Applications of the Elementary Principles of "True Civilization"* . . . *Being Part III, The Last of the "True Civilization" Series, And the Facts and Conclusions of Forty Seven Years Study and Experiments in Reform Movements Through Communism to and in Elementary Principles, found in a Direction Exactly Opposite to and away from Communism, but Leading Directly to all the Harmonic Results Aimed at by Communism* (Princeton, Mass., 1873).

77. Printed in New York, 1851.

78. Stephen P. Andrews, *Science of Society*, No. 2, "Cost the Limit of Price," p. 17.

79. *Ibid.*, pp. 14–15; 35.

80. *Ibid.*, pp. 38–42.

81. "Individuality has been misapprehended and mis-represented as 'isolation,' 'selfishness,' 'unsocialism,' etc." (Warren, *True Civilization*, p. 160). See also Andrews' repudiation of Tocqueville's interpretation of the term in Andrews, *Science of Society*, No. 1, pp. 68ff.

82. Hawkins, *Positivism in the U.S.*, p. 138.

83. See the slandering reports on the morals of "Modern Times" published in Greeley's New York *Tribune* in Martin, *Men Against the State*, pp. 74–89, and in Horace Greeley, *Recollections of a Busy Life* (New York, Boston, 1868).

84. George F. Holmes, "Theory of Political Individualism," *DeBow's Review*, 22:133–49 (1857). Holmes was well acquainted with Andrews. He corresponded with him on questions of social philosophy. See Harvey Wish, *George Fitzhugh, Propagandist of the Old South* (Baton Rouge, 1943), p. 83; and "George Frederick Holmes and the Genesis of American Sociology," *American Journal of Sociology*, 46:698ff (1941).

85. Holmes, "Political Individualism," *DeBow's Review*, pp. 138–41. He referred to Spencer's *Social Statics* and its doctrine of individualism and to Proudhon's *Idée générale de la Révolution*.

86. *Ibid.*, pp. 145–46. He quotes Nettement's *Histoire de la littérature française sous le gouvernement de juillet* in support of his views.

87. See John R. Commons *et al.*, *History of Labor in the United States* (New York, 1918–35), I, 511.

88. See Clark's "A Neglected Socialist," *Annals of the American Academy of Political and Social Science*, 5:720ff (1894).

89. Martin, *Men Against the State*, pp. 26, 80.

90. Noyes, *History of American Socialisms*, p. 94. The author calls Warren the "apostle of individualism," *ibid.*, p. 84.

CHAPTER XIV: THE GREAT DEBATE ON THE NATURE OF THE
AMERICAN IDEAL

1. To William Short, April 13, 1820. Thomas Jefferson, *Writings*, Andrew A. Lipscomb *et al.* (Washington, 1903), XV, 247.

2. See Ray A. Billington, *The Protestant Crusade: 1800–1860: A Study*

of the Origins of American Nativism (New York, 1952), p. 417. See also
Gustavus Myers, *History of Bigotry in the United States*, ed. and rev., Henry
M. Christman (New York [1960]), chaps. xiv–xvi; Howard P. Nash, Jr.,
Third Parties in American Politics (Washington, D. C. [1959]), pp. 13–20;
Theodore C. Smith, *Parties and Slavery, 1850–1859* (New York, London,
1906), pp. 109–48.

3. George F. Holmes, "Observation on a Passage in the Politics of Aristotle Relative to Slavery," *Southern Literary Messenger*, 16:195–205 (1850).

4. Holmes corresponded for two years with Auguste Comte. See Richmond L. Hawkins, *August Comte and the United States, 1816–1853* (Cambridge, Mass., 1936), p. 99; George F. Holmes, "Greeley on Reforms,"
Southern Literary Messenger, 17:257–80 (May 1851).

5. "The Nineteenth Century," *ibid.*, 17:462, 466 (August 1851). See also
Harvey Wish, "George Frederick Holmes and the Genesis of American
Sociology," *American Journal of Sociology*, 46:699 (1941).

6. See William E. Dodd, *The Cotton Kingdom; A Chronicle of the Old
South* (New Haven, 1921), chap. iii; Frederick L. Olmsted, *The Cotton
Kingdom: A Traveller's Observations on Cotton and Slavery in the American
Slave States* (New York, 1861), II, 362ff; Arthur C. Cole, *The Irrepressible
Conflict, 1850–1865* (New York, 1938), chaps. ii–iii; Avery O. Craven, *The
Coming of the Civil War* (New York, 1942); Benjamin B. Kendrick and
Alex M. Arnett, *The South Looks at Its Past* (Chapel Hill, 1935); William
S. Jenkins, *Pro-slavery Thought in the Old South* (Chapel Hill, 1935);
Chancellor Harper and others, *The Proslavery Argument as Maintained by
the Most Distinguished Writers of the Southern States* (Philadelphia, 1853);
also Margaret L. Coit, *John C. Calhoun, American Portrait* (Boston, 1950),
chap. xix.

7. See "Harper's Memoir on Slavery" in the *Proslavery Argument*, pp.
2–3, 15; and Professor Dew's "Review of the Debate in the Virginia Legislature, 1831–32," *ibid.*, pp. 287ff.

8. Jefferson to John Holmes, April 22, 1820, Jefferson, *Writings*, ed.
Lipscomb, XV, 249. See also the same attitude still expressed by many
southerners during the Missouri question in Gaillard Hunt, *John C. Calhoun*
(Philadelphia [1908]), pp. 53–55.

9. "Remarks on the State Rights' Resolutions in Regard to Abolition,
Jan. 12, 1838," in John C. Calhoun, *Works* (New York, 1853–55), III, 180.

10. See "Harper's Memoir on Slavery," *The Proslavery Argument*, pp.
6–13.

11. *Ibid.*, pp. 8–9.

12. See "A Disquisition on Government," Calhoun, *Works*, I, 9–11, 14–24, 34–42.

13. *Ibid.*, pp. 52–59.

14. *Ibid.*, pp. 54–55.

15. See *ibid.*, pp. 28–38, 63–70.

16. See *ibid.*, pp. 1–4.

17. *Ibid.*, p. 4.

18. *Ibid.*, pp. 56–59.

19. See Coit, *John C. Calhoun*, pp. 467ff; Hunt, *John C. Calhoun*, pp. 290–308.

20. See Chancellor William Harper, "Slavery in the Light of Social Ethics," in *Cotton is King and Pro-slavery Arguments*, ed. E. N. Elliott (Augusta, 1860), pp. 549ff.

21. See James D. B. DeBow, *The Interest in Slavery of the Southern Non-Slave Holder* (Charleston, 1860). Thomas Carlyle's *Latter-day Pamphlets,* especially his "Occasional Discourse on the Nigger Question" (London, 1853), were widely reviewed in the southern press. The essay was reprinted in *DeBow's Review,* in the *Southern Quarterly Review,* and in the *Southern Literary Messenger.* See also chap. xiv of David Christy, *Cotton is King; or, Slavery in the Light of Political Economy,* in *Cotton is King and Pro-slavery Arguments,* ed. Elliott, pp. 132–49; and Albert Taylor Bledsoe, "Liberty and Slavery, or Slavery in the Light of Moral and Political Philosophy," chap. iv, on the emancipation in the West Indies in *Cotton is King,* pp. 380ff. On the same, see J. H. Hammond, "Slavery in the Light of Political Science," *ibid.*, pp. 665ff.

22. See Chapter VI, sec. 4, above; see also Jenkins, *Pro-Slavery Thought in the Old South,* pp. 65–69, 81–89; Dew, "Review of the Debate . . . , in *The Proslavery Argument;* see also Calhoun, *Works,* IV, 410–11; also Bledsoe, "Liberty and Slavery," *Cotton is King,* ed. Elliott, pp. 294–96, 298–99; S. A. Cartwright, "Slavery in the Light of Ethnology," *ibid.*, pp. 691ff. See especially the appendix to Cartwright's essay, pp. 707ff, and his "On the Caucasians and the Africans," *ibid.*, pp. 717ff. See, for the development of the theory of racism, Oscar Handlin, *Race and Nationality in American Life* (Boston, 1957). Josiah C. Nott published an ambitious ethnological work, *Types of Mankind,* in 1854. Nott also collaborated in the English translation of Gobineau's *The Moral and Intellectual Diversity of Races.* See Harvey Wish, *George Fitzhugh, Propagandist of the Old South* (Baton Rouge, 1943), p. 71.

23. See the famous poem of William J. Grayson, "The Hireling and the Slave," in *DeBow's Review,* 21:248–56 (September 1856).

24. *Cotton is King,* ed. Elliott, p. 898; see also the warnings of Hammond in *Cotton is King,* p. 669, and in his speech in Congress, "Cotton is King," as quoted by Harvey Wish, *George Fitzhugh, Propagandist of the Old South* (Baton Rouge, 1943), p. 38.

25. See George F. Holmes, "The Failure of Free Society," *Southern Literary Messenger,* 21:129–41 (March 1855); "The Prospects of Southern Agriculture," *DeBow's Review,* 22:180–93 (February 1857).

26. George Fitzhugh, "The Conservative Principle; or, Social Evils and Their Remedies," *DeBow's Review,* 22:428–29 (April 1857).

27. See Bledsoe, "Liberty and Slavery," *Cotton is King,* ed. Elliott, pp. 273–89, 319–36.

28. *Ibid.*, p. 332; see also William Andrew Smith, *Lectures on Philosophy and Practice of Slavery, as Exhibited in the Institution of Domestic Slavery*

in the United States: with the Duties of Masters to Slaves, ed. Thomas O. Summers (Nashville, 1856).

29. See Holmes, "The Failure of Free Society," *Southern Literary Messenger,* 21:136 (March 1855). See also J. T. Wiswell, "Delusions of Fanaticism," *DeBow's Review,* 29:58–59 (July 1860).

30. Fitzhugh, "The Conservative Principle," *DeBow's Review,* 22:421ff (April 1857).

31. *Ibid.,* p. 426.

32. Python, "The Relative Political Status of the North and South," *DeBow's Review,* 22:118 (February 1857), and "The Relative Moral and Social Status of the North and the South," *ibid.,* 22:226ff (March 1857); George Fitzhugh, "The War upon Society—Socialism," *ibid.,* pp. 633–34, and "Centralization and Socialism," *ibid.,* pp. 692–94.

33. George Fitzhugh, *Sociology for the South, or the Failure of Free Society* (Richmond, 1854), p. 11.

34. *Ibid.,* pp. 176–77, 182–201.

35. *Ibid.,* p. 70.

36. *Ibid.,* pp. 27–28; see also *ibid.,* p. 29: "It [slavery] is a beautiful example of communism, where each one receives not according to his labor, but according to his wants."

37. *Ibid.,* p. 72.

38. See Fitzhugh, *Sociology for the South,* pp. 31–32, 177.

39. The title was taken from Carlyle's *Latter-day Pamphlets.*

40. *Cannibals All! or Slaves without Masters,* ed. C. Van Woodward (Cambridge, Mass., 1960), pp. 25–26.

41. *Ibid.,* pp. 199–200, on the Puritan revolution, which he calls the victory of exploitative capital.

42. *Ibid.,* p. 361.

43. See Wish, *George Fitzhugh,* pp. 114–21; also Hermann von Holst, *The Constitutional and Political History of the United States* (Chicago, 1885), V, 53–54, 449ff; also *ibid.,* chap. x.

44. Wish, *George Fitzhugh,* pp. 126, 204.

45. Quoted in *The Patriarchal Institution, as Described by Members of Its Own Family,* comp. Lydia M. Child (New York, 1860), pp. 5–7.

46. See "The Southern Convention in Savannah," *DeBow's Review,* 22:216–24 (February 1857); "Editorial Miscellanies," *ibid.,* pp. 554–55; Fitzhugh, "The Conservative Principle: II. The Slave Trade," *ibid.,* p. 469. See also the annual message of Governor J. H. Adams of South Carolina calling for the revival of the slave trade as quoted in Allan Nevins, *Ordeal of the Union* (New York, 1947), II, 519.

47. Wish, *George Fitzhugh,* p. 151.

48. *Ibid.,* p. 152. See also "The Counter-Current; or the Slavery Principle," *DeBow's Review,* 21:90–95 (March 1855).

49. *Documents of American History,* ed. Henry S. Commager (New York, 1948), p. 345. Though the simile had been used often before (see the instances quoted in Nevins, *The Ordeal of the Union,* II, 78), the southern

declarations inspired Lincoln and Seward to make similar statements. Lincoln, at least, claimed in his Cincinnati speech, September 17, 1859, that neither he nor Seward nor Hickman had first expressed these ideas, but the *Richmond Enquirer* of Virginia in 1856. See Abraham Lincoln, *The Collected Works* (Springfield, 1953–55), III, 451. Henry C. Whitney has pointed out in *Lincoln the Citizen* (New York, 1908), I, 267, that Lincoln was a regular reader of the *Richmond Enquirer* and that Fitzhugh's writing preoccupied him. See also Wish, *George Fitzhugh*, pp. 150–53.

50. *Orations of American Orators* (New York [1900]), II, 198.

51. "Speech at Peoria, Illinois," Lincoln, *Collected Works*, II, 275. See also Lincoln's address before the Wisconsin State Agricultural Society, Milwaukee, September 30, 1859, in which he attacked Hammond's "mud-sill" theory (*ibid.*, III, 477–80).

52. "Peoria Speech," *ibid.*, p. 283.

53. To Henry Pierce and Others, Springfield, Illinois, April 6, 1859, *ibid.*, III, 374–75.

54. Wish, *George Fitzhugh*, pp. 283–87. See also *The Republican Scrap Book* (Boston, 1856). See the section, "The Oligarchic and Anti-Republican Character of Slavery as Shown by Their Own Statesmen," pp. 51–58.

55. On this aspect of the sectional conflict see Nevins, *Ordeal of the Union*, II, 125–95, 316–23. On the interpretation of the Civil War as a conflict between two rival social philosophies and as a Southern conspiracy to destroy democracy, see Henry Wilson, *History of the Rise and Fall of the Slave Power in America* (Boston, 1872–77); James G. Blaine, *Twenty Years of Congress* (Norwich, 1884–86); Horace Greeley, *The American Conflict: A History of the Great Rebellion of the United States of America, 1860–[65]* (Hartford, 1864–66); John W. Draper, *History of the American Civil War* (New York, 1867–70).

56. See the resolutions of the South Western Liberty Convention, written by Salmon P. Chase in Cincinnati in 1845, in Theodore C. Smith, *The Liberty and Free Soil Parties in the Northwest* (New York, London, 1897), pp. 88–89.

57. Quoted by Child, *Patriarchal Institutions*, pp. 6ff; and von Holst, *The Constitutional and Political History of the U.S.*, V., 481.

58. See Richard Hofstadter, *The American Political Tradition* (New York, 1948), pp. 119–20. See also the pamphlet printed by the Republican party, *The New "Democratic" Doctrine. Slavery not to be Confined to the Negro Race, but to be made the Universal Condition of the Laboring Classes of Society* (n.p., n.d.).

59. William Trimble, "The Social Philosophy of the Loco Foco Democracy," *American Journal of Sociology*, 26:714–15 (May 1921). See also Arthur B. Darling, *Jacksonian Democracy in Massachusetts, 1824–1848*, unpub. diss., Harvard University, 1922, and *Political Changes in Massachusetts, 1824–1848; a Study of Liberal Movements in Politics* (New Haven, 1925), especially on the workingmen's party, 97–100, 172–73, 349–59; and

chaps. v–vi and pp. 349–59. See also Ralph Gabriel, "Democracy: Retrospect and Prospect," *American Journal of Sociology*, 48:411–18 (1942).

60. See Gerrit Smith, *The True Office of Civil Government* (New York, 1851); Thomas V. Smith, *The American Philosophy of Equality* (Chicago [1927]), also *The Liberty and Free Soil Parties*, p. 140, and *Parties and Slavery, 1850–1859*, chaps. viii and xix and pp. 109–14. See also Francis Curtis, *The Republican Party; A History of its Fifty Years' Existence and a Record of Its Measures and Leaders, 1854–1904* (New York, London, 1904), I, 114–19, 130, 147, and chap. vi, *passim*. Vernon L. Parrington, *Main Currents in American Thought* (New York [1927]), II, 238–46. See also the speech of Judge Emmet at the Republican Convention in Philadelphia, June 17–19, 1856, in *Proceedings of the National Convention . . . Held at Philadelphia*, pp. 3–11.

61. Henry S. Commager, *Theodore Parker* (Boston, 1936), p. 200.

62. See Theodore Parker, *Social Classes in a Republic* (Boston, n.d.); and Octavius B. Frothingham, *Theodore Parker; A Biography* (Boston, 1879), pp. 134ff.

63. Frothingham, *Theodore Parker*, p. 136.

64. Commager, *Theodore Parker*, p. 167.

65. Frothingham, *Theodore Parker*, p. 442. See Parker's letter to John P. Hale, Oct. 21, 1856, in which he described the animosity of the wealthy classes of Boston toward the Republican party and the abolition movement, in Commager, *Theodore Parker*, pp. 197–99. See also *Letters of Lydia Maria Child* (Boston, New York, 1883), p. 18; and Lydia Maria Child, *Letters from New York* (New York, 1843), I, 40.

66. Parker subscribed to the *Richmond Enquirer* and *DeBow's Review*. See Commager, *Theodore Parker*, p. 202.

67. Frothingham, *Theodore Parker*, p. 448.

68. *Ibid.*, pp. 397–98.

69. Commager, *Theodore Parker*, pp. 193, 208, 192.

70. See John R. Commons, "Horace Greeley and the Working Class Origins of the Republican Party," *Political Science Quarterly*, 24:468–88 (September 1909).

71. J. F. Rhodes, "Newspapers as Historical Sources," *Historical Essays* (New York, 1909), pp. 90–91; see also Willard G. Bleyer, *Main Currents in the History of American Journalism* (Boston [1927]), p. 228.

72. See J. R. Commons, "Horace Greeley," *Political Science Quarterly*, 24:473–74 (1909).

73. Horace Greeley, *Recollections of a Busy Life* (New York, 1868) and *Hints Towards Reform in Lectures, Addresses and Other Writings* (New York, 1850), and especially "The Organization of Labor."

74. A pamphlet carrying this name was circulated to the number of 100,000 copies. See Commons, "Horace Greeley," *Political Science Quarterly*, 24:480 (1909).

75. On the relations between George H. Evans and Horace Greeley see

the interesting material in the otherwise unreliable book by Charles South-eran, *Horace Greeley and other Pioneers of American Socialism* (New York, 1915), pp. 83–89.

76. For Evans' agrarianism see John R. Commons *et al.*, *History of Labor in the United States* (New York, 1918–35), I, 522–46. See also George Lockwood on Evans, in *The New Harmony Movement* (New York, 1905), p. 337.

77. In 1837 Evans edited Thomas Paine's writings, including *Agrarian Justice, Opposed to Agrarian Law and Agrarian Monopoly.*

78. Commons, "Horace Greeley," *Political Science Quarterly*, 24:478–84; see also Curtis, *The Republican Party*, pp. 173–74.

79. Commager, *Documents*, I, 331; Nevins, *The Ordeal of The Union*, II, 111–13.

80. See Theodore Smith, *The Liberty and Free Soil Parties*, pp. 140, 244, 245ff.

81. See *Platforms of the Two Great Political Parties, 1856–1928*, comp. G. D. Ellis (Washington, D.C., 1928), p. 12. See also *Republican Scrap Book* (Boston, 1856), pp. 16–17. See in *The Proceedings of the National Convention of the Republican Party* (Philadelphia, 1856) the speech of Hon. Caleb Smith, pp. 24ff; of Owen Lovejoy, pp. 25ff; and of Hon. Henry Wilson, pp. 28ff.

82. Speech of Owen Lovejoy, *Proceedings of the National Convention* (1856), pp. 26–27.

83. Lincoln, *Collected Works*, II, 275.

84. Lincoln, *Collected Works*, IV, 438.

85. See Chapter VII above.

86. Commager, *Documents*, I, 388.

87. See Chapter VII above.

88. See Ralph Waldo Emerson, "Abraham Lincoln," *Complete Works* (Boston, 1888), XI, 308ff; also Ralph H. Gabriel, *The Course of American Democratic Thought: An Intellectual History since 1815* (New York [1940]), pp. 407–13; and Hofstadter, *The American Political Tradition*, pp. 92ff.

89. Speech at New Haven, March 6, 1860, Lincoln, *Collected Works*, IV, 24ff.

90. See also his address before the Wisconsin State Agricultural Society, Sept. 30, 1859, *ibid.*, pp. 477–80.

91. *Ibid.*, pp. 478–79. See also speech at Cincinnati, Ohio, Sept. 17, 1859, *ibid.*, p. 459; "Fragment on Free Labor," *ibid.*, pp. 402–63.

92. Speech in Independence Hall, Philadelphia, Feb. 22, 1861, *ibid.*, IV, 240. See also T. H. Williams, "Abraham Lincoln—Principle and Pragmatism in Politics, A Review Article," *Mississippi Valley Historical Review*, June 1953.

93. Walt Whitman, "Democratic Vistas," *Complete Prose Works* (Philadelphia, 1891), pp. 213–14.

94. *Ibid.*, p. 214.

95. D. W. Draper, *History of the American Civil War*, 3 vols. (New York, 1868–70).

96. *Ibid.*, I, 207–8.

97. *Ibid.*, I, 211ff, and especially pp. 239–41.

98. *Ibid.*, I, 26–27, 419.

99. On the popularity of Mill's socio-economic theory see Joseph Dorfman, *The Economic Mind in American Civilization* (New York, 1946–59), vol. II, and *Thorstein Veblen and His America* (New York, 1934). See also Edwin L. Godkin, "The Economic Man," *Problems in Democracy* (New York, 1896), pp. 158–63.

100. John S. Mill, *Principles of Political Economy with Some of Their Applications to Social Philosophy* (London, 1852), II, 570.

101. *Ibid.*, I, 125–26.

102. *Ibid.*, II, 550–53.

103. *Ibid.*, I, 286–88; II, 338, 357–58, 379–80.

104. John S. Mill, *Principles of Political Economy* (London, 1848), I, 252–53.

105. Neither in his *Principles* nor in *On Liberty* did Mill introduce the term "individualism." He used rather the terms "sovereignty of the individual," or "individuality." The former term he had admittedly borrowed from Josiah Warren. The term "individualism" is first introduced in the unfinished chapters on "Socialism," posthumously published, and in his *Autobiography* (1873).

106. See James Schouler, *History of the United States under the Constitution* [*1783–1877*] (New York, 1880–1913), vol. V; James F. Rhodes, *History of the United States from the Compromise of 1850* (New York, 1893–1906), I, 137–61; Woodrow Wilson, *Division and Reunion, 1829–1889* (New York, London, 1893), p. 211. See also Edward Channing, *A History of the United States* (New York, London, 1905–1925), I, v–vi and *The United States of America, 1765–1865* (New York, 1896), pp. 258ff. Cole, *The Irrepressible Conflict*, p. 407. For the whole question see Thomas J. Pressly, *Americans Interpret Their Civil War* (Princeton, 1954).

107. "Democratic Vistas," Whitman, *Complete Prose Works*, II, 67.

108. A full survey of the history of the concept of individualism in America in the post-Civil War period is given in the author's unpublished doctoral thesis: *Toldoth Mussag Ha-Individualism Be-Arzoth Ha-Brith, 1840–1912* [History of the Concept of Individualism in the United States], Hebrew University, Jerusalem, 1955.

Chapter XV: Epilogue

1. James Bryce, *The American Commonwealth* (London, New York, 1888), II, 404.

2. *Ibid.*, pp. 404–5.

3. *Ibid.*, pp. 406–7.

4. *Ibid.*, p. 405.

5. *Ibid.*, p. 406.

6. *Ibid.*, p. 408.

7. *Ibid.*, p. 407.

8. *Ibid.*, p. 409.

9. *Ibid.*, p. 409–10. See also his chapter "Kearneyism in California," *ibid.*, II, 391.

10. See the list of names to which Bryce makes acknowledgement in his *American Commonwealth*. On Bryce's friendship with E. L. Godkin, see Herbert A. L. Fisher, *James Bryce* (London, 1927), I, 135–36; *Life and Letters of Edwin Lawrence Godkin*, ed. Rollo Ogden (New York, 1907); also Robert H. Murray, *Studies in the English Social and Political Thinkers of the Nineteenth Century* (Cambridge, 1929), II, 328–29.

11. Among others see: Allan Nevins, *Grover Cleveland; A Study in Courage* (New York, 1948), pp. 156ff; Matthew Josephson, *The Politicos, 1865–1896* (New York [1938]), pp. 158–66; Van Wyck Brooks, *New England Indian Summer, 1865–1915* ([New York], 1940), pp. 115–19; Ralph H. Gabriel, *The Course of American Democratic Thought: An Intellectual History since 1815* (New York [1940]), p. 178; Stow Persons, *Free Religion in American Faith* (New Haven, 1947), chaps. ii, iii, and iv; F. B. Sanborn, "Social Science in Theory and Practice," *Journal of Social Science,* 9:5–10 (January 1878).

12. Francis E. Abbott, "Organization," *The Radical*, 2:224 (December 1866).

13. Samuel Johnson, "The Spiritual Promise of America," *ibid.*, 2:453 (April 1867).

14. C. C. Shackford, "The Modern Problem Social, Not Political," *ibid.*, 6:441–54 (December 1869).

15. "The Spiritual Promise of America," *ibid.*, 2:463 (April 1867).

16. William B. Scott, "Does Social Advancement Depend upon Political Organizations?," *ibid.*, 6:242 (September 1869).

17. *Ibid.*, p. 244.

18. John W. Draper, *History of the Conflict Between Religion and Science* (New York, 1876), p. 295.

19. Harry H. Clark, "The Vogue of Macaulay in America," *Wisconsin Academy of Sciences, Arts and Letters* (1941), p. 256. A full reprint of Macaulay's letters to H. S. Randall is given in "What Did Macaulay Say About America?," *Bulletin* of the New York Public Library, 29:463–73 (July 1915).

20. Clark, "The Vogue of Macaulay," p. 256.

21. For instances of the preoccupation of American liberals with Macaulay's prediction, see: "The Communistic Movement," *Nation,* 26:302–3 (May 9, 1878); "The Dangers of Playing Tricks with the Labor Question," *ibid.*, 15:148 (September 5, 1872); William G. Sumner, "Separation of State and Market," in *Earth Hunger and Other Essays,* ed. Albert G. Keller (New Haven, 1913), pp. 306–7; also Henry George, *Progress and Poverty* (New York, 1880), pp. 320–21, 506–20; see also "German Socialism in America," *North American Review,* 127:482–83 (1879).

22. William G. Sumner, "What Is Civil Liberty?" *Earth Hunger and Other Essays,* pp. 127–28.

23. William G. Sumner, "Separation of State and Market," *ibid.*, p. 308;

also "State Interference," *War and Other Essays,* ed. Albert G. Keller (New Haven, 1911), p. 219.

24. See William James on Godkin in Ogden, *Life and Letters of Edwin Lawrence Godkin,* I, 221; also W. G. Bleyer, *Main Currents in the History of American Journalism* (Boston [1927]), pp. 270–90. See also Edwin L. Godkin, "Aristocratic Opinions of Democracy," *Problems of Modern Democracy* (New York, 1896), pp. 55–56; and "The Labor Crisis," *North American Review,* 105:183 (July 1867).

25. Godkin, "The Labor Crisis," *ibid.,* pp. 181, 186–90, 199–202.

26. "Aristocratic Opinions," in Godkin, *Problems of Modern Democracy,* pp. 55–64; and "The Duty of the Educated Man," *ibid.,* pp. 216–17.

27. Godkin, "The Labor Crisis," pp. 212–13.

28. Herbert Spencer designated his theories as philosophy of individualism for the first time in the Introduction to the American edition of *Social Statics; or, the Conditions Essential to Human Happiness Specified, and the First of Them Developed* (New York [1865]), p. x. For the early recognition of Spencer as philosopher of individualism: Henry C. Carey, *Memoir of Stephen Colwell* (Philadelphia, 1871), pp. 17–24. George F. Holmes, "Theory of Political Individualism," *DeBow's Review,* 22:133–49 (February 1857); Émile de Laveleye, "The State Versus the Man: A Criticism of Mr. Herbert Spencer," *Popular Science Monthly,* 27:165–87 (1885); Henry George, *A Perplexed Philosopher* (New York, 1892), p. 87; Arthur T. Hadley, "Individualism," in W. D. P. Bliss, ed., *New Encyclopedia of Social Reform* (New York, 1908).

29. "Herbert Spencer's Autobiography," William James, *Memories and Studies* (New York [etc.], 1912), pp. 140–41.

30. Émile de Laveleye, "The State Versus the Man: A Criticism of Mr. Herbert Spencer," *Popular Science Monthly,* 27:165–87 (1885). See also Ludwig Gumplowicz, *Grundriss der Sociologie* (Vienna, 1885), pp. 10–13.

31. For a general treatment of Spencer's influence in America see: Richard Hofstadter, *Social Darwinism in American Thought* (Boston [1955]); Vernon L. Parrington, *Main Currents in American Thought* (New York [1927]), III, 197–211; Bert J. Loewenberg, "Darwinism Comes to America, 1859–1908," *The Mississippi Valley Historical Review,* 28:352–56 (December 1941); Gabriel, *The Course of American Democratic Thought;* Brooks, *New England Indian Summer,* pp. 107–11, 262–63.

32. Quoted in Hofstadter, *Social Darwinism,* p. 21.

33. See Henry F. May, *Protestant Church and Industrial America* (New York, 1949), pp. 142–47. Bert J. Loewenberg, "Controversy over Darwinism in New England, 1859–1873," *New England Quarterly,* 8:232–57 (1935).

34. See *Lochner vs. New York,* 198, U.S. 45 in *Documents of American History,* ed. Henry S. Commager (New York, 1948), II, 221.

35. Samuel E. Morison and Henry S. Commager, *The Growth of the American Republic* (New York, 1942), II, 86.

36. See Ida M. Tarbell, *Nationalizing of Business, 1878–1898* (New York, 1936), History of American Life Series, IX, 30–31; Nevins, *Grover Cleve-*

land, pp. 357–59; Arthur M. Schlesinger, *The Rise of the City, 1878–1898* (New York, 1933), in History of American Life Series, X, 368–72; Ira V. Brown, *Lyman Abbott, Christian Evolutionist* (Cambridge, 1953), pp. 89–95; and Board of Indian Commissioners, *Seventeenth Annual Report for the Year 1885* (Washington, D.C., 1886), p. 73.

37. Lyman Abbott, *The Rights of Man; A Study in Twentieth Century Problems* (New York, 1901), pp. 219–22.

38. See M. E. Gates, "Land and Law as Agents in Educating Indians," *Journal of Social Science,* 21:119 (September 1886). The article is identical with the report of Gates in Board of Indian Commissioners, *Seventeenth Annual Report.*

39. Gates, "Land and Law," *Journal of Social Science,* 21:134 (1886).

40. *Ibid.,* p. 132.

41. *Ibid.,* pp. 134–35.

42. Board of Indian Commissioners, *Seventeenth Annual Report,* pp. 96–97.

43. *Ibid.,* p. 98.

44. *Ibid.,* p. 90 and 28.

45. See Hofstadter, *Social Darwinism,* p. 31; Hofstadter, *The American Political Tradition,* chap. iv; Charles E. Merriam, *American Political Ideas; Studies in the Development of American Political Thought* (New York [1920]), pp. 324–25.

46. Charles A. Beard, "The Myth of Rugged American Individualism," *Harper's Magazine,* 164:20–21 (December 1931).

47. Henry George, *Progress and Poverty* (New York, 1938), p. 479.

48. *Ibid.,* pp. 478–81.

49. Spencer, *Social Statics,* pp. 481–83.

50. *Ibid.,* pp. 474–77.

51. *Ibid.,* pp. 477–81.

52. Herbert Spencer to Horace Seal, quoted in David Duncan, *The Life and Letters of Herbert Spencer* (London [1908]), p. 353. See also Murray, *Studies in the English Social and Political Thinkers,* II, 25–26.

53. Ernest Barker, *Political Thought in England, 1848 to 1914* (London, 1940), p. 85. See Thomas C. Cochran and William Miller, *The Age of Enterprise, A Social History of Industrial America* (New York, 1942), p. 120.

54. Herbert Spencer, *The Man vs. the State; A Collection of Essays* (New York, 1884), pp. 65, 67; also Spencer's letter to J. A. Cairnes; Duncan, *Life and Letters,* pp. 161 and 300; see also Herbert Spencer, *Principles of Sociology* (London, 1897), III, 563–64 and pp. 570ff; Herbert Spencer, *The Principles of Ethics* (New York, 1892), pp. 148–49.

55. The influence of Spencer's theory on the elaboration of a private-enterprise ideology has been repeatedly studied and the literature on it is abundant. Among others see: Sigmund O. Diamond, *The Reputation of the American Businessman* (Cambridge, Mass., 1955), chap. iii; Alfred W. Griswold, "The American Cult of Success," unpub. diss., Yale University, 1933; Sidney Fine, "Laissez Faire and the General-Welfare State in Ameri-

can Thought," unpub diss., University of Michigan, 1948; Hofstadter, *The American Political Tradition,* 166–85; Gabriel, *The Course of American Democratic Thought,* chap. xiii; "The Gospel of Wealth of the 'Gilded Age' "; John W. Hollenbach, "A Study of Economic Individualism in the American Novel from 1865 to 1888," unpub. diss., University of Wisconsin, 1941.

56. See Andrew Carnegie, *Autobiography* (Boston, New York, 1920), p. 327, and *The Gospel of Wealth, and other Timely Essays* (New York, 1900), pp. 6, 7, 13.

57. See Herbert D. Croly, *Marcus Alonzo Hanna; His Life and Work* (New York, 1912), pp. 464ff; see Andrew Carnegie, *The Empire of Business* (New York, 1902), "The Road to Business Success," p. 18; see also *ibid.,* "How to Win a Fortune," pp. 103–23.

58. Herbert Spencer, *Principles of Sociology* (New York, 1877), II, 210–11.

59. Diamond, *Reputation of the American Businessman,* p. 53. See also Fine, "Laissez Faire and the General-Welfare State," pp. 145–88. See also Josephson, *The Politicos,* pp. 443–45.

60. Carnegie, *The Gospel of Wealth,* pp. 5–6.

61. See, apart from Carnegie's work, Robert Shackleton, *Acres of Diamonds by Russell H. Conwell. His Life and Achievements* (New York and London [1915]), pp. 18, 20; see also May, *Protestant Church and Industrial America,* pp. 199–200; Henry F. Pringle, *Theodore Roosevelt; A Biography* (New York [1931]), pp. 26ff; Gustavus Myers, *History of the Great American Fortunes* (New York, 1936), pp. 366–67, n. 17; Charles M. Schwab, *Succeeding With What You Have* (New York, 1917), p. 63; Henry Wood, *Natural Law in the Business World* (Boston, New York, 1887), p. 220; Samuel C. T. Dodd, *Combinations: Their Uses and Abuses, with a History of the Standard Oil Trust* (New York, 1888), p. 24. Cochran and Miller, *Age of Enterprise,* pp. 331–32. See also the series of pamphlets published by the N.A.M. in the first decade of the twentieth century as, for instance, Pamphlet No. 1, "Class Distinction and Americanism," N.A.M. (May 19, 1909), and Pamphlet No. 4, "The Next Step in Education," pp. 9–18.

62. Henry Clews, *Individualism versus Socialism* (New York [1907]), pp. 1–3.

63. *The American Individual Enterprise System; Its Nature, Evolution, and Future* (New York, 1946), II, 1018–21. For an identical formulation, see: *Facing the Future's Risk; Studies Toward Predicting the Unforeseen,* ed. Lyman Bryson (New York [1953]), pp. 248–73; see also "Individualism Comes of Age," in issue entitled "U.S.A., The Permanent Revolution," *Fortune,* 43:113–15 (February 1951), pp. 113–15.

64. See especially Diamond, *Reputation of the American Businessman.*

65. Frederick J. Turner, "The Significance of the Frontier in American History," *The Frontier in American History* (New York, 1920), pp. 29–32; and "The Problems of the West," *ibid.,* pp. 205–6; and "The Mississippi Valley," *ibid.,* p. 203.

66. "Pioneer Ideal and the State University," *ibid.*, pp. 271–72, 279–80; "The Contribution of the West to American Democracy," *ibid.*, p. 258; and "The Significance of the Frontier," *ibid.*, pp. 30, 35.

67. "The Mississippi Valley," *ibid.*, p. 203.

68. *Ibid.*, p. 204.

69. R. T. Ely, "Report of the Organization of the American Economic Association," in *Publications of the American Economic Association,* I (1886), 6–7.

70. See Fine, "Laissez Faire and the General-Welfare State," pp. 325–28.

71. Richard T. Ely, *The Past and Present of Political Economy* (Baltimore, 1884), vol. III, and *Recent American Socialism* (Baltimore, 1885), vol. IV; see also Ely's opening address at the founding convention of the A.E.A. in *Publications of the A.E.A.,* I (1886), pp. 15–16.

72. Ely, *Past and Present of Political Economy,* p. 48.

73. "Report," *Publications of the A.E.A.,* I, 22ff.

74. Henry C. Adams, "Relation of the State to Industrial Action," *Publications of the A.E.A.,* I (1887), 490, n. 2, and 479, 477, 482–83.

75. *Ibid.*, pp. 499–500.

76. *Ibid.*, p. 546.

77. *Ibid.*, pp. 542–44. See the change of opinions in Clark concerning individualism by comparing "The Nature and Progress of True Socialism," *The New Englander,* 38:566, 571 (July 1879), with John B. Clark, *The Philosophy of Wealth* (Boston, 1886), pp. 176, 201, 207; Woodrow Wilson, *The State* (Boston, 1889), pp. 620–38. On the influence of Clark on Wilson see William Diamond, *The Economic Thought of Woodrow Wilson* (Baltimore, 1943), p. 37.

78. Charles H. Hopkins, *The Rise of the Social Gospel in American Protestantism, 1865–1915* (New Haven, 1940), p. 319.

79. See R. H. Newton, "Communism," *Unitarian Review,* 16:485ff (December 1881); Roswell D. Hitchcock, *Socialism* (New York, 1879); Joseph Cook, *Socialism* (Boston, 1880); John B. Clark, "How to Deal with Communism," *New Englander,* 37:533ff (July 1878); Adolphus J. F. Behrends, *Socialism and Christianity* (New York [1886]); Washington Gladden, "The Strength and Weakness of Socialism," *Century Magazine,* 31:736–49 (February 1886), and "Socialism and Unsocialism," *Forum,* 3:122–30 (April 1887); Edward W. Bemis, "Socialism and the State Action," *Journal of Social Science,* 21:52–66 (September 1886); John Bascom, "The Gist of the Labor Question," *Forum,* 4:87–95 (September 1887); Frederic D. Huntington, "Causes of Social Discontent," *Forum,* 6:2–9 (September 1888); Nicholas P. Gilman, *Socialism and the American Spirit* (New York, Boston, 1893); Franklin M. Sprague, *Socialism from Genesis to Revelation* (Boston, 1893).

80. Quoted by May, *Protestant Church and Industrial America,* pp. 65–66.

81. Washington Gladden, "Socialism and Unsocialism," *Forum,* 3:122–29 (1887); see also F. D. Huntington, "Causes of Social Discontent," *ibid.*, 6:2–3 (1888); John Bascom, "The Gist of the Labor Question," *ibid.*,

4:95 (1887); and Washington Gladden, "Three Dangers," *Century Magazine*, 28:620ff (1884).

82. John Rae, *Contemporary Socialism* (New York, 1891), p. 395.

83. See, among others, Sidney Ratner, *A Political and Social History of Federal Taxation* (New York, 1942), pp. 177, 183, 186, 200; Chester McArthur Destler, "The Opposition of American Businessmen to Social Control during the 'Gilded Age,' " *Mississippi Valley Historical Review*, 39:641–72 (March 1953); Benjamin R. Twiss, *Lawyers and the Constitution; How Laissez-faire Came to the Supreme Court* (Princeton [1942]).

84. See Herbert Hoover's book *American Individualism* (New York, 1922).

85. *Platforms of the Two Great Political Parties, 1856–1928*, comp. George D. Ellis (Washington, D.C., 1928), pp. 165–66; see also correspondence between Taft and Roosevelt from 1907 to 1908 in Henry F. Pringle, *The Life and Times of William Howard Taft; A Biography* (New York [1939]), I, 341–42, 347.

86. *The Roosevelt Policy*, ed. William Griffith (New York, 1919), II, 513.

87. Theodore Roosevelt, *Works* (New York, 1926), XVIII, 393; see also "Nationalism and Special Privilege," *Outlook*, 97:145 (Jan. 28, 1911).

88. *Platforms of the Two Great Political Parties*, p. 181.

89. Elihu Root, *Essentials of the Constitution* (Washington, 1913), Senate Document No. 168, 63d Cong., 1st sess., p. 3; William Allen White, *Autobiography* (New York, 1946), pp. 469–71; George E. Mowry, *Theodore Roosevelt and the Progressive Movement* (Madison, 1946), p. 462, on Root's role in the convention of 1912. For similar views of Root see: "The Union League Club," Elihu Root, *Miscellaneous Addresses*, eds. Robert Bacon and James B. Scott (Cambridge, Mass., 1917), pp. 124–25; and "The Preservation of American Ideals," *ibid.*, pp. 259–65; also "Business and Politics," *ibid.*, pp. 249–57; and "Socialism and Its Menace: Why Government Ownership Would Not Help the Wage Earners," the views of President Taft as reported by Charles Dewey Hilles in *Century Magazine*, 84:943–48 (October 1912). The classical document of this Republican outlook is given in the new edition of Herbert Spencer's *The Man vs. the State; A Collection of Essays*, ed. Truxton Beale (New York, 1916), in which Truxton Beale, Elihu Root, Henry Cabot Lodge, E. M. Gary, Nicholas M. Butler, David J. Hill, Harlan F. Stone, and Charles W. Eliot applied Spencer's view to the contemporary scene by critical and interpretive essays.

90. *Speeches of William J. Bryan* (New York, 1890), pp. 88–89; also William J. Bryan, "Individualism versus Socialism," *Century Magazine*, 71:856–57 (1906).

91. Thomas R. Marshall, "The Automatic Citizen," *Atlantic Monthly*, August 1912, pp. 297, 300–30; also Woodrow Wilson, *The New Freedom; A Call for the Emancipation of the Generous Energies of a People* (New York, 1919), p. 57.

92. Chester McArthur Destler, "The Influence of Edward Kellogg upon American Radicalism," *Journal of Political Economy*, 40:345–63 (1932);

James J. Martin, *Man against the State,* pp. 109–10, 142–44, 202–3; John R. Commons *et al., History of Labor in the United States* (New York, 1918–35), II, 136–44, 337–400, 167–71, 244–48; Terence V. Powderly, *Thirty Years of Labor, 1859 to 1889* (Columbus, 1890), pp. 243ff; Frederick E. Haynes, *Third Party Movements Since the Civil War, with Special Reference to Iowa* (Iowa City, 1916), pp. 93–96; John D. Hicks, *The Populist Revolt; A History of the Farmers' Alliance and the People's Party* (Minneapolis [1931]), pp. 427–30; see also *The Labor Movement: The Problem of To-day,* ed. George E. MacNeill (Boston, 1887) with Terence Powderly, R. Heber Newton, Henry George and others. In chap. iv, "The Labour Movement in America to 1861," MacNeill traces the aspirations of organized labor back to the founders of the Republic and the ideals of New England civilization. Josiah Warren's ideas are fully appreciated in their significance for the labor movement (*ibid.,* pp. 67–73).

93. John G. Brooks, *American Syndicalism; the I.W.W.* (New York, 1913), p. 641 and *passim;* see also *Socialism and American Life,* ed. Donald D. Egbert and Stow Persons (Princeton, 1952), I, 497.

94. See Daniel Bell, "The Background and Development of Marxian Socialism in the United States," *Socialism and American Life,* ed. Egbert and Persons, I, 215–22; Sidney Hook, "The Philosophical Basis of Marxian Socialism in the United States," *ibid.,* pp. 450–51.

95. See Henry George's interpretation of the Jeffersonian philosophy and his confrontation with the concepts of socialism and individualism in *Progress and Poverty* (New York, 1880), pp. 316–21, 455–56; Louis F. Post and Fred C. Leubuscher, *An Account of the George-Hewitt Campaign in the New York Municipal Election of 1886* (New York, 1887), pp. 27–28, 53; Henry George, *Protection or Free Trade,* in *Complete Works,* X (New York, 1911), 304–6, 308–10; his absolute rejection of socialism in *The Science of Political Economy* (New York, 1898), p. 198.

96. Hamlin Garland, "A New Declaration of Rights," *Arena,* 3:159, 160 (January 1891).

97. *Ibid.,* pp. 167–68.

Index